Virtual Reality Madness!

VIRTUAL REALITY MADNESS!

Ron Wodaski

SAMS
PUBLISHING

To the finest kids in the world: Chris, Chanel, and Justen.

Copyright © 1993 by Sams Publishing

Trademarks

Composed in 1Stone Serif and MCPdigital by Prentice Hall Computer Publishing

Printed in the United States of America

Overview

Contents

Acknowledgments

I owe the biggest debt of gratitude to my wife, Donna, whose support was essential to completing this book. I've also received outstanding cooperation from numerous companies whose software and hardware are reviewed in this book. It takes a lot of effort to ship dozens and dozens of products in both directions, and I'd like to take this opportunity to publicly thank everyone who helped out in this regard.

A special thanks goes to our three kids, Chris, Chanel, and Justen, who had to wait sometimes while Daddy finished a chapter.

I also want to tip my hat to all the folks in the various multimedia-related forums on CompuServe. If you aren't already a member of CompuServe, you're missing out on one of the world's best idea exchanges. I visit the multimedia forums every day, both to answer questions and to learn. Multimedia in general and virtual-reality video in particular are fast-evolving fields. Electronic communication is the most effective way to keep up to date.

About the Author

Ron Wodaski currently resides in a small community on Puget Sound in Washington, where he tries to keep up with the latest advances in multimedia. He started out as a journalist but caught the computer bug when he bought one of the original Osborne computers as a word processor.

He designed and wrote custom software using BASIC and dBASE II for several years, eventually joining the dBASE team at Ashton-Tate until it was merged with Borland. Somewhere along the line, he graduated to C and then retired to Visual Basic and Toolbook. He has worn a number of different hats in the computer industry, including programming, test management, project management, and product design.

He currently writes books on a variety of computer subjects, creates a monthly multimedia column for *Nautilus* (a CD-ROM magazine), pens the occasional science fiction story, and writes documentation for several software and hardware companies. When no one is looking, he avoids computers entirely.

Introduction

Virtual Versus Artificial

If there is a phrase that is even more ambiguous than the word *multimedia*, it's *virtual reality*. These are two of the hottest buzzwords in the computer universe, and finding any two people who can agree on what they mean is a major accomplishment.

What is virtual reality (VR)? Here's my own home-grown definition:

> Virtual reality is anything that isn't real, but does a good job of faking it.

That's a pretty broad definition. Some folks would define virtual reality narrowly, in terms of goggles, gloves, and interactivity. I made my definition for a good reason. I also have some home-grown ideas about why anyone would want to mess around with virtual reality in the first place:

> Virtual reality is for stretching and enhancing the imagination.

Goggle/glove/interactive VR certainly does that, but so do a lot of other things that fake reality. A few examples from actual virtual reality (AVR)[1] will demonstrate my point:

- Chemists can view complex molecules in real time and visualize new ways of creating materials.

- Students can roam through a computer representation of the solar system to learn about things like gravity and mass.

- Pilots can train without leaving the ground, or test expensive new aircraft designs without trashing the hardware in a crash.

- An artist can create worlds that are internally logical without worrying about troublesome things like the laws of physics.

---

[1] I know, this is begging the point, but consider how you would phrase it! This is a good place to note that I have made liberal use of footnotes throughout the text. I have stuffed three kinds of material into footnotes: technical stuff for those who like that kind of thing; obscure but interesting trivia; and fun, irreverent, and editorial comments.

■ An architect and client can "see" a new building—even walk around in it—before the first spade of earth is turned.

It isn't important whether things are merely artificial or totally virtual. Debates about what is and is not virtual reality are quite beside the point. Is it fun? Is it useful? These are the kinds of questions that really matter when it comes to artificial/virtual reality.

What Virtual Reality Is

Whether you play with VR or use it as a tool, there is a common element involved: visualization. However, what you visualize may or may not actually correspond to reality. Just as a materials engineer can use VR to visualize how materials interact with each other at the atomic level, an artist can create virtual spaces that don't even obey the basic laws of physics. Does gravity always have to pull downward? Does mass really have to matter?[2]

If we set aside the term *virtual reality* for a moment, we can use these two terms:

■ **Artificial reality**—Anything that looks, feels, or operates realistically, but isn't real.[3]

■ **Virtual madness**—Stuff that breaks the rules of reality.

These are equally legitimate virtual pursuits. Both are a part of virtual reality. Some of us wish to recreate reality, either just like it is (scientific VR), or as we would like it to be. Others want to push the envelope, to use VR to stretch—maybe even to the breaking point—the human intellect and imagination. VR gives us the ability to, at least temporarily, redefine what reality is.

Let's face it—a book is a simple form of virtual reality. Pictures are a simple form of virtual reality. Ever since someone first used language, pictures, and sounds to represent things in the real world, mankind has been involved with virtual reality. Computers are extending the range to the point where we can imagine a time when it might be impossible to distinguish between the real world and a virtual one.

My point is that such extreme examples of virtual reality are not the only things to categorize as virtual reality. 3D modeling is both cool and virtual, just as 3D goggles are. So is a telerobotic arm, landscape generation, 3D home design, and so

---

[2]Pun intended.

[3]Naturally, the degree of realism will vary with the hardware available.

on. I see virtual reality as a continuum, with cave paintings at one end and total-immersion, full-body alternate reality at the other end. This book is about the stuff in the middle—it's new enough to be interesting and fun; it's (mostly) inexpensive so you can afford it; and it's virtual enough to excite and tantalize your imagination.

The Cost of Virtual Reality

It would be great if a reality built out of electrons and photons didn't cost anything, but that's not the case. You can get started in virtual reality easily and inexpensively, but if you plan to seek out a high degree of realism and real-time imaging, you had better have a decent budget. Here are the facts of life in the virtual universe:

- It takes lots and lots of pixels to create high-resolution images. If you want fancy graphics, the two most important components in your system become the video subsystem and the CPU. Get the best you can afford in both areas.

- If you plan to use video, every part of your system will need to be an above-average performer. This includes your hard disk (larger and faster are better), the video system (accelerator cards are a must; look for ones that support Video for Windows in hardware), and the CPU (486/33 or better).

- Rendering is a time-intensive process. I had no trouble creating animations with 3D Studio that required 5 or 6 hours to render. Plan on using your computer to render at night or on the weekend.

You don't need the most expensive components to work with virtual reality. Patience will often substitute for cash. The only time it won't work that way is when you need real-time performance, such as with digital video. Some of the cutting edge software on the CD may require more hardware than you have installed. It's not the software that's at fault; it's the bit-hungry, byte-mangling requirements of multimedia and virtual reality that are the problem. If you are serious about virtual reality, you'll have to either invest time and patience or upgrade your hardware. If you just want to explore, the hardware you have now may be fine. I recommend at least a fast 386 with 4 megabytes of memory if you want to create 3D images. The larger your hard disk, the better. I would recommend at least a 210 megabyte disk if you're shopping for one, but it doesn't cost much more to move up to 300 or even 500 megabytes these days. Don't shortchange yourself with false economy if virtual reality appeals to you. I use a 486/66 with 12 megabytes of RAM, a hot ATI Ultra Pro video card with 2M of memory, 16-bit color, a gigabyte of hard disk, and an Intel Smart Video recorder for video capture. Some days, I wish I had more—but that's life on the cutting edge, and virtual reality is right there on the cutting edge.

Magic, Realism, and the Imagination

This book is intended to work like a cookbook. If you want to cook a meal, the first thing most of us do is drag out a good cookbook and see what we can create with the food at hand. A good cookbook provides:

- A list of ingredients.

- The procedure for mixing the ingredients.

- Instructions for the actual cooking—oven temperature, how long to boil, and so on.

- Basic descriptions of fundamental procedures—poaching fish, sautéing onions, and so forth.

We can convert these into their computer equivalents:

- A list of the hardware and software you'll need.

- The procedures for getting things to work together.

- How to use the all this cool stuff—menu choices, file formats, and so on.

- Basic descriptions of fundamental procedures—rendering in three dimensions, interactive solutions, and so forth.

As I write this, the image that comes to mind is of the three witches in *Macbeth*. "Boil, boil, toil and trouble..." That's the recipe for virtual reality. Mix and match reality and imagination in the strongest concentrations you can stand and see what comes out—goblins and ghosts, major distortions of space-time, or a fly-through of your new kitchen. The only limit to what you can do with virtual reality is right between your ears. Hold on tight, get ready for adventure: it's time for the amazing, 16.7 million color journey into the computer/mind spaces of *Virtual Reality Madness!*

Ron Wodaski

July, 1993

I

VIRTUAL REALITY IS HERE

1

GETTING STARTED WITH VIRTUAL REALITY

Virtual Reality has arrived.[1] For decades, virtual reality has been nothing more than speculation and promises. Now, today, you can order virtual reality hardware and software from a catalog. Science fiction buffs have been waiting with barely suppressed glee for just this moment.

I have to confess that it is enormous fun to write about virtual reality. VR, as it is often called, is by far the coolest thing to happen on computers since electrons first danced to the whims of programmers. I can't tell you how many times I went storming through the house to find my wife, or one of the kids, to show them some stunning apparition on my computer screen. I can only hope you'll have as much pleasure discovering the possibilities as I did.

This book is arranged like a journey. In this chapter, you'll start with a form of VR that is easy to visualize and easy to work with. As you move through the book, you'll learn more and more about the concepts and techniques of Virtual Reality. Along the way, I've tried my best to include lots of fun stuff.[2]

Beginning at the Beginning

Virtual reality is an extremely broad term. It has come to refer to almost anything that has anything at all to do with three dimensions on computers. The original use of the word—back when VR was all in the imagination—referred mostly to complete immersion systems. This meant complex headsets to project a 3D visual space, and a bodysuit full of electronics to send and receive signals about your own body position. Using such a system, you would feel just like you were in a virtual world.

Such hardware is, in fact, available today. It requires a lot of supporting hardware, however, and represents the furthest edge of VR—both in terms of cost and capability. It is not necessary, however, to start with such complex hardware and software at all. To my way of thinking, virtual reality starts in the imagination. Mankind was born with the ability to visualize in three dimensions—that's where VR begins. The computer can only build on or enhance our own built-in VR capabilities.

---

[1] I have chosen to make liberal use of footnotes throughout the text—sometimes for fun, and sometimes to expand a thought or follow a useful tangent. You have been warned!

[2] This reflects my theory of learning: we learn better and faster when we are having fun. Remember advanced math, and how boring it probably was? What if you had been using what you were learning to build a remote controlled airplane, or to design a more efficient racing-boat hull? It seems so obvious you gotta wonder sometimes about the educational system.

One of the most fascinating aspects of virtual reality is the creation of virtual landscapes. Later in this chapter, you learn how to easily build both natural and fantastic landscapes using a product called Vistapro. Vistapro is a wonderful program that I enjoyed a great deal. It isn't often that I find a program that is this enjoyable and fun to use.

Planets 'R' Us: Vistapro 3.0

RECIPE

1 copy program
2 megabytes or more available extended (XMS)[3] memory
1M hard disk space
1t Patience

Instructions: Load the landscape of your choice and arrange ingredients in a pleasing setting. Render slowly on a fast machine until done. Serve with animations or morphing, or season with 3D Studio or Imagine for exciting variations. Good rendering is like homemade bread: it has to sit a while before it's ready.

Figure 1.1 shows a typical landscape created with Vistapro.[4] It is based on a natural landscape in southwestern Oregon—Crater Lake. The vertical scale has been enhanced to emphasize details, and the sky, lighting, and angle of view were chosen to reflect the purpose for the image: a desktop for Windows. There's lots of clear space in the sky for icons.

---

[3] It's easy to get confused between EMS and XMS memory. XMS (extended memory) is faster because your computer can work with bigger chunks of it. EMS (expanded memory) is slower because it requires a lot of juggling of memory space. If software gives you a choice, choose XMS.

[4] There are numerous generated landscapes on the CD-ROM as well. They come in all sizes, so you can have fun no matter what computer you have. Images range from basic 8-bit images to 1024x768, 24-bit photo-realistic images. There are even some 3D images for use with red/blue 3D glasses.

Figure 1.1.
A landscape
created with
Vistapro 3.0.

This image appears exactly as it was created in Vistapro. As you learn how to work with Vistapro, you can control precisely how the image appears—realistic or dreamy, sharply defined or obscured by fog. And after creating a landscape, you can enhance realism further by altering the image using paint programs, such as Photoshop from Adobe. Figure 1.2 shows a fanciful Mars landscape at local dawn—including artificial lens flare for a nice touch of ultra-realism.

Figure 1.2.
A Vistapro image
enhanced in
Adobe Photoshop
for Windows.

It's easy to create a landscape in Vistapro. The program includes mapping data for a number of real locations, from Big Sur in California to the Alps in Europe. You can also create fractal landscapes—scenes based on the science of fractal[5] imagery. To create a landscape, you only need to set a number of parameters and hit the Render button (see Figure 1.3 to view a rendering in progress). To make life even easier, Vistapro comes with presets you can use to quickly set up for rendering.

Figure 1.3.
A Vistapro
landscape
partially
generated.

I have included a demo version of Vistapro on the CD-ROM that accompanies this book. You can use the demo version to explore the capabilities of the program. Unlike most demo programs, it is full featured—you can even save your work to disk. However, it is the *prior* version of Vistapro for the PC, Version 1.0. (The first PC version was 1.0, and the second Version is 3.0. There was no Version 2.0, so you aren't getting some horribly out-of-date version of Vistapro—just the *last* version. Is that clear?) You can also get Vistapro add-on products that allow you to create morphs[6]

---

[5] Fractal comes from the word fraction. It refers to the use of fractional dimensions to create interesting, life-like images. For example, you draw on paper in two dimensions, and experience life in three dimensions. A fractal image might have dimension of 2.65, instead of a simple, straightforward 2 or 3.

[6] The term morph is a shortened version of the word metamorphasis. A morph involves a visual transformation of one image into another. The movie Terminator 2 used numerous morphs of a police officer turning into the liquid-metal terminator. Many commercials also feature morphs these days, such as a car morphing into a tiger.

and animations. This allows you to create landscapes that grow and change before your eyes, or you can animate a fly-through of a landscape.

The opening screen of Vistapro is shown in Figure 1.4.[7] The landscape is shown on the left, and various controls are on the right. In this section, we'll look at how you can use the controls to create fractal landscapes, modify existing landscapes, and render landscapes in a variety of interesting ways.

Figure 1.4.
The Vistapro
screen.

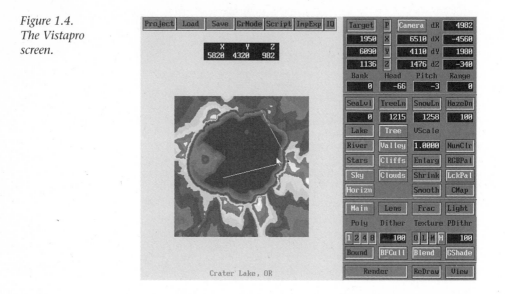

Perhaps the nicest thing about Vistapro is that you can use it to do wonderful things without having to worry a whole lot about the complexities of 3D. Drawing software is awkward to use in 3D because it requires you to think in three dimensions. With Vistapro, you can rely on basic map-reading skills.

Setting Up for Rendering

Vistapro normally involves three steps. You can spend more or less time at each step perfecting your landscape.

---

[7] Vistapro was originally written for the Amiga, so the interface isn't PC standard. However, it's easy to use and shouldn't present any usage problems once you learn a few quirks. Quick tip: A "gadget" is really a text box, and you have to press the Enter key to complete your entry.

■ Create or select a map.

■ Set scene parameters.

■ Render.

There are numerous ways to create a map, and you can always load one of the many maps supplied with the program. Vistapro uses DEM—Digital Elevation Modeling— to describe the 3D coordinates of a landscape. The sample files included with the program rely on USGS[8] mapping data and are extremely accurate.

Instant Virtual Reality

In the following sections, you'll learn how to fine-tune the various settings available in Vistapro to produce exactly the kind of landscape you desire. You don't have to twiddle the dials, however, to get results. To follow along with this example, you can use the demo version supplied on disk, or the regular version of Vistapro 3.0. To begin, load one of the supplied DEM files by clicking the Load menu and dragging to the Load DEM option. (Refer to Figure 1.4 to locate the menu bar at the top left of the Vistapro screen.) Pick any file on the list, such as craterla.dem, and click on it. Click the Load button at the upper left to load the file.

There's a tiny little button at the right of the menu, labeled IQ. Click this button to display a list of pre-defined settings:

Low—This setting will render very quickly, but the results are crude. This is useful when you want to check the general appearance of the landscape quickly.

Medium—This setting is useful for slower computers, or to get a (relatively) quick look at your landscape.

High—This setting yields useful results—images that look realistic and can be used in desktop publishing or other situations that require detailed images.

Ultra—This sets Vistapro for extremely high-quality rendering. It will take longer to render images, but the results are often stunning.

User—You can also define your own presets.

---

[8] That's the United States Geologic Survey.

The button you pick depends on what you would like to see, and also on the speed of your computer.[9] If you are using a 386/25 or slower machine, I would recommend the Medium setting for your first rendering. For faster computers, High or even Ultra would be fine.

Clicking one of the IQ buttons sets numerous parameters; you may notice some of the settings on the right side of the screen changing. Don't worry about those settings yet. The only button you are interested in is at the bottom left of the controls: Render. Click it, and watch as the landscape is created bit by bit on the screen. The speed of rendering will vary dramatically with the speed of your computer, and with the level of quality you set. It can take from a few seconds to a minute.

The border of the screen will flash when the rendering is complete. If you would like to save the rendering, press the Escape key, and then click on the Save menu. Select the image type you would like to save. For this exercise, I would suggest using Save PCX. This will save your landscape rendering as an 8-bit PCX image.

Basic Settings

There is one setting that will make a dramatic difference in the appearance of your rendered images: the screen resolution. By default, Vistapro assumes you have the most basic VGA display hardware installed.[10] However, if you have a Super VGA card, don't despair: if it includes support for VESA[11], you can use Super VGA resolutions for rendering.

There are two ways that display cards support the VESA standard:

- Right in the hardware.
- Using a TSR[12] program.

---

[9] Rendering is a CPU-intensive activity. Until recently, personal computers were simply too slow to be used for rendering. If you feel badly about the time it takes to render, consider this: until the 486 CPU came along, most rendering was done on supercomputers like the Cray.

[10] The default resolution is 320x200 and 256 colors (sometimes called MCGA). This is a standard VGA resolution.

[11] There is a long story behind VESA. Every display adapter has its own way of doing SuperVGA— for a long time, there was no standard way of implementing Super VGA. This was a big problem for software companies, who had to write different software for each Super VGA display card, or pass up support for Super VGA. VESA changed that by creating a standard interface for Super VGA resolutions (800x600, 1024x768, and so on).

[12] *Terminate* and *Stay Resident*.

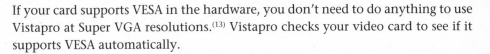

If your card supports VESA in the hardware, you don't need to do anything to use Vistapro at Super VGA resolutions.[13] Vistapro checks your video card to see if it supports VESA automatically.

If your card uses a TSR to support VESA, you'll need to load that program before you run Vistapro to get Super VGA support. Consult the documentation that came with your video card for information.

If you have VESA support—and most recent video display cards do support VESA—you gain access to the Super VGA resolutions. Vistapro supports a number of Super VGA resolutions, ranging from 640x400 to 1280x1024. However, most video cards that support 1280x1024 don't support it under VESA, so the highest resolution you are likely to be able to use is 1024x768. This is more than adequate for most needs. To set the resolution, use the GrMode menu button. This menu also enables you to turn on support for 24-bit color. If you elect to use 24-bit color, keep in mind that the file sizes for high-resolution images can get very large—1024x768x24 bits is 2,359,296 bytes (2,304K).

Not all video card drivers support VESA as well as they should. If you encounter problems—black or gray screen, vertical bars, scrambled images—you should contact the video card manufacturer for an updated VESA driver.

If you are working with the demo version of Vistapro from the CD-ROM, disk file size doesn't matter—you can't save to disk anyway. However, if you only have the minimum amount of memory required by Vistapro installed (2 megabytes) you may be limited to the lower screen resolutions.

Camera and Target

In the "Instant Virtual Reality" section earlier in this chapter, the view you saw used the default camera and target locations. In this section, you'll learn how to set up your own camera and target positions.

Figure 1.5 shows the controls for camera and target. There are three columns at the top, and a row of settings at the bottom. The first column, at the left, defines

---

[13] The demo version of Vistapro supplied on the CD may not support some or all Super VGA resolutions.

the Target location in 3D coordinates. The middle column defines the Camera location, and the rightmost column shows the delta[14] between the Target and Camera coordinates. The small buttons between the Target and Camera settings can be used to lock one or more of the settings. The bottom row of settings are used to alter the orientation (heading) of the Camera. All distances are measured in meters, and all headings are measured in degrees.

Figure 1.5.
Camera and
Target controls.

When you work in two dimensions, only two coordinates are needed to specify a location: *height* and *width*. Working in three dimensions requires three coordinates to specify a location: height, width, and *depth*. The first two dimensions, height and width, are referred to using the letters x and y.[15] The third dimension, depth, uses the letter z. These letters are a standard shorthand way of referring to the three dimensions; you'll see them over and over in this book and elsewhere.

You can see the letters x, y, and z in the columns under the Camera and Target controls. There is a column of buttons between the Camera and Target columns; these are used for locking the current position of the camera and target along any one dimension. For example, if you want to prevent any changes to height, simply click the z button before moving the camera or target.

Moving the camera or target is very easy. Click the appropriate button at the top of the column, either Camera or Target. Then click anywhere on the map; the camera or target will move to the new location. Both are marked by a tiny square, and the camera angle is displayed by two lines radiating from the camera. Objects within the angle will be included in the rendering.[16]

---

[14] Delta is a Greek letter used by scientists and mathemeticians to indicate change or difference.

[15] These are called Cartesian coordinates, as you may have learned in high school algebra or math classes.

[16] Because the camera view is 3D, and the map view is 2D, you will find that objects outside the angle may show up in the rendered landscape. For example, if you set the camera overlooking the valley, objects in the valley will show up for some distance outside the indicated angle.

The third column shows the delta, or difference, between the target and the camera. The top number, **dR**, is the actual range distance (straight line, in meters) from the camera to the target. The three figures below **dR**—**dX**, **dY**, **dZ**—represent the distance in the **x**, **y**, and **z** directions. For example, if the camera is at 1000 meters, and the target is at 500 meters, then **dZ** is equal to -500 meters.

There are four settings at the bottom of the Camera/Target area. These control the orientation of the camera, including such things as tilt and rotation. Vistapro uses the technical terms[17] for each kind of orientation. To understand the terms, imagine that you are five years old again and playing airplane with your friends. Your arms are out to the side and serve as your wings. Most of these measurements describe a rotation of one kind or another, so most measurements are expressed as degrees.[18]

Bank—If you lower your left wing (arm)[19], that is a bank to the left (counterclockwise), and is expressed as a negative number. If you lower your right wing, that is a bank to the right and is expressed as a positive number. A bank of -10 means that the left wing is lowered 10 degrees.

Head—Heading describes the direction you are facing. North is zero; south is 180 degrees. Rotation to the right (clockwise) is a positive number; rotation to the left is a negative number. If you refer back to Figure 1.4, where the heading is -66, you'll see that this means the camera is facing roughly west northwest.

Pitch—If you lean forward or backward, you can change your pitch. If you pitch forward (nose, literally, down), that's a negative number. If you pitch backward (nose up), that's a positive number. A positive pitch of 90 degrees puts your nose right on the ceiling.

Range—This is not a measurement in degrees; it uses meters. It is a setting you can use to eliminate portions of the view from the rendering. For example, if you enter 1,000 meters, objects more than 1,000 meters away will not be rendered. Similarly, if you enter -500, objects closer than 500 meters will not be rendered.

---

[17] These terms are taken from aviation and are often used to describe the movements of an aircraft.

[18] There are 360 degrees in a complete circle. Thus, a quarter rotation is 90 degress, and a half rotation is 180 degrees.

[19] Of course, the right wing (arm) goes up at the same time.

By default, the camera is placed 30 meters above the height of the landscape at the location you choose. This prevents nearby objects from obscuring the view. You can change the camera height by entering a new number in the Camera Z control.[20] You don't need to make any changes to Bank, Head, Pitch, or Range to get useful renderings. Vistapro will automatically set these when you locate the target or camera.

> **TIP**
>
> For a dramatic point of view, change the camera height to 500 or 1,000 meters above the height of the map location.

Trees and Clouds, Lakes and Rivers

The middle portion of the control panel (see Figure 1.6) contains a number of parameters that will have a major impact on the appearance of your rendered landscape. You can add a number of natural features, including such things as lakes and rivers, clouds, stars, cliffs, and so on.

Figure 1.6.
The Vistapro
middle control
panel.

The middle control panel also includes settings for various boundaries, such as the distance at which haze becomes apparent, and the tree line. Using these settings, you can create a very natural-looking landscape.

There are four different kinds of settings on the middle control panel:

- ■ Boundaries
- ■ Natural features
- ■ Scale and textures
- ■ Colors

You'll learn about each of these subsections in turn.

---

[20] You can change the settings in any of the controls manually at any time before rendering.

BOUNDARIES

These settings allow you to establish the location of basic natural boundaries in the landscape. You can use these settings to make subtle adjustments to the landscape. For example, you can add haze to increase the sense of distance in the landscape.

There are four settings you can control:

SeaLvl—Use this to change sea level. For example, if you enter 500, all portions of the landscape at or below 500 meters are changed to 0 meters. All portions of the landscape above 500 meters are lowered by 500 meters. The result is that everything at or below the sea level is flattened. To set sea level based on the map, click the SeaLvl button and then click on the map to indicate an elevation.

TreeLn—Vistapro can render trees in the landscape. This number defines the height in meters above which trees will not grow. This reflects the way trees actually grow in natural settings. As with many of its features, Vistapro uses artificial intelligence to decide where, exactly, to put trees. Steep slopes have a lower treeline, and flat surfaces have a higher tree line. Again, this reflects the way trees behave in nature. To set a tree level based on the map, click the TreeLn button, and then click on the map to indicate an elevation.

SnowLn—This is the lowest level at which Vistapro will draw snow on the landscape. As with the tree line, Vistapro will bend the rules to generate a realistic-looking snow line. To set a snow level based on the map, click the SnowLn button, and then click on the map to indicate an elevation.

HazeDn—This is the haze distance—a value of zero eliminates haze, values up to about 1,000 give progressively more haze, and values over 1,000 generate a thick fog.[21] To have Vistapro calculate a "typical" haze value, click the HazeDn button.

NATURAL FEATURES

Version 3.0 of Vistapro gives you control over a number of natural features in the landscape. Such features can make a dramatic difference in the appearance of the rendered image. Table 1.1 lists the various settings you can control.

---

[21] In most cases, such foggy scenes aren't very useful—almost all of the detail from the landscape is lost. One type of landscape that sometimes benefits from severe haze is a seacoast, where some fog and a jutting headline can look terrific.

Table 1.1. Natural Features in Vistapro 3.0.

Feature	Description
Lake	Click this button, then click on a point in the map. All points at that elevation will define a continuous shoreline surrounding a lake. Be careful with this one—if there is a break in the proposed shoreline, the lake could "spill over" into places you didn't intend.
River	Click this button, then click on a point on the map. Vistapro will calculate a river course for you. If the river isn't wide enough for your needs, click at an adjoining point to widen the river.
Stars	Use this option in place of Sky for a nighttime effect. You can choose large or small stars. Unless you intend to output to video tape, small stars are your best bet. Important: if you don't change the landscape colors, they will still render in daytime colors!
Sky	Causes Vistapro to render a sky. If you have a bitmap you want to use as a sky, turn Sky off and use the Load/Background menu selection to load your bitmap.
Horizon	Causes Vistapro to render a horizon line. If you don't want a distant horizon, or if you have your own background, click to turn this off. In most cases, you will want it on.[22]
Tree	Turning this on causes Vistapro to add trees to the landscape. You won't see the trees until you render. The dialog box that you use to define the type and density of trees is described later in this section.
Valley	Determines the extent to which a valley changes the tree line or snow line. Clicking it opens a dialog box with two values. **Valley Width** determines how much valley effect is used. Default value is 100. **Valley Scale** determines the extent of

---

[22] If you set a very high camera elevation, having Horizon on will usually improve the appearance of the image. A high camera elevation may show the edges of the map, and a carefully chosen horizon color can make this less noticeable.

Feature	Description
	valley effect at each valley point. Larger numbers expand the range of the valley effect, and small numbers restrict it. The default is 8.
Cliffs	This defines which portions of the landscape are steep enough to be considered cliffs. Special colors are used to render cliffs. In some cases, a more natural look results if Cliffs is turned off. You'll need to experiment to see the effect on a given landscape.
Clouds	Turning this on causes Vistapro to add clouds to the sky. You won't see the clouds until you render. The dialog box that you use to define the type and density of clouds is described later in this section.

All of these controls have noticeable effects on the rendered image, but several will have a big impact on the final rendered image. We'll look at those in detail now.

LAKE

The Lake setting is both powerful and dangerous, but it can add a touch of realism to a scene. You can change the colors for water to create different moods.[23] The most important thing to learn is the relationship between the point you click and the shape of the lake. Fortunately, Vistapro allows you to preview the appearance of the lake before you finalize it.[24]

RIVER

It takes a little experimentation to develop a knack for getting rivers to look right. A single click to create a river is seldom enough to get a useful river effect; it's more like a creek effect. To create natural-looking rivers, look for the characteristic land forms on the map. Figure 1.7 shows a close-up of a portion of a map, and the best areas for starting a river are marked. Figure 1.8 shows the results of a single click to create a river; Figure 1.10 shows a multi-click river. Note that there are several tributaries to the river, and that the river is wider.

---

[23] See the section, "Colors," later in the chapter.

[24] Unfortunately, the dialog box that asks you "Accept Lake?" often covers the preview area. You'll need a quick eye to determine if the lake will work for you, because you may only see the preview for a fraction of a second. If in doubt, I highly recommend saving your work before creating a lake!

Figure 1.9 shows the results of rendering the river in Figure 1.8. Note that it is almost invisible. Figure 1.11 shows a rendering of the river in Figure 1.10. In this case, the river fits the scale of the landscape much better.

Figure 1.7.
A detail of a
map, showing
good locations
for originating
a river.

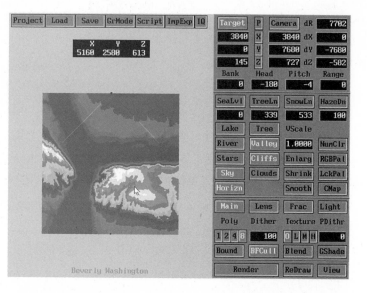

Figure 1.8.
A river created
with a single
click of the
mouse.

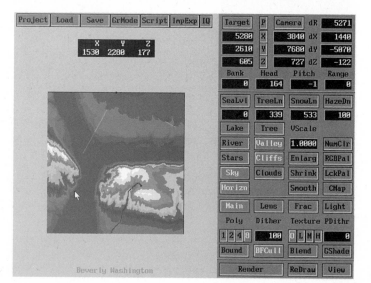

Figure 1.9.
A rendering of
the river created
in Figure 1.8.

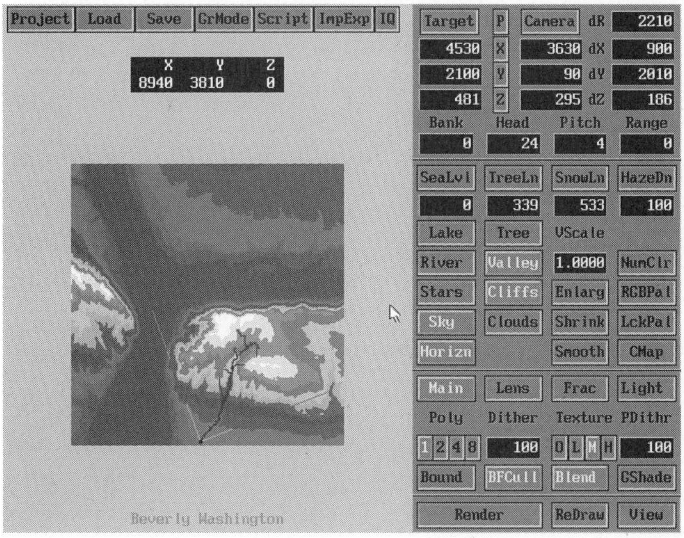

Figure 1.10.
A river created
with multiple
mouse clicks.

STARS

It's easy to add stars to your images: just click the Stars button to depress it. However, this only changes the appearance of the sky, which will now include a dark background and lots of stars. The landscape colors don't change. The resulting image won't look bad, but if you want a realistic nighttime scene, you'll need to edit the landscape colors. Refer to the section on Colors in this chapter for more information.

Figure 1.11.
A rendering of
the river created
in Figure 1.10.

Like other additions to the landscape, such as trees and clouds, the starry sky will render consistently. If you create an animation, you can count on the stars behaving like real stars. That is, they will appear to "move" as the animation point of view changes.

TREES

The newest version of Vistapro—3.0—improves greatly on the original in this area. It is capable of rendering realistic-looking trees. However, there is a price to pay for such realism: rendering time increases dramatically if you set the quality of tree images very high. Unless you are rendering a final image, you will probably want to render trees at modest settings.

Clicking on the Trees button when it is off displays the dialog box shown in Figure 1.12.

The first thing to notice is that there are four different kinds of trees: Pine, Oak, Cactus, and Palm (see Figure 1.13 for an example of pine trees). Most types of terrain in Vistapro are like this. Each terrain type has a range of colors that are used to render the terrain. The default colors for trees are four shades of green, naturally. Having several colors available allows Vistapro to generate more varied and interesting textures for the various kinds of terrain.

Figure 1.12.
The dialog box
for defining the
characteristics of
trees.

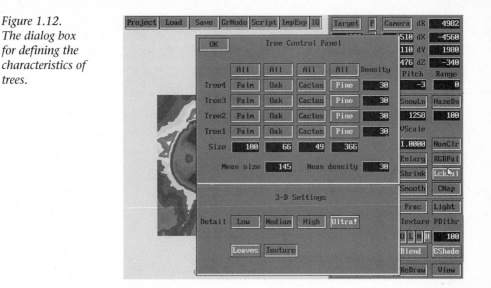

The Trees dialog box is a lot like a program within a program. It controls the rendering of trees, which are complete, discrete fractal objects. The top half of the dialog box allows you to define the types of trees that will appear at specific elevations, as well as the size and density of trees at each elevation.

Figure 1.13.
Vistapro pine
trees.

For example, if you wanted to have more pine trees at high elevations, and more oak trees at low elevations, you could set Tree4 as Pine, Tree3 as both Pine and Oak, Tree2 as Pine and Oak, and Tree1 as Oak.

The density of trees you use will vary with the landscape. If you want a sparse look, try settings of 10-30. If you want a loose forest, try a setting of 50. Higher settings take you all the way to forest, for which you will not be able to see individual trees. Size will also vary depending on the landscape. You may need to experiment with different sizes until you get a look you want. A flat landscape will probably look best with smaller trees, while a deep valley with steep cliffs may look better with taller trees. When in doubt, simply accept the default settings.

You can control the overall size and density of all tree types using the Mean size and Mean density settings.

The Tree Control Panel also contains settings for 3D rendering of trees. You can choose different levels of detail—Low, Medium, High, and Ultra. As a general rule, match the tree detail to the image size. If you are rendering at 320x200, Low will be fine. Any additional detail would simply get lost. Even at 1024x768, only the trees closest to the camera will benefit from the extra detail.

The two buttons at the very bottom of the Tree dialog box, Leaves and Texture, further refine the appearance of trees. The Leaves button does just what you would expect: it adds leaves to the trees. The Texture button adds fractal textures to leaves and branches of trees. If you don't use 3D settings for trees, they are created as stick figures, as shown in Figure 1.14. Figure 1.15 shows a rendered image with leaves, and Figure 1.16 shows the same image with texture instead of leaves. All of these images were rendered at 1024x768 with an IQ setting of Ultra.

CLOUDS

Your landscape will need a good set of natural-looking clouds to be complete. It just wouldn't do to have a gorgeous, natural landscape sitting under a completely artificial sky, now, would it? A click of the Clouds button displays the dialog box shown in Figure 1.17. There are just a few buttons and controls, but it doesn't take much to create a pleasing sky.

Figure 1.14.
Two-dimensional
trees: oak (a) and
palm (b).

a

b

Figure 1.15.
Oak (a) and
palm (b) trees
with leaves.

a

b

Figure 1.16.
Palm trees with
texture. Note that
these are not
substantially
different from
trees without
texture at this
resolution
(640x480).

Figure 1.17.
The Clouds
dialog box.

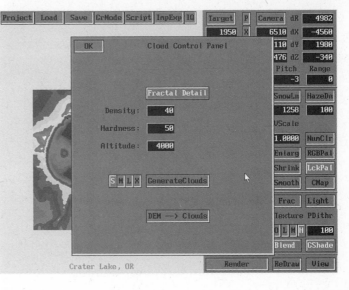

Table 1.2 lists the various cloud controls.

Table 1.2. Vistapro Cloud Controls.

Control	Description
Fractal Detail	Adds fractal details to clouds for a more realistic effect.
Density	Determines the total cloud coverage. Higher numbers result in more clouds.
Hardness	Sets fluffiness. Low settings result in fluffy, fleecy clouds.
Altitude	Determines the height of clouds. Clouds will always be created higher than the camera's height.
S/M/L/X	Click one of these buttons to determine the size of the clouds, ranging from small to extra large.
GenerateClouds	Once you have the settings the way you want them, click this button to generate the clouds.
DEM —> Clouds	Creates clouds based on the DEM data of the current landscape. You can use this to create clouds and then save them with the Save/Clouds menu item.

You can use the DEM —> Clouds button for a very interesting effect: sky writing. Create a PCX file in your favorite image editor that contains text, then load it into Vistapro using the PCX —> DEM selection on the ImpExp[25] menu. Then use the DEM —> Clouds button to create clouds shaped like the text.

Figure 1.18 shows simple, medium clouds without any fractal detail, and Figure 1.19 shows clouds with fractal detail added. The differences are subtle, but then so are clouds.

---

[25] Import/Export.

Figure 1.18.
Clouds without
fractal detail.

Figure 1.19.
Clouds with
fractal detail
(most noticeable
just to the right
of top center).

SCALE AND TEXTURES

Just to the right of the controls for natural features is the third column of buttons in the middle control panel: scale and texture. There are three scale settings and one texture setting, as shown in Table 1.3.

Table 1.3. Vistapro Scale and Texture.

Control	Type	Description
VScale	Scale	Determines the vertical scale factor.
Enlarg	Scale	Enlarges a portion of the map to full map size.
Shrink	Scale	Shrinks multipart maps to the next smaller size.
Smooth	Texture	Smoothes rough edges in the map.

VERTICAL SCALE

Every point on the map is multiplied by the number you enter into the VScale box. This increases or decreases the height of all points on the map. For example, if you enter a value of 2.0000, every point will become twice as high. If you enter a value of 0.5000, every point will be half as high. Because the lowest level on the map is always zero, numbers greater than one have the effect of increasing the vertical relief of the map.[26] Numbers between zero and one reduce vertical relief.

You can also enter negative numbers. These have the effect of turning the map "inside out." That is, mountains become valleys, and valleys become mountains. This can produce some very interesting effects.

ENLARGE

This control allows you to enlarge a portion of a map to full map size. This can be useful when you generate a map using fractals[27]—if you see an interesting portion of the map, you can enlarge it and work with just that portion of the map.

After enlargement, the map will be smoother than it was because the partial map does not have the same level of detail as the full map. You can use the **Frac**talize button in the lower control panel to artificially add realistic detail. See the section "Fractal Magic" for details.

SHRINK

Shrink is not the exact opposite of Enlarge. A little background is necessary. Vistapro can work with several sizes of maps. The smallest size, 258x258 data points, is appropriately called Small. The standard size map is called large, and it is 514x514

---

[26] This is a fancy way of saying that the mountains get higher in relation to the valleys.

[27] See the Fractal Magic section.

data points. You can load one standard Vistapro DEM file, or up to four small DEM files. The largest size, Huge, is 1026x1026 data points, and can contain up to sixteen small files, four standard files, or one giant, extra-big, huge file.

The Shrink command shrinks the current map by one step in this hierarchy. Thus, a huge file will be shrunk to large, and a large will be shrunk to a small. A small file can't be shrunk any further.

This business of combining DEM files to view larger areas is new in Version 3.0 of Vistapro. Vistapro will automatically load all files in a larger view if you set the image size to Automatic.[28]

SMOOTH

You will seldom need to use smoothing with a DEM file that represents real data, but smoothing can be very useful when you are creating maps by other means. Smoothing will remove the "rough spots" in the data. For example, look at Figure 1.20, which shows a map generated using fractals. The texture is extremely rough. Now look at Figure 1.21, after smoothing has been applied—the texture is noticeably smoother.[29]

Figure 1.20.
A map with very
rough texture.

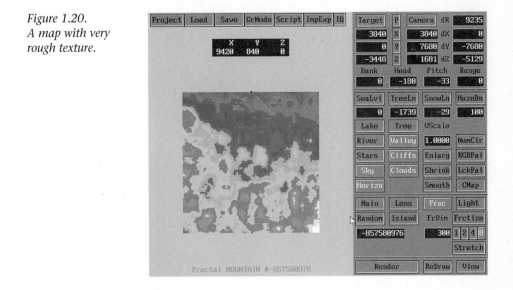

---

[28] This is set on the Project menu: Set DEM Size.

[29] You can use smoothing several times to tame a particularly rough landscape. However, smoothing tends to effect high points more than low points, so overuse can reduce the overall height of the terrain. You might need to apply a larger vertical scale after repeated smoothing.

Figure 1.21.
The same map
after smoothing
has been applied.

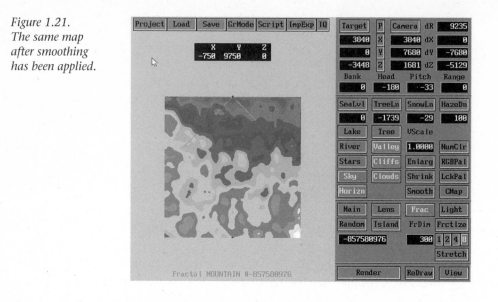

Use smoothing when the map details are too complex to make out clearly.

COLORS

This brings us to the last column of controls in the middle control panel. There are four buttons, as shown in Table 1.4.

Table 1.4. Vistapro Color Controls.

Control	Description
NumClr	Rendering normally uses all 256 colors in the 8-bit palette. If you plan to edit the image in a paint program, this setting allows you to use fewer colors for a rendering. You can then use the remaining palette slots for additional colors in a paint program. If your paint program supports 24-bit color, this is not necessary.
RGBPal	Normally, Vistapro selects the colors for a palette prior to rendering the image. This button allows you to force Vistapro to select a palette based on colors that actually appear in the rendered image. You must enable 24-bit support on the GrMode menu first, however.

Control	Description
LckPal	This locks the color palette. Normally, Vistapro calculates a separate palette for each image. This button forces Vistapro to use the current palette for rendering.
CMap	Pressing this button activates the Color Map dialog, which is described below.

Under most conditions, you won't need to do anything at all with this group of buttons. You can blissfully go on generating image after image without ever visiting this section of the screen. However, for special purposes, these are handy settings to have around.

After you have played around with Vistapro for a while, it can be fun to play around with the colors in a scene. For example, you might want to render a nighttime scene, or perhaps a Mars landscape appeals to you. The CMap button gives you the power to completely control the colors used by the system to render images. You can even save color settings to disk for later use. Figure 1.22 shows the Color Map control panel.

Figure 1.22.
The Color Map
control panel.

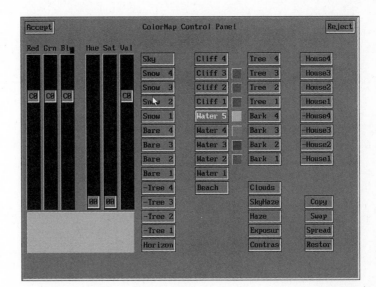

The Color Map control panel has a zillion buttons, and it's both easy and complex to use. The easy part is setting individual colors. To set a color, click the button (such as Sky) and then adjust either the Red/Green/Blue or the Hue/Saturation/Value sliders until you have the color you want. The hard part is creating a set of colors that will give you scenes that look the way you want them to look.

I've tried many different techniques for developing a coherent set of colors, and only one method works consistently well: working *within* groups of colors, and then *with* groups of colors. Generally, I make one pass through all of the color buttons, starting with Sky and working through, one color at a time. When I get to the first color in a group, I spend some time creating a color that is just right. The higher numbered colors, such as Snow4, are located at higher elevations, and are usually the brighter colors.[30] If I set a bright color in the 4 position, I can then set the exact same color in the 3 position, and then use the Value slider to darken it a little. This allows me to maintain tight control over color values inside of a group. If you want to vary Hue or Saturation instead of value, of course, you can simply change that slider instead of Value.

Using this technique, you wind up with four colors that change predictably. The color might not be exactly what you want, or it might not work well with other color groups, but you now have a controlled situation that makes it easier to edit the entire color group if that is necessary.

After I set up all of the colors in all of the color groups, I render a sample image to see the effect of the colors. If it is not the effect I wanted, I go back to the Color Map and adjust the colors in whichever groups are causing a problem. For example, if the snow is too dark, I lighten each of the colors in the Snow group by the same amount.

This process requires a light touch and some patience, but you can create some amazing-looking scenes if you are willing to take the trouble to create your own color map.

Bottom Control Panels

The bottom control panel can take on four different appearances, depending on which of the four buttons at the top of the panel you click. These panel variations are listed in Table 1.5, and described in detail in this section.

---

[30] If you have some special color scheme in mind, of course, you may want the reverse.

Table 1.5. Vistapro Bottom Control Panel.

Variation	Description
Main	Set rendering parameters, and establish basic geometry for rendering. You'll also need to have this panel active to start rendering.
Lens	Allows you to adjust angle of view for camera, and you can also create Red/Blue 3D images.[31]
Frac	Gives you access to fractal features, which include such goodies as adding fractal detail to a map, or creating a complete fractal landscape.
Light	Adjust lighting angle and set shadow style.

The controls in the bottom control panel are ones that you will use frequently. The most important panel to understand is the Main panel, because its controls will have a major impact on the appearance of your rendered image.

MAIN

Getting the right settings on the Main control panel (see Figure 1.23) can make or break your rendering. Knowing what to expect for various settings is the key to both natural and fantasy landscapes. You'll learn about the panel button by button in this section.

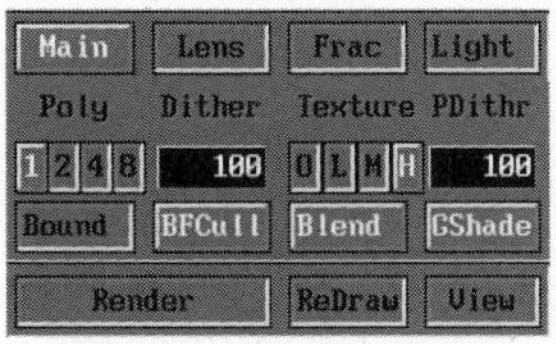

Figure 1.23.
The Main version
of the bottom
control panel.

---

[31] You'll need red/blue 3D glasses to get the stereo effect.

POLY

A properly rendered landscape won't show it, but it is made up of perfectly ordinary polygons.[32] These four mini buttons determine the size of the polygons used for rendering. Smaller polygons lead to more detailed renderings. Thus, a setting of 1 uses the smallest polygons, and a setting of 8 uses the largest polygons. Figure 1.24 shows a landscape rendered with a polygon setting of 8, and Figure 1.25 shows the same landscape rendered with a setting of 1. For these examples, to emphasize the effect of changing the polygon setting, no special smoothing or texturing capabilities were used.

Figure 1.24.
A landscape
rendered with a
polygon setting
of 8.

Large polygons are useful in the early stages of designing a landscape. You can check lighting angle, for example, without taking a lot of time for a detailed rendering. If all you want to know is whether a given cliff face is in light or shadow, a quick rendering is all you need.

Once you have the gross features of the landscape worked out, however, you'll need to use progressively smaller polygon settings to see what your landscape looks like.

---

[32] If you didn't learn about polygons in geometry class, read on. A polygon is a flat shape bounded by three or more lines that meet at vertices (a vertex is a fancy name for a corner). The simplest polygon is a triangle, and most 3D programs build more complex objects out of triangular polygons. A rectangle or an octagon are also examples of polygons. Polygons with sides of equal length are called regular polygons.

Figure 1.25.
A landscape
rendered with a
polygon setting
of 1.

DITHER

Vistapro determines what color to use for a given polygon based on its altitude.[33] By itself, this would create a banding effect that would not look natural. You can use this setting to determine the amount of dithering between adjacent bands of color.[34]

A value of 100 provides a modest amount of dithering—just enough to blend adjoining areas slightly. Higher values will smooth the transitions more; values over 1,000 will make it impossible to distinguish one area from another. A value of zero turns off dithering completely.

TEXTURE

Texture is a very powerful feature that has a lot to do with how natural your landscapes look. Without texture, color alone will be used to suggest landscape features. Unless you want an unnatural look for your landscape, texture is a good idea. However, texture adds quite a bit of time to the rendering process.

---

[33] Strictly speaking, this is not true. Vistapro considers other things besides altitude when deciding what color to use. For example, a polygon on the side of a mountain might be below the snow line, but Vistapro may decide to render it as snow or as a cliff instead of the color based on height. Vistapro takes a large number of values into consideration during rendering. Many of these values are intended to create the most natural looking landscapes.

[34] Dithering is a simple mixing of pixels from one area into those in an adjoining area.

There are four mini-buttons for setting texture levels. "O" stands for Off, and the remaining buttons set texture levels of Low, Medium, and High. When you set the texture level to Low or more, you are asked to choose between Shadow and Altitude texturing.

Shading texture is less CPU-intensive than Altitude texture. If you click on Shading, Vistapro will break each polygon into smaller polygons, and use a slightly different color for each polygon.[35] Altitude shading uses fractal technology to break the larger polygon into smaller polygons, each of which is shaded and colored individually. This creates extremely realistic features. If realism is your goal, make sure you set Altitude shading on.

PDITHR

This stands for pixel dithering. It is different from regular dithering. Regular dithering affects the boundaries between landscape colors. Pixel dithering applies to every pixel in the image. Generally, a little pixel dithering—100 to 250 units—is a good thing. This is particularly useful in the sky. Vistapro uses only a few colors for the sky, and pixel dithering improves the situation.

BOUND

Clicking this button allows you to mark—set a boundary for—an area. During rendering, only the portion of the map within the boundary area will be rendered.

BFCULL

This stands for "back face culling." When this button is depressed, polygons facing away from the point of view will not be calculated. It's hard to think of a situation where you wouldn't keep this feature turned on. The only one that comes to mind involves putting the camera *inside* a mountain, where you would want to see the complete underside of the mountain.

BLEND

This is yet another control that is easy to confuse with dithering. If the Blend button is depressed, Vistapro will average the colors of a polygon with those of the polygons surrounding it. This improves the appearance of distant potions of the rendering, and you'll have to decide for yourself if the reduced intensity of color in the foreground is worth the result.

---

[35] If you elect to use Shading texture, try clicking the GShade button as well. This turns on Gourand shading, a technique that is very effective for fantasy style landscapes. It is not normally useful to use Gourand shading with Altitude because Gourand will obliterate the details generated by Altitude shading.

GSHADE

This button controls Gourand shading. This form of shading is used by a variety of 3D software products including 3D Studio. It is very effective at eliminating boundaries between polygons. However, it also has a tendency to make the landscape look less realistic because it decreases the apparent level of detail in the image. It is very useful for creating fantasy landscapes with a romantic feel to them. For example, Figure 1.26 shows a landscape generated with a realistic effect, and Figure 1.27 shows the same landscape using Gourand shading.

Figure 1.26.
A landscape
rendered without
Gourand
Shading.

LENSES

Vistapro uses the metaphor of a camera to describe the point of view used for the rendering. The metaphor isn't carried very far,[36] but it is useful and does make it easier to get a feel for what the rendering will look like. After all, who hasn't had at least some experience with a camera these days?

Figure 1.28 shows the appearance of the bottom control panel when the Lens button is clicked. There are a number of buttons, but most of them are special purpose. In fact, for most uses, you probably won't need to mess with the lens settings at all.

---

[36] For example, 3D Studio uses extensive camera terminology and technique. You can roll or dolly the camera, and you can set a very wide range of lens characteristics.

Figure 1.27.
A landscape
rendered with
Gourand
Shading.

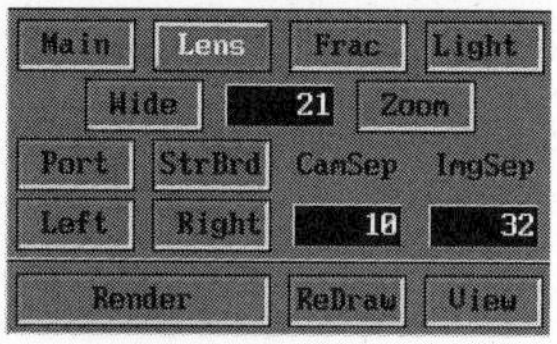

Figure 1.28.
The Lens version
of the bottom
control panel.

The primary control you have over the lens is focal length. In nontechnical terms, your choices range from wide angle to telephoto. However, the numbers don't correspond to the focal length values for the most common lens in use today for 35mm cameras. Lower numbers represent wider fields of view, and higher numbers represent narrower fields of view. If you click the Wide button, you'll get a 90 degree field of view. This is useful for most situations. In real life, a wide-angle lens is the lens of choice for landscape photography, and that's generally true for Vistapro as well.

The manual for Vistapro points out that you can set very, very high values for the focal length, but you'll need to move the camera very far away from the scene. For example, you can enter a value of 30,000, but the camera will have to be a million meters away from the scene to get any kind of useful image.

The remaining controls allow you to create 3D images using red/blue images (you'll need red/blue glasses to view the images) and panoramic images. The procedure for creating red/blue 3D images is straightforward, and is explained well in the manual. However, even though the actual procedure is simple, it takes some intense experimentation to determine the right values for effective 3D images. Expect to spend some time getting the hang of it. The key variables are camera separation and image separation. To get started, follow the manual's instructions exactly, and then vary the settings for your own viewing requirements.

> **TIP**
>
> If you do render 3D images, avoid large foreground objects when you are getting started. They can make it difficult to get a good 3D effect. I also suggest making sure there is no glare on the screen—bright reflections will almost certainly spoil the 3D effect.

Figure 1.29 shows what a red/blue 3D image looks like. This image is in black and white, but there are a number of images on the CD-ROM that you can view with special glasses.

Figure 1.29.
A red/blue 3D
image (see text
for explanation
of double image).

To create a panoramic series of images, you'll need to render three times: once in the usual way, then once with the Port[37] button depressed, and once with the StrBrd (starboard) button depressed. To make sure the images will meet properly at the edges, use a setting of 16 for the focal length (just click the Wide button to do so). Figure 1.30 shows a single image created from three views (port, normal, starboard).

Figure 1.30. A panoramic image created from three separate renderings.

FRACTAL MAGIC

The Fractal bottom control panel allows you to either modify an existing landscape with fractal details, or to generate random landscapes. Figure 1.31 shows the controls available in this control panel.

Figure 1.31. The Fractal version of the bottom control panel.

The Random button allows you to generate random fractal landscapes. Directly below the Random button is a text window where a random number will appear if

---

[37] Do you, like most of us, get confused when it comes to port and starboard? As a public service, I am offering some assistance in getting these two terms into your brain. Ignoring the fact that "left" and "right" would be just as easy to put on the buttons in Vistapro, there are some easy mnemonic devices you can use to tell your port from your starboard. Device 1: the word "left" has four letters, and so does "port." Ergo: port is left. Device 2: Left comes before right in the dictionary, and port comes before starboard, so port is left and starboard is right. Device 3: As Phil, my development editor noted, "the ship left port" is also a convenient way to remember that port is left. The interesting thing about both of these words is that they are based on words that describe both sides of a ship. Port comes from the word porthole, meaning a small circular hole in the side of a ship—portholes can be on any side of a ship. Starboard comes from "steer bord." A bord is the side of a ship (any side), and steering is just what you think it is. How these came to refer to specific directions is anyone's guess; the terms have been in use in English for more than 400 years! I guess it's too late to make a change.

you click the Random button.[38] Vistapro automatically generates the fractal landscape as a new map. The other controls in the Fractal control panel affect the nature of the new landscape.

A number such as 1,232,832 will generate a completely different landscape than its opposite, -1,232,832. You can also enter numbers directly into the text window, and press Enter to generate a landscape.

The Island button generates the landscape as an island—that is, the edge of the map is all at zero elevation. As with all landscapes, you'll have to fill the sea with water yourself; use the SeaLvl button, or the Lake button—either will work well.

The FrDim setting controls the height and roughness of the generated terrain. The default value is 100. Higher values will result in higher, rougher, landscapes, and lower values will result in smoother, lower terrain.

The Frctlze button will add fractal detail to existing landscapes. It uses the setting of FrDim to determine what to do. High values of FrDim will result in roughening of the landscape, whereas low values will smooth out the landscape. This button also relies on the setting of the Fractal Divisor buttons immediately below it. The Fractal Divisor buttons determine the scale of the fractalization. A setting of 1 adds fractal noise in very tiny changes, whereas a setting of 8 will probably completely alter the overall look of the landscape. This button works exactly in reverse when you generate a landscape—a small fractal divisor will generate large landscape features, and a high setting will result in many small mountains.

The Stretch button changes a landscape by stretching it vertically. Peaks get higher, and valleys get deeper. If you set a low value in the Fractal Divisor buttons, only small features get stretched—a good effect for nightmare landscapes. At high values of the Fractal Divisor, only larger features are stretched. You can stretch repeatedly with different Fractal Divisor settings to get different effects. Figure 1.32 shows a landscape before stretching, and Figure 1.33 shows the same landscape after stretching. Yes, that's Mt. St. Helens in both figures.

---

[38] You can enter your own number here as well. In fact, if you find a random landscape that you like, you can note the number and re-create it anytime you like.

Figure 1.32.
A landscape
before stretching.

Figure 1.33.
A landscape after
stretching with a
fractal divisor of
4 (twice) and
with a fractal
divisor of 1
(once).

LIGHTING

The lighting control panel also affects the appearance of the landscape map. A set of concentric circles is overlaid on the map, as shown in Figure 1.34. Each circle represents a different lighting angle. At the zero circle, the light will be right on the horizon. At the circle marked 45, the light will be exactly halfway between zenith[39] and the horizon. The number represents the number of degrees the light is above the horizon; zenith is 90 degrees. To set the light location,[40] click the Custom button on the Light control panel, and then move the mouse around on the map until the light is coming from the direction you want, at the angle you want.

Figure 1.34.
The Lighting
version of the
bottom control
panel.

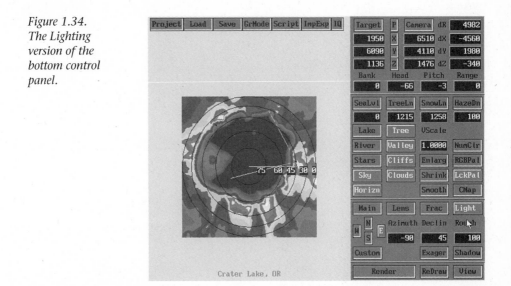

The angle of lighting, and the direction in relation to the camera, can make a huge difference in the appearance of the landscape. Generally, you will want to light from the side at intermediate angles. However, a bad lighting location can ruin your rendering, while a creative lighting angle can create a mood or effect that enhances the appearance of the rendering. For examples of the effects of different lighting setups, refer to Figures 1.35 through 1.40. In all figures, shadows are turned on, and exaggeration is off. Roughness is set to 100 in all figures.

---

[39] YATT: Yet another technical term. Zenith is the point in the sky directly overhead.

[40] It might help to think of the light as the sun on a cloudless day, because that's the effect you will get from setting the lighting angle and position.

*Figure 1.35.
A landscape with
the light right
behind the
camera; note how
flat-looking the
scene is.*

*Figure 1.36.
The same
landscape as
Figure 1.35, but
lit from the right
side at a 45
degree angle.*

*Figure 1.37.
The same
landscape as
Figure 1.35, but
lit from the left
side at a 45
degree angle.*

*Figure 1.38.
The same
landscape as
Figure 1.35, but
lit from overhead
(high noon).*

*Figure 1.39.
The same
landscape as
Figure 1.35, lit
from behind and
slightly to one
side.*

*Figure 1.40.
The same
landscape as
Figure 1.35, lit
from a low angle
to simulate
sunrise.*

You can set basic lighting positions using controls in the lighting control panels. The "N/S/E/W" buttons will put the light at North, South, East, or West, respectively. The Declination is the lighting angle, expressed as degrees away from the horizon (which is zero). The Azimuth control refers to the rotational angle of the light, with south being zero and north 180 degrees. The Rough setting controls the apparent roughness of the landscape, and is used in conjunction with shading texture.[41] Useful values range from 0 to 300; higher values should only be used when you need an unnatural look. Figures 1.41 and 1.42 illustrate the effect of different roughness settings.

Figure 1.41.
A landscape
rendered with
shadows on and
a roughness
setting of 0.

The Exager button exaggerates the effects of lighting. Instead of a gradual transition from light to shadow, the transition will be more abrupt. This enhances the apparent detail in the image, but you should experiment with each landscape to see if it works. In particular, using exaggeration with low lighting angles can put large flat areas into near-total darkness.

The Shadow button does just what you would expect: it adds shadows to the landscape. This is a must for natural-looking landscapes. Only terrain casts shadows; trees and clouds do not. Rendering will take longer with shadows on.

---

[41] In case you forget, you set shading texture in the Main bottom control panel when you select the amount of texture to apply—the O/L/M/H buttons control texture, with "O" being off (no texture), and the other buttons set Low, Medium, and High texture values, respectively. When you click on L, M, or H, you will be asked to set either altitude or shading texture.

*Figure 1.42.
A landscape
rendered with
shadows on and
a roughness
setting of 300.*

Figure 1.43 shows a landscape rendered with shadow off, and Figure 1.44 shows a landscape rendered with shadows on.

*Figure 1.43.
A landscape
rendered without
shadows.*

*Figure 1.44.
A landscape
rendered with
shadowing
turned on.*

Using PCX Files as Maps

This is one of the coolest features of Vistapro. You can import PCX files for a variety of applications and in a variety of ways. For example, you can import a PCX graphic that has nothing at all to do with a landscape, such as the face in Figure 1.45.

*Figure 1.45.
The face of the
programmer of
Vistapro im-
ported as a
landscape.*

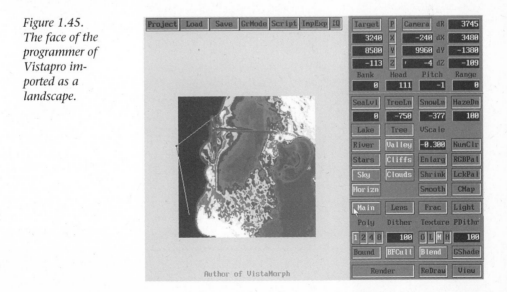

Although the map looks like a face, the rendered landscape doesn't resemble a face at all; Figure 1.46 shows a cliff corresponding to the nose in the map. Before rendering the image, I created a sea in front of the nose, and added fog to obscure the medium and distant portions of the landscape. Note that the scale setting in Figure 1.45 is set to -0.300. This means that the original peaks were turned into valleys, and the original valleys were turned into mountains.[42] Figure 1.47 shows how the landscape would look with a scale setting of +03.00; it is a photo negative of Figure 1.45.

Figure 1.46.
A rendered
landscape from
the PCX file
imported in
Figure 1.45.

As a matter of fact, I preferred working with this version of the file. Figure 1.48 shows why. I call it "The Valley of the Ear in Morning Light." As you can see if you look at the original on the CD-ROM,[43] this image is lit by a low light angle. I also massaged this image slightly in Adobe Photoshop for Windows. I selected just the portions of the "snow" that are facing the sun, and tinted them ever-so-slightly pink to make it look more like an authentic sunrise. Vistapro does not support such detailing, but it's not hard at all to add such effects in a photo-realistic paint program—all you need is a "magic wand" tool that will select areas of similar color.

---

[42] Which hints at a more general consideration: Just importing a PCX file is seldom all you have to do to get a good landscape. You may have to make major adjustments in order to get good results. Be prepared to play and massage until you have something workable. Instant art this is not!

[43] To find images on the CD-ROM, look for them by the figure number in the index.

Figure 1.47.
Reversed scale
setting for the
map in Figure
1.45.

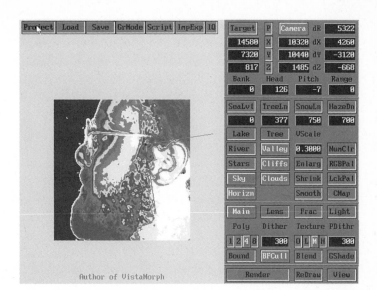

Make sure that the PCX file is large enough to fill the map area (which is usually 514x514). If it is smaller, you may get skewing or other undesired distortion.

Figure 1.48.
The Valley of the
Ear in Morning
Light (see text for
an explanation).

It's not as easy as it might look to get a map that looks like the PCX file you import, however. I took a frame from a video I prepared for a different book I wrote (see Figure 1.49), converted it to a PCX file, and imported it. The resulting map (shown in Figure 1.50 from a very high camera angle) bore only the slightest resemblance to the image, but as you can see in Figure 1.51, it nonetheless provided some interesting renderings. Figures 1.52 and 1.53 show details from a landscape generated from a slightly different version of the same image. Before converting the image from a .bmp to a .pcx file, I loaded it into BitEdit[44] and reordered the palette according to brightness. Vistapro maps the incoming image according to order that colors exist in the palette. If they are in random order, you'll set a random result as shown in Figure 1.50. If you order the palette entries in some way, you'll get more consistent results.

> **TIP** If you don't think you have an interesting landscape for rendering, try different camera angles and target locations. Almost every landscape has features in it somewhere that will give you a pleasing rendering.

Figure 1.49.
An image of the
author for
importing into
Vistapro.

---

[44] This is a bitmap editor that comes with the Video for Windows retail package.

Figure 1.50.
A rendering of
the image from
Figure 1.49; note
that it bears little
relation to the
original image.

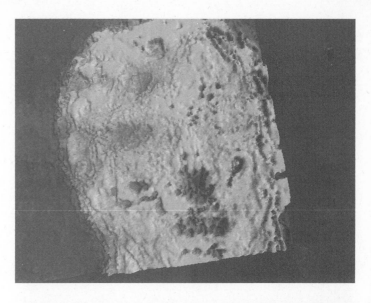

Figure 1.51.
A rendering at a
low camera angle
at a point just
below the "nose."

*Figure 1.52.
A rendering of a
broad valley from
a different PCX
image of the
author.*

*Figure 1.53.
The same valley
as in Figure 1.52,
but from a much
lower camera
angle.*

Figures 1.52 and 1.53 illustrate how important it is to experiment with different camera angles and targets. The mood of your image can vary dramatically with different placements.

Animation

Vistapro does a great job rendering single images, but the program really comes into its own when you generate a series of images and combine them into an animation. You could do this manually, of course, by adjusting the camera angle to a slightly different position for each image. However, you'll need at least 15 frames for each second of animation.

If you use fewer than 15 frames per second, the image will flicker too obviously. Even more frames per second would be better (cartoons and movies use 24, and video uses 30), but many computers won't support such high frame rates—see my book, *PC Video Madness,* for a complete discourse on this subject—and that could get mighty tedious to do manually. The answer is a Vistapro add-on program called Flight Director. Flight Director, also available from Virtual Reality Labs, uses Vistapro's script capabilities to generate a series of images that correspond to a flight path through a landscape.

Figure 1.54 shows a Flight Director screen. It looks something like the Vistapro screen, but only superficially. The concept behind Flight Director is simple. You click on a series of points on the landscape map, and this becomes a flight path which a Vistapro camera will follow. You can see the flight path superimposed on the map in the left half of the screen in Figure 1.54.

*Figure 1.54.
The Flight
Director screen.*

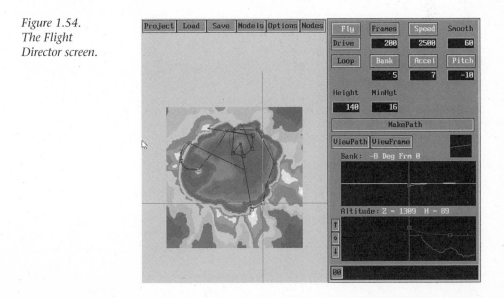

The crosshairs over the map mark the current cursor position. Each of the small squares along the flight path is called a node, and each node can have its own target. Flight Director will interpolate camera and target positions between nodes, creating a smooth flight path. Once you have placed all of the nodes, and added any targets,[45] click the MakePath button to generate a path. To see the result in *wireframe*[46] mode, click the ViewPath button, which will fly you through the animation in the space normally occupied by the map (see Figure 1.55).

Figure 1.55. Wireframe animation of the flight path.

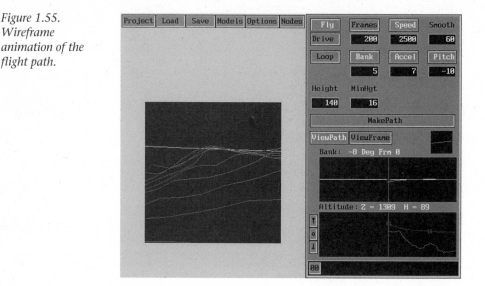

Flight Director allows you to choose the type of imaginary vehicle making the journey from the Models menu (see Figure 1.56). Not all of the vehicles fly; in addition to a glider, jet, cruise missile, helicopter, you'll find a dune buggy and a motorcycle.[47]

---

[45] If you don't add any targets, Flight Director assumes you simply want the camera to point forward.

[46] Wireframe refers to the act of rendering 3D objects using outlines instead of solid shapes. It's a lot easier and faster to render wireframes than solids.

[47] Use caution when working with the land-based vehicles—the path is close to the ground, and may actually go underground if the landscape is very rough. This does not look very good, so watch out for it in the wireframe preview. You can tell you're underground if the landscape is suddenly overhead instead of below.

Figure 1.56.
Choosing the
kind of vehicle.

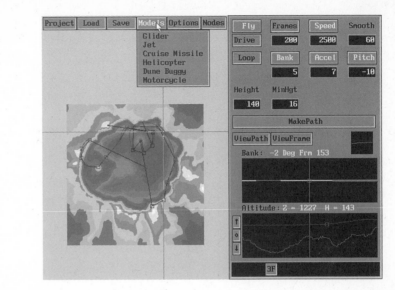

Let's take a moment to look at the controls in Flight Director. You may never use them; when you pick a vehicle, Flight Director sets default parameters that match the vehicle's characteristics. However, you may wish to fine-tune those characteristics, or you may want to try something completely different.

Refer to Figure 1.56, where you can see a number of buttons and text windows at the top right of the screen. You can choose to set Fly or Drive buttons, which correspond to the two different types of vehicles on the Models menu. You can also determine if the pace of the fly-through[48] will be adjusted for the number of frames, or if it will proceed at a constant speed and generate as many frames as are needed. If you want the number of frames to control the animation, click the Frames button and enter the number of frames. If you want speed to be the deciding factor, click the speed button and enter an appropriate speed. I find that 2,500 is a good starting point for speed, but you can change it for different effects.

You can also set numeric values for Bank, Accel, and Pitch, which control the limits of these activities for the vehicle. Banking refers to action in turns. Aircraft bank one way, while land-based vehicles bank in the opposite sense. A motorcycle, for example, banks into a turn, while a glider banks the opposite way. Acceleration controls the degree to which a vehicle changes speed as it rises and falls. A high Accel value means the vehicle will change speed more dramatically.

---

[48] Granted, you can fly or drive, but for simplicity's sake I'll use the phrase fly-through in this section to refer to both.

Pitch changes can also be controlled. Higher values allow the vehicle to pitch forward or backward to a greater degree as it ascends and descends.

The Height text window tells Flight Director how high above the ground elevation to place nodes. For flying vehicles, a good range is from 100 to 200 meters. For ground vehicles, set a low value like 15 to 30. Keep in mind that these numbers are for nodes only. Flight Director makes an effort to insure that the path doesn't go through the ground, but this is not a guarantee. Raise these numbers for rough terrain to avoid running into the ground. The MinHgt text window tells Flight Director the minimum height above ground to maintain; this is also an effective way to keep from running into the ground. Settings of 16 to 50 feet will work, but use higher numbers for rough terrain.

The Smooth button will also effect the relationship between the vehicle and the ground. High values of smoothing will round off the rough edges of the path, but in rough terrain this can run you into the ground. If in doubt, check the path in preview mode (click the View Path button).

The loop button will cause the last node to loop back to the first one, creating an animation that can be looped.

If you don't want to purchase Flight Director, but would still like to create animations, see the section below on Scripting in Vistapro for some ideas that may help you create simple animations.[49]

The procedure for creating a flight path is simple:

- Click to place nodes indicating the path you want to follow.
- Select a model, or set the various control settings manually.
- Click the MakePath button to create the path.
- Check the path with the ViewPath button.

If you find that you want to change a node, you can either delete it and add a new one using the Node menu, or you can use the Bank and Altitude windows (see Figure 1.56) to move the node with the mouse. After moving a node, you must use

---

[49] Scripting won't be useful in the demo version of Vistapro that is on the CD-ROM, since you need to save animation frames to the disk before you can link them into an animation. You'll need the full working version of Vistapro to create animations with either Flight Director or scripts.

the MakePath button again to re-create the path. Use the Save menu to generate a script that you can load into Vistapro.[50]

Figure 1.57 shows four frames from an animation from one of the files on the CD. If you look closely, you'll see that each frame is slightly different. The sequence is taken from one of the Crater Lake fly-throughs.

Figure 1.57.
Four frames from
an animation (a
fly-through over
Crater Lake, OR).

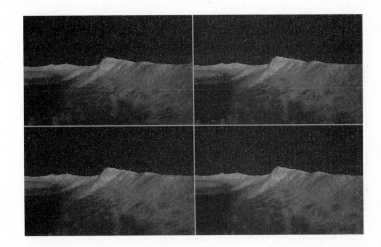

TIP

Lock the palette before creating animations.[51] This insures that a single palette will be used for all the files. This is necessary for using the animation player that comes with Vistapro, and makes life easier with most other programs. You may, however, get better results with some programs that can create a single palette from multiple palettes. Examples include Animator Pro and good old VidEdit.

---

[50] To load the script, just use the Script menu in Vistapro. Select one of the Run items (which one you use depends on the kind of file you want to generate—Targa, BMP, or PCX), then click on the name of the Script file you created in Flight Director. You'll need to supply a base name, such as PIC, to which Vistapro will append numbers for each file—PIC00001.PCX, PIC00002.PCX, etc. Vistapro will now happily create all the images necesary for the animation. You can load the resulting files into a program such as Animator Pro or VidEdit to create a FLI, FLC, or AVI file. Before you start, make sure the image size and all settings are correct. The most common mistake with a script is to have the wrong landscape loaded!

[51] Use the LckPal button in Vistapro to lock the palette. If you are using Vmorph (next section) to create the animation, set Lock Palette on the Setup menu.

See Chapter 6, "I Can Fly!", for an exciting use of a landscape animation in 3D Studio.

Morphing

Now you're gonna learn something that will literally make the earth move—morphing landscapes. It won't exactly happen under your feet, but you can create animations of a wide variety of landscape changes. In this section, you'll learn how to create an animation that grows a rugged, mountainous landscape out of flat terrain using Vmorph, another add-on program for Vistapro.

Figure 1.58 shows the starting landscape. However, this is not the place to get started; you start with the *last* frame, for reasons that will be clear shortly. Figure 1.59 shows the last frame.

Figure 1.58.
The starting
landscape for
a morph.

I created this landscape using the Fractal Control Panel; I simple clicked the Random button and took what showed up. Because the morph is intended to show a landscape rising up, the key is to use the vertical scaling capabilities. It's very simple: for the ending image, I used a vertical scale of 2.0, and saved the file as end.dem. For the starting image, I used a vertical scale of 0.2, saved it as start.dem.

Figure 1.59.
The ending
landscape for
a morph.

Don't save the file as an extended DEM file. Vmorph can't handle the extended file format.[52] If you want to include such things as clouds in the morph, you'll need to use scripts. See the section *Scripting in Vistapro,* below, for an example.

Figure 1.60 shows the opening screen of Vmorph. Vista Morph is not included on the CD. It is an add-on program that you can purchase from Virtual Reality Laboratories, the folks who sell Vistapro. It's much easier to work with than it looks. There's a menu at the top, frame numbers from left to right,[53] and buttons with actions you can take on the left. You'll only need to use one of the buttons to create a morph—LOADDEM. You'll load start.dem to start the morph, and end.dem to complete it.

---

[52] Extended DEM files contain information beyond simple landscape data—cloud settings, tree settings, etc.

[53] The frame numbers are confusing; they read from left to right and bottom to top. That is, the number 10 shows up with 0 on the top and 1 on the bottom.

Figure 1.60.
The opening
screen of
Vmorph.

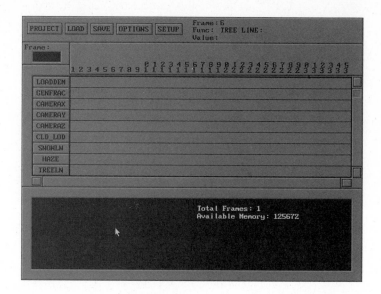

Step 1: Click on the line marked LOADDEM in the space for frame one (see Figure 1.61). This will open a dialog; enter the name of the file to load (start.dem). Click OK.

Step 2: Click again on the line marked LOADDEM, but this time in the space for frame 60 (see Figure 1.62).[54] This will open a dialog; enter the name of the file to load (end.dem). Click OK.

Step 3: Click the right mouse button to toggle the menu, then click on the Morph button. This will display the dialog box shown in Figure 1.63. Don't enter text into the text windows directly. Click on the LOADDEM line in frame 1, and then in frame 60. The values will be entered into the Morph dialog automatically. You'll need to change only one value: set a value of .75 for Ease.[55]

Step 4: Set global values for the morph on the setup menu: Lock Palette On, and Graphics Mode 320x200. Set the palette to frame 1.

---

[54] Use the slider button at bottom right to move to frame 60.

[55] Ease controls the pace of the morph. If the Ease value is less than one, the morph will start fast and then slow down. If the Ease value is greater than one, the morph will start slow and then speed up.

Step 5: Time to generate the script. Click the save menu, and enter a name for the script file in the text window (see Figure 1.64). When the script has been saved, exit Vmorph.

Step 6: Load Vistapro. Click on the script menu selection Run PCX, which will display the dialog box shown in Figure 1.65. Click on the filename of the script file you created in Step 5.

Step 7: After the script loads, you'll see a dialog asking for the base picture name. This is a three-character prefix that will be used for each of the image files that are generated. For example, the first filename in the example would be pic00000.pcx, the next pic00001.pcx, and so on. When you click OK, the script will run. The script will repeatedly use Vistapro to create frames; the process can take a long time. I once created a very long fly-through of the Big Sur area. It had more than 1600 frames, and took two and a half days to generate. This isn't as bad as it seems; I added trees, which can triple the rendering time.

Step 8: Enjoy! You can use the `pcx2flc` utility to create an animation, or you could load the bitmaps into VidEdit (Video for Windows) as a DIB sequence[56] and add sound appropriate to such earth-shattering goings on. The `pcx2flc` utility is easy to use—it has a command line interface. To create an animation, use the command line:

```
pcx2flc pic -b -s
```

where "pic" is the base picture filename, `-b` tells the program to use compression to reduce file size, and `-s` tells the program to optimize for playback speed. These settings will insure playback on the widest variety of hardware. The output file in this example would have the filename pic.flc.

See the last section in this chapter for an example of a script created by Vmorph.

---

[56] You can use a utility like Image Pals in Windows to convert all of the files in one shot, or you could use the Run BMP24 menu choice instead of Run PCX to generate bitmap files directly. However, 24-bit files are much larger so you'll need much more disk space. 192,000 bytes per frame, to be exact, for a 320x200 animation.

Figure 1.61.
Loading a DEM
file in Frame 1.

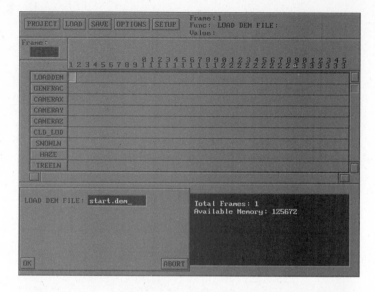

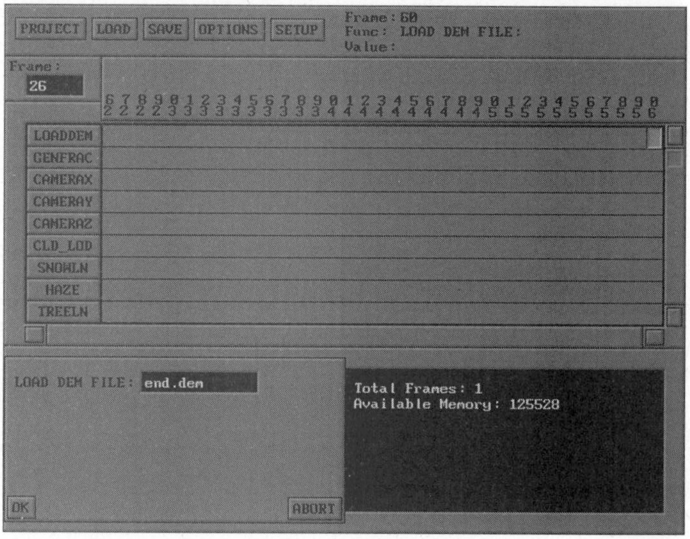

Figure 1.62.
Loading a DEM
file in Frame 26.

Figure 1.63.
Setting the morph
values.

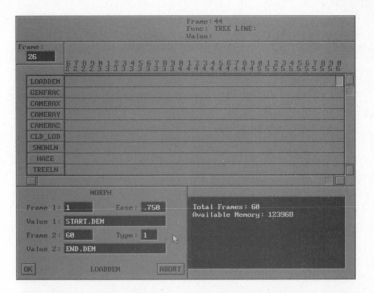

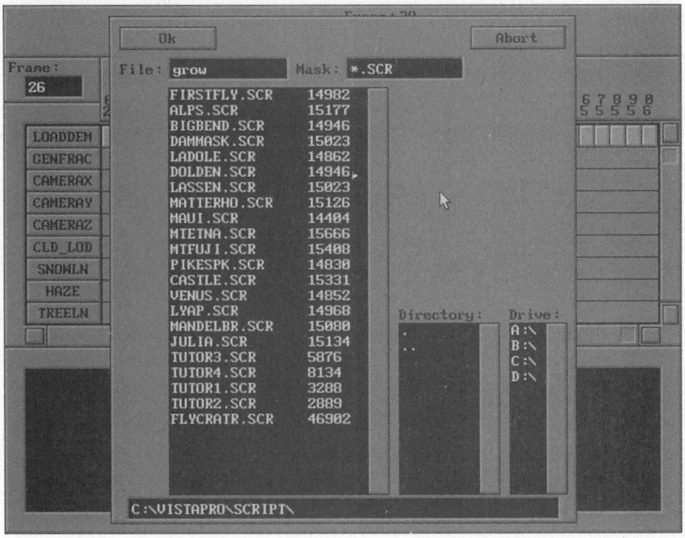

Figure 1.64.
Generating the
script file.

Figure 1.65.
Selecting a script.

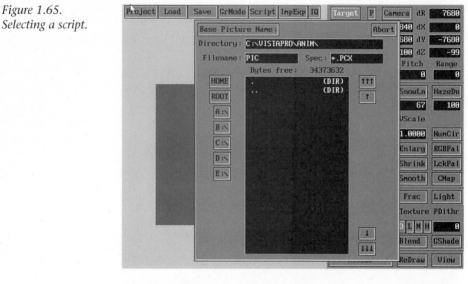

Figure 1.66.
Four sample
frames from a
morph animation
(Frames 1, 20,
40, and 60).

Vistapro Gallery

All of the images in this section were created with Vistapro. Some of the images were further modified in a paint program. Typical reasons for using a paint program include adding a sun, adding special effects such as lens flare, adding objects or people to the landscape, and using the landscape as a background.

*Figure 1.67.
A view of El
Capitan, a
famous rock-
climbing
destination.*

*Figure 1.68.
The same view as
in Figure 1.67,
but using
Gourand
shading. Note
how this softer
shading gives the
image a very
different feel.*

*Figure 1.69.
A fractally
generated
landscape in late
afternoon light.*

*Figure 1.70.
This landscape is
similar to that in
Figure 1.69, but
there are no
cliffs, and a body
of water gives it a
much more
serene look. Note
that there is no
sky haze, giving
the landscape a
hyper-real look.*

Figure 1.71. Even the simplest landscape looks good in a Vistapro rendering.

Figure 1.72. This is a slightly fractalized version of the Mandelbrot set.[57] A Mandelbrot DEM file is one of the sample files that comes with Vistapro. As supplied, the landscape has sheer cliffs and isn't too exciting. I applied smoothing and a little fractal texture to create a more realistic appearance.

---

[57] The Mandelbrot set is a famous set of points in fractal history. See Chapter 7 for information about fractals.

Figure 1.73.
Two renderings
of a valley using
the same data.
The rendering on
the left was done
using normal
height, and the
rendering on the
right with a
height setting
of 2.000.

Figure 1.74.
A fanciful
landscape created
from one of the
DEM files
supplied with
Vistapro 3.0.

Scripting in Vistapro

One of the most powerful aspects of Vistapro is its support for scripting. Just about every feature of Vistapro can be controlled in a script. The easiest way to create a script is to use Vmorph to generate a script. If necessary, you can edit the generated script in a text editor to make final changes. However, you can usually accomplish everything you need to right in Vmorph.

*Figure 1.75.
This landscape
was created from
a PCX image
that was
imported with the
PCX->DEM
menu selection.
The extreme
vertical drop is
typical of an
abrupt change in
the PCX from a
light shade to a
dark shade.*

*Figure 1.76.
This landscape is
also based on an
imported PCX
that was
converted to a
DEM file. The
image has a
haunting quality
that I really like;
it's one of my
favorite Vistapro
landscapes.*

In the section on morphing earlier in this chapter, I outlined an eight-step procedure for creating a morph in Vmorph. In this section, you'll learn how to tweak the script to produce the most realistic-looking animation.

Remember that column of buttons at the left of the Vmorph screen? Refer back to Figure 1.61. To set up the necessary parameters, all we need to do is click in frame one in the rows corresponding to several important buttons. The most important settings are shown in Table 1.6.

Table 1.6. Morph Settings.

Setting	Description
Altitude Texture	One of the most important settings for photo-realism is altitude texture. We are rendering at 320x200, so there's no need for ultimate quality. I used a setting of ALTITUDETEXTUREMEDIUM.
Blending	Blending is most effective on distant portions of the landscape. With a setting of BLENDON, distant objects will not be too sharply defined.
Dithering	With only 256 colors in a palette, dithering is critical for realism. This is one of two dither settings, and it controls dithering between color bands. I used the same value that Vistapro uses as a default: DITHER 100.00.
Shadows	Just for fun, I used Vmorph to create a varying sun angle during the animation. Setting SHADOWSON emphasizes the movement of the sun.
Lighting angle (azimuth)	Moving the "sun" during the animation gives the impression of time-lapse photography. A setting of SUNAZIMUTH 90.00 starts the sun in the east. It will move approximately three degrees (1/60*180) in each frame. The exact change from frame to frame will be affected by the Ease setting of .75.

Setting	Description
Pixel dither	This is one of two dither settings. This setting controls the amount of dithering in all pixels, whereas the Dither setting refers only to the color bands. I used a setting of PIXELDITHERRANDOM 100.00. This provides a modest amount of dithering—too much dithering would ruin the realistic effect.
Polygon size	All of the settings listed here are important, but none is more important than polygon size. For realism, always use a setting of POLYGONSIZE1 when rendering. This creates the smallest possible polygons.
Backface culling	Rendering speed increases if you set BACKFACECULLINGON. This means that unseen portions of the landscape will not be rendered.
Palette locking	Setting LOCKPALETTE insures that all frames will use the same palette as Frame 1. This is necessary if you will be using pcx3flc to create the animation.

You can set each of these values by clicking in Frame 1 in the corresponding row in Vmorph. An appropriate dialog box will appear allowing you to enter or click on the required value or setting. The only exception to this is the lighting angle. This works just like the morphing you did on the LOADDEM line. Click Frame 1 in the row marked SunAzimuth and enter a value of 90 (that's east). In the same row, click Frame 60 and enter a value of -90 (west). Then click the Morph menu button at the top of the screen to display the morph dialog. Click Frame 1, then Frame 60, and then click OK in the dialog to create the intermediate settings in Frames 2 through 59.[58]

---

[58] You can use this technique to morph any numeric values in a script, between any two frames.

If you set these values correctly, you will see the following script lines for Frame 1, following the default settings:

```
ALTITUDETEXTUREMEDIUM
BLENDON
DITHER 100.00
SHADOWSON
SUNAZIMUTH 90.00
PIXELDITHERRANDOM 100.00
POLYGONSIZE1
BACKFACECULLINGON
RENDER
LOCKPALETTE
; Frame: 1 END
```

This gives you a high degree of control over scripting. With a little effort, you can create some amazing animations. You can also use Vmorph to add such things as cloud map loading for each frame to increase realism. To load a cloud map, all you need is a command like this for each frame:

```
CLOUDLOAD CLOUD\MORPH1
```

The filename is "morph1." You do not need to specify the .cld extension.

Creating animations is fun, but it's also fun just to play them. I have included a number of animations created with Vmorph (as well as an animation player) on the CD-ROM for your enjoyment.

Listing 1.1. A Vistapro script generated by Vmorph.

```
Vista Script File
CamX,  CamY,  CamZ, Bank, Hdng, Ptch,
; Frame: 1 BEGIN
DEFAULTDIRDEM DEM\
DEFAULTDIRCMAP CMAP\
DEFAULTDIRCLOUD CLOUD\
DEFAULTDIRSCRIPT SCRIPT\
DEFAULTDIRFOREGROUND TGA24\
DEFAULTDIRBACKGROUND TGA24\
DEFAULTDIRIQ IQ\
LANDSCAPESIZEAUTO
GRMODEVGA320X200
GRMODEVESA640X480
LOADDEM DEM\START.DEM
ALTITUDETEXTUREMEDIUM
BLENDON
DITHER 100.00
SHADOWSON
```

```
SUNAZIMUTH 90.00
PIXELDITHERRANDOM 100.00
POLYGONSIZE1
BACKFACECULLINGON
RENDER
LockPalette
; Frame: 1 END
; Frame: 2 BEGIN
SPAWN META DEM\START.DEM DEM\END.DEM DEM\METALTMP.DEM 1 59 1 0.75 1
LOADDEM DEM\METALTMP.DEM
SUNAZIMUTH 83.90
LOCKPALETTE
RENDER
; Frame: 2 END
; Frame: 3 BEGIN
SPAWN META DEM\START.DEM DEM\END.DEM DEM\METALTMP.DEM 2 59 1 0.75 1
LOADDEM DEM\METALTMP.DEM
SUNAZIMUTH 80.85
RENDER
; Frame: 3 END
;
; Frames 4 through 57 are pretty much the same.  For each
; frame, the parameters for the SPAWN command are
; incremented, and the sun azimuth angle is changed to give
; the impression that the sun is moving across the sky
; ;during the morph.
;
; Frame: 58 BEGIN
SPAWN META DEM\START.DEM DEM\END.DEM DEM\METALTMP.DEM 57 59 1 0.75 1
LOADDEM DEM\METALTMP.DEM
SUNAZIMUTH -86.95
RENDER
; Frame: 58 END
; Frame: 59 BEGIN
SPAWN META DEM\START.DEM DEM\END.DEM DEM\METALTMP.DEM 58 59 1 0.75 1
LOADDEM DEM\METALTMP.DEM
SUNAZIMUTH -90.00
RENDER
; Frame: 59 END
; Frame: 60 BEGIN
LOADDEM DEM\END.DEM
SUNAZIMUTH -90.00
RENDER
; Frame: 60 END
```

Hitch Your Wagon to a Star

I hope I have been able to convey the excitement and pleasure I experienced using Vistapro. Software comes and goes, but there are certain packages that offer more than usual—and I certainly put Vistapro in that category. There's something about creating photo-realistic renderings that I found exciting, and Vistapro is both easy to use and powerful. It doesn't offer every single feature you might want, but then again it doesn't cost a fortune, either. The retail price is $129. In my opinion, this is one program no Virtual Reality enthusiast should be without.

There is a demo version of Vistapro on the CD-ROM; give it a whirl and see if you don't agree.[59]

---

[59] You might think I get a commission, I'm selling this program so hard. Unfortunately, I don't get a penny.

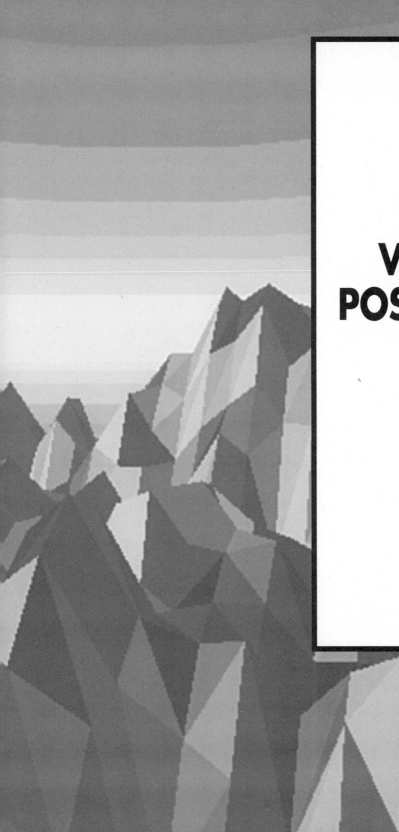

2

VIRTUAL POSSIBILITIES

In Chapter 1, you learned how to get a running start in virtual reality using Vista Pro. In this chapter, virtual reality moves indoors with Virtual Reality Studio. Like Vista Pro, Virtual Reality Studio offers an inexpensive way to explore virtual spaces.

There are two versions of VR Studio. This chapter covers the latest version, 2.0. This version is available at many software outlets and by mail order. Another version of VR Studio, 1.0, is included on the CD-ROM that comes with this book. You can find information about that version in the appendix to this book, and the complete manual is supplied on the CD-ROM. Including Version 2.0 of Virtual Reality Studio would have driven the price of the book quite high. Version 1.0 allows you to play and explore inexpensively.

Artificial Reality

Virtual reality is a buzzword these days, and a hot one at that. It's so hot, in fact, that the meaning changes almost daily as companies try to associate their products with the words. I'd like to step back from the craziness and intensity of buzzwords and talk in a more generic sense about the underlying concepts of virtual reality. I use the term *artificial reality* as a starting point.

Not only does using this term avoid the confusion surrounding *virtual reality*, in many ways *artificial reality* is more accurate. I don't expect everyone to suddenly switch to using new terminology, but it might take some of the heat, confusion, and too-high expectations out of the air. To that end, a definition of the term artificial reality is necessary.[1]

> **artificial reality**—anything at all that stimulates the mind or senses to create a simulacrum of reality *in the imagination*.

I have deliberately created a definition that stresses results, not the technique used to achieve those results. The emphasized phrase—in the imagination—stresses the *kind* of results that matter. Virtual reality need not be virtually real to be interesting, useful, or fun.[2]

---

[1]Truth be told, I hate definitions because as soon as you create one, someone will come along and point out the deficiency of the definition. Defining terms such as *artificial reality* is doubly dangerous because the terms are so vague.

[2]The day when virtual reality becomes virtually indistinguishable from reality is a long way down the pike. We can't let that little fact spoil the party!

For some time, virtual reality had a very definite meaning: full-body suits, helmets, and other paraphernalia associated with full-body total immersion into an electronic reality.[3] Pieces of that total picture have begun to arrive, and the term *virtual reality* has shifted to describe those first arrivals. The term has then been stretched further to mean just about anything 3D. This is an extremely broad range of meaning, and it is useful to break artificial realities into categories. The following sections cover these categories, beginning with the most modest forms of artificial reality and ending with the ultimate forms of virtual reality. It reflects the current state of the art, and projections of what might be possible in the future.

Text

Text may strike you as an unusual form of artificial reality, but it is useful to look at how text serves in that role. For centuries, books have been the cutting edge of artificial reality. Think about it: you read words on a page, and your mind fills in the pictures and emotions—even physical reactions can result. Text is important because all of our expectations[4] are based on what we've experienced with books.[5]

Text forms a baseline upon which we can measure the success of various kinds of artificial reality. Although there are many ways that images, sounds, and other sensory communication can expand the capabilities of text, there are qualities of the reading experience that will be challenging to reproduce. If you are not convinced, think about books that have been converted to movies. Most of the time, even if the movie is regarded as being as good as the book was, the movie has to leave a lot of the story out—the overhead of telling a story in pictures is a lot higher than for text.

---

[3]In some ways, I like that term—*electronic reality*—best of all. But buzzwords have never thrived on accuracy, have they?

[4]Except those based on television.

[5]Kids, of course, who are growing up today don't necessarily base their expectations on books. Many do, however—my son Justen loves books, but he's also a nut about his Sega and Nintendo systems, as well as PC games like Stunt Island. Books provide a depth of stimulation that most games and PC programs can't match. The non-visual, low-tech nature of text actually gives it an advantage over all other forms of artificial reality. It's a lot easier to simulate, and stimulate, if the technical overhead is reduced. This seems obvious, but it's a critical obstacle that must be overcome in the development of virtual reality.

2D Still Images

Photographs have been with us for a little more than a century, and their capabilities are described in the phrase "a picture is worth a thousand words." This is true in two senses: a picture—specifically, a photograph—is both accurate and detailed. Nonetheless, comparing pictures and words is, to drag in another old bromide, like comparing apples to oranges. Text is good at certain things, and pictures are good at others. You can't, for example, look behind what is in a 2D picture, nor can you take pictures of many things—the state of a man's mind, the inside of a volcano, a molecule.

Most of the time, pictures and text are used together. This reflects their complementary aspects. Each is good at different things, and best when used together. Neither one is truly superior to the other.

3D Still Images

This is a technology that is both common and in its infancy. Primitive 3D still images have been with us for decades, but it has been holograms that have made quality 3D images possible. However, from a commercial standpoint, holography is mostly a failure—there are no widespread commercial uses of holograms as images. Holograms are used for such things as credit cards and packaging precisely because they are complicated to reproduce.

Technically speaking, however, 3D images represent an interesting twist in the move toward more sophisticated artificial reality. The simulacrum of the third dimension is vivid, even if the image quality is often second rate or worse.

Animation

Neither 2D nor 3D images have a quality that reality thrives on: movement. Animation—the trick of using flickering images to fool the eye—adds the dimension of time to artificial reality in ways that still images can never do. A series of still images on a page, for example, or even a series of slides, provides only an intellectual sense of movement and change. Animation, even when very abstractly done, conveys a sense of immediacy that is very powerful.

Video

I was tempted to include video with the discussion of animation, but the two technologies are different enough to merit separate consideration. Video, after all, captures an image of reality and preserves it, and that is an entirely different kind of artificial reality than animation. Animation is truly and totally artificial—most of the time. Some of the most fascinating animation sequences are actually based on video.

The process starts with a standard video of some real action—a fish swimming, a couple dancing. An artist then uses this as an underlayment for an animation, substituting a series of drawings for the video frames. The effect looks like a virtuoso animation, when in reality it is just a series of tracings.

Sound

Multimedia computers, upgrade kits, and sound cards are in the process of revolutionizing the way we think of computers. The ability to listen to sounds appropriate to a context can make the computer interaction much more pleasant, and often more interesting, effective, and informative as well. For example, you can use sound for everything from using a cat's meow instead of a beep for errors to controlling your computer with voice commands.

Unfortunately, the majority of the sound cards installed on computers today isn't of very high quality, and most uses of sound do not use high-fidelity recording techniques. Speaking from experience, high-quality stereo sound is as important for computer use as it is in a home stereo system. Until there is general use of noise-free, accurate sound equipment on computers, we'll be missing something. In terms of numbers, we must move from the 8-bit, mono, 22 KHz sounds of today to true CD-quality sound (16-bit stereo, with 44KHz sampling).

3D Motion

We are just beginning to witness serious efforts to portray the third dimension in ordinary media. Films such as Jaws III featured 3D using special glasses, but the investment in equipment to create such films made them unusual. Technology has just begun to swing to the point where you can create 3D motion pictures on your own.

In most cases, some form of glasses are required to decode the 3D information in each image of an animation or video sequence. Unlike conventional 3D glasses, video 3D glasses are high tech. They use shutters that direct subsequent frames of the video to each eye in turn. Chapter 13, "The Virtual Future," covers this kind of technology in greater detail.

This kind of technology is right at the edge of what is available to the average computer enthusiast today. Developments in this area will make up the bulk of serious progress in virtual/artificial reality over the next several years.

3D Input Devices

One of the most frustrating aspects of current 3D technology is the lack of a convenient way to manipulate 3D objects. Whether you are using a simple 2D video monitor or sophisticated, 3D head-mounted displays, if you do not have the ability to manipulate objects with a 3D input device,[6] your capabilities are limited.

For example, as you will see repeatedly in the examples in this book, programmers and game designers have developed many clever techniques for manipulating 3D objects using 3D tools. Almost without exception, this is a tedious, frustrating, and inexact way to work. Current experiments with head-mounted tracking devices, 3D mice, and interactive gloves have not yet resulted in a low-cost, easy-to-use solution to the problem.

Head-Mounted Display

Often called *HMD*s, these range from goggles to full-sized, head-encircling units. You can buy a head-mounted display today for under $10,000, but most of the software that uses such expensive hardware is highly specialized. You can, for example, find software that will allow you to visualize complex organic molecules in 3D, but there is nothing available yet that addresses more pedestrian activities. The high cost of HMDs is the current root of that problem.

There are a very few inexpensive head-mounted displays, but they tend to make serious compromises. For example, human vision is marvelously wide-angle. Creating a screen that is small and light enough to be placed in front of your eyes, and still curved enough and wide enough to give you a natural field of vision is beyond the range of affordable technology. Some simple units are available for under $1000, but they were just being announced as this book went to press.

Another serious problem involves data rates. Filling larger displays with data takes serious computing power—more than is currently available, particularly if the HMD is at all light and portable.

---

[6]The world is waiting for a 3D manipulation device that will make 3D interaction as easy as 2D mouse-based or pen-based interaction.

Wide-Angle Displays

Thus, the next step after HMDs are HMDs with a field of vision approximately the same as we humans take for granted. Personally, I would expect this to be a major step, and one that has the potential to revolutionize artificial reality. Until the field of vision is wide enough to engage the two kinds of vision we possess, the experience will be marred by whatever shows up in our peripheral vision—whether it be simply blackness, or "real reality."

Display technology will also have to advance to a point where the large numbers of pixels needed for true wide-angle displays can be displayed cheaply and, just as important, instantly.[7]

Tactile Feedback

What would life be like if your mouse went *bump* when you reached the edge of the computer screen? That's tactile feedback—a physical sensation coming back from the computer to tell you what's going on. Vibrating mice are with us today, but there is a real lack of software that supports such technology.[8]

A mouse represents just the barest beginnings of tactile feedback technology. Gloves that give you a sensation of picking up objects are a much more advanced form of tactile feedback.

Head and Body Tracking

If only the computer could, like a friend in a conversation, keep track of our head or body position, we could communicate so much more easily with the computer. Voice recognition is nice, but what if you could signal the equivalent of an OK button by just nodding your head? Pointing with a finger is one of the most natural gestures, but it is completely mysterious to a computer.

---

[7]The very nature of digital imaging is both a blessing and a curse. The blessing comes in the form of very exact image representation. The curse takes the form of high data rates to reproduce precise colors and large, complex—and therefore interesting—images.

[8]What we really need is a mouse that will resist movement if you try to do something inappropriate. For example, wouldn't it be great if the mouse offered resistance when you tried to move the mouse cursor out of a modal dialog box? (A modal dialog is one that you must deal with before you return to the program that spawned it.)

Current ideas about how to implement tracking are somewhat intrusive. For example, video games are making use of large (3-4 feet in diameter) circular sensors placed on the floor. Experimental head-tracking devices often require you to wear something on your head, although there are experiments with video cameras built into monitors.[9] The computer analyzes the video image to try to determine where your head is facing.

Non-Visual Sensory Output

Now we are moving into the realm of future possibilities. Senses such as smell and touch are a lot harder to integrate into a computer connection. The sense of smell, for example, is extremely complex—and very personal. One person's great smell is another person's stink.

Given that we are only just beginning to be able to reproduce a limited number of scents chemically, and that the most desirable scents are tremendously subtle and natural, the sense of smell may wait a long time to be computerized. Touch is equally complex. Touch receptors are located all over the body, with different kinds of touch in different areas. It seems highly likely that initial attempts to integrate touch will focus on areas of the body with large numbers of touch receptors, such as the hands.

"Extra-Sensory" Input and Output

There also exists the possibility of involving non-sensory data in the loop. This can be done as a simulation or by mapping—for example, converting infrared data into sounds (mapping objects bright in the infrared to high pitches, and dim objects to low pitches), or mapping it to the visible spectrum (bright as blue, dim as red, for example). Ultimately, this could possibly be done more directly by mapping sensor data right into the brain.[10]

Total Immersion

The ultimate goal of artificial reality would be to create an experience that would be indistinguishable from the real McCoy. This seems like total hype at this stage

---

[9]How would you feel if the computer were constantly watching you with a video camera?

[10]This is far out, highly speculative stuff. It is, however, interesting to think about the possibility of extending human senses via computers.

of the game, and the proper forum for such ideas may well have to remain on the holodeck of the Enterprise for the time being.

Artificial Is a Matter of Degree

If there is anything to be learned from my attempt at classifying the forms that virtual reality might take, it is that there are many degrees of *artificial*. Some are more realistic than others, and some do a better job of creating the experience of reality than others. The "reality" is that there are multiple dimensions involved, and there is no single line from the simple to the complex. Artificial reality is made up of a large number of intersecting needs and technologies, and all of it is bounded by what we can actually afford to do, as individuals and as a society.

Creating Virtual Spaces with VR Studio 2.0

One of the things I did not emphasize in my progressive section of artificial reality technologies was image resolution. There is a simple rule that explains the importance, and the problems, of high resolutions: For a given CPU, the higher the image resolution, the longer it will take to display a single image. It may be acceptable to take a second or two to display a high-res image when you are using a paint program, but when you want 15 or more frames displayed per second, that's no good at all.

Virtual Reality Studio 2.0 allows you to move your viewpoint around a virtual space. This means that it is constantly changing the display to reflect the new position of your viewpoint. To make the movement fluid, it operates at low (standard) VGA and MCGA resolutions. You have a choice of 640x480 and 16 colors, or 320x240 and 256 colors. Neither of these is what anyone would describe as realistic, so we must ask the question: without realism, is this virtual reality at all?

That's really a trick question, because we are operating under the definition given earlier for *artificial reality*. By these standards, Virtual Reality Studio qualifies. There is an even more important standard that also applies: is it fun?[11] VR Studio is fun.

---

[11]This standard comes into play (sorry for the pun) again in Chapter 4 where you'll learn that even inexpensive games can be a fun dose of virtual/artificial reality.

It takes a bit of learning to get comfortable with VR Studio, however. The interface suffers from the usual difficulties of manipulating 3D objects with 2D tools. The approach used by VR Studio uses indirect object manipulation. Instead of picking and dragging objects, you select an object and move it using control buttons. For example, to move a cube, you select it, and then use the object mover controls to move it up, or down, or to lengthen it or rotate it. You can also use similar controls to change your point of view. Truth be told, this system works better for changing your point of view than it does for moving and changing objects. Nonetheless, it does work.

VR Studio is one of the software packages that has its own personality. This is evident in the unique user interface, and in the manual. For example, the following passage is taken verbatim from the manual.

> *The commands for making absolute moves are detailed in the reference manual, which, as you may be realizing, will have to be digested in full with gravy and two vegetables before you get the maximum out of this rather horrifyingly complex program that you thought "might be a bit of fun."*

Learning a complex, idiosyncratic program is a bit less of a strain when the manual seems to reflect the situation clearly.[12]

I must also warn you that VR Studio has some bugs. They are more frustrating than serious, but you should keep an eye out for anomalies. Save your work often. The calculations for visual representation of a 3D space in two dimensions are complex, and VR Studio will sometimes get things wrong. An object that should be on one side of a wall, for example, will wind up on the other side, but only at certain angles. This is unfortunate, but when you consider the cost of VR Studio relative to other 3D packages, a little tolerance of such things is reasonable. In other words, despite such problems, I think that VR Studio is a useful and interesting program. However, the door of opportunity for an inexpensive and fun VR package is still open.

---

[12]Just adding silly comments, of course, isn't enough to make me feel better. The documentation for Imagine is also spotted with silly comments, but, unlike the VR Studio docs, Imagine's aren't possessed of a painfully accurate self-knowledge.

The opening screen of VR Studio is shown in Figure 2.1. There is a menu at the top, a view in the middle, and whole lot of controls at the bottom. There is also a small information window imbedded in the control panel.

Figure 2.1.
The opening
screen of Virtual
Reality Studio
2.0.

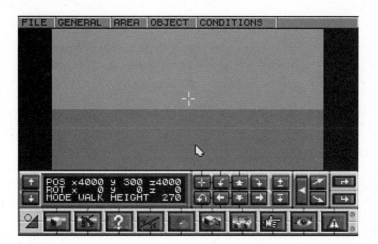

It would be fun to start creating some object, but it is a lot more sensible to look closely at that control panel first. You live and die by the control panel—if you learn to use it right off the bat, if you treat it as an end in itself, you will suffer a lot less frustration. It's very much like learning to play the piano—if you can't relate the notes on the page to the keys on the piano, you are in trouble.

There are two chunks of controls worth knowing about. The chunk to the right of the little display panel controls the movement of your viewpoint. The chunk arranged in a line at the bottom are buttons that access some of the most commonly used features of the menus. Let's look at the controls for moving around in the scene first.

Moving your viewpoint is tricky. I used the piano analogy earlier, but that doesn't quite capture the experience of learning how to move around in VR Studio. The best analogy for that part of the process is learning to ride a bicycle. There will be times when you mean to turn left, but you'll turn right by mistake.[13] Once you learn the nuances of the controls, however, you'll find it easy to set a useful

---

[13]Just after I learned how to ride a bicycle, and was oh so proud of myself, someone behind me yelled, "Your back wheel is turning backwards!" Rube that I was at the tender age of seven, I turned around to look and crashed ingloriously.

viewpoint. The key is to learn to use controls in groups. For example, if you want to get a better look at a part of your universe, you may need to rotate left, look "up," back up, look "down," and then zoom in. This all becomes second nature after a few hours.

Here's a list of the controls that explains what each one does.

 Cross hairs—A small cross hair marks the center of the viewport. Clicking this button toggles the cross hairs on and off. Most of the time, you can leave them off.

Reverse—Turns you 180 degrees from your current heading. In other words, it reverses your direction. This is useful for navigating in architectural spaces. For example, after you enter a door, you can turn right around with no fuss or bother.

Rotate Left—Rotates your view to the left, which has the effect of rotating the universe to the right. It takes some practice to get this correct. There is a tendency in most people to associate the rotational direction with the universe rather than one's own point of view. Don't be surprised if you find yourself reaching for the wrong rotate button for the first few sessions with VR Studio.

Forward—Moves you forward. This is a relative forward, not absolute. This has subtle, but important, effects on your navigation. If you are looking down on a scene, moving forward will move you down—forward is whatever direction you happen to be facing. If you are looking from above, and want to move "forward" instead of down, you'll need to look ahead before moving forward, and then look down again. The keys that look up and down are near bottom right (with diagonal arrows in them).

 Rotate Right—Rotates your view to the right, which has the effect of rotating the universe to the left. (See the explanation for Rotate Left.)

 Up—Moves you straight up. No matter what direction you are facing, this button will move you vertically. See the forward button for an important difference between these two buttons. You will almost always need to look down if you make large vertical movements.

Left—Moves you to the left. Leftward movement is always relative to your current position. Since the rotate keys rotate your point of view, not the universe, you will almost always need to use the rotate controls with the left and right controls to walk "around" an object.

 Back—Moves you backward. This is a relative backward, not absolute. This has subtle, but important, effects on your navigation. If you are looking down on a scene, moving backward will move you up—backward is the opposite of whatever direction you happen to be facing. If you are looking from above, and want to move "backward" instead of up, you'll need to look ahead before moving backward, and then look down again. The keys that look up and down are near bottom right (with diagonal arrows in them).

 Right—Moves you to the right. Rightward movement is always relative to your current position. Since the rotate keys rotate your point of view, not the universe, you will almost always need to use the rotate controls with the left and right controls to walk "around" an object.

 Down—Moves you straight down. No matter what direction you are facing, this button will move you vertically. See the backward button for an important difference between these two buttons. You will almost always need to look down if you make large vertical movements.

 Level—This button faces you forward without changing other aspects of your viewpoint. For example, if you are looking down from a great height, and click this button, you will be looking straight ahead at a great height.[14]

 Rotate Up—This button rotates your point of view upward.

 Rotate Down—This button rotates your point of view downward.

 Roll Right—Rotates your point of view clockwise.

 Roll Left—Rotates your point of view counter-clockwise.

---

[14]And you will most likely see nothing at that point, unless you have some very tall objects in your universe.

I strongly suggest practicing with these controls to move around in a simple universe. Let's create a cube. Click on the little cube icon control at the bottom left of the screen (see Figure 2.1 for the location of this control). This will display the dialog box shown in Figure 2.2.

Figure 2.2.
Creating an
object in VR
Studio 2.0.

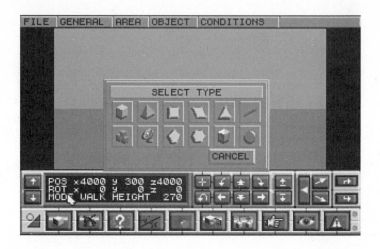

The dialog box displays icons for the 12 kinds of objects you can create in VR Studio. Select the icon of the cube at the upper-left corner. This will deposit a cube in the virtual universe (see Figure 2.3).[15]

Now you have a reference point that allows you to see the effects of using the various controls. If you try to move up or down, you will discover that your movement is very limited. That's because VR Studio's default *vehicle* is walking. Use the General|Mode|Vehicle menu selection to change your vehicle to Fly2 (see Figure 2.4). This allows for more natural movement—particularly the ability to move up and down. When you are creating a virtual universe, it is critical to move up and get an overview of your handiwork. The best use of the walk mode is for cruising through a virtual universe that has already been built.

---

[15]Although VR Studio only has a limited number of basic shapes, you can change their size and relative proportions, and you can combine objects into groups to form more complex shapes. In general, however, the limited number of basic shapes means that you won't be able to create very realistic images.

Figure 2.3.
A virtual cube in
a virtual space.

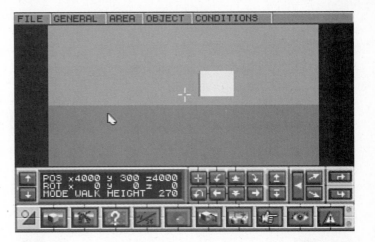

Figure 2.4.
Changing your
vehicle type.

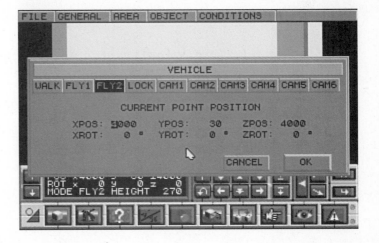

To test your maneuvering skills, try the following movements using the point of view controls. If you like to solve puzzles on your own, you may want to try to find a method to make the movements listed on the left before peeking at the methods I used, listed in the right-hand column.

Movement	*Method*
Move down to the ground	Press the down control until you can't move down any further.
Look at the cube from above	Move forward, left, up, down, and/or right until the cube is right in front

Movement	Method
	of you. Then press the up and rotate down controls in tandem[16] until you are above the cube looking down.
Look at the cube from the right side	Use the right and rotate left controls in tandem to gradually shift your point of view around to the right side of the cube. This is a tricky set of moves, but you will often find the need to use it.
Look at the cube from below	Move forward, left, up, down, and/or right until the cube is right in front of you. Then press the down and rotate up controls in tandem until you are below the cube looking up.
Move to one of the cube's faces and then shift to a view looking out from that face	Move forward, left, up, down and/or right until the cube is right in front of you. Then press the reverse control to change your point of view 180 degrees.

Before you learn how to modify the cube's shape, take a look at that bottom row of controls. From left to right, these controls do the following:

Create object	Displays a dialog that let's you choose what kind of object you want to create.
Delete object	Lists current objects and allows you to select one for deletion.
Set/modify conditions	This is covered in detail in Chapter 9, "The Model is the Thing." By setting conditions, you can control what happens to an object during an interactive session.

---

[16]"In tandem" means click one, then the other, and repeat until you are where you need to be.

Object attributes	Displays a dialog that allows you to set a variety of object attributes. Two of the most important attributes involve sensors and transposers, topics covered later in this section.
Object color	Displays the controls for changing object colors. You can change the color of each face of an object.
Modify object	Displays the controls for modifying the shape and orientation of an object.
Copy object	Creates a copy of the selected object.
Select object	Changes the currently selected object.
View full screen	Displays the current workspace without the controls.
Reset point of view	Resets your point of view to ground level. It also resets your vehicle mode to walk.[17]

The very first thing to do is to make that simple little cube more interesting. Let's build a house with Virtual Reality Studio—it will show off the program's features and capabilities. Start by clicking the Modify object icon at the bottom of the screen. This displays the most common VR Studio dialog: Select Object (see Figure 2.5).

Before you carry out a command, you must always specify what object the command applies to. Even though you have created only one object—a cube—you will note that there are two objects listed, and our cube is number 2. Object number 1 is something called a cuboid. This is a default object that exists in every new virtual space—it is the ground.[18]

---

[17]This is frustrating, especially if you ever click this button by mistake.

[18]What is the difference between a cube and a cuboid? After a thorough review of the too-brief documentation that comes with VR Studio, I could find no reference to explain cuboid. Unfortunately, there isn't an index where I could look it up. I give VR Studio a B- (B minus) for the documentation. What documentation there is, is clearly written. However, the lack of an index and the omission of a comprehensive reference section will frustrate you sometimes.

*Figure 2.5.
Selecting on
object.*

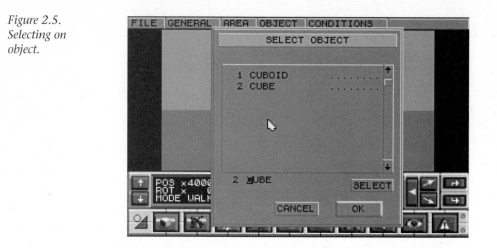

To select the cube, you can either click object number 2, or you can click the Select button and then click the cube in the scene. Once you have many objects, it is much easier to select objects in the scene.[19] You can use the Object Attributes button to access a dialog that will allow you to name your objects, but in the heat of creation it's often easy to overlook this step.

Once you have selected the object you plan to modify, the Object Editor appears and takes over the lower half of the screen (see Figure 2.6). This awesome array of buttons and controls looks imposing, but after a little practice I found it easy to use. The top portion of the Object Editor should look familiar—it is nothing more than the controls for moving your viewpoint. The bottom half consists of five clusters of similar controls. Each set of controls modifies related attributes of the currently selected object.[20]

The labels for each of the control clusters are not easy to distinguish in black and white. From left to right, they are:

Point   Moves individual points
Turn   Rotates objects

---

[19]One exception to this is the group. When you group objects, the group exists, but cannot be selected by clicking in the scene. You must choose the group by name from the Select Object dialog. If you click on a group in the scene, you will merely select the object of the group that you happened to click on.

[20]Once you are in object edit mode, the rules for selecting objects change. You can select objects simply by clicking on them. Groups, however, must still be selected "the old fashioned way"— use the Select button at the lower right of the Object Editor.

Shrink   Reduces the size of objects
Stretch   Increases the size of objects
Move   Moves objects

Figure 2.6.
The Object Editor
screen.

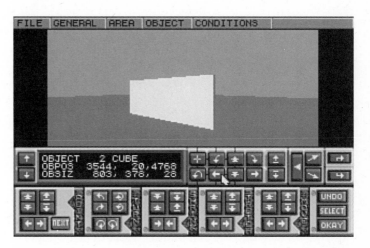

Each of these control clusters contain six buttons that behave identically, with the exception of the rotation controls, which I will describe separately. A typical cluster (Move) is shown in Figure 2.7.

Figure 2.7.
The Object
Editor's Move
control cluster.

The two buttons at the left move the object away from you or toward you. The two buttons at the right move the object up and down. The two buttons at the bottom move the object left and right. The other controls have similar functions. For example, consider the Stretch controls. The top-left button stretches farther out the object edge farthest away from you, whereas the button immediately under it stretches the face closest to you. The two buttons at the right stretch the object vertically, and the remaining two buttons stretch it horizontally. This enables you to stretch in two directions along each of the three axes—up/down, left/right, and in/out. The shrink control cluster is the exact opposite—it pulls in where the stretch controls push out. The point controls move individual points on an object, and the rotate controls rotate to varying degrees as specified on the icon for each button.

The point control cluster adds a Next button, which will advance you to the next movable point on the object.[21]

To create a house, the cube must be transformed into an exterior wall. This is easily done using the Stretch and Shrink control clusters. Use the left and right stretch buttons to pull the cube out horizontally, and then use the stretch up button to increase its height. Use one of the shrink toward/away buttons to slim down the thickness of the wall. You can use the viewpoint controls to move around and see what you are doing from a different perspective. Because several adjoining faces of the cube have identical colors, you may not be able to see clearly without changing your point of view. The wall should look like the example in Figure 2.6.

> **TIP**
>
> If you will be adding any of the clip objects that come with VR Studio (such as couches, tables, and chairs), you can load one of them now to check the size of your wall. To load an object, refer to the clip art handbook that comes with VR Studio to find the filename, and then use the File|Load Object menu selection to load the object (see Figure 2.8). Figure 2.9 shows a desk and chair loaded and placed into the scene.

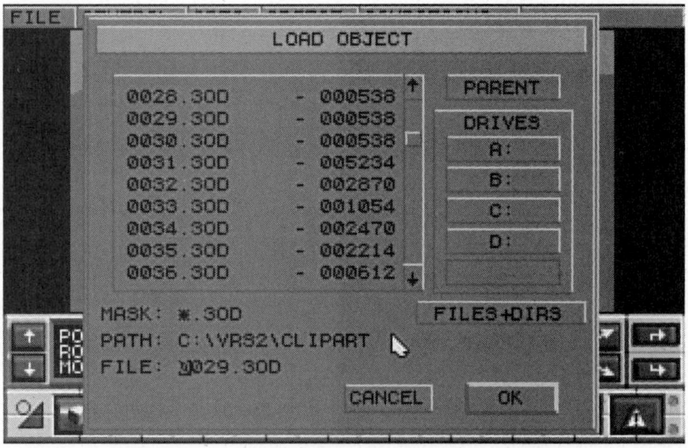

Figure 2.8.
Loading an object
from available
clip art.

```
FILE                              LOAD OBJECT

        0028.30D    - 000538           PARENT
        0029.30D    - 000538
        0030.30D    - 000538           DRIVES
        0031.30D    - 005234             A:
        0032.30D    - 002870             B:
        0033.30D    - 001054             C:
        0034.30D    - 002470             D:
        0035.30D    - 002214
        0036.30D    - 000612

      MASK:  *.30D                    FILES+DIRS
      PATH:  C:\VRS2\CLIPART
      FILE:  0029.30D

                         CANCEL        OK
```

---

[21]Not all objects have movable points, and not all points on an object will be movable. The Next button will take you only to legally movable points.

Figure 2.9.
A desk and chair
loaded into the
scene.

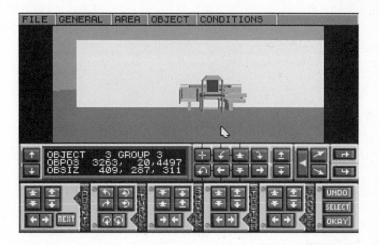

Once you have your first wall, you can simply duplicate it over and over, stretching and shrinking the copies to make the remaining walls. Clicking the Copy Object icon at the bottom of the screen displays the dialog shown in Figure 2.10.

Figure 2.10.
Copying an
object.

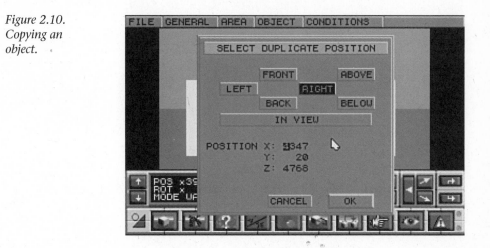

When you copy an object, you can specify the relative position of the new object. You can also specify the object position in coordinates. In Figure 2.10, the selected relative position for the new wall is Right. Figure 2.11 shows the result. The new wall is placed immediately to the right of the old wall.

This looks like one big wall, but it is not. Click the Modify object button at the bottom of the screen, and select the new wall. Move it to the right using the Move control cluster in the Object Editor (see Figure 2.12).

*Figure 2.11.
Adding a second
wall to the right
of the first one.*

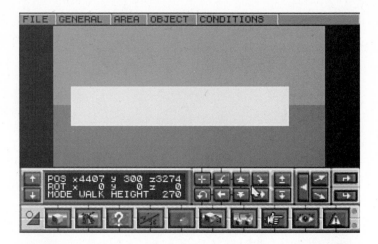

*Figure 2.12.
There are now
two walls.*

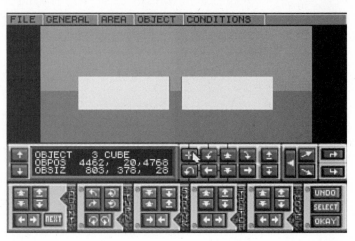

You can now use the Rotate control cluster to rotate the new wall 90 degrees (see Figure 2.13) and then Move it next to the first wall and align the corners (see Figure 2.14).

You can add objects to the scene at any time. Figure 2.15 shows a couch being added.

*Figure 2.13.
Rotating an
object.*

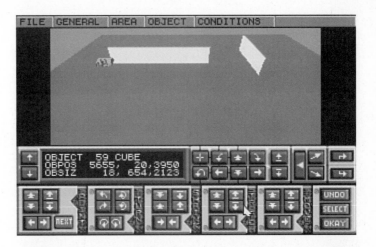

*Figure 2.14.
Aligning the two
walls.*

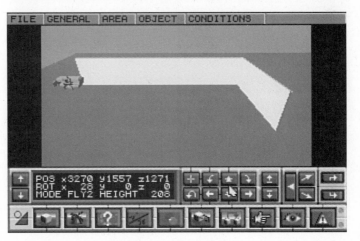

Figure 2.16 shows the scene after a chair and a third wall have been added. The
third wall was added by copying the second wall, and specifying Left for the placement. VR Studio finds the nearest position to the left of the wall where it can place
the new wall, which is (conveniently!) at the edge of the first wall, just like in Figure 2.16.

Figure 2.15.
Adding a couch.

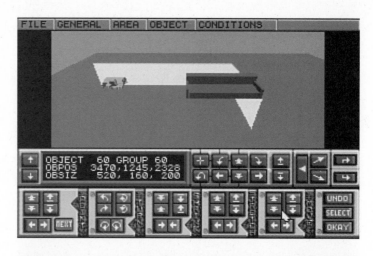

Figure 2.16.
Adding a third
wall.

The house would be a little small, however, if you do not stretch out the new wall. Figure 2.17 shows the third wall stretched out (done, of course, with the Object Editor), and yet another wall added. This new wall is an interior wall, but it was added like the previous walls and then stretched and shrunk to fit. You can see the beginnings of the floor plan.

Figure 2.18 shows a few more walls added in the same fashion. To make the house interesting, I deviated from a simple square.

Figure 2.17.
You can stretch
and shrink new
walls once you've
added them.

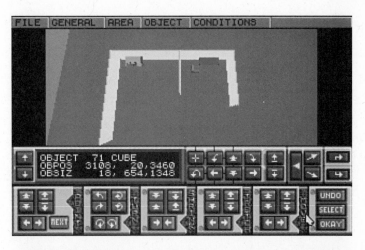

Figure 2.18.
Additional walls
give further
definition to the
room.

There is no grid in VR Studio, so it can be challenging to correctly line up walls at the corners. Here is where whatever practice you have at moving around will come in very handy. If you take a moment to position the point of view near the corner (see Figure 2.19), it becomes very easy to line up walls and other objects precisely.

Figure 2.20 shows how to add a bedroom, complete with bed and closet, to the house. The bed was added using the same steps used to add the desk (way back in Figure 2.9), and the walls were made from copies of existing walls.

Figure 2.19.
Lining up walls
at the corners.

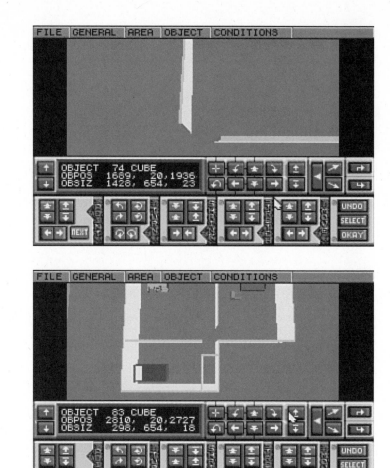

Figure 2.20.
Creating a
bedroom.

Figure 2.21 shows the addition of walls for a bathroom (on the left) and a kitchen. I have also added a rather overdone dining room table[22] opposite the soon-to-be-finished kitchen. This is yet another stock object from the clipart that accompanies VR Studio.

---

[22]As my editor noted, the table would make an excellent TV tray for Henry VIII.

*Figure 2.21.
Adding a
bathroom and
kitchen to the
house.*

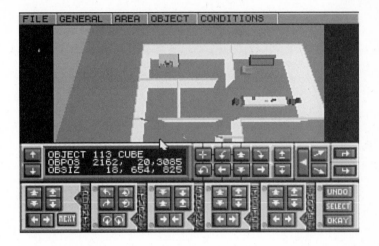

The kitchen really ought to have cabinets. To create them, you can return to the basics. Create a cube, as shown in Figure 2.22. Figure 2.22 also shows the Color Editor. The available colors are shown at the bottom center of the screen. The six faces of the current object are shown at the left, and you can put a different color on each face. To pick a color, click with the left mouse button. To set a color, right-click on the corresponding face at the lower left.[23]

*Figure 2.22.
Using a cube as
the basis for
kitchen cabinets.*

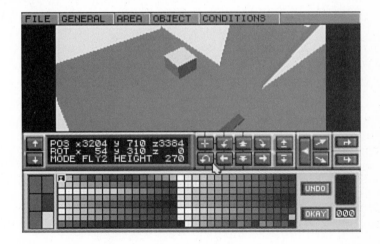

[23]This arrangement of coloring the faces by clicking on one of the squares at the lower left is bothersome. It is almost impossible to keep the faces straight (sorry; another pun just slipped out). Fortunately, you can right-click on an object face to set its color.

To create cabinets, use the Object Editor to stretch the cube into a counter. You can then copy and Shrink/Stretch to put a U-shaped set of counters in the kitchen. If you like, you can add a refrigerator or stove from the clip art collection.

To add a roof to the house, Create a pyramid[24], and then Stretch it to extend just a bit past the edges of the floor plan. The final result should look something like Figure 2.23.

Figure 2.23.
An outside view
of the completed
house.

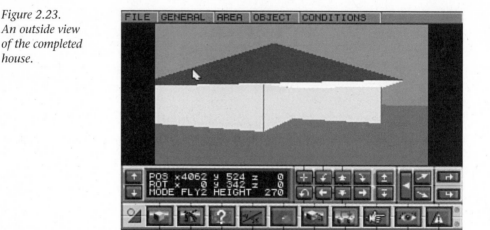

Once you have added a roof, you can locate the point of view inside the house to continue adding furniture, appliances, or whatever you like to the decor. Sometimes, just to be perverse, VR Studio will place the new object or group above the roof. VR Studio uses rules to make sure it doesn't place one object where another one already exists, and the results are therefore sometime unpredictable. If this happens, just lift your point of view above the roof to find the object. Then slide the roof aside and drop the object through the opening (see Figure 2.24).

This exterior view is quite plain. The house needs some windows and doors. You can add these using the Create Object button at the bottom of the screen. Instead of using a solid object, simply add a few rectangles. These can be sized and colored to suit your tastes. Figure 2.25 shows an outside view with a door and a window added at the front entrance of the house.

---

[24]You can create a pyramid just like you create a cube—click on the pyramid shape instead of the cube shape in the dialog for creating objects.

Figure 2.24.
Adding an object
after the roof
is on.

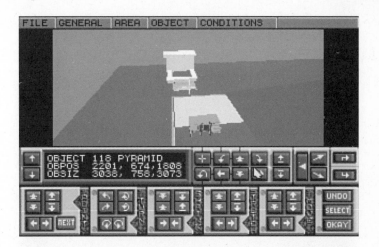

Figure 2.25.
An outside view
with a door and
window added.

So far, this door is just a flat rectangle placed against the house. However, VR Studio allows you to create Entrances, and Transporters that move you to an entrance. To create an entrance, move to the position that represents the entry point. In this case, that's the inside of the wall where the door was placed—just inside the living/dining room. Click the Area/Create Entrance menu selection to make this spot an entrance. To see the attributes of the entrance, click the Area/Edit Entrance menu selection. This displays the dialog shown in Figure 2.26.

Notice that both the position and rotation coordinates of the entrance position are editable. This means that to create an entrance, you must set not only the position but the orientation as well. In this example, the entrance is intended to mimic the act of walking through a door, so the orientation points into the room.

Figure 2.26.
Editing the
attributes of an
entrance.

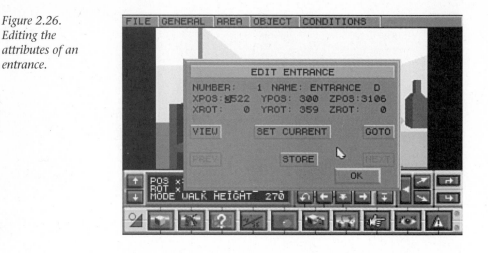

Now that you have an entrance, you can create a transport that will take you to it.[25] Select the exterior door, and modify its attributes using the Object/Edit Attributes menu selection or the Object attributes button at the bottom of the screen. Either method displays the dialog box shown in Figure 2.26.

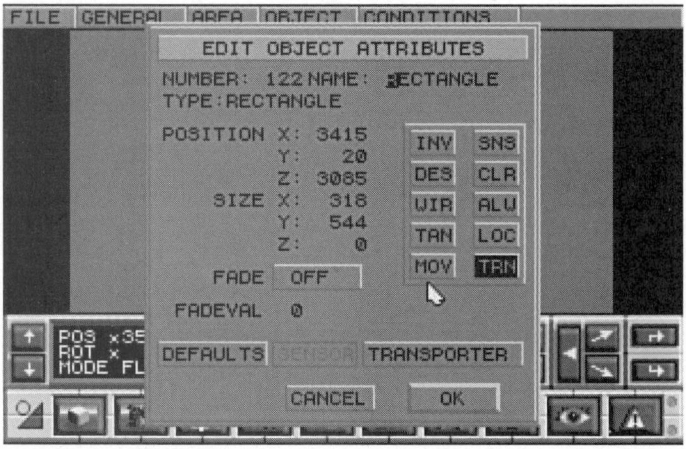

Figure 2.27.
The Object
Attributes dialog
box.

---

[25]The term entrance is a little misleading. An entrance need not be located in an entry point. You could, for example, move to a point far away from the house, and make that an entrance. Such jumps lend themselves well to game situations.

You can also create multiple areas in a project. You can create one kind of space in one area, and a completely different kind of space in a different area. A transporter in one area can take you to an entrance in a different area.

There are many attributes available for editing, but only one is of interest for creating a transporter: the TRN button. Click it to activate the Transporter button. Clicking the Transporter button allows you to select the area and entrance that the object will transport to (see Figure 2.27).

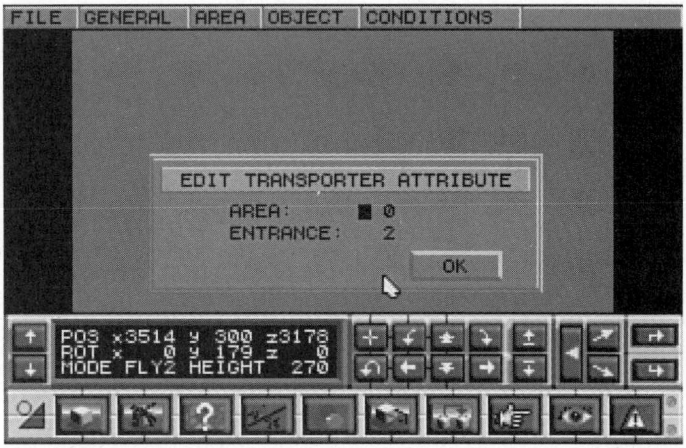

Figure 2.28.
Selecting the
entrance for a
transporter.

Now, when you collide with the door (that is, when you "walk" into it) you will be transported to the living/dining room, at the location you set as the entrance. To create a way back out, you must create another door on the inside of the wall,[26] create an entrance near the outside door, and then make the inside door a transporter.

This concludes the tour of the basic features of Virtual Reality Studio 2.0. For information about the advanced features of VR Studio, please see Chapter 9. Even if you never do anything beyond creating interesting custom universes, however, you'll get a lot of enjoyment out of VR Studio.[27]

---

[26]Don't copy the outside door to make the inside door. VR Studio will not be able to properly keep track of the entrances, and you won't be able to transport properly no matter how much you edit the various attributes and objects.

[27]However, a warning to the wise. VR Studio has some bugs that can be frustrating. Most of these don't show up until you try to create a large number of objects. I strongly suggest that you save your work frequently, and that you check the state of all objects before saving over an older version of the scene. This will allow you to restore from an older version if something goes wrong. You should also contact Virtual Reality Laboratories to see if you have the latest version of the package. The latest version I received was 2.07. They are making an effort to clean up the bugs.

3

VIRTUAL POWER

3D Modeling

Most of the history of art took place without any accurate attention to the third dimension. At best, the third dimension was stretched in virtually[1] unrecognizable ways. There are good reasons for this. The most important reason is simple to state:

Drawing in three dimensions is not natural.

Before you start calling me an idiot for making such an inane pronouncement, think about this for a minute. What is natural about 3D is viewing in three dimensions. *Living* in three dimensions does not automatically qualify anyone for *drawing* in three dimensions. There is some effort involved. If you don't believe me, pull out pencil and paper and draw a circle. Heck—don't even worry too much about getting the sides straight; if you were working on a computer, the computer could straighten things out for you.

Done with the circle? Good. Now draw a sphere.

Not as simple, right? Good. Now we're on the same wavelength.

I am making this point as a warning. If you have never drawn in three dimensions with a pencil, don't expect the computer to suddenly make it easy to do. Because its not the mechanics of drawing in 3D that's difficult; it's thinking in 3D that's hard. Once you break through the barrier, however, and start thinking in 3D, it gets easier and easier. If you haven't already had a 3D-drawing "Aha!" experience, you will at some point. It may seem like work until you reach that stage, however. So don't give up if it seems frustrating—you'll miss the best part of 3D if you do. Which leads me to the following statement:

With a little effort, you can make drawing in three dimensions a perfectly natural activity.

In other words,[2] 3D drawing is an acquired taste.

---

[1] Unintentional play on words, but I'll take credit for it anyway.

[2] And in keeping with the recipe idea, of couse.

Working in Three Dimensions

There are two ways to work in three dimensions: *intuitive* and *mechanical*. The intuitive method is exciting once you acquire the skills, but good old mechanical drawing has its advantages, too. For starters, it offers a frame of reference that I can describe. It's like the notes in a musical score—it's a way of describing something, but it is not that something. Just as it takes practice to turn notes into music, it takes practice to turn mechanical drafting into interesting virtual spaces.

When working in two dimensions, we traditionally use Cartesian[3] coordinates to define points in the 2D plane. Figure 3.1 shows a typical Cartesian coordinate system. There is a vertical axis, called the y axis, and a horizontal axis, the x axis. The point where these two axes meet is called the origin. The origin is at distance zero on both axes, and we can describe this point as (0,0).

To define a point, we need merely mention its distance from the origin along both axes. For example, a point 5 units to the right of the origin along the x axis, and 3 units below the origin on the y axis has the coordinates (5,-3). By convention, the x coordinate is given first. There are an infinite number of such points in the 2D plane.

To describe points in 3D space, we merely add a third dimension. The third axis is called the z axis.[4] A three-dimensional coordinate system is shown in Figure 3.2.

To specify a point in a three-dimensional system, we need to supply three numbers. Each number represents the distance from the origin along each respective axis—x, then y, then z. For example, if we take the same point as in the previous example, and lift it 83 units up from the origin, its coordinates are (5, -3, 83).

Now, we have not merely an infinite number of points in a plane, but an infinite number of planes in space—and each plane has an infinite number of points in it. The level of complexity has just gone from infinity to infinity-squared.[5]

---

[3] Named after the great mathematician René Descartes, who slept until noon. They never tell us those things about famous people, and we don't find out until it's too late to develop such delicious eccentricities in ourselves.

[4] I'll bet you saw that coming.

[5] Of course, I'll leave the questions of how one squares infinity to the mathematicians.

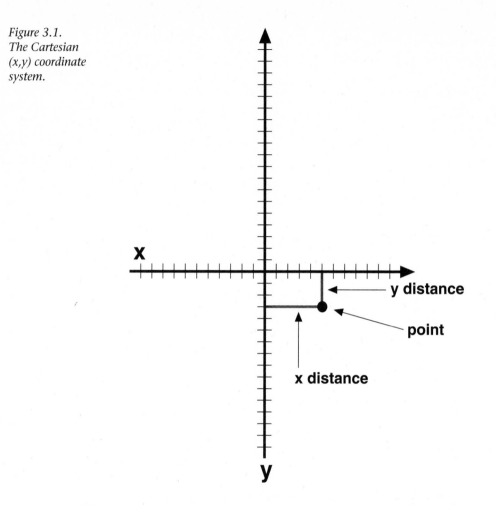

Figure 3.1.
The Cartesian
(x,y) coordinate
system.

I suppose all those infinities would be more manageable if we didn't have to find a way to represent them on two-dimensional surfaces. Paper is two dimensional; the computer screen is two-dimensional. Thus the allure of fancy virtual-space-creating goggles: they offer the promise of being able to draw and work in three dimensions using clever tricks to fool the eye (see Chapter 8, "Seeing is Believing").

Figure 3.2.
A three-
dimensional
coordinate
system.

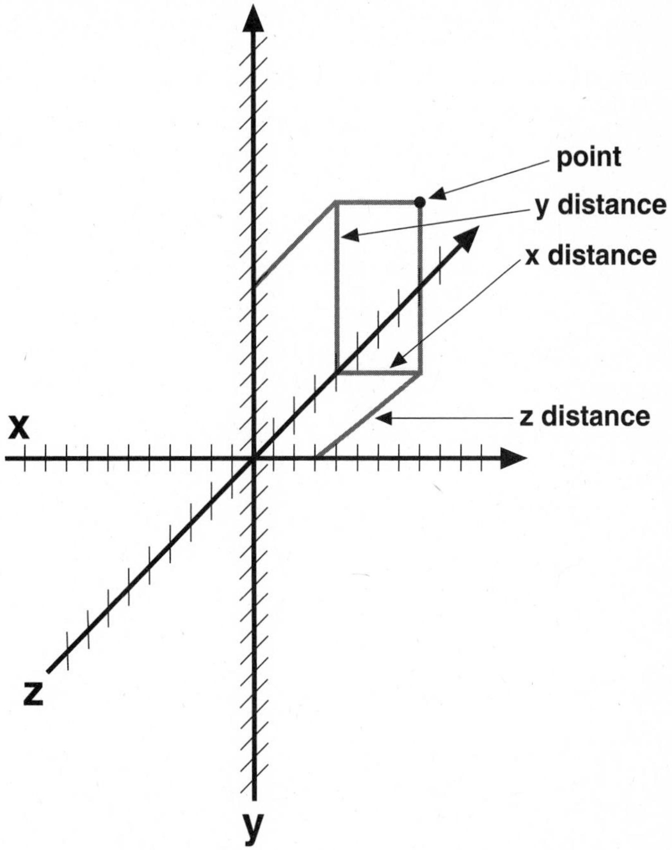

point

y distance

x distance

x

z distance

z

y

The problem is, such goggles cost thousands of dollars, have limited capabilities,[6] and the range of software written for them is, well, almost zero.[7] For a while yet, we'll have to make do with representing three dimensions in two. The rest of this chapter is dedicated to the proposition that as long as we're calling it *virtual* reality, *degrees* of virtuality are a reality—for the time being. After all, a perfectly rendered, highly detailed 3D scene on your computer monitor beats the heck out of nothing at all.

---

[6] Don't move your head too quickly, for example—the computer will choke trying to update the scene to keep up, and shatter any illusion of reality.

[7] Not that there aren't software programs, of course, but, so far, there aren't any spreadsheets or word processors—that is, the kinds of software you and I use everyday. Drawing programs are limited to special-purpose applications, such as rendering the chemical structure of complex molecules.

Video and 3D Modeling Software

One of the most fascinating ways to work with 3D modeling packages is to add video images. Many 3D packages support some form of animation, and video allows you to mix virtual and real in sometimes powerful ways. In this chapter, you'll explore ways to use 3D modeling to enhance videos. In Chapter 10, you'll learn how to put video images into a virtual space. You can put an image of yourself in a dream reality, or you can put a product video inside a virtual-space presentation for a sales meeting.

Working with video adds a whole new dimension to 3D modeling.[8] And the reverse is true as well: adding 3D modeling to video creates some visually stunning possibilities. In this section, you'll learn how to use several 3D modeling packages to create digital special effects for video files.

Issues with Video

Using video is not a trivial step. The results can be stunning, but if you are not already working with video, you may be surprised by the effort and technology required. It's not daunting by any means; with a minimum investment of time and money, you can definitely add videos, or use 3D software to enhance your videos. Read through this section carefully, however, to see if you will be able to assemble the components you'll need. A minimum setup requires:

- A video source. Right now, it's expensive to buy video clips, so you'll probably want a video camera. You can spend anywhere from $400 to $2,000 for a new camera (more if you want professional equipment), and from $100 to $750 for decent used equipment.

- A tripod. This is a minor item that can make a huge difference in quality. A tripod insures steady images, which is very important when working with small image sizes. Make sure you get a true video tripod, with a fluid head.[9]

---

[8] Did he really say that? Ouch!

[9] A fluid head will smooth out motion when you pan the camera. Don't get a tripod for a still camera; it probably won't have a fluid head.

■ A video capture card. A card that compresses video in real time is ideal; expect to spend around $500 for such a board. The Intel Smart Video Recorder is a good choice, but more boards are coming out all the time.

■ A fast computer. I recommend at least a 486/33, 500 megs of hard disk space, a fast (12 millisecond average seek or better) hard drive, 8 megs of memory (16 is better), and a very, very fast Windows accelerator video display card.

■ Video for Windows software. The retail price of this piece of the puzzle is the least of your worries—street prices are around $100, and it may even wind up as an integral part of Windows.

■ 3D modeling software. Good choices include the two packages I describe in detail later in this section—3D Studio 2.0 from Autodesk, and Imagine 2.0 from Impulse. Imagine is much more affordable ($495 retail) than 3D Studio ($2995).[10]

Some optional goodies to make life a little easier:

■ A video monitor for displaying the incoming video signal

■ Remote controls for all of your equipment so you're not jumping up and down all the time to adjust things

■ A video output card to send animations to videotape

■ A second deck for dubbing and editing of video material outside the computer. (If you do this, consider Video Director from Gold Disk; it could make your life substantially easier.)

■ A high-end video capture system. Standard video capture cards, like the Intel Smart Video Recorder, are limited to image sizes of 320x240 and 15 frames per second (fps). Full-motion, full-frame video is 640x480 and 30 fps. For many applications, the smaller image size is fine—it allows you to display text as well as the video image on your computer screen. If you want to output edited video to tape, however, you'll need high-end equipment. Expect to pay from $5,000 to $50,000 for a full setup.

---

[10] Don't let the price difference fool you—Imagine is extremely powerful. Autodesk markets 3D Studio to folks who are already using things like AutoCAD, which is a limited market—thus the high price. If all you want to do is work in 3D modeling, then Imagine may be all you need. However, a word of warning: Imagine is *extremely* idiosyncratic. If you don't have an artistic orientation, you might find it frustrating. It is also challenging to learn to use well.

Obtaining Source Material

If you haven't worked with video before, you may be surprised to find out what's involved. It's not as simple as pointing a camera and hitting the record button. Once you get the steps down, however, it's pretty easy to do. There are many nuances to learn, of course, but I've had so much fun integrating video into my applications that it's never been a bother.

Let's assume that you are working with the Intel Smart Video Recorder,[11] and that you have a video tape with a sequence you'd like to capture. It might be a shot of a new product, showing how it is used, or it might be the president of a company making pithy comments during a keynote address at a symposium on flywheel manufacturing. The complete process works like this:

0. Before you do anything else, defragment the hard disk you will use for capture. This is a must! A fragmented disk can seriously cut into your ability to capture video. The time spent hunting for the next available sector results in lost data. After you defragment, run VidCap (the Video for Windows capture program) and use File/Set Capture File to create a large capture file. Allow from 10 to 25 megabytes per minute of video, depending on the card you are using, and the image size you plan to capture. Refer to the manual that comes with your capture card for guidance, or experiment.

1. Queue the videotape to a point several seconds before the beginning of the sequence you want to capture. Most decks take a few moments to get started. Pause the tape.

2. Run the VidCap application that comes with Video for Windows, (or any other application that supports video capture). Click on the Capture Video icon, or click on Capture/Video on the menu.

---

[11] I keep mentioning this card because it is far and away the most convenient to use. Just in case you think I'm biased, or that Intel is paying for the endorsement, I'll mention some other cards that also do a good job. The Video Spigot, from Creative Labs, has excellent image quality, and comes with some clever options that give you more choices when it comes to playback. The Pro Movie Spectrum, from Media Vision, also does a good job, but I thought the image quality wasn't quite as good as for the Spigot. If you need overlay, consider the Bravado 16 from Truevision. It comes with an add-on real-time compression module, has room for a VGA-to-video daughter card, and has excellent image quality. The only hassle is that it won't allow you to have more than 15 megs of memory in your system.

3. Set the capture options you want to use. For general use, I suggest Video Options set to 15 fps, 160x120, and the Indeo Video codec.[12] For audio, start with 8 bits, 22kHz, and mono. Once you get this much working, you can experiment with other settings. Click OK when everything is set the way you want it.

4. Another dialog box pops up; clicking OK will start recording. Don't do that yet! Every second of video capture will chew up lots of disk space. Start video playback, and after about a second (or when your deck is up to speed and playing with a clean image), click the OK button to start capture. When you have the entire sequence (plus a little extra, just in case), hit the escape button on your keyboard and then the stop button on the video deck.

5. You now have the video sequence on your hard disk, but you are not done. Run VidEdit (it also comes with Video for Windows), and open the capture file. Use Video/Compression Options to set parameters for the file. If you want the file to be able to play satisfactorily on 386 machines, set the following compression options:

- CD-ROM 150K/second

- No change

- Key frame set to 1

Now use File/Save As to save the file with a new name. The capture file can now be used to capture another sequence. This technique has the advantage of letting you use the same unfragmented capture file over and over. In addition, it gives you the most compact file sizes and data rates for best playback on slower machines.

If you want more detailed information about using video, you can find it in my book, *PC Video Madness*, also from Sams Publishing. It contains a wealth of information about working with video on the PC.

---

[12] "Codec" is a made-up word that has two possible origins. Some say it refers to encoding and decoding, and some say it refers to compression and decompression. Either way, it refers to a computer algorithm that handles both capture and playback. Take your pick.

Image Quality

Because you will almost certainly be working with video image sizes in the range of 160x120 to 320x240, you'll need to pay special attention to image quality at several steps in the overall process. When you are shooting video, try to fill the frame with the subject. This makes the subject stand out, even at smaller image sizes. A steady camera is also very important—use a tripod whenever possible. You can find a decent video tripod for as little as $50.

During or after capture, when you compress the video,[13] you'll need to make some decisions that will affect image quality. Uncompressed video isn't practical; full-motion, full-frame video occupies 1.5 gigabytes *per minute!*[14] The more you compress, the lower the image quality. You'll need to find a balance point between quality, image size, frame rate, and the speed of the playback machine.

Life with Palettes

I have a saying regarding video playback: "24 bits or bust." A little history is necessary to explain why this is so.

When Windows was born, only 4 bits of data were available for specifying colors. That yields a grand total of 16 possible colors. You cannot do photographic-quaity images with 16 colors. You can fake it using dithering, but the results are not very pleasing.

The next step forward was to 8-bit color; that gives us 256 colors to work with. Actually, it's a little better than that; the design used to implement 256 color support lets you pick which 256 colors you want to use at any one time from a universe of more than 16 million colors. The selection of colors in use at any one time is called a palette. If you want to display an image that uses colors different from those in the current palette, you need merely switch to a different palette. Presto! You can display images that use a wide variety of colors.

The reality isn't quite so presto. If you have an image displayed on-screen when you change the palette, the colors in that image get changed—there's only one palette, and if you change it, everything changes. This is the Achilles heel of using

---

[13] Compression is a complex area. There are no general guidelines for how to compress. There are tradeoffs involved. Higher compression results in smaller files, and allows you to play back on slower machines. However, image quality is reduced. You'll have to experiment to find out what you prefer.

[14] That's why video is supported mostly in small sizes like 160x120 or 240x180.

palettes. Every time you change the palette, any images already on the screen get their colors scrambled. This can be so severe that you can completely lose any suggestion of what the first image actually shows.

Thus, my slogan: 24 bits or bust. 24-bit color gives you instant, simultaneous access to all 16+ million colors. And at today's prices—less than $130 for 24-bit video at 640x480—24-bit color is very affordable. Not only that, 24-bit color looks dramatically better than any palette ever will. If you don't want the overhead of pushing all 24 bits around for every pixel on your screen, 16-bit color will do a good job. It avoids the palette problems, provides enough color for general use, and has 1/3 less calories than true color.

And here's the clincher: the best codecs automatically store video data as 24-bit color. If you don't have 24-bit in your system, they will fake it—they will dither the image to use the current set of 256 colors to display the image. This is OK, but you'll miss seeing how good the video image really is. If you are going to work with video, use the best possible video display card you can afford. The results are worth it. If you must keep costs down, or if you want to work at high resolutions like 1024x768 or 1280x1024, 16-bit color is also very good, and is an excellent compromise.

3D Studio 2.0

Have you ever been in a situation where you knew what you had to do, didn't like doing it, and had to do it anyway? That's the position that I'm in when it comes to writing about 3D Studio from Autodesk. First, the good news: I love what I can do with this program. Next, the bad news: the software costs almost $3,000, and uses a hardware *dongle*[15] as well. These are major inconveniences in this day and age of $99 software. Why, in the very next section I'll be describing the wonders of a product that retails for one-sixth of that. The question becomes, why bother with an expensive product like 3D Studio?[16]

Because there are times when nothing else will do. As you'll see in this section, 3D Studio can do some really fantastic effects.

---

[15] The word dongle has an interesting origin, or so I've read in the ads from a company that sells them to software vendors. The ad said that the inventor of the little hardware clump (which you attach to your parallel port so the software knows you are the true and legal owner of the software) was named Don Gull. I'm just a teensy-weensy bit skeptical on that one.

[16] Especially when Autodesk sent it to me at no cost, and I should be grateful and keep my mouth shut.

RECIPE

1 video file (.AVI)
1t Video for Windows
1t Animator Pro
4 cups 3D Studio
4-8 megs of memory
1 Math Coprocessor/486 CPU
1 VESA-compatible video display card

Instructions: Convert the AVI file to a FLC file, and then attach it as a texture map to an object in 3D Studio. Animate the object to create a digital special effect—wipes, explosions, flips, flying videos—you name it. Convert back to AVI and serve.[17] Makes an excellent appetizer in multimedia titles, or serve between courses to clear the palette.

Getting Started

Before you can use a video file in 3D Studio, you need to convert it to a file format that 3D Studio can read: .FLC or .FLI. These are animation file formats. The conversion process is easy, but you'll need extra software to pull it off. The easiest method uses Animator Pro, but there is a slower method that you can use if you don't have Animator Pro. I'll explain both methods in this section.

Start with the file open in VidEdit. From the File menu, select Extract. This will display the dialog box shown in Figure 3.3. The list box titled "List Files of Type:" is the key to the process. Select DIB Sequence. Then enter a filename of the form

xxxxnnnn.bmp

where *xxxx* is a unique name, and *nnnn* is the first number in a sequence, such as 0001 or 0000. The name you enter becomes the first filename in a numbered sequence of files. In the example in Figure 3.3, the filenames will be face0000.bmp,

---

[17] Actually, this concoction might be best described as a kind of club sandwich: 3D Studio in the middle, Animator Pro on both sides of that, and VidEdit on the outside. A little mayo, and you've got lunch at your desk.

face0001.bmp, and so on. There will be one file for each frame in the video. It's a good idea to verify that you have enough disk space for the bitmaps. There's a formula for estimating how much space you'll need:

<width> * <height> * <bit_depth/8> *<number_frames>

For example, if you have a video sequence that is 160x120, using 24-bit color and 103 frames, you'll need:

160 * 120 * (24/3) * 103

or

15,820,800 bytes—that's 15.5 megabytes.

Remember to use the .bmp extension; some programs don't know to look for the default .dib extension that VidEdit uses. You can use more or less than 4 characters for each portion of the name; just make sure that there are enough characters in the numeric portion. For example, if you have 103 frames in your video, you must have at least 3 characters for the numeric portion of the name. All of the following are valid sequence names:

```
face01.bmp
x000001.bmp
v1.bmp
icefall1.bmp
```

When you have a satisfactory name entered for the initial file in the sequence, click the OK button. You'll see a message box telling you the progress of the operation.

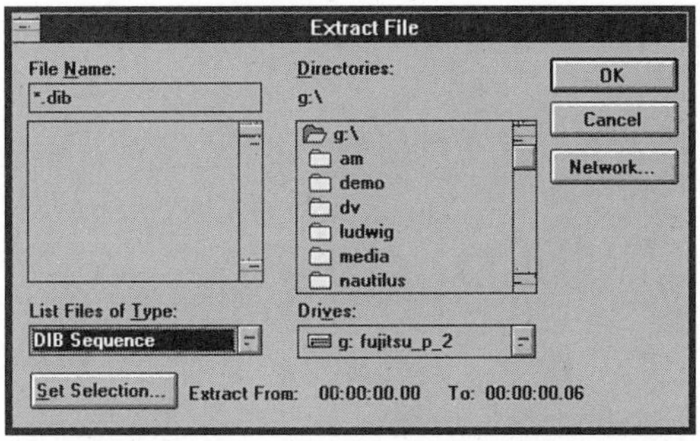

Figure 3.3.
The File/Extract
dialog box in
VidEdit.

Once you have the DIB Sequence, you have two choices about how to get it into 3D Studio:

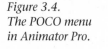
■ Load the bitmaps into Animator Pro to create an animation (.FLC) file;

■ Convert the bitmaps to a file format that 3D Studio can read.

Let's look at how to use Animator Pro to handle this task first. Open Animator Pro and click on the POCO menu. Click Numpic, as shown in Figure 3.4.

Figure 3.4.
The POCO menu
in Animator Pro.

This opens a dialog box (see Figure 3.5) that allows you to work with numbered file sequences. To load the images you created in VidEdit, select choice 2: Load Pics as Flic. If the current animation is not the same size as the incoming images, you'll be asked if you want to resize the .flc file to match the incoming image size; answer yes.

Wait patiently while each file is read; this is especially necessary if you saved the bitmaps as 24-bit images because Animator Pro analyzes each image and performs color reduction to 8-bit color.[18]

---

[18] VidEdit also gives you the option to perform color reduction. Use the Video/Video format menu selection to make the change. If you are wondering which program does the job better, all I can say is that VidEdit does it a lot faster, although you do have the extra step of creating a palette after you reduce the number of colors (otherwise you'll wind up with a gray scale image). There is an advantage to using Animator Pro, however. Animator Pro creates a separate palette for each frame. 3D Studio is capable of handling creation of a unified palette during rendering. Because you can use lights in 3D Studio, the colors needed for the final images are likely to be different from the colors used earlier in the process.

*Figure 3.5.
Animator Pro
dialog box for
importing/
exporting
numbered files.*

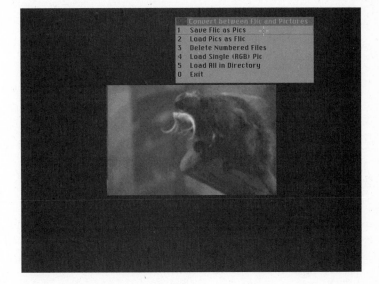

Once you have a FLC file, it's time to run 3D Studio.

If you don't have Animator Pro, and want to use AVI files in 3D Studio, follow this procedure:

1. Create a DIB sequence as described previously using VidEdit.

2. Use an image program to convert each of the bitmap files to a file type that 3D Studio can work with. I suggest Targa files (*.tga). You can do this one image at a time with a paint program,[19] or you can use a utility like Graphic Workshop (shareware) or Image Pals (commercial software). Either of these products allows you to perform mass conversion operations. The process still takes time, but you don't have to sit there and initiate each conversion.

3. In 3D Studio, instead of specifying an FLC file for the texture map, you would specify a file containing a list of the image files, in the order you want to use them.

---

[19] Talk about tedious! I had three AVI files, each with 562 frames, that I used in a single 3D animation. Converting one at a time would have taken me, let's see, at 35 seconds per image, and 3x562 images, that's—16.4 hours! Whew!

Creating Objects in 3D Studio

The opening screen of 3D Studio is shown in Figure 3.6. There are four viewports, a menu at the upper right, and several icons at the lower left.

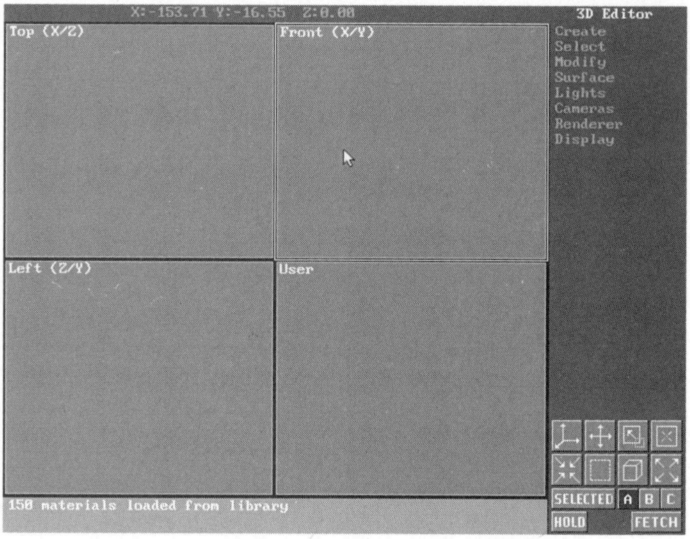

*Figure 3.6.
The opening
screen of 3D
Studio.*

The standard types of viewport are:

> **Top**—This shows your 3D creation from above.
>
> **Front**—A front view of the scene.
>
> **Left**—A view from the left side.
>
> **User**—A 3D view, sometimes referred to as an orthographic projection.

There are additional viewport types available, but you can only display up to four at one time.

Unlike the menus you may be familiar with in most graphic programs, 3D Studio's menu is vertical. Clicking on a top-level menu item, such as Create, displays the next level of commands (look ahead to Figure 3.9 to see an example).

The icon group at the lower right of the screen gives you access to a number of common actions (see Figure 3.7).

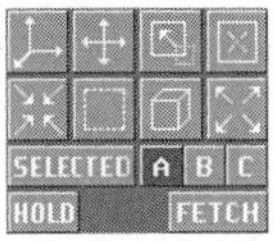

Figure 3.7.
The 3D Studio
icon group.

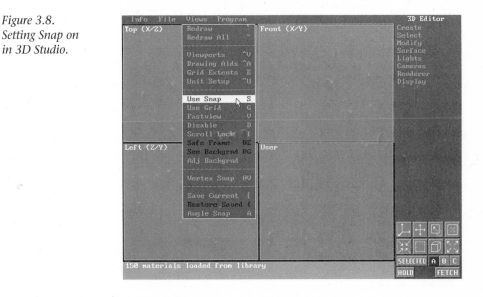

In this example, you'll learn how to use 3D Studio to create one style of video transition. However, you can apply the same basic techniques to a wide variety of special effects. I'll offer some suggestions at the end of this section. In the example, we'll shrink one video to reveal another one behind it.

You'll need precise sizes for your objects, so turn on Snap using the View menu (see Figure 3.8). I also turn on the Grid points to show the locations that I'm snapping to. The most common video file size is 160x120 pixels, so we'll create an object with exactly those dimensions. To create an object, select Create on the menu at upper right, then click on Box (see Figure 3.9).

Figure 3.8.
Setting Snap on
in 3D Studio.

Click anywhere in the upper left of the Front viewport, and drag the mouse until you have a rectangle that is exactly 160 wide and 120 high. You can verify the exact size at the top of the screen (see Figure 3.9). Note that 3D Studio prompts you for the required action at the bottom of the screen in a status bar. After you have defined the rectangular shape, you are asked to set the depth of the box. Unless you want to attach the video to a box with depth, set the depth to be minimal by clicking twice in the same place, once to anchor the depth setting, and once to define its length as zero. The completed ultra-thin box is shown in Figure 3.10.

Figure 3.9.
Creating a box.

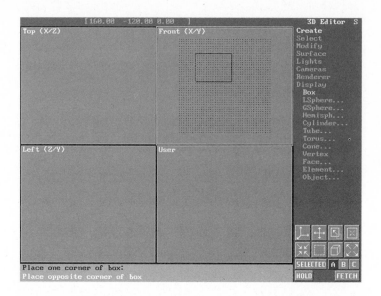

Figure 3.10.
A 160x120 box
defined in 3D
Studio.

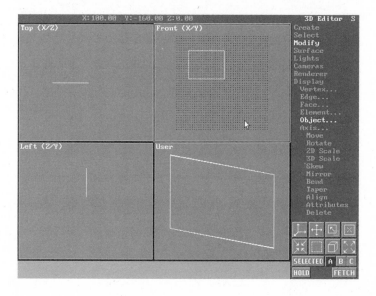

Now click on the Modify menu, and choose Object/Move. To create the second object,[20] hold down the shift key when you click on the object we just created. This will clone the object, giving us a second ultra-flat box just the right size, as shown in Figure 3.11. After creating the clone using move, you will need to reposition the new object to cover the first object.

Figure 3.11.
A cloned object.

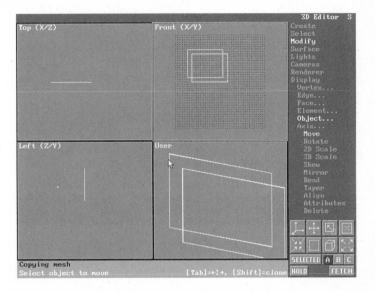

Mapping

You add a video sequence to an object as a texture map. To apply a map, you'll need to define mapping coordinates so 3D Studio knows where to position the bitmaps, and at what scale. In this case, the object is the same proportion as the video—160x120—so the easiest way to do this is to fit the map to the object. Use the Surface/Mapping/Aspect/Region Fit[21] menu selection to display the mapping coordinates. Figure 3.12 shows (in the upper right viewport) mapping coordinates that are both offset from and larger than the object. The cross hairs are located at the upper left corner of the object to define the upper left extent of the map, and you need only click and drag to the lower right corner of the object to properly fit the mapping coordinates.[22]

---

[20] For the second video sequence, of course.

[21] This business of putting slashes between menu commands is the standard way of referring to 3D Studio menu selections, and will be used throughout this section.

[22] If you try to render an object that has a map but no mapping coordinates, you'll get an error message. It can't be done!

Figure 3.12.
Default mapping
coordinates.

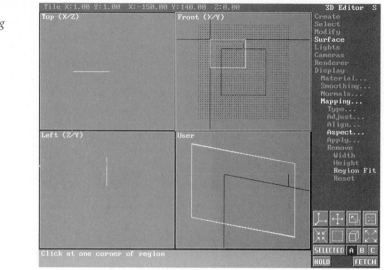

Figure 3.13 shows mapping coordinates properly applied. The image has been zoomed to show just the object being worked on. Note that there is a small vertical line at the top of the rectangle; this little handle defines "up" for the map. Fortunately, it's already pointing in the right direction. If it weren't, we would use the Surface/Mapping/Adjust/Rotate selection to change it.

Figure 3.13.
Mapping
coordinates fitted
to an object. Note
"handle" at top
indicating "up."

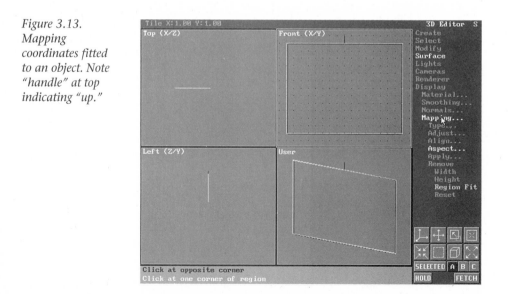

The next step is to apply the coordinates to both objects, using Surface/Mapping/Apply/Object. In order to apply the mapping coordinates, we need to select an object. However, with one object on top of the other, as in this case, you can't do that by clicking—the click will always select the object on top. To select an objects by name, simply press the h key instead of clicking. This will display a list of objects to pick from (see Figure 3.14). When you select the object from the list, the action specified by the current menu selection will be applied to that object. You can apply the same mapping coordinates to both objects.

Figure 3.14.
Selecting objects
by name.

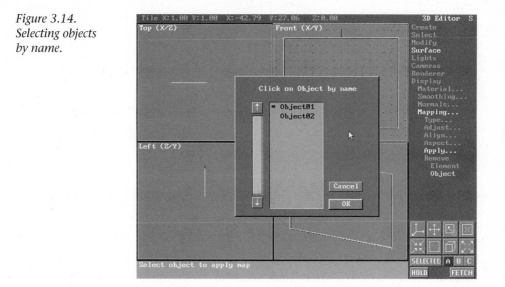

Materials

You can use the materials editor to create new surface materials in 3D Studio. To start the materials editor, press the F5 key. The materials editor screen is shown in Figure 3.15.[23] The blank squares at the top of the screen are slots for new materials. The controls at the middle of the screen are used to set the color and characteristics of the material. The four groups of buttons at the bottom of the screen are the ones we are interested in—they control mapping. However, before we start, move the mouse to the top of the screen to activate the menu, and click on Option/Cube. The default setting renders to a sphere; because you'll be rendering to a flat surface, the cube gives a more representative example.

---

[23] Due to the limitations of the screen capture software, I had to use a reduced screen resolution to show 256 colors in the materials editor. The images in this section were taken at 320x240x256 colors; if you have a SuperVGA adapter you will almost certainly want to use 640x480x256 colors.

Figure 3.15.
The materials
editor screen in
3D Studio.

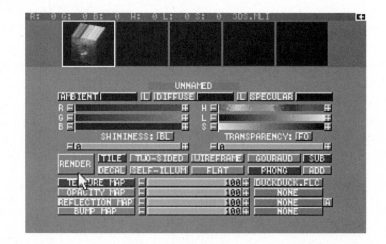

It's very easy to create a texture map. Click on the texture map filename button (see Figure 3.16). This will open a dialog box that allows you to select the file you want to use. Click on the filename, then click OK. The filename will be displayed on the texture map filename button. To see what the texture map will look like, click on the render button (see Figure 3.6). A small-scale rendering will be displayed in the current material slot at the top of the screen.

Figiure 3.16.
An example
rendering of a
texture map.

That's all there is to it. We won't be using any of the other features in the materials editor for this example. If desired, we could set characteristics such as shininess, rendering quality, transparency, and more. We could also create bump maps (to determine surface texture based on an image file) or reflection maps (to determine what will reflect off of the surface), etc.

To save the material, press the 'P' key to Put the material into the material library. A dialog box will ask you for the material name; enter any name that you like that fits in the space provided. Spaces are OK. Because we have two objects, each with a different AVI file, in this case you would also create a second material using a second FLC file. When you have put both materials into the library, press the 'F3' key to return to the 3D Editor.

Next, you'll want to apply the new material to the objects. Use Surface/Material/Choose to select one of the new materials, as shown in Figure 3.17. In this case, the material is called Monkey Antics. Click OK when you have the right material selected.

Figure 3.17. Selecting a new material with the material selector.

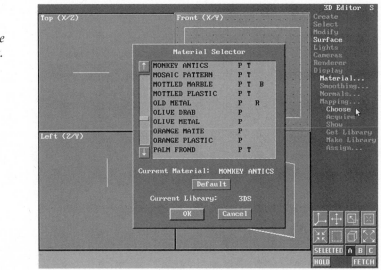

To apply the material to an object, use Surface/Mapping/Assign/Object. Then choose the second new material, and apply it to the other object.

At this point, both rectangles are in the same plane, and you'll need to move one of them in front of the other. You can use Select/Object/Single to make one of the rectangles the current object, and then move the selected object. Press the 'H' key to open the "Click on Object by name" dialog, and select whichever object you want to move to the front, and click OK.

Now use Modify/Object/Move, which changes the cursor to a small box with arrows, as shown in Figure 3.18. Click in the Top viewport to activate it,[24] then press the 'Tab' key until the little arrows are pointing up and down. To move the currently selected object, press the Selected button at bottom right, then use the mouse to move the selected object just ever so slightly downward. Because we are working in the Top viewport, this has the effect of moving the object toward the Front. Figure 3.18 shows how little of an offset is necessary.

Figure 3.18.
Moving an object.

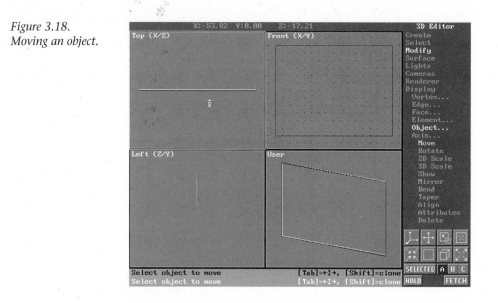

This is a good time to check your work. Use the Renderer/Render menu choice, and click in the User viewport to select it as the view to render. You should see the "Render Still Image" dialog box (see Figure 3.19); if you don't, click the User viewport a second time.[25] Make sure that the Disk button is not highlighted, and then click the Render button. This will render to the screen. During rendering, you'll see a progress dialog (see Figure 3.20).

---

[24] Only if it is not already activated.

[25] If the User viewport wasn't the active viewport, it won't render on the first click. The first click in a viewport always has the effect of activating it, rather than carrying out a menu action. This is a safety feature; it prevents you from taking actions you don't want to take, and allows you to move to a different viewport and continue the current operation there.

Figure 3.19.
Rendering a still
image.

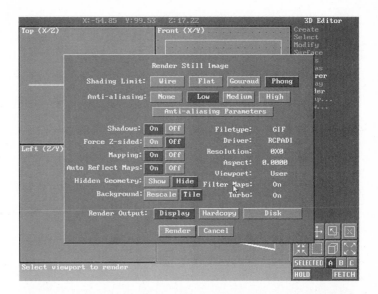

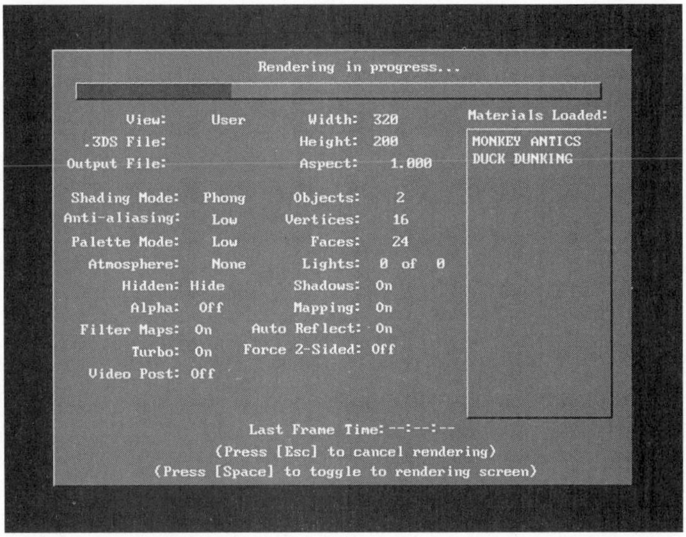

Figure 3.20.
The Rendering in
Progress message
box.

After a few moments, you'll see a rather dim image, as shown in Figure 3.21. You probably won't be able to recognize the image at all. The reason for this is simple: this is virtual reality—there is almost no light to illuminate the scene unless we add the light.

*Figure 3.21.
A rendered scene,
but with inad-
equate lighting.*

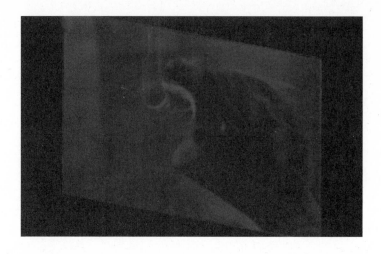

By default, the ambient light in a scene is set to a value of 77. There are 256 possible values, from 0 to 255; a value of 77 represents 77/256 or 30% of full lighting—not much at all. The default value is displayed if you select Lights/Ambient from the menu, as shown in Figure 3.22. I would suggest a setting in the range of 200-255 for adequate lighting. If you want colored lighting for special effects, use the RGB or HSL settings to create the color you want.

*Figure 3.22.
Adjusting
ambient lighting.*

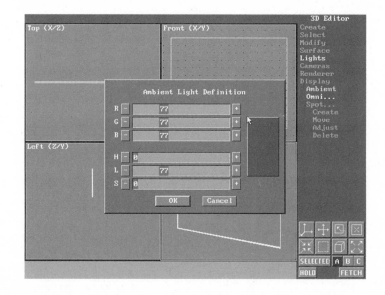

If you select Renderer/Render again, and render the scene to the screen, you'll see more natural results (see Figure 3.23).

Figure 3.23.
A scene rendered
with adequate
lighting.

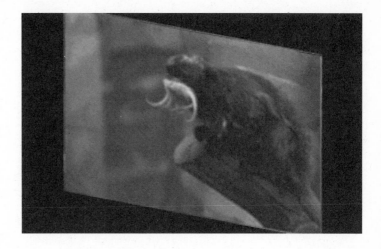

3D Studio also allows you to create two special types of lights. These are Omni lights, which are point sources of light, and Spotlights, which cast shadows and have adjustable light cones. You can create quite intricate lighting arrangements by using several different kinds of lights in different positions.

Animating

Here's a summary of what we've done so far:

- Converted the AVI file to either an FLC file or a series of .tga files
- Created two objects the same size as the video images
- Applied mapping coordinates to the objects
- Created two new materials using texture maps, one for each video file
- Assigned the new materials to the objects
- Adjusted lighting values.

Everything is now in place; it's time to animate. Animation takes place in the Keyframer, which you can access by pressing the 'F4' key. The opening screen of the Keyframer is shown in Figure 3.24. It's similar to the 3D Editor screen, but there are some important differences. The four viewports are the same, but the menu is different. There are two new buttons above the icons—Track info and Key info. These buttons allow you to modify key points along the animation track to fine-tune the animation, or to delete key animation events.

The buttons below the icons are standard VCR-style controls for moving from frame to frame, or playing the animation sequence.

Figure 3.24.
The Keyframer
screen.

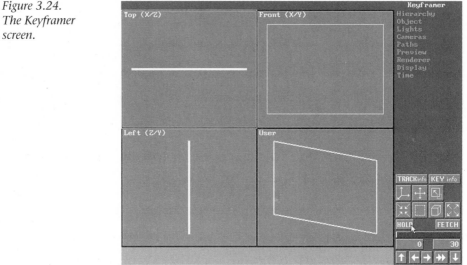

There are several ways to view an animation. You can use a standard viewport, such as Front view, which will give you a plane view (flat, no perspective). You can also render from the User viewport, which will give you an orthogonal view (3D, no perspective). You can also create a camera, which will give you full 3D and perspective. For our purposes, the flat, no perspective view is ideal—there will be no distortion of the rectangle during the special effect. The Front viewport is best, of course, but there is empty space around the objects. We want to fill the frame with the image.

Figure 3.25 shows the Zoom icon in action. The upper-left corner of the object has been clicked, and you can then drag the mouse to mark the lower-right boundary of the viewport.

Figure 3.26 shows the result of this zoom. The left and right borders of the object are now coincident with the viewport. Don't worry about the fact that the top and bottom of the objects aren't lined up with the viewport. You can set the aspect ration of the rendering so that only the actual object will show in the scene. Of course, if you wanted black space around the image, you would adjust the zoom factor accordingly.

Figure 3.25.
Adjusting the
zoom factor of a
viewport.

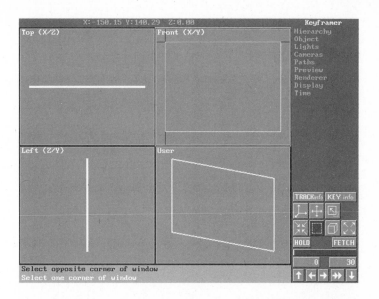

Figure 3.26
The zoom has
been adjusted to
match the object
and the viewport.

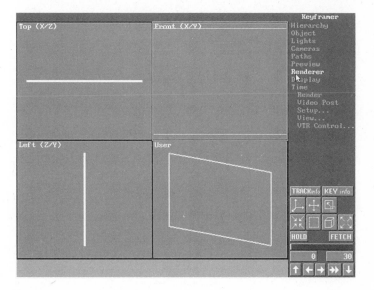

Using the Keyframer, you do not have to create every frame of the animation. In fact, in this case, we can create a single key frame and the Keyframer will generate all of the intervening frames. Use the controls at bottom right to move to the last frame. By default, the Keyframer creates 30 frames. At 30 frames per second, that's two seconds of video—about right for an effect.

This is a good point to talk about how to select the proper parts of your video sequence for the effect. Let's suppose that you have one video sequence that is 33 seconds long, and a second sequence that is 14 seconds long. For this example, you would export the last two seconds of the first video, and the first 2 seconds of the second video. After you have completed generation of the effect, you would splice the pieces together like this:

31 sec. of first video + 2-second effect + last 12 sec. of second video

This yields a total of 45 seconds of video. We lost two seconds because two seconds of each video are now playing simultaneously.

Back to the Keyframer: we are now at frame 30, the last frame in the sequence. The desired effect is to have the front video shrink away to nothing at the center of the other frame. Select Object/Scale, and then click on the front object (use the 'H' as described earlier if you want to select it by name). Drag the mouse sideways to change the scale of the object. Depending on your screen resolution, you may need to zoom in and scale the object a second time to make it small enough to "disappear" during the rendering. Any size below 1 unit will be smaller than a single pixel in the final rendering. Figure 3.27 shows the scaling operation in progress, and Figure 3.28 shows the completed scaling.

Figure 3.27.
Scaling operation
in progress.

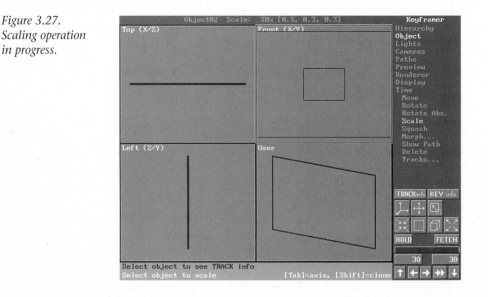

*Figure 3.28.
The scaling
operation
completed.*

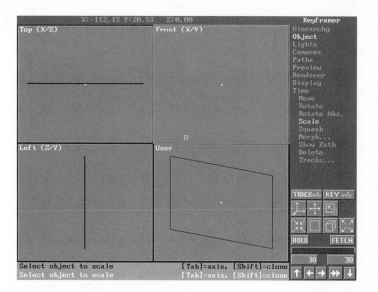

To show that the Keyframer really does create all of the intervening frames, look
at Figure 3.29. It shows frame 15 of the animation—yes, the front object is exactly
half way along in the shrinking process.

*Figure 3.29.
Frame 15 of the
animation.*

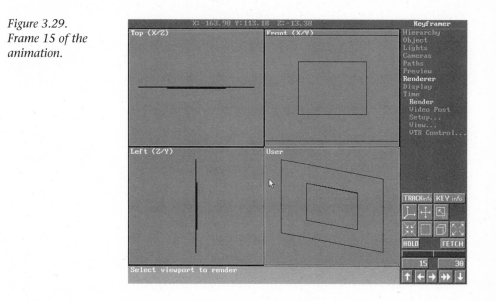

Rendering the Animation

Once you have created the animation sequence as a wire frame model, as outlined above, you are ready to render the animation as an FLC file. Before you render, you'll need to configure the system. Select Renderer/Setup/Configure, which displays the dialog box shown in Figure 3.30.

Figure 3.30. Configuring for rendering.

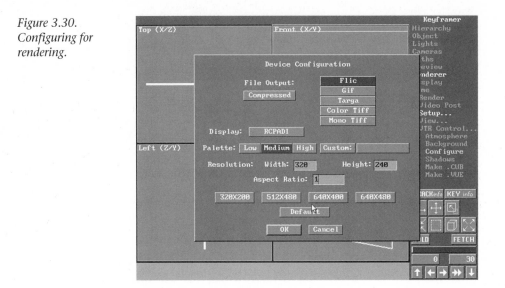

I suggest turning off compressed output—make sure the Compressed button is not highlighted. This keeps image quality at the highest possible level. You have the option of outputting as either an FLC file or a series of images. If you plan to use Animator Pro to output .bmp files, go ahead and save as an FLC file. If you want to use a utility to convert numbered files to bitmaps, select the desired file format: .gif, .tga, or .tif.

There are three palette choices listed, but only two of them are worth considering: Medium and High. Refer to Table 3.1 for information about the palette choices. For most cases, the Medium setting is fine.

Table 3.1. Rendering Palette Choices.

Choice	Description
Low	The Renderer will create an optimal 256-color palette for the first frame, and then use that palette for all subsequent frames. Unless the first frame is highly representative of the remaining frames, this is not a good option.
Medium	The Renderer will create an optimal 256-color palette for each frame in the animation, and then combine the palettes into one optimal palette.
High	Each frame will be rendered with 24-bit color. After rendering is complete, a single 256-color palette will be calculated. This option takes the most time, but gives the best results. It also uses a lot of disk space—72 megabytes in the case of a 562-frame animation I did.

You'll also need to set an appropriate image size. There are three parameters to set: Width, Height, and Aspect Ratio. Width and height are obvious: use numbers that are in the same proportion as the objects. In this example, I have used 320x240, exactly twice the size of the originals. The primary consideration when deciding on image size is the machine you plan to use for playback. The smaller the image size, the better it will play on slow machines. Set the aspect ratio to 1. This is the ratio of pixel width and height.

Once you have the configuration set, it's time to render. Select Renderer/Render on the menu, and click in the viewport you want to render (Front). This displays the dialog box shown in Figure 3.31.

For this example, accept the default settings for rendering. You can test the animation by picking a representative frame and rendering a single frame. Click the Single button, make sure the Disk button is not highlighted, and then click the Render button. You'll be asked if you want to render to the screen only; click OK. When rendering is complete, you'll see an image like the one in Figure 3.32. This is frame 15—the front image has shrunk halfway.

If the image meets your approval, it's time to render the complete animation. Select Renderer/Render to redisplay the render dialog. This time, click on the Disk button to highlight it, and click the All button. When you click the Render button, you'll be asked to supply a filename. If you chose to render as a series of numbered frames, enter a name like file*.gif or file*.tga, depending on the file format you want. Otherwise, enter a filename of up to eight characters. Depending on the complexity of the animation, the image size, and the palette setting, the time to render each frame can vary from a few seconds to a few minutes.

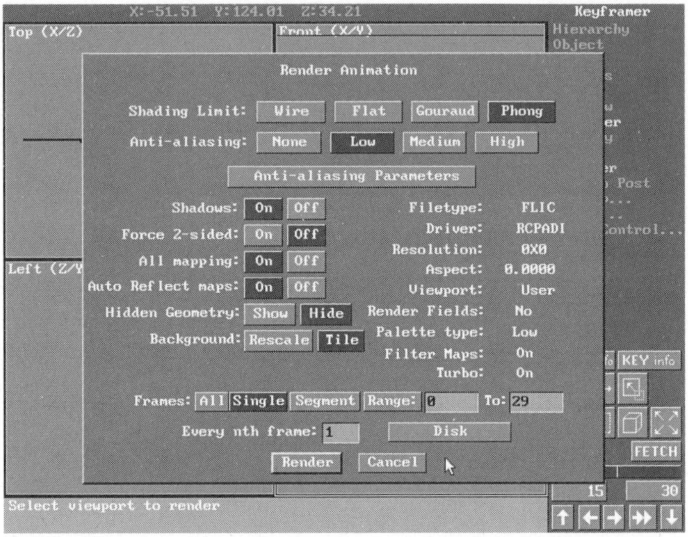

*Figure 3.31.
Setting up for
rendering.*

*Figure 3.32.
A rendered frame
from the anima-
tion.*

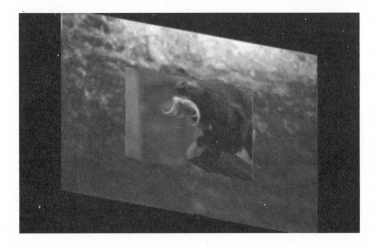

If you rendered the animation as an FLC file, there are two ways to import it into VidEdit. You can run Animator Pro, and use the POCO/Numpic menu selection to save the file as a series of .bmp files. You can then load the files as a DIB Sequence in VidEdit using the File/Insert menu selection (see Figure 3.33). Or you can simply use the File/Open command, and load the .flc file into VidEdit. In many cases, using File/Open will work just fine. In some cases, you may find that the conversion did not work properly.[26] In such a case, you'll have to go back to Animator Pro and create bitmaps to Insert.

If you rendered the animation as a series of image files, use a utility like Image Pals or Graphic Workshop to convert them to DIBs with a .bmp extension. You can then use File/Insert (see Figure 3.33) to import the images.

Figure 3.34 shows the entire 30-frame animation as a series of bitmaps loaded in the Image Pals utility program. The first frame is at the upper left, and the animation progress from left to right, top to bottom.

Figure 3.33.
The File/Insert
menu in VidEdit.

Finishing Up with VidEdit

Once you have a series of bitmaps, you are ready to finish up the process using VidEdit. Figure 3.33 shows the File/Insert menu selection, and Figure 3.35 shows the dialog box that this menu selection opens. To load a DIB sequence, first select DIB Sequence in the list box at the bottom left of the dialog. Note that the default

---

[26] Symptoms of incorrect import include bits of prior frames floating around in the current frame, misalignment of images (horizontal or vertical offsets within the image frame), size distortion, etc.

extension is "*.dib." Change it to "*.bmp" and press the Enter key. This will display all .bmp files (see Figure 3.35) in the current directory. Click on the first filename in the sequence you want (fade0001.bmp in Figure 3.35) and click the OK button. This displays the dialog box shown in Figure 3.36. Click on DIB Sequence in the list, then click OK.

*Figure 3.34.
A 30-frame
animation as a
series of bitmap
images in Image
Pals.*

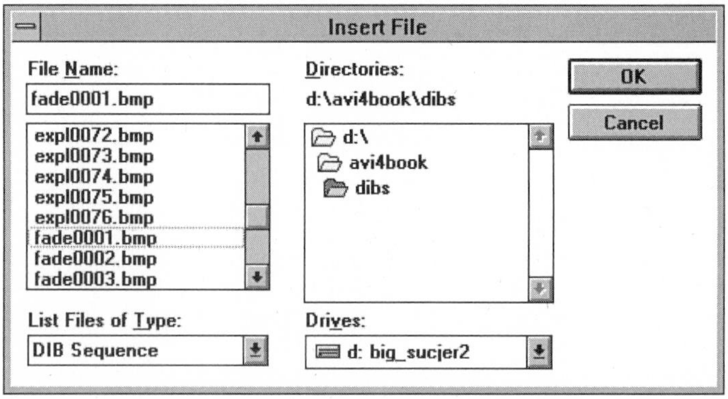

*Figure 3.35.
Selecting the first
file in a DIB
sequence.*

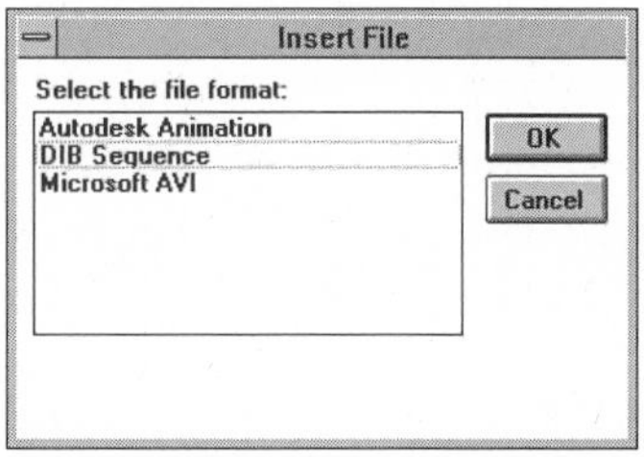

Figure 3.36.
Inserting a DIB
sequence.

Insert File

Select the file format:

Autodesk Animation
DIB Sequence
Microsoft AVI

OK

Cancel

VidEdit will read in the file. A message box will appear showing progress of the operation if there is a large number of DIBs to load. Figure 3.37 shows the sequence loaded into VidEdit. Once you have the sequence in VidEdit, you can fine-tune frame rate, add audio, and so on—all the things that VidEdit is designed for.

Figure 3.37.
A video special
effect loaded into
VidEdit.

If we assume that we started with one video sequence 33 seconds long, and a second one 14 seconds long, you would need to perform the following steps in VidEdit in order to complete the process:

■ Open another instance of VidEdit and use Edit/Copy to copy the first 31 seconds of the first video to the Clipboard.

■ Go to the original instance of VidEdit, move to the beginning of the special effect, and Edit/Paste.

■ Go to the second instance of VidEdit, and open the second video file. Edit/Copy the last 12 seconds of the video to the clipboard.

■ Go to the original instance of VidEdit, move to the end of the file, and Edit/Paste.

■ If you will be saving the video using a 24-bit codec, skip to the next paragraph. If you will be using an 8-bit codec, select Video/Create Palette and click on the Paste Palette button when it appears. Then save the file as described in the next paragraph.

■ To save the file, use appropriate settings. If you want to insure that the video will be viewable on the widest range of computers, use the parameters shown in Figure 3.38. When using Indeo in particular, a key frame setting of 1 insures you will avoid any ghosting or weird *delta frame*[27] effects on slower machines.

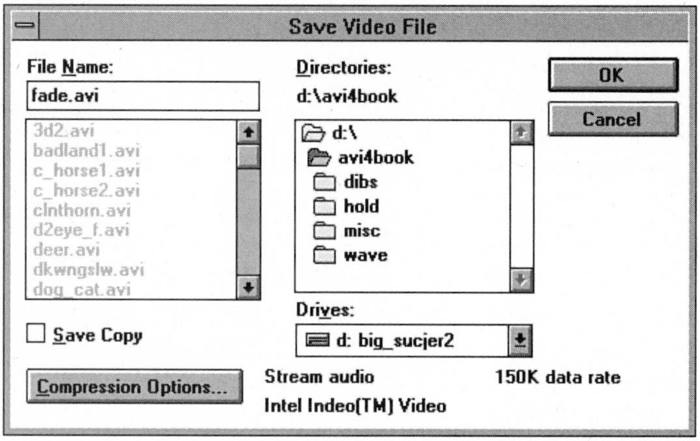

Figure 3.38. Setting compression options in VidEdit.

Imagine 2.0

Imagine is a 3D modeling package that originated on the Amiga. I can sum up Imagine in one sentence: it is a really cool product that can be frustrating to learn how to use. A love/hate relationship is almost inevitable with Imagine. There are times, while using the program, when I ask myself, "Why am I using this program?" Sooner or later, the answer comes knocking: I'll find a way to create a truly organic object that would be nearly impossible to create using a different program.

---

[27] A delta frame is a frame between key frames. The Greek letter Delta has been used for many years by mathematicians and scientists to indicate change; a delta frame only contains information about changes, not an entire frame of data.

But that doesn't quite describe what it's like to get started with Imagine. After all, you can't use a program until you learn *how* to use it! Without qualification, I would say that Imagine was the hardest program to learn that I have encountered. You would have to think that it would have to be pretty darn useful to still get reviewed in this book, and you would be correct. To give you as clear an idea of how Imagine works, I will take you through its operations one tiny step at a time. For that reason, this particular section will be much more detailed than many other sections.[28]

RECIPE

4 cups Imagine
4-8 megs of memory
1 meg expanded memory
1 Math Coprocessor/486 CPU
1 VESA-compatible video display card
1 Truckload patience

Instructions: Allow adequate time for preparation; ingredients may not blend properly at first. Using Imagine is a lot like making whipped cream: stop too soon, and you'll have nothing but the time you spend; get it just right, you'll have a delight. This is a real chance to let out your inner artiste.

---

[28] I almost feel obligated to do this—the manual that comes with Imagine has a long list of faults. Number one, the manual was written for the Amiga, where Imagine was born, and there is absolutely no attempt to translate for the PC user. Number two, there is no index. Number three (and I'm just getting started), it's nearly impossible to find the information you need in the narrative because it wanders around quite a bit. Number four, the manual is written as though the author knows what you want to do and why, and I think that's patronizing and out of place in a good software manual. Number five, the entire manual is written as a single tutorial. There's no reference section at all. One good point: The information is all there if you can be patient enough to extract it. At the same time I was writing this book, author Phillip Shaddock, a good friend of mine, was writing a book that should tell you everything you want to know about Imagine; you should strongly consider it if you want to do more with Imagine than what I've outlined in this chapter.

The opening screen of Imagine is appropriately perplexing. It's just a logo, with no menu in evidence. To access the menu (see Figure 3.39), you need to click at the top of the screen. To get started, click on the Project menu, then click New.[29] If you never even got to the opening screen, chances are you don't have any expanded memory. It's easy to add. Look at the line for emm386 in your config.sys file. If it says "noems," change it to "1024" instead. This will give you 1 megabyte of expanded memory. You can allocate more if you have 8 or more megabytes of system memory.

Figure 3.39.
The Imagine
opening screen.

Once you name the project, you'll see the screen shown in Figure 3.40. Click the New button to create a rendering sub project, which will display the dialog shown in Figure 3.41. There are many buttons and text windows, but you only need to understand a few of them to get started. Most important: Rendering method, and Picture size. Set Scanline for the rendering method; this gives you most of the features you want in solid modeling, but without ray tracing features.[30] This is good for seeing what your image looks like without spending a lot of time getting there. When you finish the design, you can render with the Trace setting, which will give you full ray-tracing capabilities. Set an image size that meets your needs; 320x200 or 640x480 is a good starting place.

Figure 3.40.
Project editor
screen.

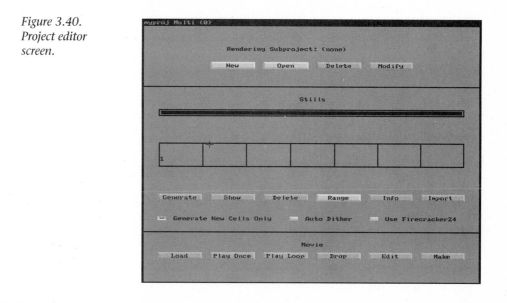

Imagine comes from the Amiga, so the text windows will take a little getting used to. You can't just enter text; you must press the Enter key to "lock in" the text you've entered. If you don't press the Enter key, the text change will not take place. Exiting an Imagine dialog is a two-step process: press Enter to exit the text Window, and click an OK button to exit the dialog.

---

[30] Ray tracing involves creating an image by tracing the path of light rays in the scene. This is a very exact way of handling complex phenomena like reflections, but it takes longer to render this way.

Figure 3.41.
Creating a
rendering sub
project.

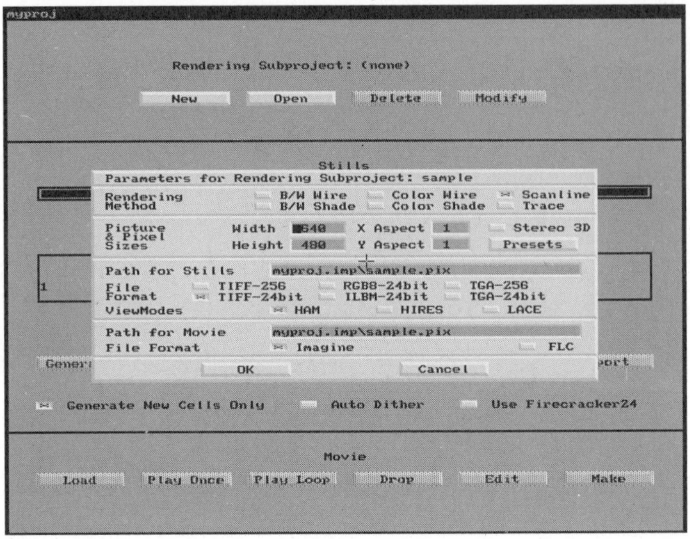

This takes you back to the project editor. Click at the top of the screen to activate the Editor menu, shown in Figure 3.42.

Figure 3.42.
The Imagine
Editors.

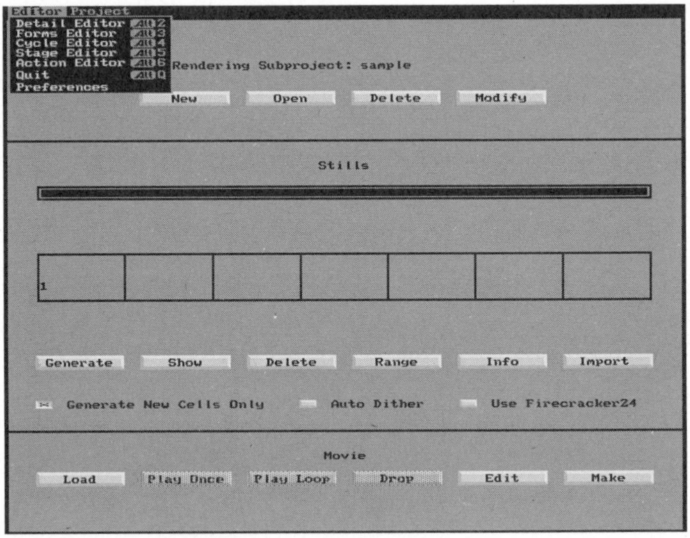

Imagine uses a number of what it calls editors. Each one is its own distinct program, although some editors resemble each other. Table 3.2 contains a brief description of each editor and its capabilities.

Table 3.2. Imagine Editors.

Editor	Description
Project	This editor (shown in Figure 3.40) is where you manage your entire 3D project.
Detail	The detail editor does just what its name implies: allows you to finish the details on objects that you have created elsewhere. You can apply surface textures, for example, to objects you created in the Forms editor.
Forms	This is where you can create "forms," or objects, interactively, by moving the points on the surface of the object. You can create amazingly organic objects with this editor. Typically, you'll create a basic form for an object here, and then finish it in the detail editor.
Cycle	This editor allows you to set up repetitive motions for an animation.
Stage	This editor allows you to load various objects and put them into motion. It uses tweening[31] to create intermediate frames.
Action	You can apply the finishing touches to your animation here, including many special effects like explosions and rotations.

For this example, you'll start with the Forms Editor. In many ways, it's one of the most impressive aspects of Imagine. Short of the day when you can have a headset and gloves that allow you to modify a 3D object directly, Imagine gives you some interesting tools to work with in the Forms editor. That's the good news. The bad news is that it's going to take time and practice, practice, practice to get good at it.

Figure 3.43 shows the opening screen of the Forms editor.[32] There are four windows on the screen. Clockwise from the upper left, they are:

---

[31] Tweening is a common concept in animation programs. It's similar to morphing: you create a start position and an end position, and the software creates all of the intermediate positions.

[32] To get to the forms editor from any other editor, use the click menu at the top of the screen. It's right there on the Editor menu.

Top—The object viewed from above

Perspective—An adjustable perspective view of the object

Right—The object viewed from the right side

Front—The object viewed from the front

Figure 3.43.
The forms editor
screen.

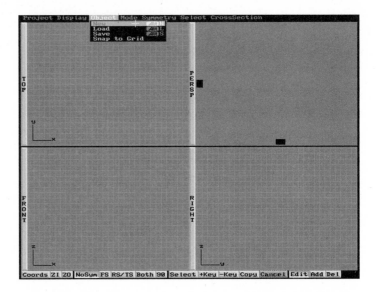

This is a fairly standard variation on the presentation of 3D objects, but, as you'll see shortly, it's not exactly what it seems to be. To create an object, use the click menu at the top of the screen and choose Object/New. This displays the dialog shown in Figure 3.44.

There are a lot of things going on in this dialog box that require an explanation. What are slices? What's a "former view?"[33] Let's interrupt the tutorial for a bit here to talk about how Imagine creates objects.

---

[33] It's not the last view, I'll tell you that much!

Figure 3.44.
Creating a new
object in the
forms editor.

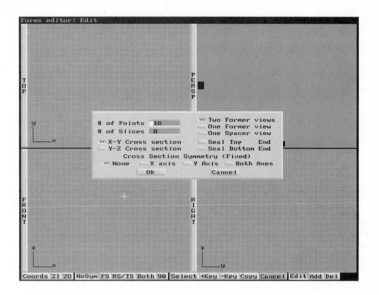

An object is made up of *points* and *slices*. Points are just what you expect—a point is a point is a point.[34] Slices are also just what the name implies. They are important because they enable you to establish some degree of control over your 3D objects. Think of a cucumber. It's basically a cylinder with its ends closed over. But it's a rounded shape; where do you put the points? The answer: at the slices. Take that cucumber and slice it up at intervals of, say, one inch. Then put it back together and you've got a typical forms editor object.

Keep that image in mind and refer back to Figure 3.44. You are being asked to supply the number of points, and the number of slices. If you enter 8 for the number of slices, it's like cutting the cucumber into 8 equally spaced slices. If you enter 16 for the number of points, you'll get 16 points—*on each slice.* That's a total of 128 points for the object.

As for the other items in the new object dialog, a former view is nothing more than a view window in the forms editor. For certain kinds of objects, you can work with fewer windows when you only need to modify one or two dimensions of the object. For now, click the button marked One former view. X-Y and Y-Z cross sections refer to the orientation of the object in the forms editor view windows; for now, accept the default. As for sealing the Top and Bottom ends, all that does is close off the object instead of making it a hollow tube.

---

[34] With apologies to Gertrude Stein.

The buttons near the bottom of the dialog regarding symmetry can be safely ignored for now; click none. These buttons allow you to create objects that are symmetrical in one or two directions. For example, your face is bilaterally symmetrical—there is a single axis down the middle of your face with the same features on either side of that line.

Click OK to close the dialog box, and you'll see something like Figure 3.45.

Figure 3.45.
A newly created
object in the
Imagine forms
editor.

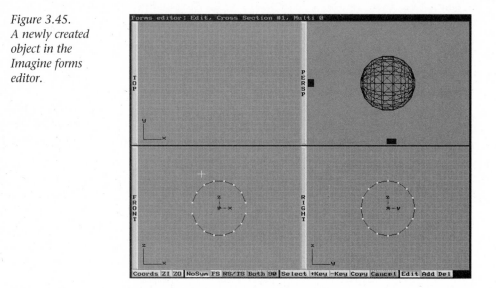

It's time for another digression into the ways and means of Imagine. There are some minor points about the display that make a big difference in how you work with Imagine compared to, say, 3D Studio.[35] The first thing to notice, if you can make it out in the figures, is that each of the view windows[36] has a small "axis indicator" in the lower left-hand corner. There are two axes in each view, one pointing up and one pointing to the right. Each axis is labeled with a letter: x, y, or z. It takes a while to get used to thinking in terms of axes, but this might help: the x axis goes from left to right, the y axis goes from front to back, and the z axis goes up and down.

---

[35] Think of it this way: Imagine is a right-brain kind of program. Any sense it makes will likely appeal to the creative side of your brain. 3D Studio is more of a left-brain, intellectual type of program. Here's another way to look at it: Learning to use Imagine is like learning to play a musical instrument. Learning to use 3D Studio is like learning calculus.

[36] Except for the perspective window, which uses sliders to adjust the point of view.

Look closely at the Front view, enlarged in Figure 3.46. This is not just an ordinary front view of the object. Notice that the last two points on the right and left of the circle are not connected like the other points are. Let's go back to that cucumber idea. Think of Figure 3.46 as a front view of a very, very fat cucumber. Those unconnected points are the two tips of the cucumber, and each pair of points defines a slice of the cucumber. Here's the punch line: if you move one of these points, you aren't really moving a point. You are adjusting a *slice*. We'll move some points and slices around shortly; for now, let's get back to describing the interface.

Figure 3.46.
The Front view of
the forms editor.

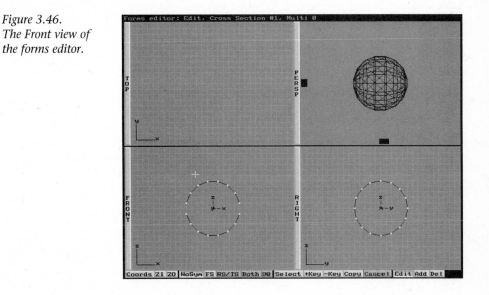

The perspective view in Figure 3.45 uses wireframe modeling. This makes it hard to visualize the object when there are many points, and in 3D modeling there are almost always too many points. Imagine also lets you display the perspective view as a solid, or even shaded.[37] Use the Display/Shaded menu choice to change the perspective display (see Figure 3.47 for the result).

Clicking on the left margin of any view window enlarges it to full screen, as shown in Figure 3.48. Since we selected shading, a light source has been added to show the object more clearly as a 3D object. You can switch to the other view windows using the buttons at the right of the screen labeled Front, Right, and Top.

---

[37] The shaded view actually only shows up under certain circumstances. You can enlarge any one view window to full screen by clicking on the vertical bar to the left of the view window. In full screen mode, the perspective window shows shading. If you must, peak ahead to Figure 3.48.

Figure 3.47.
Using solid
modeling to
display the
perspective view.

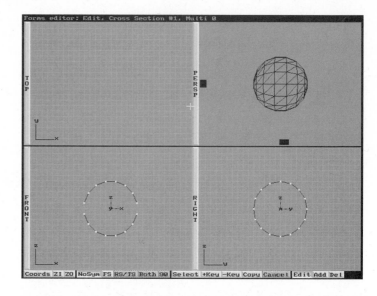

Figure 3.48.
A shaded view of
the object.

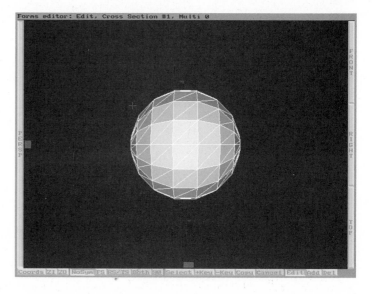

Let's get daring and move a point. Click on a point near the middle top of the Front view and move it close to the center of the object.[38] When you are done moving the point, look at the perspective view (see Figure 3.49). Notice that you didn't move just one point; you adjusted an entire slice of the object. Figure 3.50 shows a 3D shaded view of the object.

Figure 3.49. Moving a point on a slice in the Front view.

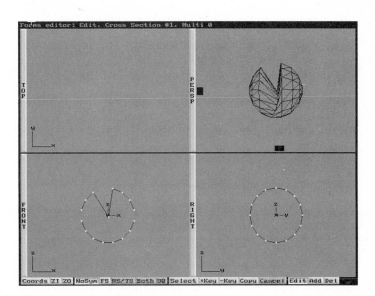

Because we created this object without any symmetry, we are free to move any point on any slice. If we create an object with bilateral symmetry, moving one point on a slice moves the corresponding point on the other side of the slice like a mirror image. For example, look at Figure 3.51. It shows an object that is bilaterally symmetrical.[39]

---

[38] While you are moving it, you'll see a little axis indicator indicating that the z axis is up, and the x axis is to the right. This duplicates what is already being displayed in the lower left of the Front view window, so I don't exactly understand why it happens.

[39] Most of the time, when you create a new object it will show up as a sphere. You can then deform it to whatever shape you desire. You can use a kind of "snap to grid" feature to make perfectly square or rectangular objects easily.

*Figure 3.50.
The result of
moving a point
on a slice.*

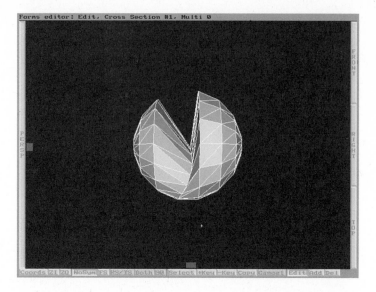

*Figure 3.51.
An object with
two-fold symme-
try.*

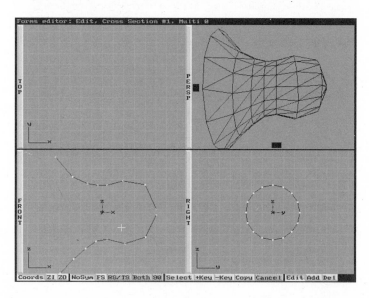

Time for another lesson in the ways and means of Imagine. Notice that the Right
view window hasn't changed one bit even though we have made dramatic changes
to the shape of the object. Remember that the Front view isn't really a true front
view. The Right view isn't really a true right view, either. You aren't seeing a front

view of the entire object. You're seeing a front view of a single slice. Because all the slices are still circular (even if they are different sizes), the Right view is still circular, too. To change the slice that is shown in the Right view, use the Select button at the bottom center of the screen. You can only display key slices in the Right view. To make a slice a key slice, click the +Key button (to the right of the Select button). You can use the -Key button to make a slice a non-key slice again. The idea behind key slices is simple. If a slice is not a key slice, it will adapt itself to changes made to key slices. In other words, non-key slices assume positions intermediate between key slices.

Figure 3.52 shows a shaded 3D view of the new object.

Figure 3.52.
A shaded view of
the new object.

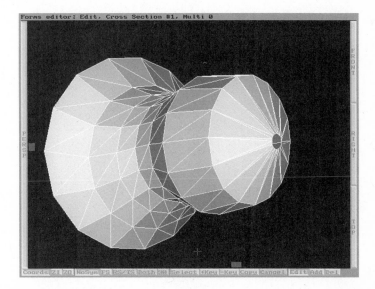

You can work with more than one point at a time in Imagine. The Select menu allows you to pick the method you'll use for selecting active points: Click, Drag Box, and Lasso. Click is the method we've used so far; to modify a point, you just click on it. The drag box method will be familiar to anyone who has used a Windows drawing program (refer to Figure 3.53). To drag a box around some points, select Select/Drag Box from the click menu at the top of the screen, and then click and drag a box around the points you want to select.

Figure 3.53.
Selecting points
with a drag box.

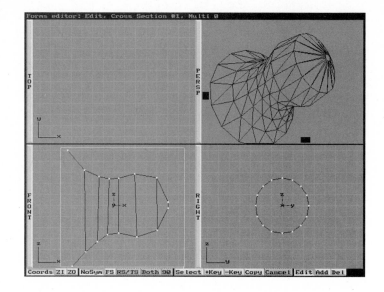

The points you selected, and the lines between them, are now highlighted and you can work with just those points. For example, the Object/Snap to Grid menu selection would operate on the selected points, moving them to the nearest grid points.[40]

You can create some pretty fancy shapes with the forms editor. Look at Figure 3.54, which shows a car form from the samples that come with Imagine. A shaded view of the form is shown in Figure 3.55. It doesn't look exactly like a car; you would add things like wheel wells and fenders in the detail editor.

Fun with the Forms Editor

Let's try a little experiment to see if I can make it clear how an object responds to your manipulations in the forms editor. To start, create an object with 8 slices and 8 points. Before you click OK to create the Object, select One former view. In the Front view, rearrange the points to make a rough outline of the letter A (see Figure 3.56).

---

[40] This is dangerous! If more than one point gets moved to the same grid point, you'll have no indication of the situation. This can get very confusing if you are not aware of the possibility.

Figure 3.54.
A more complex
shape created
with the forms
editor.

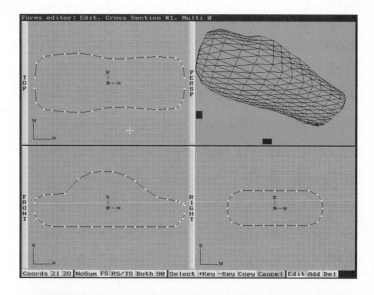

Figure 3.55.
A shaded view of
the object in
Figure 3.54; it's a
car! Sort of.

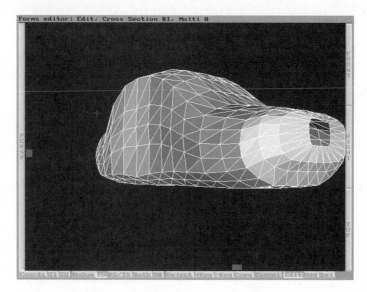

Make one of the slices near the center of the letter form a key slice, and then use the Select button to select it. This slice is now the one showing in the Right view. Click Select/Lock to turn on snap to grid. Now move the points in the Right view to form a square. Look at the perspective view, and note the contortions the form makes to switch from a circular slice, to a square slice, and then back again.

Figure 3.56.
Fun with the
forms editor.

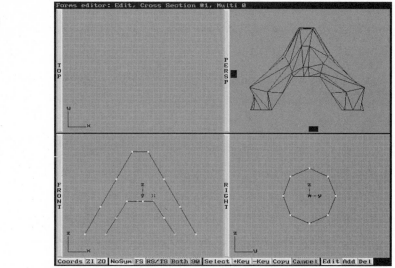

Now rearrange the points in the Right view to form a diamond shape, as shown in Figure 3.57. In addition, change the angle of view in the perspective view to show the object more clearly. Note that the middle slice does, indeed, now have a diamond shape.[41]

Figure 3.57.
Yet another
variation of the
middle slice.

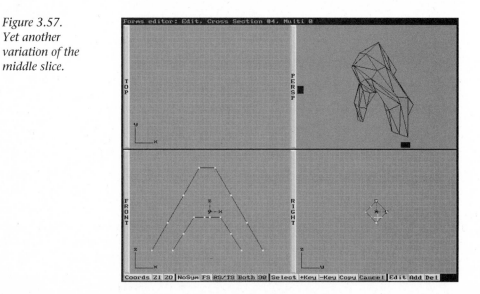

---

[41] With a little more effort, we could have a great robot shape here!

Now let's get weird. Move the top point of the diamond in the Right view way to the right, as shown in Figure 3.58. Look at the perspective view—there is the point way out to the right. Notice how the lines from other slices automatically adjust themselves to create intermediate positions.

Figure 3.58.
Far out to the
right in the forms
editor.

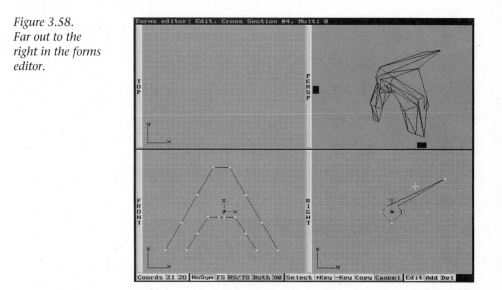

Let's try a more useful set of transformations in the forms editor. Create a new object, again with eight slices and eight points. Choose no symmetry, and Two former views. In the Front view, rearrange points until you have something like what I've done in Figure 3.59. That's right: we're making a fish. Figure 3.60 shows a shaded view of the fish form.

The form is a little fat for an angel fish. In the Top view, move the points to narrow each slice (see Figure 3.61). Align the points that define the tail until they actually touch each other. Note how this changes the appearance of the slice in the Right view. This is not thin enough, however; you'll also need to move the points in the Right view to about the same distance apart as you did in the Top view.

Figure 3.59.
Creating a fish in
the forms editor.

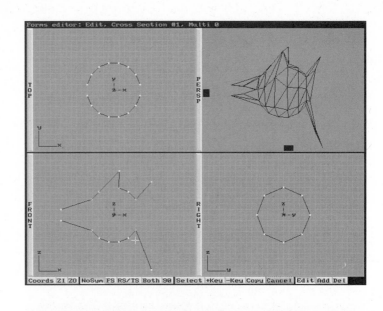

Figure 3.60.
A fish form.

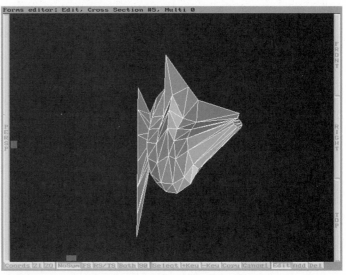

So far we have just a fish floating in space. There is no reference point, but we can create one easily by adding something called a Ground. The result in shown in Figure 3.62.

*Figure 3.61.
Narrowing the
fish form for a
realistic appear-
ance.*

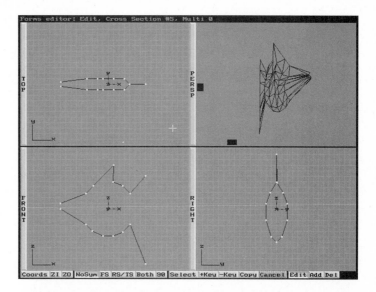

*Figure 3.62.
Oops—fish and
ground share a
common center.*

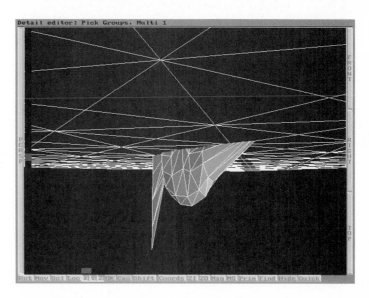

Because objects are all created at the origin of the workspace, the ground cuts the fish in half. We need to move either the fish or the ground, and it's easy to do. Click the Move button at bottom left, and then use the mouse to click and drag the ground below the fish (see Figure 3.63). The result of the move is shown in Figure 3.64.

Figure 3.63.
Dragging the
ground to a new
position after
clicking the Move
button.

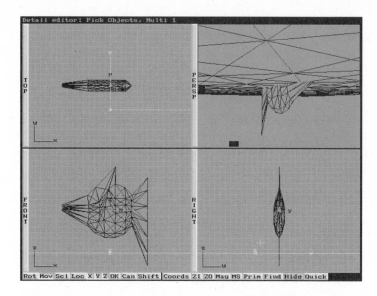

Figure 3.64.
The result after
moving the
ground below the
fish.

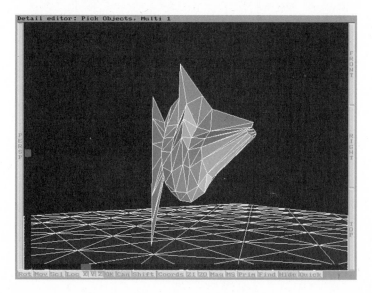

Now you can do a quick render by clicking the Quick button at the lower right of the screen. The result is shown in Figure 3.65. Hmm... it sort of looks like a fish, but we're definitely not done yet! It's time for detail editor.

Figure 3.65.
A fish rendering.

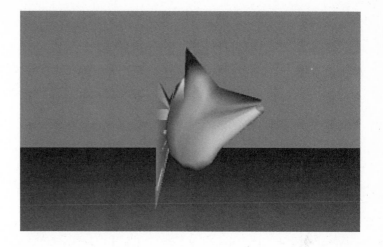

The detail editor looks exactly like the forms editor, but the menus are quite different. Once again, there are strange but important new concepts to learn. The most important concepts are Select and Pick. Selecting appears to mean nothing more than making an object appear orange, but you can't Pick an object unless it's Selected. There's a menu selection that says "Pick selected," and that's what it does.[42] There are also several other methods for picking an object, such as Pick Last. Whatever method you use, Pick the fish. This entitles you to access the Object/Attributes menu selection, and this is where the fun really starts. This displays the Attributes Requester (Amiga talk for the Attributes dialog box). (See Figure 3.66.) You can set a large number of attributes—color, reflectivity, hardness, shininess, textures, and more. Providing a complete description of attributes is beyond the scope of this book, however. For this example, I gave the fish a bright blue color, and made it mildly reflective and shiny. This gives a quick approximation of the surface attributes of a typical tropical fish.

Even so, there's more to do. At the very least, we should add an eye to our fish. We can create a simple sphere, and then Move it and Scale it so it looks just right (see Figure 3.67). I set attributes of color black, shininess 100%, and white specular reflection for the eye. Again, these are just quick approximations of the natural characteristics of an eye. The result isn't too bad (see Figure 3.68).

---

[42] Editorial comment: this complexity about selecting and picking makes the detail editor more painful than it needs to be, but, like the other quirks of Imagine, you'll get used to it if you stay with it long enough. It adds significant difficulty to the learning process.

Figure 3.66.
The Attributes
Requester in the
detail editor.

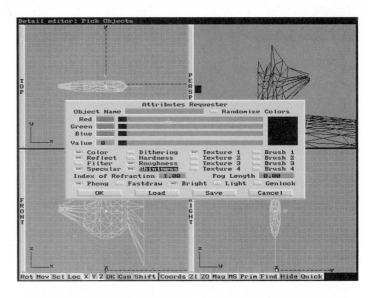

Figure 3.67.
Adding an eye to
the fish object.

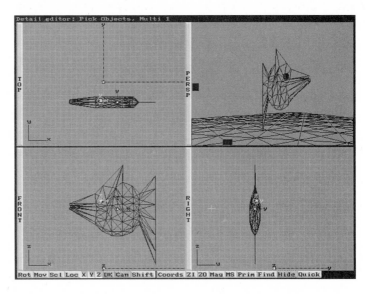

Figure 3.68.
A rendering of
the fish, eye, and
ground.

Summary

This section only hints at what you can do with Imagine. Despite its idiosyncratic interface, and poor documentation, Imagine has some interesting and powerful capabilities. If you have time and patience, you can do much more than what I've shown here, including sophisticated animations.

Architectural Space

Computers are digital. That means that some things are easier than others. When it comes to virtual reality, straight lines are easier than curves. For that reason, some of the most advanced VR applications involve architecture. Not that buildings don't have curves, but the vast majority of the lines, edges, and faces are straight. This makes for a certain degree of simplicity.

Not so simple is the sheer number of those lines, edges, and faces. In fact, this is a good place to illustrate the volume of data involved in creating a virtual space. Consider, for example, the lowly cape cod style of home. What would it take to simulate the process of opening the front door, crossing the living room, walking up the stairs, and then examining the details of an upstairs window frame?

Indoors

The answer is: it would take a lot. However, I want to impress on you just how much it does take, because this is the central issue of virtual reality. Until there are ways of handling the massive amounts of data involved, all the headsets in the world won't help a bit.

Let us go then, you and I, up to that front door. What do we see as we stand before it? There's the door itself, of course. This one is made of wood. What kind of wood, we must ask. And is the wood painted, stained, oiled, varnished, or covered in some other way? Is there a window in the door? How many panes of glass are in the window? Is the glass simple clear, flat glass, or is it stained glass, or perhaps cut or etched glass? How fancy is the frame around the window? What about the hardware on the door—brass, pewter, chrome, or something else? Is there weather stripping at the base of the door? What about the threshold at the base of the door frame. And what about the door frame—what kind of wood is used there, and is it a fancy molding with difficult to reproduce, complex curves? And then there's the latch and the notch for it in the door frame. And don't forget to consider where the light is coming from. Is it a sunny day? Are there any clouds? Is there a porch light—or, for that matter, a porch? Light surfaces reflect light; what effect does that have on the scene?

Assuming we've been able to generate an image that can handle all of that, now we have to put it in motion—and that means starting all over again. Even a little motion changes things. As we open the door, the lighting angle changes constantly. But that's just part of the problem. As the door opens, it reveals a bit of the living room inside—with its rugs and walls and paintings and trim and couches and chairs and baseboard and electrical outlets and more.

Now that I have you convinced of the difficulty of the task, it's time to look at a software package that does (sort of) just the things I've described. If you think this was merely a clever ploy to prevent you from being overly disappointed with the limited capabilities of low-end architectural rendering software, you're right.[43] In order to render 3D scenes, or to allow you to move through the scenes, low-end software had to make some serious compromises.

Let's look at a software package called 3D Plan, from Autodesk. It's a very easy program to use, and it provides some intriguing VR capabilities in an inexpensive package. Figures 3.69 and 3.70 show two views created with 3D Plan. Figure 3.69 shows a view across a backyard pool, and Figure 3.70 shows a view through sliding glass doors into the interior of a cabin.

The opening screen of 3D Plan is shown in Figure 3.71. The bulk of the screen is the area where the 3D view will be shown. Information about the current view is displayed at the bottom, and the menu is located at the right of the screen. There are five menu choices, and they are listed in Table 3.3.

---

[43] It's easy to expect too much from VR software if you don't consider the true nature of the task at hand.

*Figure 3.69.
A backyard
virtual reality.*

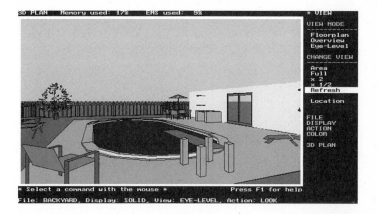

*Figure 3.70.
A view into the
interior of a
cabin.*

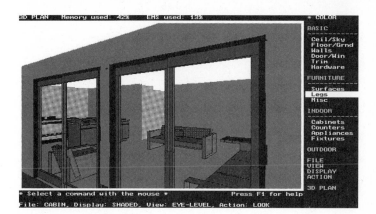

Table 3.3. 3D Plan Menu Selections.

Menu Item	Description
File	Used for loading and saving files.
View	Used to establish your point of view and the basic type of rendering.
Display	Contains parameters for fine tuning the rendering.
Action	Allows you to move your point of view.
Color	Change the colors of objects in the rendering.

RECIPE

1 .dwg file
4 cups 3D Studio
2 megs of expanded memory
1 EGA of better display card

Instructions: This is an easy-to-prepare, light dessert. Images aren't very detailed—no Super VGA support—but the results are quick. Plan ahead: you can't do anything unless you have prepared some .dwg files in advance. Use Generic 3D, AutoCAD, or any of the Home Design modules available from Autodesk.

3D Plan will work with any EGA or better color display card, but I highly recommend using a VGA display. 3D Plan will not use any Super VGA capabilities you may have. This is unfortunate, because VGA resolution—and its 16 colors—doesn't provide a very realistic image.

Figure 3.71.
The 3D Plan
opening screen.

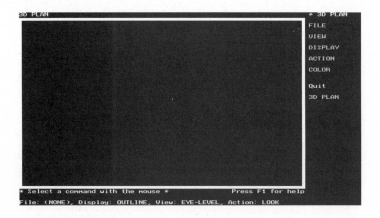

To create a rendering, click on the File menu at the upper right of the screen. This displays a menu with several items; click on Load 2D. You can only load a 2D drawing that uses the .dwg file format. You can use products like Generic CAD (also from Autodesk) to create plan drawings, or you can use the much simpler Home Series of drawing products (yes, also from Autodesk). The Home Series software comes in packages labeled Kitchen, Bathroom, etc. You can create a plan in one of the Home Series packages, and then view it in 3D with 3D Plan.

3D Plan comes with several sample .dwg files. Figure 3.72 shows the plan file home.dwg during the loading process. 3D plan applies a little artificial intelligence during the loading process. It follows a few simple rules to determine what is, and is not, a wall in the plan drawing. When it has got things pretty well figured out, 3D Plan will display only the walls. Most of the walls will be in bold, indicating that they are selected. You can click on a wall to deselect it, and it will not appear in the 3D rendering. This can be useful. For example, if you want to look at a kitchen in 3D, it might be easier if you eliminate a wall or two. If you deselect a wall accidentally, just click on it again to reselect it.

Figure 3.72.
Selecting walls
during loading.

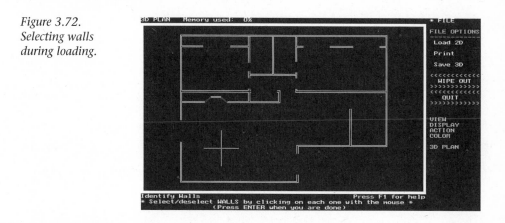

Press the Enter key when you have the walls the way you want them.[44] 3D Plan will then complete the loading process. You'll see the complete plan view, including any 3D objects that were placed in the view with the drawing program used to create the plan. For example, Figure 3.73 shows a complete plan view from the home.dwg file.[45]

---

[44] If the drawing has no walls—for example, a landscape drawing, showing just trees and shrubs—3D Plan will not pause during loading to inquire about walls.

[45] This is a good spot to put in a few words about what a "plan view" is. If you have ever taken a class in mechanical drafting—I had one in high school—you are familiar with floor plans. That's all a plan view is—a view from above showing the location of objects in the plan. Objects include walls, furniture, electrical lines, and anything else that might exist in an architectural drawing.

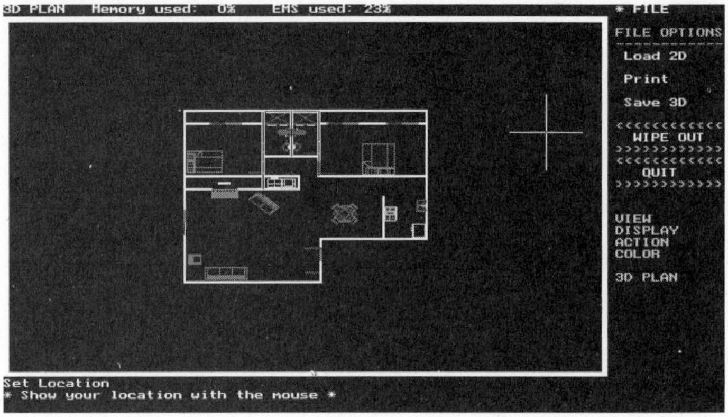

Figure 3.73.
A plan view in
3D Plan.

Your next task is to establish your position and point of view. Click anywhere on the plan view to set your position; a cross hair with one long leg (see Figure 3.74). Slide the mouse back and forth to face the long leg in the direction you want to view. In this example, the view point is just inside the front door in the living room, looking off toward the dining area.

Figure 3.74.
Setting the point
of view.

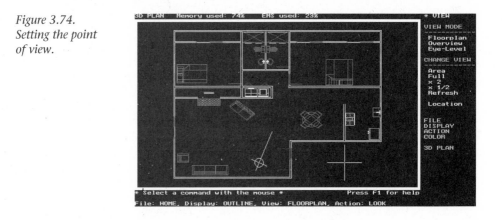

Click on View to go to the View menu, where you will see three possible View Modes:

Floorplan—Shows the plan view. This is a 2D viewing mode.

Overview—A 3D view of the entire plan. This view ignores the viewpoint you just set.

Eye-level—A view at eye level from the viewpoint you just set.

You can also use this menu to change views. You can zoom in or out, for example, or use the Area selection to pick a specific area to view. To select an area, just click and drag out a box with the mouse.

Click on eye level, and you'll see something like the view shown in Figure 3.75. The first thing you will no doubt notice is that it is a wireframe view. If you have even a moderately fast computer, you can switch to a more pleasing rendering mode.

Figure 3.75.
An eye-level view
in 3D Plan.

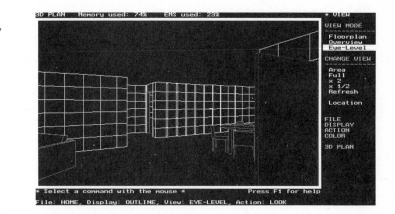

Click on Display, which will switch you to the display menu. You'll see three display modes listed on the menu:

Outline—This is wireframe mode.

Solid—Colors all objects in the scene using the current color scheme.

Shaded—Shades the solid view using simple rules about lighting. There is also a sub-choice, Edge. If edges are on, you'll see a black line at the edge of each object.

Figure 3.76 shows a view using the Solid display mode. This is an improvement, but it's hard to tell where one wall ends and the next begins. Let's try shaded mode (see Figure 3.77). This is as good as it gets. 3D Plan isn't a photo-realistic rendering program. It does, however, provide an inexpensive way to visualize what a new kitchen layout will look like, or to get an idea of what your new house will feel like. You could even use it to try out a new furniture layout. These are minor, but worthy, applications for virtual reality.

Figure 3.76.
The Solid display
mode.

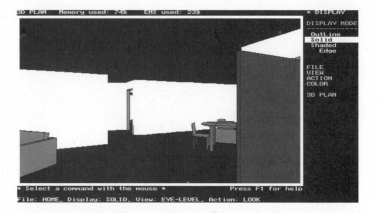

Figure 3.77.
The Shaded
display mode.

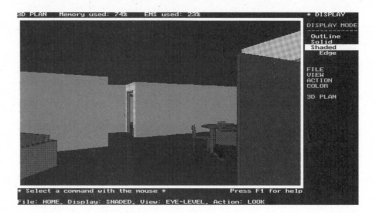

The rendering quality may not be detailed, but 3D Plan does have some additional VR features. For example, you can move through the virtual space using the arrow keys. There will be a short delay while the program recalculates the view. The left and right arrow keys turn left and right, and the up and down arrow keys move the point of view forward and backward. For example, Figure 3.78 shows a view of home.dwg from the dining area into the living room. Figure 3.79 shows the view a few steps toward the living room.[46] This is much more intuitive than resetting the viewpoint using those cross hairs. In fact, it is this simple feature of being able to move through the 3D space that makes 3D Plan useful.

---

[46] This movement is precise. Each keypress moves you the same number of feet, or rotates you the same number of degrees. You can use the Control key to magnify the motion. For example, pressing the left arrow key rotates you one degree to the left, while holding down the control key and pressing the left arrow rotates the view 15 degrees.

Figure 3.78.
Another view in
3D Plan.

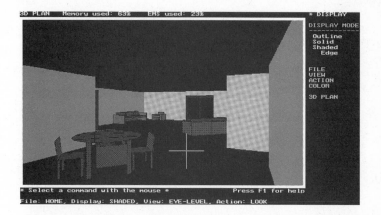

Figure 3.79.
A step forward in
the virtual space.
Compare to
Figure 3.78.

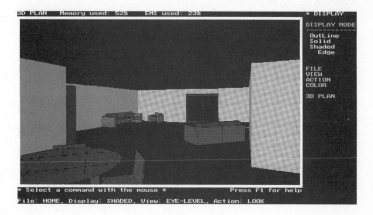

If you aren't happy with the appearance of the image, you have limited control over the colors used. 3D Plan is limited to VGA's 16 colors, and there are more than twice that number of object categories, so colors have to be shared. You can set the color of a variety of object types. For example, you can assign different colors to furniture, carpet, walls, ceiling, doors, and door frames, and so on. Figure 3.80 shows the same view as in Figure 3.79 but with different colors.

In addition to the eye-level view, you can look at your project using the Overview mode, as shown in Figure 3.81.

3D Plan is one of the plainer programs that makes use of virtual reality, but it does a great job within its limited sphere.

Figure 3.80.
Setting different
colors in 3D
Plan.

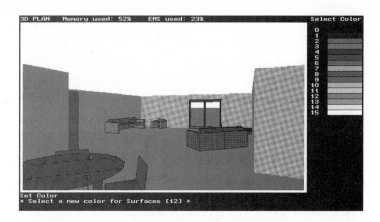

Figure 3.81.
Using the
Overview mode.

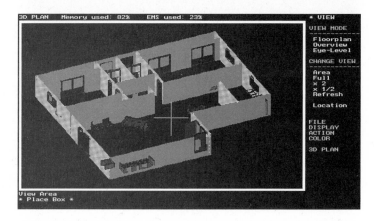

Outdoors

If rendering indoor spaces is challenging, outdoors is even more so. The variables that are so overwhelming indoors only become more numerous. In addition, nature enters the picture—grass, clouds, trees, and other detailed, complex objects.[47] Granted, there are techniques for dealing with such objects, but this greatly increases the load on the computer.

---

[47] The science of fractals is what enables computers to render such objects in anything even approaching a reasonable amount of time. It would be impossible to render every blade of grass in a lawn, or every leaf on a tree. See Chapter 7 for more on fractals.

One way around this is obvious: don't bother to render all of the details. Of course, it helps if you do a great job with what you do render—the missing details will be less noticeable. Figure 3.82 shows a rendering of a cathedral created in 3D Studio.[48]

Figure 3.82.
A rendering of a
cathedral in 3D
Studio.

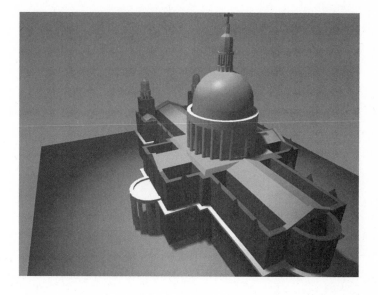

There's no lawn, no trees, and the windows look glued on, but this rendering is still impressive.[49] If the rendering itself isn't sufficient to impress you, there's a flying animation of a trip around and over the cathedral on the CD-ROM.

Sometimes, the problem isn't too many details; sometimes, in order to achieve a realistic rendering, you need to remove details. For example, objects fade with distance—in the real world, a distant mountain shows almost no details.[50] Fog is similar (see Figure 3.83).

---

[48] The source file is one of many, many samples provided with 3D Studio. 3D Studio comes with a CD that has hundreds of files of all kinds that you can use either to create renderings, or within your own renderings.

[49] It's even more impressive in color, of course.

[50] You can create a hyper-real landscape by leaving out the haze, of course.

Figure 3.83.
Virtual fog.

Unfortunately, a lack of detail is sometimes simply unavoidable. It takes time to add the little details that add the extra touch of realism, and time isn't always available.[51] Figure 3.84 shows a portion of the same virtual space used for Figure 3.83. This portion of the file doesn't have a lot of detail. That doesn't matter in the view of Figure 3.83 because the street level is so far and away, and obscured by fog as well. If you look at Figure 3.83 carefully, you'll see that there are several cars down there on the street—just enough to suggest the idea of cars in the street. You don't realize how empty the streets are until you get down there and look.

Speaking of details, I decided to render a view of this cityscape at night, using low light levels. The first rendering looked wrong, and it didn't take long to figure out why: there were no lights at street level. The cars didn't have headlights or taillights. There were no streetlights. The traffic signals (you can see a few in Figure 3.84) didn't signal. It would take a lot of effort to add all of those lights. To see just how much work it would take, I added headlights to each of the cars.

---

[51] At least right now it takes time. Perhaps someday, after we've all taken the time to create all the wonderful details of everyday life electronically, all we'll have to do is pull virtual stuff out of a virtual library—lightbulbs, sidewalks, front doors, pottery, sofas, and ice cream cones.

Figure 3.84.
A cityscape
without a lot of
details.

There was a lot more work involved than I expected.[52] I couldn't just go to the car menu and click on headlights; I had to use what was available to create headlights. I'll describe what it takes to create a single headlight. Step one is to create a light located just above a car's bumper. This involves clicking in one view to place the light, then clicking a second time to place the light's target.[53] I then had to zoom in and out a bit to make sure that the light was, in fact, next to that car's bumper. Why, you ask? When working in Front, or Top, or Side view, an object may look like it's where it is supposed to be, but it may actually be a million miles away—there's no way to tell what's going on in the third dimension without switching to another view. This is the bane of existence in the virtual fast lane.

Once the list exists, you must adjust it. A light has a couple of nested cones: the central cone (the hotspot) where the light is brightest, and the outside cone, where the light is weaker (called falloff). I set the width of the hotspot at 15 degrees, and the falloff at 45 degrees. I then made sure the light was aimed slightly downward, just like a real headlight. Unfortunately, when I rendered the scene, I couldn't see any evidence whatsoever that I had just spent some time creating headlights. I had to make two changes to make the lights visible.

The first problem was with the street. A very dull black material had been created to simulate the street, and it wasn't reflecting any of the light. A real street, of course, is black but it reflects some light. So I had to go into the Material Editor and muck

---

[52] I did this in 3D Studio; I don't know why I expected it wouldn't take time.

[53] In 3D Studio, lights have targets.

around with the characteristics of the street. It had to add a little shininess, and modify the way that the material responded to light. I went back and forth a few times until I had it right.

The second problem involved the nature of lights in 3D Studio. You can see the effects of a light, but you won't see the light itself. So I had to add little globes just behind each light, and set properties in the materials editor so the globes glowed enough to look like a headlight.

The result of all this effort is shown in Figure 3.85. It's like one of those Waldo books: can you find the headlights? After all of the work, you can't even see them at this point in the animation (frame 92 of 150). That's more of life in the virtual fast lane.

Figure 3.85.
The city at night,
courtesy of 3D
Studio.

In the last few frames of the animation, when the point of view is much closer to street level, the headlights are quite noticeable (see Figure 3.86).

Of course, while working with the model in wireframe mode, I had little idea of what the headlights would look like. Figure 3.87 shows a screen from 3D Studio during the creation process. The view at upper left shows a car from above, with two lights and two targets (the vertical lines connect lights and targets). The view at bottom left is a closeup from the side of the small spheres that show up as the bright lights in Figure 3.86, and the view at bottom right shows an overview of a portion of the city with cars in it.

Figure 3.86.
Virtual head-
lights in frame
143 of 150.

Figure 3.87.
Creating
headlights in 3D
Studio.

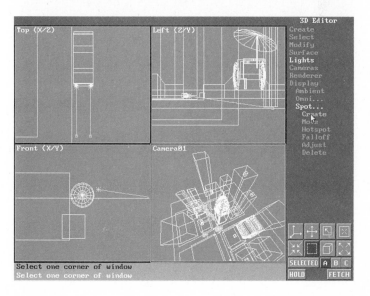

The point of this is that there is an enormous amount of effort and care that goes into a photorealistic virtual space. It gave me a real appreciation for the details of everyday life. Virtual Rome will not be built in a day.

4

VIRTUAL FUN

Even the most hard-core computer user probably wishes computers were more fun. Not that software vendors haven't tried—the next time you visit your local software store, compare the shelf space used for business software and for games. In most cases, you'll see at least as much space devoted to games as to business software—sometimes more.

While you're in the store, ask the manager a simple question: which games are selling the best? The answer: 3D games sell better than any other category. The same is true of shareware games—titles like Wolfenstein 3D are the hottest thing going. As a public service,[1] you'll find a number of 3D shareware games on the CD-ROM that comes with this book. Check the table of contents on the disk for instructions.

3D and the Inner Child

A little kid lurks inside every computer user. That much is clear from the huge number of games on dealer shelves. What is it about 3D games, and even the use of 3D in business software, that makes it so appealing? Was it the new features that made Windows 3.0 such a smashing success, or was it really those 3D buttons?

Without a moment's hesitation, I'll assert that Windows succeeded because it used 3D in small but important ways. The 3D look gave Windows legitimacy in a way that no other feature could. Think about it: before the 3D look, Windows was an interesting also-ran, sitting on as many bookshelves as hard disks. Put a little 3D in, and wham!—a revolution occurs.

Microsoft offers a lot of reasons for the success of Windows 3.0, such as:

- The huge product roll-out, with live video conferences in cities all over the United States;

- The all-new GPF to replace the all-too-common UAE;

- The addition of sound and other multimedia support.

---

[1] As if putting games on the CD is anything but a cold-blooded appeal to the child in every reader. Hi. I'm the author's alter-ego, Clarence. The author has certain obligations to his editor and society, but I don't. I'll be watching over Ron's shoulder throughout this chapter, and you can count on me to give you the *real* story.

These are *not* the reasons why Windows became a success. No one who actually *buys* Windows ever goes to such conferences; they're for guys in suits with big offices. GPF, UAE—gimme a break here; a crash is a crash, even if it only brings down the system half as often. As for multimedia, how many computers were already set up for multimedia when Windows was introduced?

I'm exaggerating here, of course,[2] but I'm doing it to make a point. Maybe 3D didn't put Windows on tens of millions of computers overnight, but it makes a Big Difference:[3] Buttons are really *buttons* now, not just little pictures with lines around them.

More precisely: virtual buttons. Remember those Fisher-Price crib toys that provide a row of buttons? Each button does something cute when the baby pushes it—a cow makes a "moo" sound, a door opens to reveal a picture of a turkey,[4] or a bell rings. That's what a toolbar is: the adult version of that old crib toy.

Many[5] psychologists define play as "anything that provides a large reward for a small effort." Do you see the connection? A simple little click on a toolbar button gives you big dialog boxes. No need to hunt through menus to find the commonly used tools (that's work); just click on a picture (that's play).

What does all this have to do with virtual reality? The answer is coming right up.

Virtual Reality as a Game

When a new computer product enters the market, it tends to sputter and flop around a bit before it becomes well known and successful.[6] During this time, whole legions of news reporters, computer columnists, and magazine editors spend infinite hours of their time theorizing about:

■ Why the new product came into being;

■ Whether or not it represents an Entire New Category of software;

---

[2] Like heck! He's silly enough to believe every word of what he's saying.

[3] With apologies to Douglass Adams for stealing the device of capitalizing Big Ideas.

[4] Hey—this is sounding more and more like software as we go along!

[5] Some.

[6] Unfortunately, some flounder, sputter, and do painful things to your computer even after they become successful!

■ Who will use the new software;

■ What implications for the industry are inherent in the new software; and

■ Whether or not anyone will actually spend money on it.[7]

If you look through the computer press, you find exactly these kinds of discussions going on about virtual reality. Everyone is acting as though VR is some kind of New Thing. It's not new at all. In fact, at every stage of computing, as soon as the CPU power grows enough to support the next level of VR, it gets added. The most notable additions of VR to the common computing repertoire are listed in Table 4.1.

Table 4.1. Virtual Reality that We Already Use.

Item	VR Justification
The mouse[8]	A device which, although not as sophisticated as a Power Glove, still allows you to move around in a virtual space
GUI (Graphical User Interfaces)	Virtual desktop—that's what they called it at first, remember?[9]
3D buttons	Buttons have evolved from a mere box-shaped outline to a complete simulation with an animated click—how virtual does it have to be?
The Toolbar[10]	Crib toy for adults

---

[7] Do you know why we face a glut of monstrously huge software products these days? It's harder to pirate a piece of software that requires 10 pounds of documentation. If you ever spent some time at the photocopier making pirate documentation, those days are now officially over.

[8] Can anyone explain why the price of a mouse varies from $19.95 to over $100.00 for exactly the same functionality??? I mean, let's get real here.

[9] And you thought virtual reality was new...

[10] Didn't anybody patent this thing? They're everywhere—even places where they *don't* work. Somebody could've made a mint on this idea.

Soon, we'll have useful speech recognition and other advances, too. Speaking of speech, there's an interesting demo program on the CD-ROM. As with all stuff on the CD-ROM, just check the table of contents on the disk to find what you need.[11]

Enough preamble.[12] Time to get to the point: virtual reality isn't just part of the game scene. Virtual reality *is* a game. It's called Stunt Island, and it's from Disney Software. Oh, all the usual game stuff is there, of course—planes you can fly, maps, interesting and cute touches—but this is extremely inexpensive[13] software that you can use to create virtual spaces to play around with. Forget mere flight simulators—how about a virtual space in which the plane crashes into a building and fire trucks scream to the rescue! Crashing your plane isn't necessary, of course. You could also set up a rescue operation at an evil warlord's castle.

Stunt Island

I purchased a copy of Stunt Island for less than $40, and if you aren't interested in spending $3,000 for your virtual reality software, it's a heck of an economical start. You give up some things, naturally. You can't create your own objects; all you can do is place pre-existing objects into a scene. The graphics aren't high-resolution; you'll have to settle for MCGA (320x240 and 256 colors). Fortunately, Stunt Island contains a huge number of objects—trees, human figures, animals, machines, buildings, and more—so you won't run out quickly. The image quality is good (especially considering it's only MCGA), especially the navigation screens (see Figure 4.1).

Stunt Island contains 32 predesigned stunts, each of which typically contains a large number of props. If that were all Stunt Island did, it would still be a fun game. The virtual fun starts when you create your own stunts. Before you learn how to do that, however, there are some memory issues to address.

Setting Up Memory

Stunt Island is a DOS program, and it needs a whole lot of memory to run—570K. I had to reconfigure my machine to run Stunt Island with a screen capture

---

[11] Isn't organization wonderful? If he really cared, he'd tell you where it was.

[12] No kidding, author/turkey person.

[13] Ahem. I believe the term is "cheap."

program, but if you're using DOS 5 or higher you shouldn't have a problem. To configure for best use of memory, try the following:

■ Make sure that you have a memory manager, such as himem.sys, loaded in your config.sys file.

■ Use emm386.exe or a similar program to open up the upper memory area for drivers and TSRs. Make sure you load DOS high (DOS=HIGH,UMB in config.sys) when you do this, of course.

■ Load all the drivers and TSRs high that you can using DEVICEHIGH (config.sys) or LOADHIGH (autoexec.bat) as appropriate.

■ Use the mem command with the /c switch to examine the layout of your machine's memory. This will tell you how much memory each driver or TSR is using, and the size of contiguous memory blocks available for loading high. For best results, type

```
mem /c ¦ more
```

to avoid information scrolling off the screen. To run Stunt Island, verify that you have at least 570K of conventional memory available.

■ Make sure that your mouse driver is loaded because you'll really want to use it with Stunt Island. You also can use a joystick or a special throttle/yoke device for flight simulators.

Figure 4.1.
A typical
navigation screen
from Stunt
Island.

Playing with Stunt Island

Stunt Island is software with a sense of humor. It comes with a large number of stock aircraft, and some of them aren't airplanes. There's a hang glider (see Figure 4.2), a duck, and even a pterodactyl. If you decide to try bombing with the duck, you'll find out that the bombs are really, well, *eggs*.[14]

Figure 4.2.
A hang glider about to take off from Stunt Island.

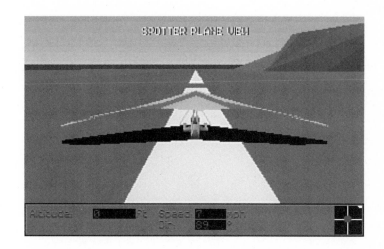

I'm going to skip over a lot of the features of Stunt Island, however, and get right to the virtual meat: the Scene Editor. Figure 4.3 shows the Scene Editor without any elements in the scene. Stunt Island refers to a scene as a stunt, of course. The Scene Editor contains four general areas you need to know about:

Placement Window | This window displays a map of Stunt Island. You can use the View Controls to position the cross hairs, and to zoom in or tilt the point of view.

View Controls | The two boxes on the left side are used to enter coordinates for the cross hairs. (You also can click and drag to move the cross hairs.) The two boxes on the right control the orientation (left/right) and tilt of the Placement Window. The slider is used for zooming.

---

[14] Yuck! There need to be some limits to virtual messes!

Prop Display Window   The current prop is displayed in this window.

Prop Controls   These controls allow you to add a prop, place a prop, and make various adjustments. You also can delete a prop if you make a mistake.

Figure 4.3.
The Stunt Island
Scene Editor.

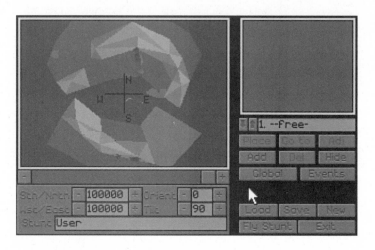

Getting Started

The first task in creating a scene/stunt is to zoom in on the part of the island where you plan to set up. Figure 4.4 shows a small island located in the lagoon in the middle of Stunt Island.

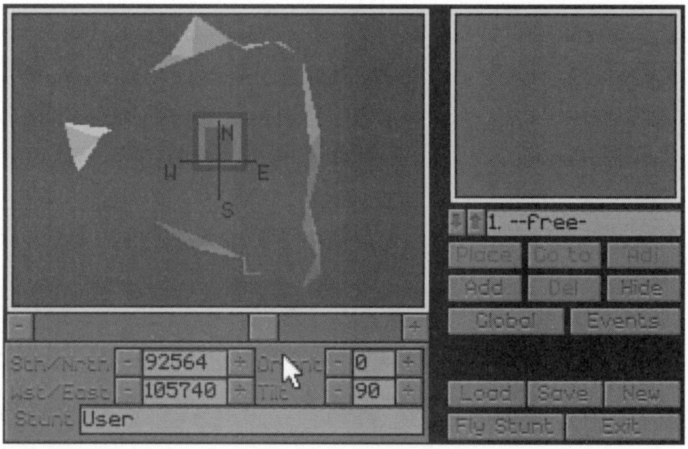

Figure 4.4.
Zooming in to
set up a stunt.

We can zoom in even further, as shown in Figure 4.5. This figure shows part of a castle wall, with turrets and crenellations. This progression is typical of Stunt Island—there are lots of interesting details that you will run into as you zoom in.

Figure 4.5.
Zooming in on a
castle on the
island.

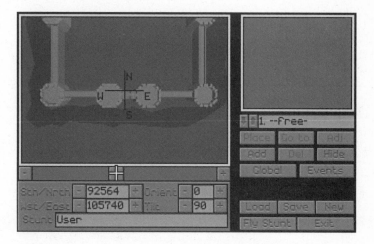

So far, the views in the Placement Window have been from directly overhead. You can use the tilt box in the view control section to change the tilt angle, as shown in Figure 4.6.

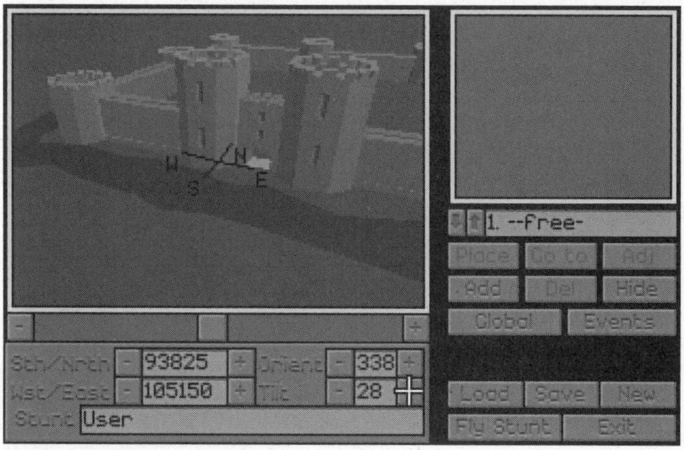

Figure 4.6.
A zoomed-in
view with a
different point
of view.

We'll set up our scene right here at the front of the castle. The first step is to add a prop. Click the Add button (see Figure 4.6) to display the prop categories (see Figure 4.7).

Figure 4.7.
Prop categories in
Stunt Island.

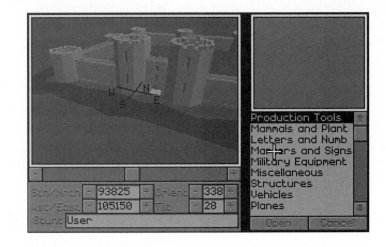

There are nine kinds of props in Stunt Island, and each category has a wide variety of props in it. I do have one criticism of the prop selection: at MCGA resolution, the difference from prop to prop is sometimes pretty minor. For example, it's pretty hard to tell one tree from the next,[15] as you can see in Figure 4.8. That's an Ash #3 on top, and a Lime #2 below it.

Props Have Properties[16]

Once you have selected a prop, you can set a variety of properties, as shown in Figure 4.9. There are various kinds of props, and you can set different properties for each kind. For example, I've defined an Ash #3 as a *free prop*. A free prop has no dependencies—it does not rely on any other prop to determine its actions (or lack thereof). Other kinds of props include *attached*, which are literally attached to some other prop and act just like a part of that other prop, and *follow* props, which, although not attached, follow another prop wherever it goes.

To position the prop, we'll need to set its altitude. Unfortunately, the Scene Editor doesn't give us any clues about the altitude of the virtual earth at the position of our prop. In the case of the ash tree, I had to experiment to determine that the

---

[15] And don't even try to tell the forest from the trees.

[16] Don't forget that the word "prop" is actually short for "properties." That means the section title is really "Properties Have Properties," which is pretty dumb.

elevation of the island was about 850 feet.[17] The best technique is to place the prop, and then raise the elevation until you can see the prop. Then you can zoom in to position it exactly. If you don't set the correct altitude for a prop, you won't see it (it will be under the virtual ground), or it will be up in the air. Figure 4.10 shows the Ash #3 prop in place at the correct elevation, along with a few other trees.

Figure 4.8.
Use the box at
the upper right of
each figure, with
07 on the left
and 11 on the
right. Two
different kinds of
tree props, an
Ash (a) and a
Lime (b).

a

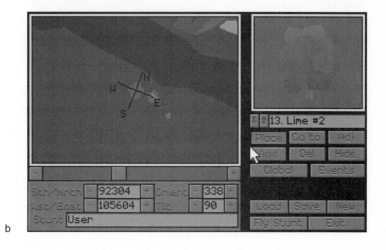

b

---

[17] This is as much of a hassle as you would expect it to be. Some of my guesses about height weren't very good—I wound up with props floating in the air. That cuts the reality part out right there. Are you guys at Disney listening? It would be a Really Neat Idea to be able to position a prop at ground level, not sea level.

Figure 4.9.
Setting a prop's
properties.

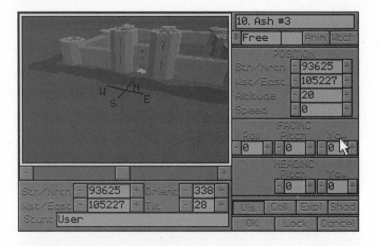

Figure 4.10.
A prop has been
placed at the
location marked
by the cross
hairs.

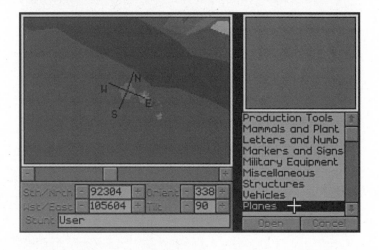

You also can set the speed of a prop, and set its direction, but that's not much use for the average tree. There are, however, plenty of props that need to move, such as cars and trucks.

Flying Through the Scene

One of the most important props is the aircraft you will fly through the scene. Stunt Island comes with a large collection of aircraft, as you can see in the pull-down list at the right of Figure 4.11. One of the more amusing choices—a pterodactyl—is included in the list, as is another favorite of mine, the space shuttle. Stunt Island isn't a fancy flight simulator, however. This game is about stunts, and the flying is pretty simple. You won't, for example, encounter any crosswinds, or be able to adjust trim for precision flying. The flying you'll do will involve fast reaction time and tight turns more than the theory of flight.

Figure 4.11. Selecting an aircraft to fly.[18]

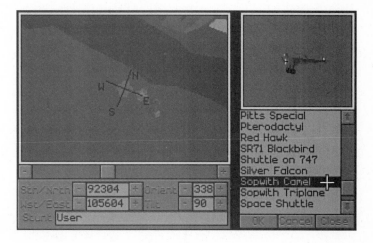

For this example, we'll use a Sopwith Camel as prop number one; you always put the aircraft you'll fly in this prop slot. There are 40 slots for props; you can't use any more than that. It's best to zoom out to place the aircraft, as shown in Figure 4.12.

Figure 4.12. Zooming out to place an aircraft.

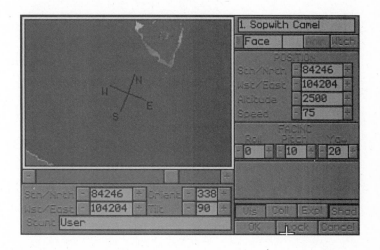

---

[18] Which begs the question: Is a pterodactyl an aircraft? My editor didn't think so, and I don't either, but as far as Stunt Island is concerned, a pterodactyl is, indeed, an aircraft. Ducks are aircraft, too, if you are curious.

For this scene, you'll put the plane about a half-mile up and well out from the island. This gives you time to react to the situation as the scene starts. To create a more challenging stunt, you could position the plane lower and closer to the island. You can enter the numbers after clicking the Adjust button; this displays the entry boxes you see in Figure 4.12.

The Spotter Plane

Prop number two is always a spotter plane. The spotter always follows the aircraft in slot number one. This is a good time to mention another really neat feature of Stunt Island: cameras. Up to eight props can "carry" a camera; all eight cameras record at the same time. Later, you can edit the clips into a movie. See the section "Editing" near the end of this chapter for more information. If you don't want to edit, Stunt Island uses a default sequence for editing the take from a stunt, and it's not half bad for the stock stunts.

Whenever you place a prop with a camera, you can display the camera view and set up the view to meet your requirements, as shown in Figure 4.13. The Sopwith Camel can be just barely seen at the center of the frame, under the cross hairs. By changing the Pitch, Yaw,[19] and Distance settings at the right in Figure 4.13, you can change the view to the one shown in Figure 4.14. Once you set the view from the spotter plane, it will follow the stunt plane like a well-trained puppy.[20]

A useful prop for a camera is a balloon, as shown in Figure 4.15.

To make this a useful camera, we need to face the balloon in the right direction. You can place the balloon near the castle and then set a compass direction (+263[21] in this case, as shown at the middle right of Figure 4.16) to enable the balloon to face the castle. The *facing pitch* has been set to -13; this points the camera 13 degrees below true horizontal. If desired, you can put the balloon in motion; I set mine drifting at a lazy 12 miles per hour. This makes the balloon an animated prop.

---

[19] You had better get used to using such terms if you're going to create your own stunts. Pitch and yaw refer to rotational movement—you change pitch when you rotate something up or down. When you nod your head to say yes, you are changing the pitch of your head. Yaw refers to side-to-side changes, such as when you shake your head to say no.

[20] Is that why they call it "Spot?"

[21] The number 263 refers to degrees, just like with a compass. Zero degrees is due north.

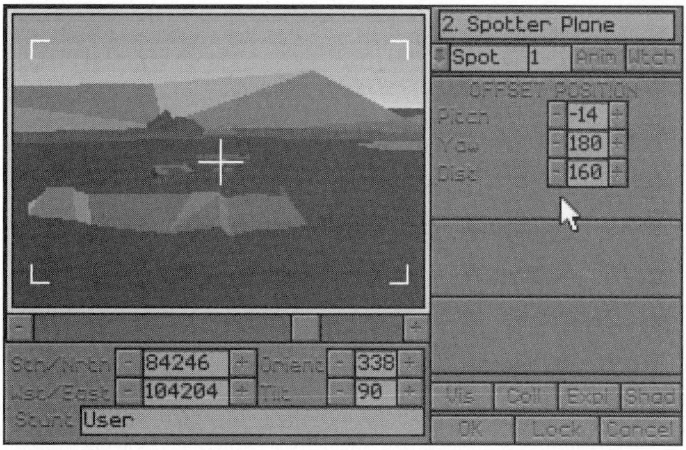

Figure 4.13. Setting the camera view for the spotter plane.

Figure 4.14. Setting the spotter plane position.

There are two kinds of animated props: static and dynamic. A static animated prop moves for the duration of a scene in the direction and at the speed you set in the Scene Editor. A dynamic prop changes direction or speed, or it may explode—it does whatever you tell it to do. For example, you might want a car to explode when it crashes into another object. You edit dynamic props using the event editor, a separate tool.

Adding Characters

So far the scene is pretty tame. Let's add a bad guy, and let's give him a camera to keep him busy because he really can't do anything nasty to our aircraft—he's just a prop. We'll set his camera to view the trees at the castle gate, just in case anything ever crashes into them.[22] I set the bad guy on one of the castle turrets; Figure 4.17 shows the view from this location. This figure also shows that, indeed, the official name for this prop is *Bad Guy*.

Figure 4.15.
Adding a balloon
to the scene.

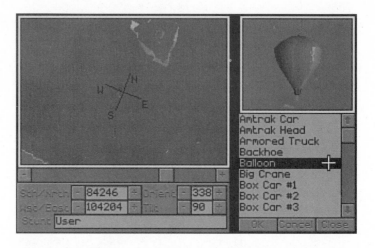

Figure 4.16.
Setting the
camera view
from a balloon.

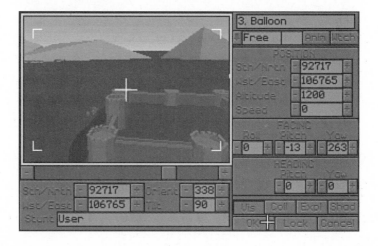

We don't have a focus for the stunt, so we'll add one: someone to rescue. There's a prop called Hook Man: a man holding a hook, you can use to pick him up with

---

[22] This author guy seems obsessed with crashing and burning.

the airplane.[23] Figure 4.18 shows what the Hook Man looks like, and the cross hairs are located on the turret next to the bad guy. Naturally, we'll set a camera view for this prop as well.

Figure 4.17.
Positioning the
bad guy's
camera.

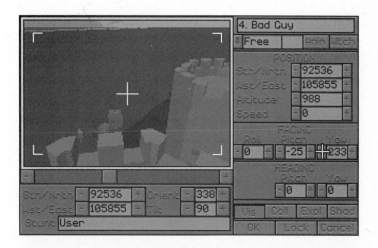

Figure 4.18.
Adding a Hook
Man to the scene.

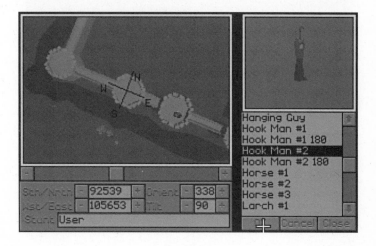

---

[23] Making the pickup is tricky—unless you think to switch the view to the spotter plane. You can easily judge your height correctly with the little expedient. Strictly speaking, it's cheating, but, hey, I'm an alter ego; I can do things like that.

This ability to put in a large number of recording cameras is one of the things that makes Stunt Island fun. When the time comes to put together a movie based on your attempts to carry out the stunt, you'll have plenty of footage and numerous camera angles to work with. For any game to be consistently interesting, it has to have a certain depth of features, and Stunt Island goes well beyond that basic point.

You can add additional props, some with and many without cameras, until you have the scene the way you want it. Figure 4.19 shows the final setup for the example scene we've been working on. I added a few goodies, including a large cathedral in the courtyard of the castle. Otherwise, it would be too easy to swoop in and perform the rescue—now you'll have to avoid the cathedral's towers immediately after the pickup.

Figure 4.19.
The final scene
ready to be saved.

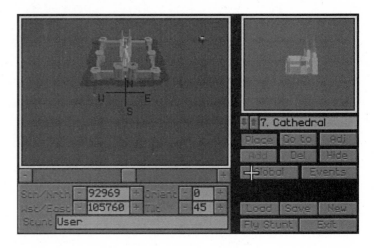

Stunt Time!

Once you have set up a scene, you can try it out. The graphic for shooting on location is shown in Figure 4.20.

You start a stunt at the controls of prop number one,[24] as shown in Figure 4.21. This figure shows a complete view, without the cockpit; you also can display a cockpit view by pressing F9. However, the cockpit obscures half or more of the screen.[25]

---

[24] That's your airplane, dummy.

[25] A classic case of over-engineering. All of the cockpit designs are fantastically detailed, but nearly every one of them is so darn big you can't see anything!

Figure 4.20.
Getting set
for action!

Figure 4.21.
The beginning
of the stunt.

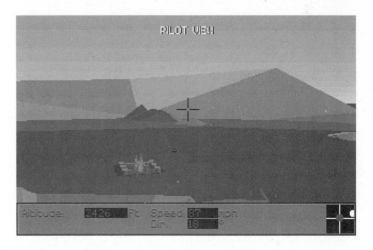

Flying the stunt is fun;[26] Figures 4.22a-d show four scenes from one attempt to do the stunt. It's no trivial feat to carry out a stunt; you can easily crash and burn if you don't pay attention. That's as it should be; I found that Stunt Island offers a nice balance between challenge and action.

---

[26] That's putting it mildly. There may be some things you'll have to put up with along the way, but once you settle into the pilot's seat and go for it, this game really shows where its focus is. The interactivity is great, and stunts are well thought out, and they offer quite a challenge.

Editing

Once you have a stunt completed, you can head for Post Production (see Figure 4.23). This leads to the editing room, where you'll find two editing decks (see Figure 4.24).

Figure 4.22.
Scenes from a
stunt in Stunt
Island.

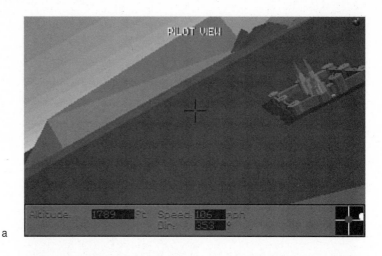

a

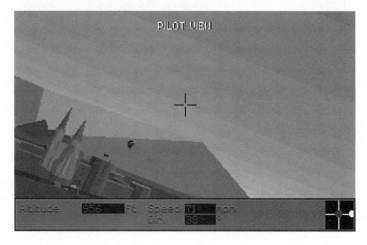

b

Figure 4.22.
continued.

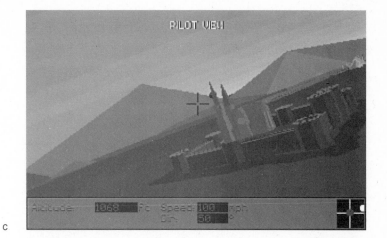

c

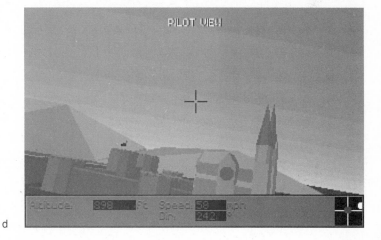

d

In Figure 4.24, the deck on the left is the source deck, and the deck on the right is the destination deck. Each deck comes with a complete set of controls for moving forward and backward, as well as markers that allow you to define the segments for editing. The editing process is straightforward.[27]

---

[27] Straightforward, yes; easy to explain, no. Once you get the hang of it, it's a lot of fun to put together a clip based on your stunt work. This was a very clever addition to the program.

Figure 4.23. The Post Production navigation screen.

Figure 4.24. The two-deck editing studio of Stunt Island.

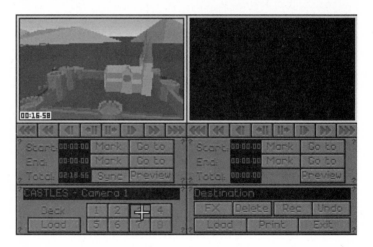

1. Load a *take* into the source deck. A take consists of the film from all of the cameras during a single stunt attempt.

2. Play the views from the various cameras until you find footage you want to keep. Click the Start/Mark button when you find a good starting point.

3. Continue playing from the starting point (you must stay with one particular camera) until you reach the end of the clip you want; then click the End/Mark button.

4. To copy the clip to the destination deck, simply click the Rec (record) button.

You can add as many clips, from as many different cameras as you like, to create a movie. You then can save the movie and play it back at your leisure.

Summary

Some folks might say it's stretching a point to call Stunt Island virtual reality, but I don't think so at all. There are important compromises—MCGS resolution is one of the most serious—but all the important ingredients are there: 3D modeling and interactivity. If you can take your virtual reality without a heavy dose of realism, then this program provides an outstanding bang/buck ratio.

There are also quite a few 3D games coming out on the market. Some of the more interesting shareware efforts are coming from Apogee software. I've included a few of their games on the CD-ROM, and you also can find their games on many bulletin boards across the country. I tried Wolfenstein 3D recently, and the game is very well designed. Unlike many cave-type adventure games, this one works in real time, which makes it very exciting and a pleasure to play. Unfortunately, I got nailed from behind by some Nazi criminals and didn't get too far with the game. The 3D action of turning to shoot is much more fun than the traditional arcade-style games. I recommend the entire series of games from Apogee highly. If you enjoy action/ skill games, you won't be disappointed.

II

VIRTUAL FANTASIES

5

CREATING YOUR OWN REALITY

RECIPE

1 copy program

Instructions: This chapter is about space—creating it, modifying it, moving around in it, and having a little fun with it. There will be a tour of the solar system, including a wild ride through an exploding planet.

Give Me Some Space!

Virtual reality is very convenient. It doesn't have the same limitations as regular reality. Gravity, for example, is actually a serious bother when it comes to programming for VR. Friction is another real hassle. Sometimes, of course, these are highly desirable. If you are an industrial engineer designing parts for a new jet, things like friction and gravity are the point of the VR process—you want to learn about the performance of your designs in the real world by messing around with them in a virtual world. If the correspondence between real and virtual is not accurate, and that jet crashes…

For the rest of us, the stakes are so low as to be negligible. Fun is the order of the day. And when it comes to fun, things like gravity and friction can get in the way or be part of the game—rules become arbitrary. You can omit the rules, make up new rules, or give the rules a new twist. For example, if you would like to fly through the solar system, the distance between the planets in the real universe is inconveniently large. Things like the mass of propellant required to accelerate quickly, the effects of acceleration, and the speed of light all contribute to making a real-time simulation not much fun. But if we were to conveniently ignore such details, the solar system could be as accessible as an amusement park ride.[1]

The Solar System

Speaking of the solar system, why don't we create one of our own. This is a big project, and I'm going to pull out the big guns to do it "right"—3D Studio, to be exact. This does not mean that you couldn't use such software as REND 386 or Imagine to create your universe, but 3D Studio has some advantages that I like for this project. The first of those is space itself. 3D Studio is quite expansive about its use of space. The scale of objects within a 3D space can be anything you want it to be. If we want to work at a scale of millions or billions of miles, that's OK with 3D Studio.

---

[1] Time to discuss the moral side of virtual reality. I recently read an editorial regarding the existence of nature shows on television. Surely, the author suggested, if there were an unmitigated good on television, it would be nature shows. He then shot down that argument by pointing out that nature shows are actually quite artificial, and are giving people an incomplete—and often a staged—picture of reality. For example, nature shows are dramatic, while nature itself consists of vast stretches of very undramatic time punctuated by short, intense dramas. Only the latter are presented to the television viewer, and the result, the author suggested, is a twisted, inaccurate, and sometimes dangerous view of nature.

Can the same be said of virtual reality? Does the twisting and altering of the rules of the nature of reality carry some kind of price tag? I won't pretend to have an answer, and the whole issue is so uncertain that I almost don't have an opinion on the matter. If pressed, I would mention that overuse of carrots can lead to serious trouble, too. I can't buy the idea that adults are credulous enough to buy that nature shows represent reality. If we have become so civilized that we can be fooled extensively about the nature of reality itself, then, yes, we ought to back up a little and reconsider. Heck, a walk in the woods will disabuse just about anyone of false views of nature, and an occasional slip on a banana peel ought to be enough of a reminder of the effects of gravity for even the most jaded VR fanatic.

RECIPE

4T 3D Studio
1 Astronomy book
1 CompuServe account
dash Photoshop
1 part disdain for pure celestial mechanics

Instructions: Create a series of spheres in 3D Studio, then apply texture maps corresponding at least roughly to planetary features. Consult a book on astronomy for things like relative sizes of the planets. For a gourmet touch, download planetary images from Compuserve, or create your own in Photoshop or other photo realistic paint program. Unless you want to spend an enormous amount of time on the recipe, leave out exact details of celestial mechanics.

I'm going to introduce some inaccuracies into this version of the solar system for the sake of simplicity. If you are following along at home, check the footnotes to see how to add more "reality" to the project.[2] For this demonstration, I'll take you as far as the Earth. That leaves Mars and the gas giants for an extra credit project.

In the beginning, there was the opening screen of 3D Studio (see Figure 5.1). Into this reality came the cursor, and the cursor said to the menu, Create/GSphere.[3]

---

[2] What is reality, anyway, in these days of quantum mechanics, wave-particle duality, and string theory? Not to mention the uncertainty principle. At the subatomic level, we're living in an "unpredictable, many-dimensioned world that isn't even continuous, or even consistently solid." If these terms are unfamiliar, they are part of the lingo of nuclear physics. Here's a rough translation into ordinary English: the universe is made up of little bitty particles that jump from here to there, even when there's no actual connection between here and there. How they do that, when they do that, and whether they stay as little bitty particles while they do it is all open to question. There. Doesn't that give you a nice, cozy feeling about the nature of reality?

[3] 3D Studio lets you create two kinds of sphere. One kind is constructed of faces that are oriented to lines of latitude and longitude (LSphere). The other kind is more like a geodesic sphere (GSphere). For our purposes, there isn't much need to distinguish between the two. If you planned to deform the sphere into a different shape, then the way that the sphere is constructed would be more important. In our case, I'm not planning anything worse than a planetary explosion. Either kind of sphere will be fine, although there are subtle differences in how they explode.

And the result was good (see Figure 5.2). This is going to be the sun. When you are asked to provide a name, use "Sun." Before it acts like the a sun, however, you'll need to set some attributes.

Figure 5.1.
The 3D Studio
opening screen.

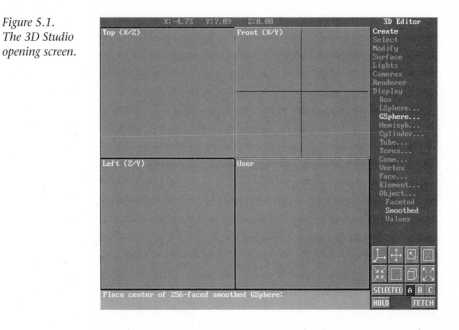

The first step is to put a light inside of the sun. Place the light at the center of the sphere. Make it an omni light, which does not cast shadows and will therefore illuminate the scene even though it is inside an object. Set the brightness of the light to 255.

Use the Surface/Material/Choose menu to access the Material Selector (see Figure 5.3). This is a list of the materials available in the current library. Believe it or not, Yellow Glass will make a good start—you'll need to modify it a bit in the Materials Editor, however. For now, choose Yellow Glass as the current material, and then assign it to the sphere. You'll be adding some surface texture to the sun in the Materials Editor, so you will also need to apply mapping coordinates to the sphere. Set the mapping type as Spherical, scale the coordinates to be just slightly smaller than the sun, and then locate the center of the mapping coordinates coincident with the center of the sun sphere. Check both the Front and Left viewports to make sure the mapping coordinates are located properly, and then assign them to the sun sphere.

Figure 5.2.
A geodesic
sphere.

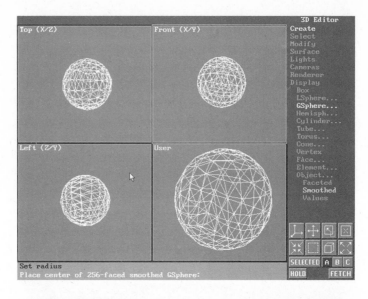

Figure 5.3.
The Material
Selector.

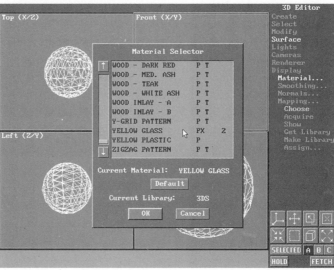

To check your work, render the User view at a small size, such as 320x200.[4]

You'll need to modify the settings for Yellow Glass in the Materials Editor. Press the F5 key to change to the Materials Editor now. To modify the Yellow Glass

---

[4] You can set the rendering size using the Render/Setup/Configuration dialog.

material, load it using the Material/Get Material from Scene menu selection (see Figure 5.4).

Figure 5.4.
Getting a
material from the
current scene.

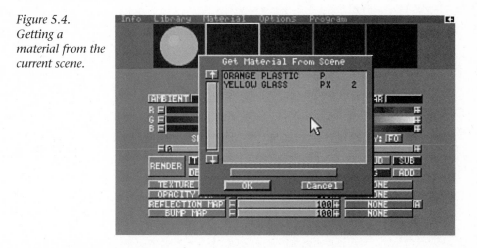

Make the following changes to the Yellow Glass material:

- Reduce the shininess to 0.

- Add a texture map using the Texture button at the bottom of the screen. Choose one that seems appropriate for a sun. I would suggest using the file granite.cel which is about as close as you can come without using a sun-specific image. You can create a texture map from scratch using a paint program, or download an image of the sun from one of the CompuServe graphics forums.[5]

- Add a bump map using the Bump button at the bottom of the screen. In most cases, you'll want to use the same image you used for the texture map, or a variation of it. Granite.cel works great.

- Click the Self-Illum button to make the sun a self-illuminating object. This is the only way to create a sun that is at all realistic. Putting multiple lights inside the sun and making it partially transparent does not give you a bright enough result.

---

[5] There are a number of NASA images in various forums on CompuServe. You can also check the Astronomy forum for possibilities.

To see the results of your tinkering, click the Render button. When you have the material just the way you want it, use the menu at the top of the screen to Put the material into the current library. Give it an appropriate name, such as Sun Texture. You must put a material into the library in order to be able to use it in the 3D Editor. You could also Put the revised material Yellow Glass back into the scene, but only do this if you do not need the original material for other objects.

"Let there be light" is only the beginning—it's on to Mercury. Create another GSphere (see Figure 5.5). In the real solar system, the size difference between Mercury and the sun is enormous. In fact, the real solar system is made up mostly of empty space. This makes for a challenging simulation, and the easiest way to solve it is to make the planets larger. The goal of this simulation is to tour the inner solar system. Since a realistic model would spend most of its time on the way to the next planet, a model with enlarged planets makes more sense for this example. If your goal was to show the empty space, instead of the planets, a realistic model would do a better job.

Figure 5.5.
Creating Mercury
as another
GShpere.

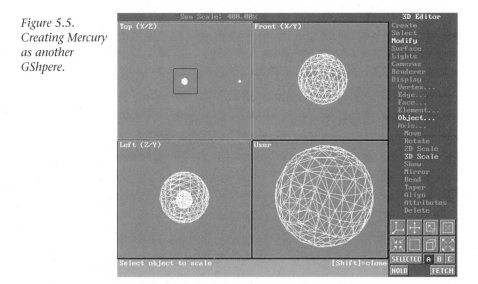

For example, I initially tried creating Mercury at the size shown in Figure 5.6. The object representing Mercury is so small I thought it might be hard to find, so I put the mouse cursor next to it—Mercury is the tiny little dot just in front of the mouse cursor.

Figure 5.6.
A smaller version
of Mercury.

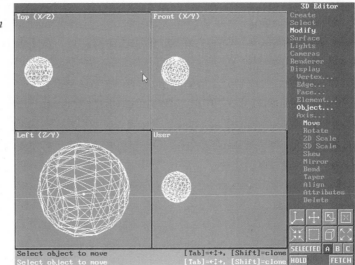

The material Orange Plastic makes a reasonable starting point for Mercury. I made some modifications in the Materials Editor (see Figure 5.7). I set the shininess down a bit to 7, and added a texture map and a bump map. I used the same file for both: tile009.tga. This is a standard texture file that comes with 3D Studio. It gives a nice planetary look to the surface of Mercury. As with the sun, you can explore CompuServe for interesting planetary images. The Astronomy forum (ASTROFORUM) would be a good place to look; you can find many NASA images there.

Figure 5.7.
Setting material
attributes for
Mercury.

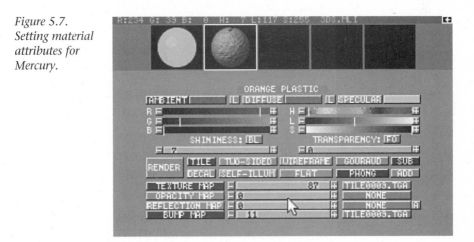

*Figure 5.8.
Setting up a
camera for test
renderings of the
planets.*

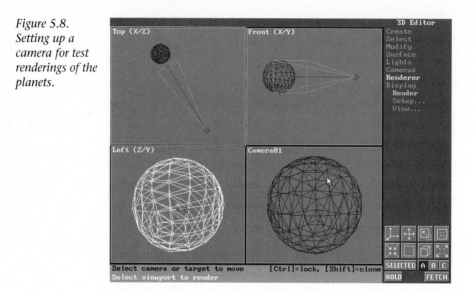

The solar system model is very large, and rendering can be a pain if you don't add a camera or three. I would suggest adding a camera for each object you want to test during development. Figure 5.8 shows a camera set up for viewing mercury. The Top and Front viewports show the camera in relation to the planet. The Left viewport shows the extreme difference in size between the sun and Mercury. The lower-right viewport, labeled Camera01, shows the view through the camera.

Once you have a camera set up, you can render to see how well the choice of materials works. Figure 5.9 shows an artfully arranged camera view, with both Mercury and the sun in the camera frame. The only problem with viewing Mercury from the back is that it is lit from the front by the sun—all you will see from this angle is a dark disk.

To apply the revised material to Mercury, you will need to follow the same steps you used for the sun. Don't forget to set the mapping coordinates. While we are on the subject of mapping coordinates, I'd like to point out a common source of frustration in renderings. Figure 5.10 shows the wrong way to set up spherical mapping coordinates for an object in 3D Studio—the coordinates are trying to be exactly the same as the object they will be assigned to. It is better to make the mapping coordinates either a little larger or a little smaller than the object. If the size difference is too small, part of the mapping coordinates will wind up on the inside of the object, and part on the outside. This results in a fractured appearance during rendering. Using different sizes avoids the problem.

Figure 5.9.
Composing a
view for the
camera.

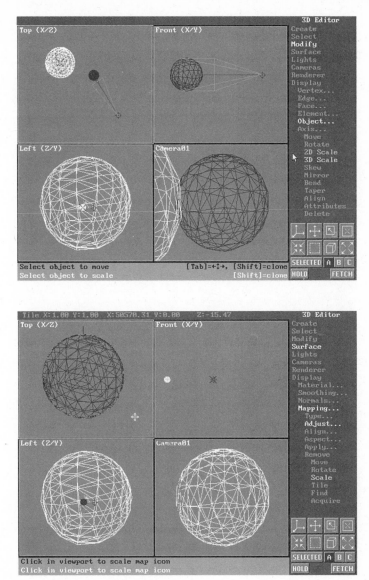

Figure 5.10.
Incorrect setting
of mapping
coordinates.

The next step, of course, is to create Venus. Venus is larger than Mercury, so size the GSphere accordingly. There is a useful material, Blue Planet, that makes an excellent starting point for Venus (see Figure 5.11).

Figure 5.11.
Setting material
attributes for
Venus.

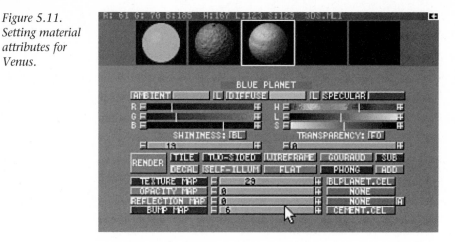

I suggest a few changes to Blue Planet to make it look more like Venus:

■ Reduce the shininess to 19.

■ Reduce the texture map percentage to 29.

■ Use cement.cel as a bump map, with a percentage setting of 6.

■ Set the Ambient and Diffuse lighting to a light bluish cyan.

As with the sun and Mercury, you will need to put the revised material back into the library or the scene, and you'll need to set appropriate mapping coordinates for Venus. Check your work by creating a camera for Venus and rendering. To set the camera viewport, use the Camera Selector shown in Figure 5.12. You can access the Camera Selector by pressing Control-V and clicking on the Camera button, and then on the viewport to be used for a camera view.

Finally, create the planet earth as yet another GSphere. Figure 5.13 shows the Earth before a camera has been created for Earth. Earth is the tiny dot at the right of the Top viewport. 3D Studio comes with a map of Earth that you can apply as a spherical texture map in the Materials Editor (see Figure 5.14).

Figure 5.12.
Selecting the
camera to use for
the camera
viewport.

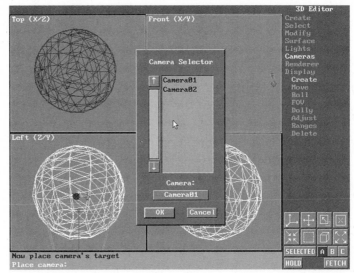

Figure 5.13.
Creating Earth.

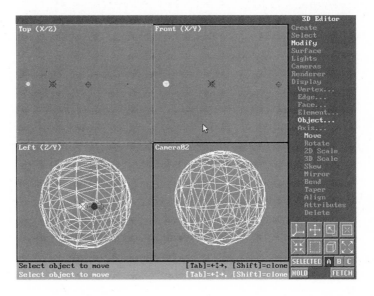

Figure 5.14.
Creating an earth
material in the
Materials Editor.

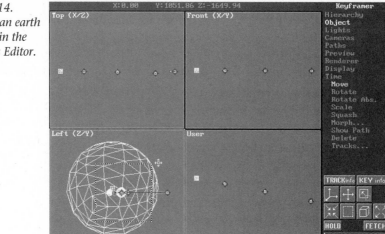

Set the texture map to the file earthmap.tga, using a texture map setting of 85 and bluish colors for the Ambient and Diffuse attributes. You may also want to add a bump map for visual interest; I used mum.cel which has the humorous effect of making the earth look like a slightly under-inflated beach ball. You can see all four materials in small-scale renderings in Figure 5.14.

As with the other objects, I would suggest creating a camera to test the rendering of the earth before moving on. You can continue to create the additional planets in the same manner shown for the inner solar system. For this example, the Earth is the last planet you'll create. Once you have enough planets to satisfy your cravings for creative power, add a camera a little further out than the Earth (see Figure 5.15). You'll use the Keyframer to fly this camera through the model of the solar system in the Keyframer.

*Figure 5.15.
Adding a camera
for the fly-
through.*

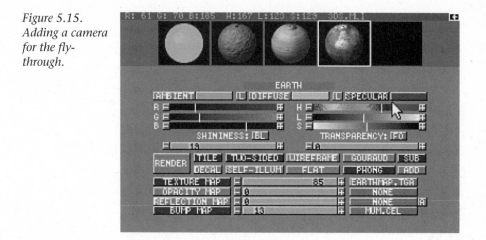

Figure 5.16 shows the camera attached to a dummy object,[6] and a path that takes it past the earth. The current frame number is 120 out of 480[7] total frames. This view is from above, and shows the first stage of creating the camera path.[8] I have labeled the various objects in the view to make it easier to follow along. Note the small squares along the path. They are key frames that I created using the Paths/ Add Key menu selection. I added the key frames at approximately even intervals along the path, and they can be used to adjust the path.

Not only would this straight path be boring, it happens to go right through the Earth—not good. There are several approaches you can use in this situation. One is to orbit the Earth and then fly away again, as shown in Figure 5.17. This was done by simply clicking and dragging the various key frame indicators to new positions.

This isn't enough, however, because the camera angle remains the same—that is, pointing toward the sun. To face the camera toward the Earth, use the Object/Ro-

---

[6] Dummy objects can be created in the Keyframer using the Hierarchy menu. A dummy object is required because you cannot create a unified path for the camera and its target, but you can create one for a dummy object. You only need to use the Hierarchy/Link menu selection to link both the camera and the target to the dummy object. Wherever the dummy goes, the camera/target will follow.

[7] I later adjusted the animation to use 600 frames. 480 frames wasn't enough to provide a smooth trip over more than 100 million miles. The earth is only 93 million miles from the sun, but I took the long way around.

[8] I will call it the camera path for the sake of clarity, but keep in mind it is actually the dummy object's path that is being adjusted.

tate menu selection to rotate the dummy object so the camera faces the earth at each of the key frames.[9] Figure 5.18 shows the camera angle properly adjusted.

Figure 5.16.
Setting up the
camera for a
flight through the
solar system.

Figure 5.17.
Orbiting the
earth.

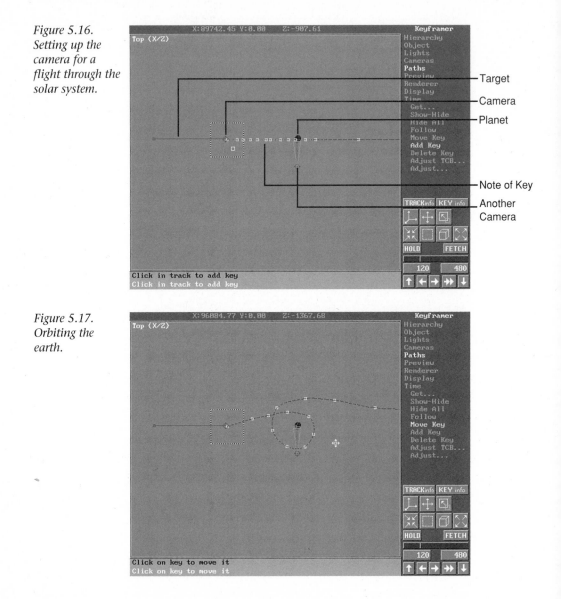

---

[9] Unless you have managed to lay out the key frames in a perfect circle, you may also need to adjust the camera position in additional frames. Step through this portion of the animation one frame at a time to check the camera angle. If the camera angle isn't consistent with respect to the earth, the earth will appear to jump from frame to frame.

Figure 5.18.
Adjusting the
camera angle
while in orbit.

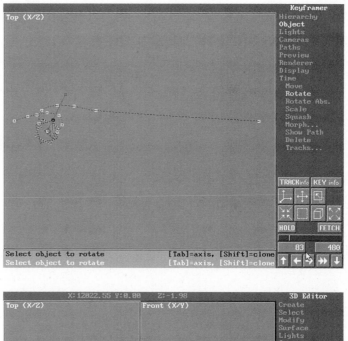

Figure 5.19.
Adjust the
camera.

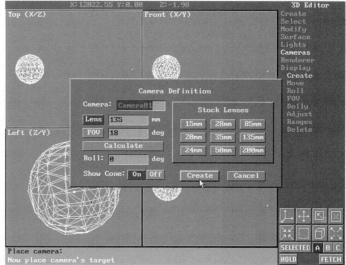

You can also make changes to the camera to make life easier. Figure 5.19 shows the Camera Definition dialog, which allows you to set various camera parameters. If the orbit is too close to the planet, for example, you can use a wider lens angle. The Stock Lenses listed correspond in their behavior to typical lenses for a 35mm camera. That is, the lenses with focal lengths ranging from 15mm to 35mm are considered wide-angle lenses, the 50mm lens is a "normal" lens, and the remaining lenses are considered as telephoto lenses.

Another possible approach for a fly-through is to create a path that weaves from planet to planet. To create such a path, move to the last frame, and position the dummy object (and therefore the attached camera) between Mercury and the sun using the Object/Move menu selection (see Figure 5.20).

Figure 5.20.
Setting the
camera position
for the final
frame.

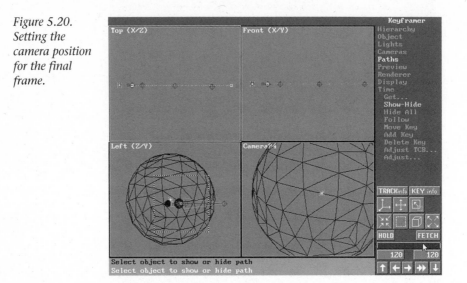

Add a series of new key frames using the Paths/Add Key menu selection as shown in Figure 5.21. These should be spaces at approximately equal intervals.

Figure 5.21.
Adding addi-
tional key
frames.

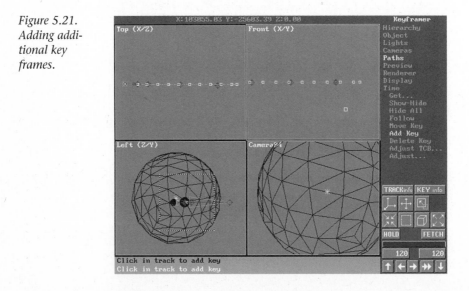

You can now enlarge the Top view to adjust the position of the camera in the corresponding key frames. Press Control-V to access the viewport dialog box shown in Figure 5.22. You can choose from any of the viewport arrangements shown in the top two rows of the dialog. To determine which view shows up in a port, choose a view from the list at the bottom, and then click in a viewport in the diagram at bottom left. If you choose Camera and there is more than one camera, you will see a dialog asking you to specify which camera to use for that viewport.

Figure 5.22.
Adjust viewport
configuration.

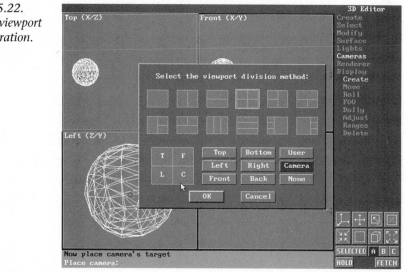

Figure 5.23 shows an enlarged Top view with the key frames adjusted to take the camera on a weaving path through the inner solar system. You can enlarge the view to show just a portion of the path as shown in Figure 5.23. This allows you to adjust the relative positions of the camera and planets very precisely.

Using this technique, you may not need to adjust the camera angle at all. If you adjust the angle of approach correctly, the approaching planet will be framed nicely in the Camera view. If necessary, of course, you can change the camera angle or lens focal length to get the views you desire.

The two methods for moving the camera through the solar system mentioned so far do not animate the planets in any way. There are two kinds of planetary animation that you can add: rotation on an axis, and an orbit around the sun.

Axial rotation is easy to add. Use the Top view, and zoom in on each planet in turn. Determine an appropriate number of frames to use for one rotation, and then move to that frame. Use the Object/Rotate menu selection to rotate the planet 360 degrees in the Top viewport. Click the KEY Info button, then click the planet you just rotated. Click the Repeat button in the dialog box that appears, then click OK. I used a 50-frame repeating rotation for the earth, and 100 days and 25 days for Venus and Mercury, respectively.[10]

Figure 5.23. Zooming in to adjust camera position.

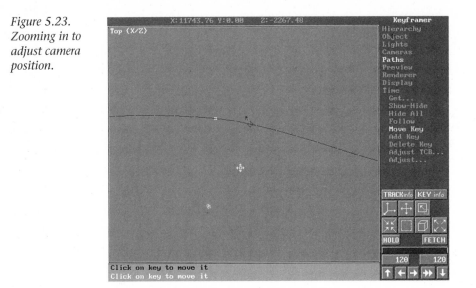

To create an orbital rotation, I first create a very thin torus (doughnut) shape (see Figure 5.24). I used the 3D Editor to scale the torus so that it corresponded to the size of Earth's orbit.[11] This will serve as a guide shape for placing the orbital path. I used a total of 600 frames, and set that as a full orbital period for Venus. Because the earth moves more slowly in its orbit, you can have the earth move through 75 percent of its orbit. Because earth is starting at the 3 o'clock position (seen in the Top viewport), that would take it to the 6 o'clock position if we rotate it counter-clockwise. To place the earth along the path correctly, move to the one-third point (frame 200) and move the earth to the 12 o'clock position, using the torus as a guide for placement. Move to frame 400, and place the earth at the 9 o'clock position, and then move to frame 600 and place the earth at the 6 o'clock position.

---

[10] For an added dimension of realism, you can tilt the Earth's axis by 22.5 degrees in the Front view before you add the rotation. You can also add appropriate axial tilts for the other planets if you so desire.

[11] In real life, the Earth's orbit is slightly elliptical.

Figure 5.24.
Using a torus to
guide placement
of a path.

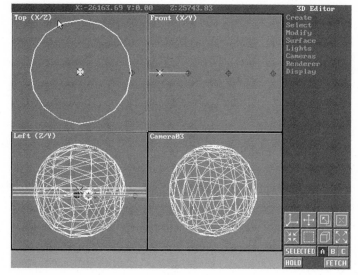

To view the path, use the Paths/Show-Hide Path menu selection. Click on the Earth to display its path. You will probably need to add additional key frames to make the path into a rough circle. Repeat this process for the other planets, changing the positions in frames 200 and 400 according to the speed at which each planet will move. For example, I moved Mercury through one and one-third rotations over the 600 frames. You can scale the torus prior to adjusting each path to give yourself a guideline.

Figure 5.25 shows the orbital paths for all three planets. Note that all of the paths are in the same plane (check the Front viewport). Note also that the path for the Earth does not close. You can't see it in this view, but the path for Mercury overlaps itself from the 3 o'clock position to the 12 o'clock position. Delete the torus when you are done.

The final task is to create a path for the dummy object/camera. The process is similar to that used for the planets, with one important difference. Instead of following a circular path, the camera should follow a spiral path from one planet's orbit to the next. Figure 5.26 shows the complete path for all objects—three planets and the camera—in an expanded Top viewport.

*Figure 5.25.
Orbital paths in
place.*

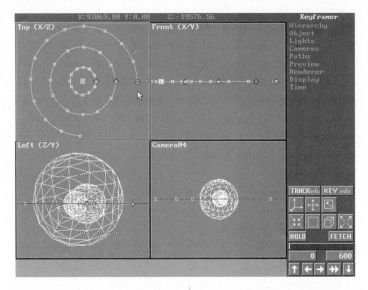

*Figure 5.26.
The paths of all
objects in the
scene.*

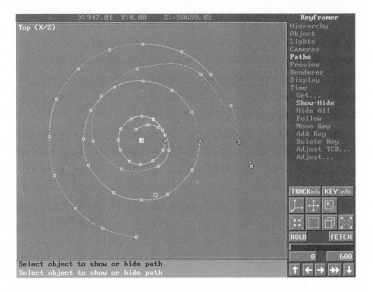

> TIP
>
> To make sure the camera makes a close approach to each planet, set the dummy object's position every 100 frames. For example, move to frame 100 so you can see the positions of the planets, and then place the dummy object near the earth. Move to frame 200, and now move the dummy object past the earth and inside the earth's orbit. Move to frame 300, and move the dummy object near Venus. Continue this until you have a rough spiral path to frame 600. You can then add additional key frames to smooth out the spiral.

For a final touch, I created a star map in Adobe Photoshop.[12] I then created a material using it as a texture map. You can add a GSphere a little bigger than Earth's orbit, and apply the material (make it two-sided, of course, since you'll be seeing the inside of the sphere) to it. If you make sure to apply spherical mapping coordinates, you'll see stars in the background of your animation. This adds a nifty touch of realism. However, if you get too close to the star background, the stars get bigger which isn't very realistic at all—be careful where you aim that camera!

The Gallery Tour

Figures 5.27 through 5.32 show various scenes from the resulting animation. The walnut-like appearance of Mercury was accidental, but since we're going to learn how to blow it up in the next section, I thought that it fit right in so I left it that way.

---

[12] Nothing fancy, just some white dots on a black background, 1024x768, and saved as a 24-bit Targa file.

Figure 5.27.
A frame from the
solar system
animation. This
is a view of the
Earth from the
beginning of the
animation.

Figure 5.28.
A frame from the
solar system
animation.
Another view of
Earth. The
camera has
moved closer on
its trip to the sun.

*Figure 5.29.
A frame from the
solar system
animation. A
distant view of
Venus after the
camera turns
away after
passing Earth.*

*Figure 5.30.
A frame from the
solar system
animation. A
close view of
Venus.*

*Figure 5.31.
A frame from the
solar system
animation. This
is a view of the
sun while passing
between Venus
and Mercury.*

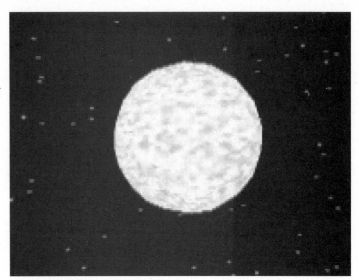

*Figure 5.32.
A frame from the
solar system
animation. A
view of the planet
Mercury from
near the end of
the animation.*

A Solar Overview

There is another way to view the solar system that is quite interesting to look at,
particularly if you have any fascination with astronomy. It uses a modified version of the solar system you just created.

Begin with the final animation of the preceding section of this chapter. Delete the sphere with the stars, and create instead a flat plane to use as a background.[13] Use the Top viewport, and the Create/Box menu selection. The flat plane should be quite large to make sure it will be visible from all angles, as shown in Figure 5.33. About three to four times the size of the solar system is about right.

Figure 5.33. Creating a background for the overview of the solar system.

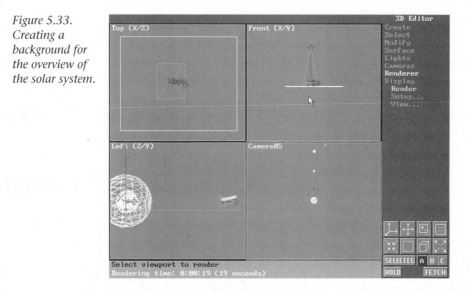

You will also need to create a camera located above the solar system. The best place to create it is in the Front viewport. Place it directly above the sun, and place the target on the sun (see the Front viewport in Figure 5.33). Finally, create a "rocket" parallel to the camera that travels along the spiral path (see the Left viewport in Figure 5.33). I used a simple cylinder. Looking from high above the solar system, a cylinder is fine. If you plan to zoom in for a close look, you can take some time to create a fancier-looking rocket or spacecraft.

The Camera05 viewport in Figure 5.33 shows the view from the camera that you placed above the plane of the solar system. The sun is at the center, and the planets above it are Mercury, Venus, and Earth. The little line above and to the right of the Earth is the spacecraft that matches the original camera's position. To make the rocket follow the camera, use the Hierarchy/Link menu selection in the Keyframer.

---

[13] 3D Studio also allows you to specify a background, but such backgrounds don't move with the camera. Although this exercise doesn't move the camera, it would be a simple thing to animate the camera and zoom in on the planets.

To render from this new point of view, simply choose Renderer/Render from the menu. That's all there is to it! Figure 5.34 shows a frame from the resulting animation. It's not much to look at, but in the actual animation you can make out the phases of the planets as they circle about the sun, as well as the movement of the camera/rocket.

Begin with the final animation of the preceding section of this chapter. Delete the sphere with the stars, and create instead a flat plane to use as a background. Use the Top viewport, and the Create/Box menu selection. The flat plane should be quite large to make sure it will be visible from all angles, as shown in Figure 5.33. About three to four times the size of the solar system is about right.

Figure 5.34.
An overview of
the solar system.

Other variations you can try from this vantage point include:

■ Zooming in on the spacecraft as it approaches Mercury.

■ Viewing the solar system from a lower angle than 90 degrees.

■ Starting out with a view close to Earth, and then moving above to show the entire solar system. You could link the camera target to the spacecraft with good results.

There is actually no end of interesting approaches to working with the model of the solar system. Comets, asteroids, alien spacecraft, or runaway planets are all interesting possibilities to explore.

A Wild Ride

And now for something completely different: a wild ride through an exploding planet.

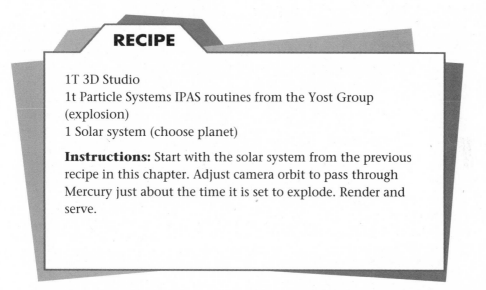

RECIPE

1T 3D Studio
1t Particle Systems IPAS routines from the Yost Group (explosion)
1 Solar system (choose planet)

Instructions: Start with the solar system from the previous recipe in this chapter. Adjust camera orbit to pass through Mercury just about the time it is set to explode. Render and serve.

The software for the explosion uses a special feature of 3D Studio. During rendering, 3D Studio can call an external process to modify the object or its properties. There are four kinds of callable external processes:

Image processing—Adds 2D effects to rendered scenes. Examples include halos, contrast enhancement, motion blur, and so on.

Procedural modeling—Changes a 3D object in some way. Used to implement fractal mountain generators, object builders, object deforming tools such as rippling, etc.

Animated stand-in—Creates an animation based on an object in a 3D scene. That is, the object is a "stand-in," or substitute, for the animation. The animation will appear only in the rendering, not in the 3D Editor or Keyframer. Useful for such things as snow, fireworks, explosions, etc.

Solid texture—These are static or animated 3D patterns. You can assign them to materials in the Materials Editor. Examples include wood, marble, variable color, etc.

As a group, these external processes are called IPAS routines. The name is taken from the initial letter of the four kinds of processes. An explosion is an AXP (Animated stand-in external process).

The explosion AXP will break the object into pieces, and they will move outward from the origin of the explosion. The smallest possible piece of an object will be a single face. There are a number of parameters you can set for the explosion, and they are listed in Table 5.1. To create a large number of faces, you can *tessellate* an object. Use the Create/Object/Tessellate menu selection (see Figure 5.35). Then click on the Mercury sphere to break each face into three faces. Accept the default values. Tessellation triples the number of pieces that an explosion can create from an object.

Figure 5.35.
Tessellating the
Mercury sphere.

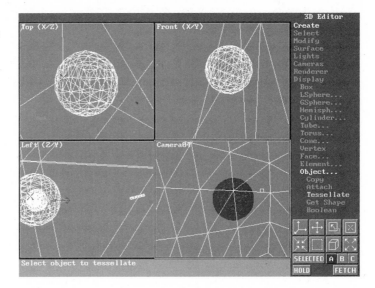

As you can see in Figure 5.35, after the tessellation, Mercury has many more faces than the other spheres. In fact, there are so many you can't really tell one face from another.

To apply the explosion AXP to Mercury, use the Modify/Object/Attributes menu selection. Figure 5.36 shows the Object Attributes dialog. The bottom third of the dialog contains information about the external process. To add an external process, click the button next to the word Name.[14]

---

[14] 3D Studio comes with a number of sample IPAS routines, but the explosion routine is not one of them. I obtained mine from the Yost Group. You can obtain a complete catalog of IPAS routines by writing to them at 3739 Balboa St. #230, San Francisco, CA 94121.

Figure 5.36.
Setting object
attributes to an
external process.

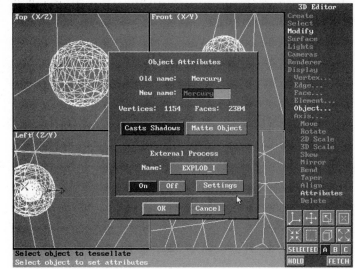

To change the settings for the explosion, click the Settings button. This will display the dialog shown in Figure 5.37. The purpose of each setting is explained in Table 5.1.

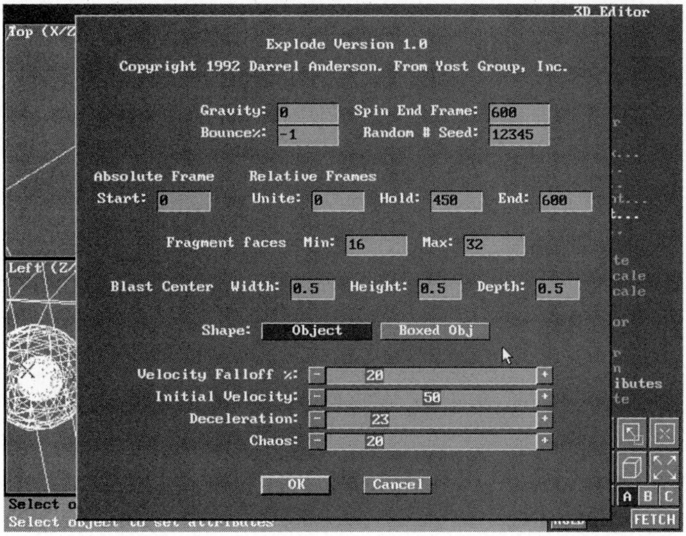

Figure 5.37.
Settings for an
explosion.

Table 5.1. Explosion Settings.

Setting	Description
Gravity	After the initial explosion, the pieces will be affected by gravity. If you want the pieces to fall quickly, set gravity to a large number. "Normal" gravity is 1. To eliminate gravity, enter a value of zero.
Bounce %	Controls bounce characteristics. A setting of -1 eliminates bouncing entirely; pieces will continue to move indefinitely in the direction they start with .[15] A setting of zero causes the pieces to stop when they reach the "ground," defined as the portion of the original object's bounding rectangle with the lowest Y axis value. Positive values cause increasingly larger bounce. A setting of 50%, for example, means that the piece will bounce to 50% of the height it fell from.
Spin End Frame	The pieces spin off from the original object. The rate of spin decreases from the explosion frame to the spin end frame.
Random # Seed	If you have multiple objects using the same AXP external process, you can vary the initial conditions by using a different random seed number.
Absolute Frame Start	This specifies the Keyframer frame number where the effect will start. Until this frame, the object will be hidden.[16]
Relative Frames Unite	This and the next two settings are relative to the absolute frame start setting. If Unite is set to 50,

---

[15] If deceleration exists, the objects will eventually come to rest, however.

[16] The start of the effect and the start of the explosion can easily be two different frames. Unless you want to object in question hidden, use zero for this setting.

Setting	Description
	for example, the object will start in pieces at the absolute frame, and then come together over the next 50 frames.[17] A setting of zero will avoid any kind of Unite action.
Relative Frames Hold	This determines the number of frames that the object will stay intact after the Unite frame. For example, if absolute frame start is zero, and Unite is zero, a setting of 100 for Hold means that the object will start to explode at frame 100.
Relative Frames End	The object explodes to nothing during the interval between the Hold frame and the End frame. Expanding on the example cited above for Relative Frames Hold, an end setting of 200 would result in the object beginning to explode in frame 100, and finishing in frame 200.
Fragment Faces Min/Max	This setting allows you to control the size of the pieces. Each piece will have at least the number of faces specified in the Min setting, and no more faces than the number specified in the Max setting. In the case of an exploding Mercury, with its many tessellated faces, good numbers would be 10 for Minimum and 100 for Maximum.
Blast Center Width/ Height/Depth	These settings control the center of the explosion. They are relative to the bounding box of the object. A setting of .5 in each item places you at the center of the object.

continues

---

[17] The position of the pieces, and therefore the appearance of the object, is exactly the same 50 frames before coming together as it is 50 frames after blowing apart. This means that if you use these settings to pull an object together and then explode it, the two actions will be mirror images of each other. This is not very natural looking, so keep that fact in mind when you design your animation.

Table 5.1. continued

Setting	*Description*
Shape	For certain situations, you can add a special boxed object that will control the parameters of the blast, rather than a real object. These buttons tell the AXP process which of the two to use. In this example, you would select Object to allow the Mercury sphere to control the explosion.
Velocity Falloff %	Each fragment starts with an initial velocity based on the Initial Velocity setting. If a falloff % greater than zero is used, a fragment's initial velocity is less if it is further from the blast center. A setting of zero gives all fragments the same initial velocity.
Initial Velocity	Determines how fast each fragment moves as the explosion starts. A setting of 100 means that a fragment will move 1/10th of the object's size per frame.
Deceleration	Controls the rate at which fragments slow down over time. If you enter a value of 100, fragments will lose 10% of their speed per frame.
Chaos	Introduces random variation in several of the settings, including initial velocity, tumbling and spinning, and gravity.

A starting set of values for the Mercury explosion is shown in Figure 5.37. Some different settings to try include:

■ Change the origin of the blast to be on the surface of the planet. For example, change the Blast Center Depth setting to 0. Experiment with different settings for Velocity falloff if you try this.

■ Lower the deceleration value and increase the initial velocity to cause the fragments to fly off into space.

■ Change the size limits (Min and Max) to see what kinds of fragment shapes result.

To add a little zest, you can add a light inside Mercury. This will reflect off of the object fragments, resulting in a more realistic explosion. The easiest way to do this is to add an omni light at the center of the planet. This will affect the appearance of other objects since omni lights shine "through" objects. You would need to turn the light off until the Hold frame to avoid unwanted light on other objects.

For a more realistic effect, you can put one or more spotlights inside the planet. Spotlights are capable of casting shadows. This takes longer, but yields a more realistic result. Figure 5.38 shows what it's like to add spotlights to the scene—all those lines make it difficult. The circles in the Top viewport are the cones showing where the spotlights will illuminate the scene. The lines in the other views are simply other objects in the scenes.

Figure 5.38.
Adding lights to
the inside of
Mercury.

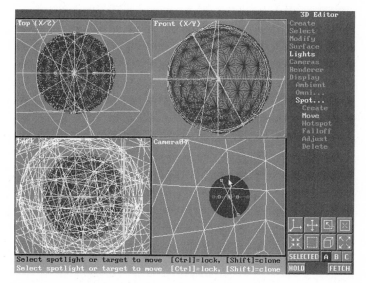

TIP

When you are dealing with masses of lines from multiple complex objects, there are two solutions. One, you can change the display geometry of individual objects to box mode. Two, you can simply zoom in—way in, as shown in Figure 5.39—until you can find what you are looking for. The lights are the four small square objects in the Front viewport at upper right.

*Figure 5.39.
Zooming in to
find objects
(lights in this
case) amid the
maze of lines.*

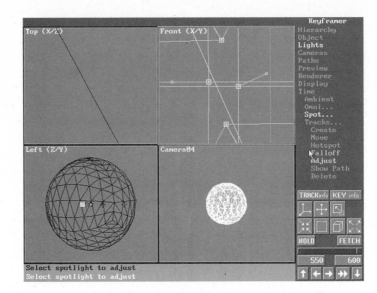

The reason for zooming in so far in Figure 5.38 is to locate the lights for making adjustments. You should set the lights to a light level of zero in frames 0 and 449, and to 255 in frame 450 (that's the frame in which the explosion takes place). That way, the lights won't interfere with other objects.

*Figure 5.40.
A self-illumi-
nated object
inside an
exploding planet.*

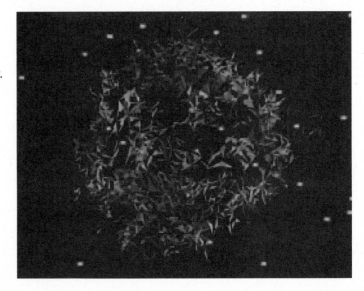

Yet another option is to create a self-illuminated object inside the planet Mercury. This might provide some of the justification for the planet exploding.... See Figure 5.40 for an example of such an object inside the planet.[18]

Figures 5.41 through 5.44 show four frames from the animation of the explosion of Mercury. Figure 5.41 shows the planet in the frame immediately preceding the breakup, and the subsequent figures were taken at eight-frame intervals thereafter.[19] The most important things to notice about the explosion are:

■ That the fragments are made up of triangles[20]

■ That the larger fragments sometimes take on an accordion-like shape

Figure 5.41.
The frame
immediately
preceding the
beginning of the
explosion.

---

[18] That spiked object is created in an interesting way that is worth an explanation. I first created a GSphere, and then selected it (Select/Object/Single). I then used Create/Object/Tessellate, and clicked the Edge button in the resulting dialog. The appearance of the sphere won't change much—apart from the new faces, that is—but if you look carefully you will see that the vertices are selected. Click the Modify/Object/3D Scale menu selection, then click the Selected button at bottom right. Click in a viewport, and then drag the mouse to the right to enlarge only the selected vertices—the result is a nice set of spikes.

[19] These frames were taken from a "trial run" of the explosion animation and do not include the object inside the planet.

[20] Why? Because faces are triangles, and fragments are made of faces.

The only way to reduce such effects is to edit the object by hand, creating the fragments yourself by welding pieces together and making groups of faces into elements, and by creating your own faces out of larger faces.

Figure 5.42.
Seven frames
after the explo-
sion.

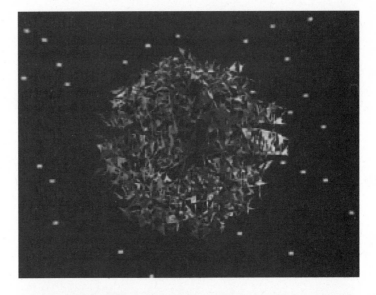

Figure 5.43.
Fifteen frames
after the explo-
sion.

Figure 5.44.
Twenty-three
frames after the
explosion.

The Solar System Gallery

During the development of the solar system model, there were many wrong turns and many interesting ones. I have collected some of the interesting images, and a few instructive ones, here for your enjoyment.

Figure 5.45.
A rendering of
the earth from an
early fly-through.

Figure 5.46.
A view of all
three inner solar
system planets.
From left to right:
the sun, Mercury
(the small dot in
front of the sun),
Venus (the larger
dot in front of the
sun), and the
Earth.

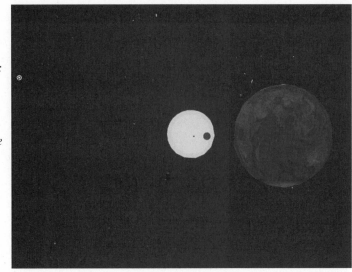

Figure 5.47.
A rendering of a
planet based on
Saturn. The
rings are merely a
flat, circular
object that was
created with
Object/Create/
Boolean. Object
one was a very
thin, square box,
and object two
was a sphere.
The boolean
operation
Intersection
results in a flat,
round object that
you can apply a
map to.

Figure 5.48. A rendering of a planet that uses a portion of the surface of Jupiter as a texture map (with a Bump setting of 1% to give some sense of height to the surface). The moons use the Bumpy Camouflage material, with the color revised toward brown to be more "plan-etary."

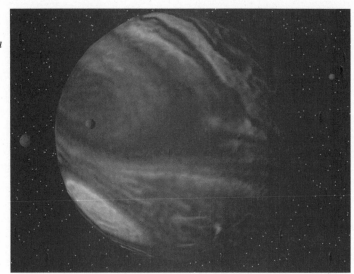

6

I CAN FLY!

Flights of Fancy

I love to fly.[1] And I know I'm not alone. So despite the fact that I've used up lots of superlatives describing various aspects of virtual reality, virtual flight is at the top of my list of Cool Stuff. As you learned in Chapter 1, it's not even hard to do. A fly-through is really an animation. This is not the same as an interactive virtual flight, where the visuals are recalculated for every frame. Because a fly-through is just an animation, it is relatively easy to play it back. You don't need hot hardware to play a fly-through, though a decent graphics subsystem doesn't hurt.

The holy grail of near-term virtual reality, however, is real-time, interactive movement, whether it be simulated flight, or walking, or driving, or whatever. On a personal computer—even one sporting a souped-up Pentium and all the hardware you can load into a single case—there just isn't enough horsepower to do all of the processing that's required to move within a virtual space in real time and still handle such mundane tasks as updating the screen. Some systems come close, but the closer they come, the more they cost. Thus, the value of the fly-through. If you insist on interactivity, you'll have to settle for lower-quality graphics. If you insist on high-quality graphics, you'll have to settle for a fly-through.[2]

Even if a fly-through isn't the holy grail, it is one of the interesting and challenging aspects of virtual reality. It takes patience and a willingness to learn a huge number of details if you want to create a sophisticated fly-through, but you can also have fun with products like Vista Pro. In this chapter, I'll show you how to fly with 3D Studio, and how to use Vista Pro and 3D Studio together for some interesting effects. For other examples of fly-throughs, see Chapters 1 and 8.

---

[1] And I'm not talking about airplanes! Maybe I should say, "I'd love to fly." But after spending so much time virtually flying, "I love to fly" is more accurate.

[2] You can simulate real-time interactivity using fly-through technology. Create an animation for every possible interactive choice, and then play the appropriate animation based on the interactive input. For example, if the user desires to enter a room, you would play an animation that moves through a door and forward into the room. If the user signals turn right, you play an animation of the viewpoint turning to the right. If the user signals turn left, you play that animation. I've included a sample of this kind of fly-through with the sample files for this chapter.

Setting Up a 3D Studio Fly-Through

You can create a complete virtual space in 3D Studio, but there are easier ways of going about the process. You can import .DXF files[3] created with other software, such as AutoCAD and many other engineering and architectural programs. A number of low-end programs also export 3D images in DXF format, such as 3D Concepts and Generic CAD. For this example, I chose the 3D image file from Chapter 3—the house and yard. This image has quite a genealogy. It started as a floor plan in the Home Design series from Autodesk, and was turned into a 3D file (with a .3DD extension) in 3D Plan. It was then loaded into 3D Concepts, and saved as a .DXF file. Now it can be loaded into 3D Studio.

3D Studio can load .DXF files directly, using the File/Load menu option (see Figure 6.1). If you accept the default values, the file will be loaded with many of the image characteristics intact. For example, objects will still be objects—the refrigerator will not decompose into its separate parts.

Figure 6.1.
Loading a .DXF
file into 3D
Studio.

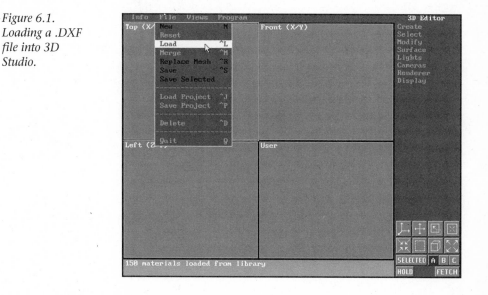

Figure 6.2 shows the house file loaded into 3D Studio. All of the pieces are there, though not always in ways that you might expect. The walls, for example, are constructed of many, many tiles. Unfortunately, this creates a lot of visual clutter, as you can see in Figure 6.2. You can get some relief from this by setting the Display/ Geometry to hide backfaces (faces on the hidden side of objects). 3D Studio also allows you to set individual objects for box display. The object is displayed as, yes, a box, which is very fast but there are no details. If you aren't working on a particular object, this is a convenience.

Figure 6.2.
The .DXF file
has been loaded
into 3D Studio.

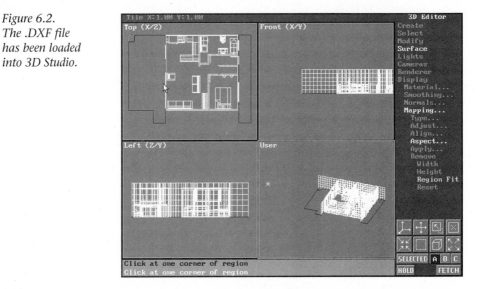

Although the file is largely intact,[4] one key element of virtual reality is missing at this point. There are no surface colors or textures on any of the objects. 3D Studio allows you to associate specific materials to objects. In fact, it has a materials editor where you can specify the characteristics of a wide variety of materials. The materials editor is sophisticated, and only the basic features are discussed in this chapter. See Chapter 8 for more on materials engineering in a virtual space.

---

[4] There were a few bugs in the loaded image. For example, several faces on the bathtub object were missing, and had to be corrected by hand. In other cases, the "face normal" of an object was set incorrectly. The face normal is the direction that a face faces. If it faces away from the camera, then you won't see anything there unless the material you chose for that face or object is two-sided. If you ever see missing objects, or missing parts of objects, it's a safe bet that some face normals are facing the wrong way. You can easily set all of an object's faces to normal normals using the Unify Normals command that uses it.

3D Studio comes with a large number of ready-to-use materials, and for the most part you can use them for this example. Specifying existing materials is easy. Select Surface/Material/Choose to select a material, and then use Surface/Material/Assign/Object to apply it to an object.[5]

3D Studio supports extended objects. That is, you can group objects together. 3D Studio calls the component objects *elements*. In the file used for this example, objects with similar characteristics are grouped together.[6] Grouped objects don't have to be "physically" together—they can be anywhere in the virtual space. Figure 6.3 shows the doors, door frames, and window frames are actually one object. The floor plan in the Top view shows this clearly, even including the bifold doors in the bedroom at the lower right. You could assign the material Teak to all of these at one time using the menu choice Surface/Material/Assign/Object, or you could assign specific materials to any one element using Surface/Material/Assign/Element.[7]

Figure 6.3.
Assigning the
material Wood -
Teak to a 3D
Studio object.

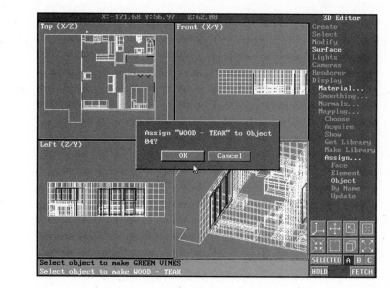

---

[5] You can apply materials to portions of an object as well. 3D Studio is extremely flexible about such things once you learn the ins and outs of the menus.

[6] This was done in the original floor plan software when groups of objects were given similar physical characteristics, such as color.

[7] This is typical of the depth (and complexity) of 3D Studio. The menu structure is not something you can learn in a day or a week; knowledge of the pathways and byways comes with experience over several months.

You must repeat this process for every group of objects in the virtual space.[8] You can draw on the extensive library of material included with 3D Studio, or you can make up your own.

Once you have added materials, the next task is to create lighting. 3D Studio offers a range of lighting options, but the most interesting are Spotlights, since they cast shadows. You can place a spotlight in the same kinds of locations that you would find in a many homes—near the ceiling, in the center of a room. Figure 6.4 shows the dialog for setting the attributes of a typical spotlight.

Figure 6.4.
Setting the
attributes for
a spotlight.

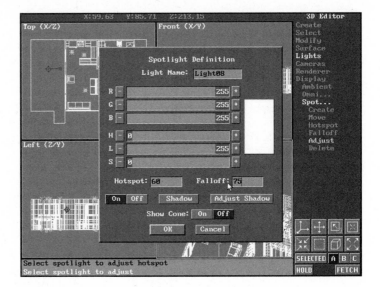

The hotspot refers to the portion of the light cone that is the brightest, while falloff refers to the zone where the light fades from bright to dark. To simulate a typical room light, the values for both should be large—large enough to brighten just about the entire room the light is in. Figure 6.5 shows the lights in place. Each light is connected to a target which determines the direction that the light shines. For this example, the target is the floor directly underneath the light. The Top view at upper left shows the lights in plan view, while the User view at bottom right shows them (and their targets) in a 3D perspective view.

---

[8] Perhaps you could try some Blue Marble for the bathroom fixtures, or a nice Almond for the appliances in the kitchen. If you don't find the color, texture, or material you want, you can probably create using the various tools in the materials editor.

Figure 6.5.
Adding lights to
a virtual space.

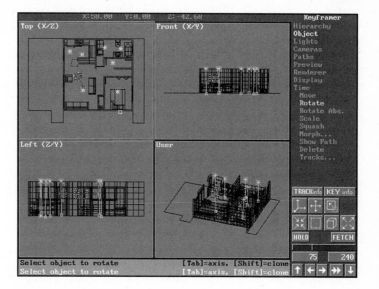

We have the set, we have the lights—the next step is a camera.

Flying the Camera

Before you can fly the camera, you need to create one with the Camera/Create menu choice. As with lights, you place both the camera and the target at which it is aimed.[9] Figure 6.6 shows a camera and a target. I set the camera for the beginning of the fly-through, on the patio outside the doors. It is at approximately eye height. The target is only a short distance away. This was a deliberate choice—it wouldn't work very well to have the target very far away since the camera will be moving about in a relatively cramped space. You may, however, set the target arbitrarily far from the camera. For example, you could move the camera a large distance away and use a zoom lens setting to bring the subject closer in the camera view.

Once the camera has been created, you have all of the ingredients needed for the fly-through. Move now to the Keyframer by pressing the F4 key. In the Keyframer, you can create animation frames for the fly-through.

---

[9] 3D Studio has some interesting support for camera features. One of my favorite features is the ability to set the focal length of the lens, using the same values you would use for a standard 35mm lens. For example, for interior shooting, you would typically use a wide-angle lens. For this example, I used a 28mm lens. A wider lens would show more of the room, but it also adds distortion—just like a real lens.

Figure 6.6.
Adding a camera
and target to the
virtual space.

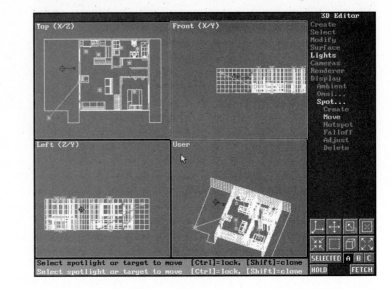

Strictly speaking, 3D Studio does not allow you to fly cameras as part of an animation. Nor can you move or fly a camera target. The trick is to create a *dummy object*,
using the Hierarchy menu. A dummy object has many of the characteristics of a
real object—you can move it, scale it, rotate it, etc.—but it is invisible when the
scene or animation is rendered. Figure 6.7 shows the Keyframer screen, and a
dummy object has been created. It is marked by a dotted outline, to make it stand
out from normal objects.[10]

Once you have created the dummy object, link the camera and the target to it using
the Hierarchy/Link menu selection. Do this once for the camera, and once for the
target. Once you have created the links, be careful to move only the dummy object, not the camera or target individually.

It is very easy to create the path the camera will follow for the fly-through. There
are at least two useful ways to do it, and I will explain both of them. The first method
involves setting specific camera positions at regular frame intervals. In this example,

---

[10] It is obvious that the dummy object was created in the Top view. That is the only view where
the dummy object and the camera line up. This is a hazard of using a 2D interface to create 3D
objects: you can only work in one plane at a time. If you look at the Front or Left views, you can
see that the dummy object was created at the default zero level in the 3D space. It's a simple matter
to move the object in, say, the Front view to put it in the same position as the camera. In fact,
since it is invisible, you can put it right over the camera with no ill effects.

I set a new camera position every 15 frames. The second method involves setting the initial camera position in frame 1, and the final camera position in the last frame, and then creating camera positions along the default path and moving them into position. The second technique requires a deeper knowledge of the way the 3D Studio works, but it can be very useful as a first-draft for a path.

Figure 6.7.
Adding a dummy
object to the
scene.

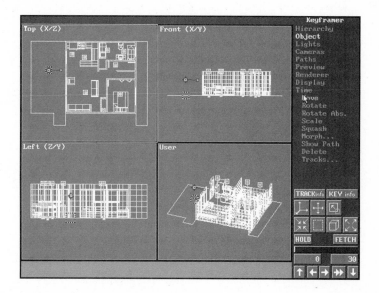

You can use the Time menu or the buttons at the bottom right of the Keyframer screen to move to specific frame numbers. You can also set the total number of frames to be used for the animation. A typical animation uses 15 frames per second. If you want the fly-through to move at a natural speed, you'll need to calculate the distance of the total flight and decide how long it should take. In this example, it should take about eight seconds to move from the patio to the bathroom, which will require 240 frames. The final version of this fly-through, which you can find on the CD-ROM, is somewhat longer and uses 360 frames.

At each camera position (every 15 frames in this example), there are two camera settings to adjust: position and rotation. For example, after the camera "walks" in through the patio door, it must turn left. If you do not rotate the camera to follow the change in direction, it will give the appearance of facing sideways. Sometimes, this will be the effect you want, but it is often awkward for the viewer.

To change the camera position, use the Object/Move menu selection. Then click on the dummy object and move it to the new location. Fifteen frames is just one second, so you shouldn't move it too far. In fact, sometimes you may want to leave the position of the dummy object unchanged, and simply change the rotation. This mimics a person turning in place. As a general rule, if you move fast, don't use rotation. If you use a fast rotation, don't use much other movement.

To change the camera rotation, use the Object/Rotate menu selection. You then can click on the dummy object to rotate it. There are three axes of rotation available; press the Tab key to change from one to the next. Use the Top view for best results and control. Most rotation will be from side to side, either to match changes in the camera path, or to look at interesting objects in the virtual space. You can simulate looking up and down by applying rotations in the Left or Front views, depending on which direction the camera is facing at the time.

Figure 6.8 shows a set of views in the Keyframer that have been set up for working with a camera path. The view at the upper left shows the patio, and the camera is inside the dummy object at upper left. The Front view shows the entire home, with the camera located just to the left of the house. The lower-left view is a plan view that shows the entire camera path,[11] starting at the top left-center of the view, and moving toward the bottom of the view. The view at bottom right is a view through the camera lens from the current camera position on the patio.[12]

Figure 6.8.
The Keyframer
set up for
working with a
camera path.
Note the exist-
ence of a path in
the lower-left
view, marked
User.

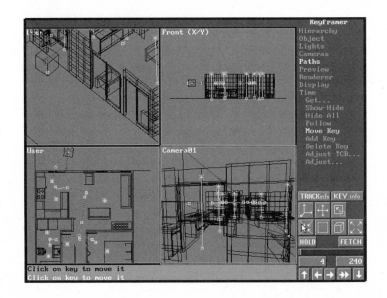

---

[11] To see the camera path, you must use the Paths or Camera menu and click on Show Path. Normally, an object's path is hidden.

[12] This view is of frame 4, so the camera hasn't really begun to move yet. It is still very close to its starting position.

You can use the Paths/Move Key menu selection to adjust the camera position at key frames. 3D Studio will automatically alter the intervening points between the key frames.[13] To see a very rough approximation of your animation, make the Camera view the active view by clicking in it, and then click the double-arrow icon at bottom right to play the animation. For a complex scene, playback may be delayed in order to draw all of the objects in the scene. If this is the case, playback speed may vary depending on how many objects are in the scene at any given frame.

To see a rough, but real-time preview, click the Preview/Make menu selection. This will take some time to create, but not nearly as long as it takes to render the scene.

You also can have a little fun with a fly-through. Before you render the animation, find places in the scene where you can personalize the virtual space. For example, you might want to hang a painting, or display a vase full of flowers. Adding details to just a few objects can transform a dull, dreary scene into one that is interesting.

For example, I couldn't resist adding a painting to this particular fly-through. Despite the presence of furniture and appliances, the walls were inescapably bare. Figure 6.9 shows how it is done.

*Figure 6.9.
Adding a
painting to a
scene.*

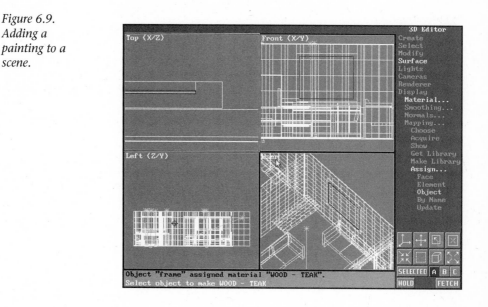

---

[13] A key frame is any frame in which you have established a position for the object. In this example, that would be 15, 30, 45, ... and so on.

The view at bottom right shows the painting selected; these are the darkest lines in the viewport. The object that will be the painting itself is the only object selected, but there is also a frame around it. You can see one corner of the frame in the Top viewport. Note that the painting is recessed inside the frame to help yield a 3D appearance. In addition to this painting, I added a wall mirror to the bathroom.

But these are just objects, created in the 3D Editor and modified slightly until they are just the right size.[14] The materials editor is where the magic takes place. Figure 6.10 shows a materials editor screen.[15] The currently selected material is called "Painting of Me." This is the material that gets applied to the thin rectangle inside the frame (see Figure 6.9). It has the following characteristics:

Figure 6.10. Creating a material with texture and reflection maps.

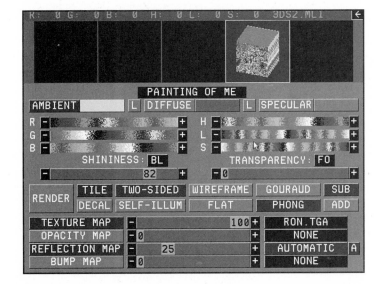

■ The shininess factor is set to 82 out of 100. This insures that the painting will reflect the scene around it, just as you would expect of a real painting behind glass. You also could create a glass object, but this is easier.

---

[14] All of these added objects started out with the Create/Box command. I did a little nipping and tucking with the Create/Object/Boolean command to make everything fit properly.

[15] Please excuse the appearance of the scroll bars near the center of the image, and of the samples at the top of the image. They don't actually look like that. In order to capture the screen, I had to use a 16-color VGA graphics mode. Normally, you would use the materials editor in a 256-color mode.

- For safety's sake, I made this a two-sided material. That means that no matter which way the face normals point, you will see the painting. This is a cheap but common trick.

- Two of the four buttons at the bottom of the image are highlighted: texture map and reflection map. The texture map is set to a file, ron.tga, which is an image of me taken from a video file that accompanied an earlier book. The texture map slider is set to 100, which means that the image will be used 100 percent of the object. If it were set to a lower number, the colors set above for ambient, diffuse, and specular would show through to some degree.

- The reflection map is set to automatic. This tells 3D Studio to handle reflections of the surrounding space automatically. The reflection map slider is set to 25, which means that only a partial reflection will occur— this is intended to imitate the behavior of real glass, which only reflects a similar small percentage of the light that strikes it.

To save this material in the materials library, use the Materials menu at the top of the screen. Choose Put Material from the drop-down menu. You must re-put a material if you change it in any way after creating it.

TIP

If you create a reflection map for a flat object, there are special rules to follow when you assign the material to an object. The most important is to make sure that you attach the material with a reflection map only to the actual faces that will do the reflecting. If you apply it to the whole object, 3D Studio will decide which face to apply reflections to, and it may not be the one you want!

Figure 6.11 shows the dialog box that appears if you click on the automatic button. For most reflection maps, you can use an anti-aliasing setting of Low—objects in a reflection map are usually small, and don't require much anti-aliasing. However, for objects that are flat, you *must* click Yes for Flat mirror, or you will not get acceptable results. 3D Studio uses a different reflection algorithm for flat objects.

If the object with reflection map will be stationary, then click on the First Frame Only button to activate it. This instructs 3D Studio to create the maps used for reflections only once, which will avoid a lot of unnecessary rendering time.

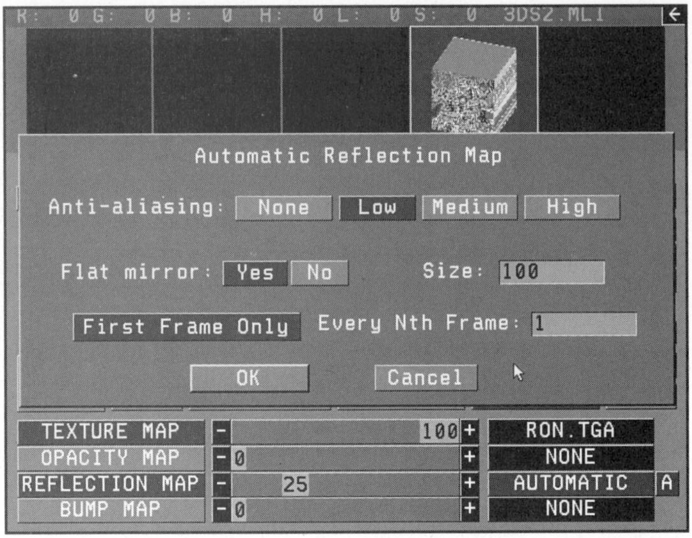

Figure 6.11.
Automatic
reflection map
settings for a
material used
with flat objects.

For the mirror in the bathroom, I modified an existing 3D Studio material called Chrome Sky (see Figure 6.12). The settings are similar to that for the painting, but there is no texture map and the reflection map is set to 100 percent. This material is also two-sided,[16] and the settings for automatic reflection map are the same as shown in Figure 6.10.

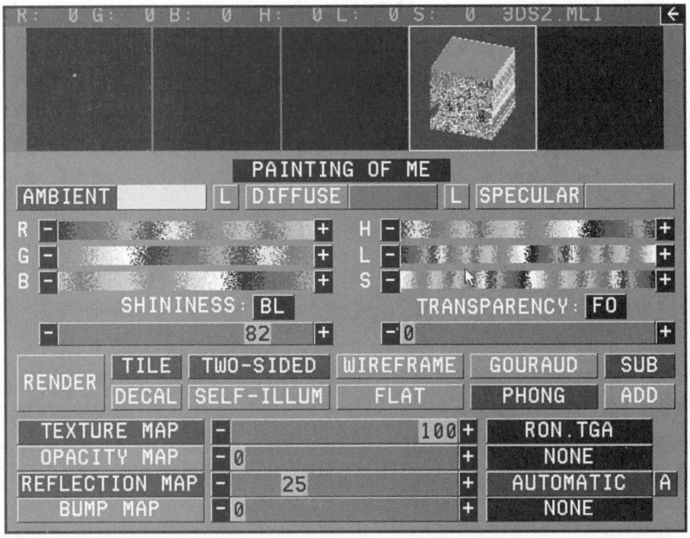

Figure 6.12.
Settings for a
mirror material.

---

[16] More out of laziness than necessity.

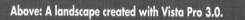

Above: A landscape created with Vista Pro 3.0.

Below: The "Valley of the Ear in Morning Light," a landscape created with Vista Pro 3.0 (and based on a PCX image of a man's head).

Above: A Vista Pro 3.0 rendering in progress.

Below: A view of Mt. St. Helens created with Vista Pro 3.0.

Right: Another view of Mt. St. Helens, using a low lighting angle to simulate sunrise.

Figure 1.66: Four sample frames from a morph animation (frames 1, 20, 40, and 60).

Above: Four frames from a Vista Pro morph (created using Vista Morph). This is a sample screen from the CD-ROM application that allows you to view figures. It uses Compel, from Asymetrix, for the presentation.

Left: A view of El Capitan, rendered in Vista Pro 3.0 from USGS data in DEM (digital elevation model) format.

Above: An example of a landscape rendered with a polygon setting of 1.

Above right: a polygon setting of 8.

Right: A DEM landscape exported as a PCX file.

Below: A panorama created using three Vista Pro images, rotating the viewpoint 90 degrees for each subsequent image.

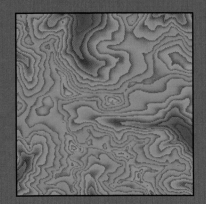

Above: A Vista Pro 3.0 rendering of Crater Lake, Oregon.

Below: A view of a house under construction with Virtual Reality Studio 2.0.

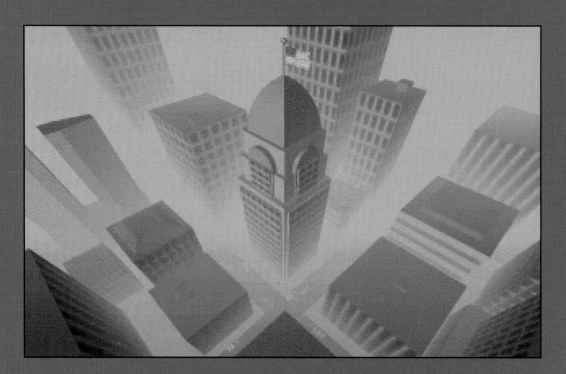

Above: A fanciful cityscape rendered in Autodesk 3D Studio 2.0.

Below: St. Paul's Cathedral rendered in 3D Studio 2.0.

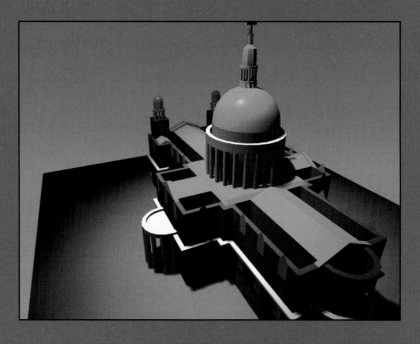

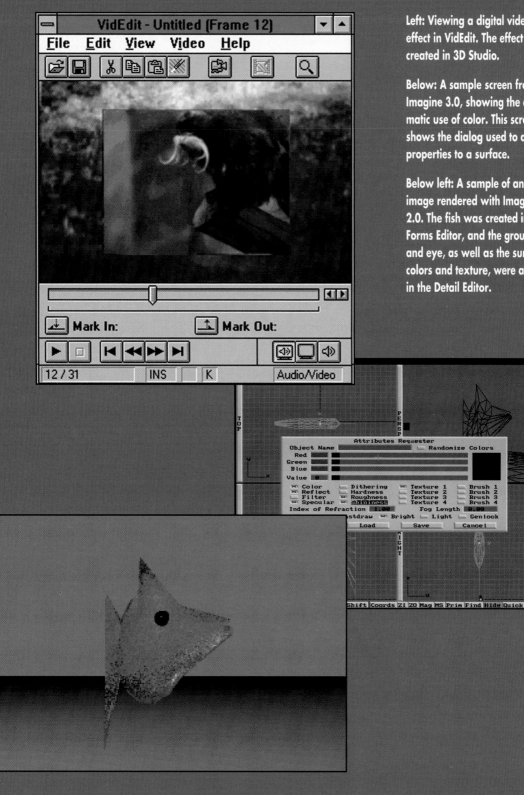

Left: Viewing a digital video effect in VidEdit. The effect was created in 3D Studio.

Below: A sample screen from Imagine 3.0, showing the dramatic use of color. This screen shows the dialog used to assign properties to a surface.

Below left: A sample of an image rendered with Imagine 2.0. The fish was created in the Forms Editor, and the ground and eye, as well as the surface colors and texture, were added in the Detail Editor.

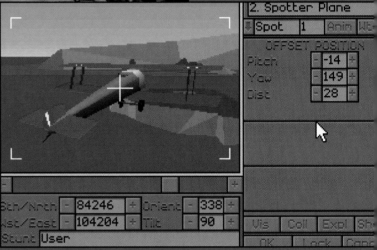

Above: A sample navigation screen in Stunt Island.

Right: Setting up a prop in Stunt Island.

Below: A frame from a video that combines a Vista Pro landscape and a 3D Studio object (the helicopter).

Above left and above right: Two frames from the animation of the exploding planet.

Left: An overview of the solar system animation, showing the three innermost planets and the camera-carrying rocket.

Below: A sample screen shot of the 3D Studio Materials Editor, showing the creating of the surface of planet Earth.

Sun

Earth

Venus

Rocket/Camera

Mercury

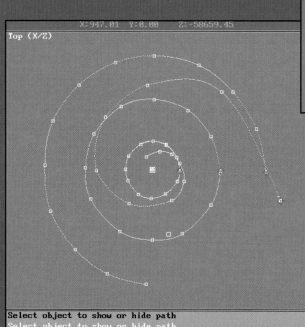

Left: A sample 3D Studio screen, showing the paths of the various planets and rockets in the Solar System animation.

Above: A fanciful landscape created with Vista Pro 3.0. The artificial lens flare was added using PhotoShop 2.5 for Windows.

Left: A 3D red/blue image created with Vista Pro 3.0. When viewed through red/blue 3D glasses, the 3D shape (Mt. St. Helens) is evident.

Left: Successive magnification of the Mandelbrot fractal set.

Below: A series of images showing a morph from a frog to a chick.

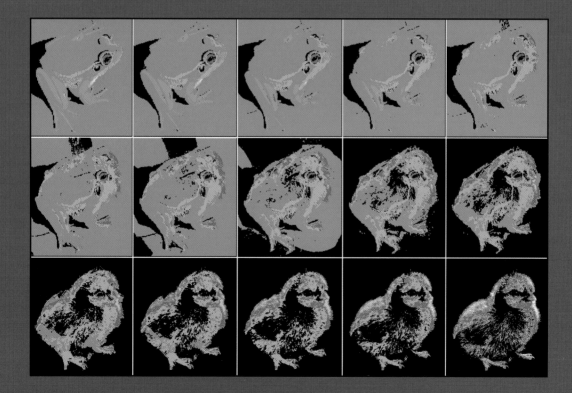

Above: A scene from a Virtual Reality Studio world. The background is a bitmap that has been loaded as a border.

Right: An example of a video frame being altered in Photoshop.

Below: A sample view of a Media Merge Story Board session, showing eight video files loaded.

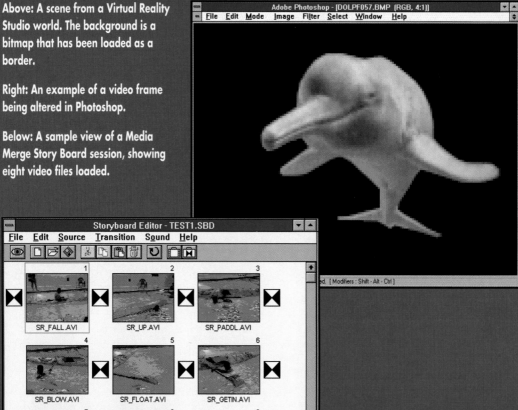

Above: A sample view of a Media Merge Scene Editor session, showing two video files being overlaid. Chroma Key was used to eliminate the background of the video in Track 2.

Leftt: A three-video composite.

Right: A sample frame from an animation that uses a morph in 3D Studio. The morph allows the solid figure (a cylinder) to appear to move.

Below: A sample 3D Studio screen, showing the use of color. Yellow is used to indicate lights, and blue to indicate a camera. Black represents objects.

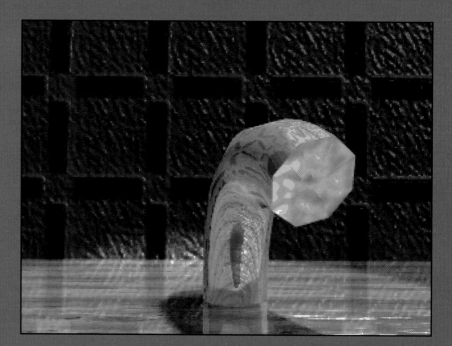

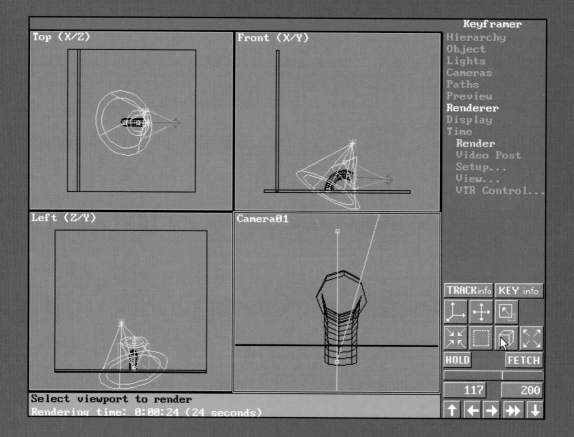

Top (X/Z)

Front (X/Y)

Left (Z/Y)

Camera01

Keyframer
Hierarchy
Object
Lights
Cameras
Paths
Preview
Renderer
Display
Time
  Render
  Video Post
  Setup...
  View...
  VTR Control...

TRACKinfo KEYinfo

HOLD   FETCH

117   200

Select viewport to render
Rendering time: 0:00:24 (24 seconds)

Right: That's my wife, Donna, showing how to work with a Power Glove and 3D glasses. This and the photographic image on the next page were created by capturing video from a camcorder using the Video Spigot.

Below: An example showing how the on-screen hand mimics the actions of the Power Glove in Rend 386.

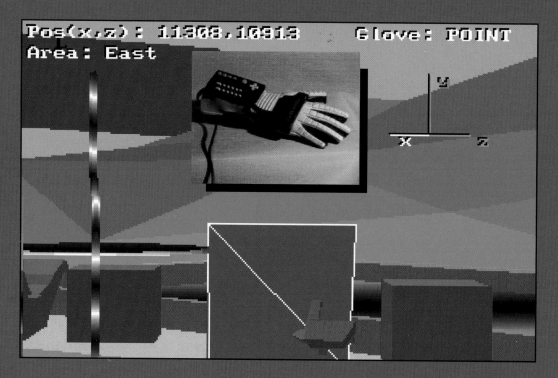

Above: A sample screen from Rend 386, and a photo of a Power Glove superimposed.

Below: A view of the Morph/Warp Editor in Photomorph.

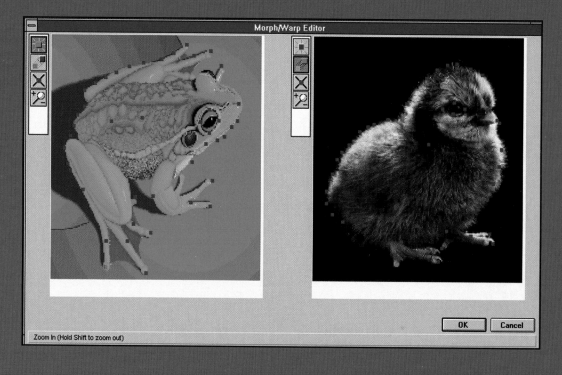

The fly-through animation file is on the CD-ROM with the files for this chapter. Figures 6.13 through 6.16 show various scenes from the animation.

Figure 6.13. Frame 5 from the 360-frame animation of the house fly-through.

Figure 6.14. Frame 83 from the 360-frame animation of the house fly-through.

Figure 6.15. Frame 283 from the 360-frame animation of the house fly-through.

Figure 6.16. Frame 360 from the 360-frame animation of the house fly-through.

Fly-Through via Helicopter

The last section was more of a walk-through than a fly-through, but this section will more than make up for that with an exciting helicopter fly-through of Crater Lake, Oregon. It will take the combined resources of both Vista Pro and 3D Studio, but it's worth it.

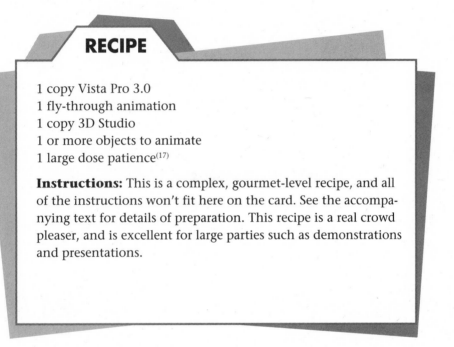

RECIPE

1 copy Vista Pro 3.0
1 fly-through animation
1 copy 3D Studio
1 or more objects to animate
1 large dose patience[17]

Instructions: This is a complex, gourmet-level recipe, and all of the instructions won't fit here on the card. See the accompanying text for details of preparation. This recipe is a real crowd pleaser, and is excellent for large parties such as demonstrations and presentations.

Chapter 1 covered the details of creating an animation with Vista Pro, and you'll build on that in this section. The basic steps in the complete process are:

■ Create the fly-through animation using Vista Pro and Flight Director.

■ Analyze the data in Flight Director to determine the lighting angles on the helicopter at various points in the animation.

■ Record the relative positions of the sun and the helicopter in a table for reference in 3D Studio.

---

[17] This is a frequently needed ingredient in VR recipes—keep plenty on hand in the cupboard.

- Create a helicopter as an object in 3D Studio, as well as a screen and a camera. Position the helicopter between the camera and the box.

- Create a material that uses the fly-through animation as a texture map.[18]

- Apply the material to a box the same relative size as the animation (320x240 and 320x200 are the two most common sizes).

- Create a light and position it according to the table you created from studying Flight Director for frame 1.

- Animate the helicopter to create realistic lighting and motion.

- Render!

Admittedly, this is a long list of tasks, but the results are well worth it. The entire process isn't as tedious as it sounds; some of these steps are easy. Others, of course, will tax your patience heavily.

Analyze the Data

Figure 6.17 shows the map portion of the Flight Director screen after the path has already been created. Since the goal is to track the relationship between the helicopter and the sun, I have taken the liberty of putting icons into the map image to indicate their relative positions at the start of the animation. The sun is located to the east (north is at the top of the map), and stays there throughout the animation. The helicopter, however, twists and turns as it follows its path. If you don't add a light that moves, the helicopter won't look very realistic. The lighting on the scene will be coming from one direction, and the lighting on the helicopter will be coming from a different direction. This is subtle, but it is an important consideration if realism is your goal.

It would be more precise to consider the sun angle for each and every frame, but that's not realistic—there are 615 frames in the animation! Instead, you only need to identify key points along the path where the sun angle on the helicopter changes. Figure 6.18 shows the key points along the path, with the frame numbers for those points.[19]

---

[18] Yes, you can use an animation as a texture map. You can either save the animation as a .FLC file, or you can use a series of bitmaps by providing a list of the bitmaps in a text file.

[19] Finding the frame numbers is easy. As you move along the path in Flight Director, it displays the frame number on the screen.

Figure 6.17.
A path in Flight
Director.

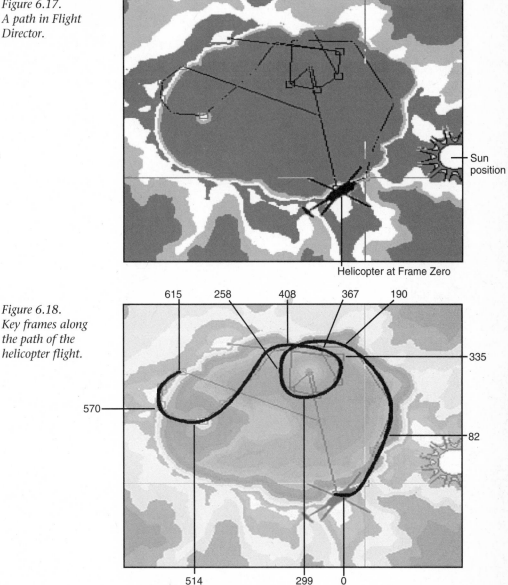

Sun
position

Helicopter at Frame Zero

Figure 6.18.
Key frames along
the path of the
helicopter flight.

There's a second level of analysis that you may also wish to perform: banking. The Flight Director will bank the virtual aircraft during turns. This causes an apparent tilt of the landscape. If you want the last touch of realism, you can record the bank angles for various frames and then use that list to adjust the bank angle of the helicopter in 3D Studio.

Record Relative Positions

The easiest way to record the sun angle is to create a chart. Figure 6.19 shows the kind of chart I use, although the pretty helicopter and sun pictures are replaced with an arrow and a small circle, drawn by hand. In Figure 6.19, the left most column is a frame number. In the middle column, the sun is held constant on the east side of the box, and the position of the helicopter at each frame changes.[20] These positions are easy to determine—the process doesn't require much thinking. With so many variables to keep track of, a minimum of thinking is a good thing.

Figure 6.19. Determining and normalizing the angle between the sun and the helicopter.

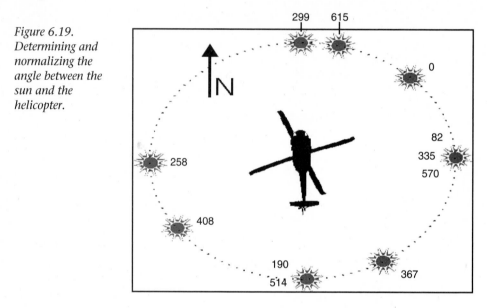

The next step is to normalize[21] for the helicopter; the reason for this will be evident in a moment. To normalize, use your imagination to rotate the helicopter and the sun together until the helicopter is facing straight up. This keeps the angle between the helicopter and the sun constant, resulting in a nice, neat normalized column of figures (the right column).

---

[20] The position of the helicopter is assumed to be tangent to the direction of motion for this example. If you set targets for nodes, this will change the situation. The direction the helicopter is facing, toward the target, is used as the position instead of the tangent.

[21] Normalizing is a common mathematical operation. Normally, it means keeping one variable constant and adjusting all of the other variables appropriately.

You're almost done now. The final step is to combine all of the images from the right column into a single image, as shown in Figure 6.20. I added the frame numbers to the diagram to make it easier to work with the illustration in 3D Studio. If you want to look ahead, Figure 6.24 shows how this drawing corresponds to the location of the light in various frames.

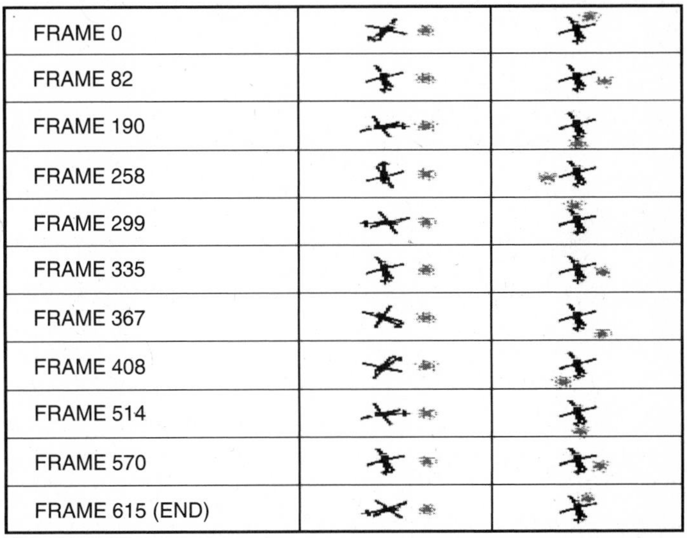

Figure 6.20.
Illustration to
keep at hand
while working in
3D Studio.

FRAME 0		
FRAME 82		
FRAME 190		
FRAME 258		
FRAME 299		
FRAME 335		
FRAME 367		
FRAME 408		
FRAME 514		
FRAME 570		
FRAME 615 (END)		

If you want to also add bank angle for that extra touch of realism, you'll need to step through the frames in Flight Director and record the frames in which the bank angle changes. Table 6.1 shows the variation of the bank angle for the first 100 frames of the animation.

Table 6.1. Bank Angle Changes in an Animation.

Frame	Bank angle
0	-8
2	-7
4	-6
7	-5
12	-4

continues

Table 6.1. continued

Frame	Bank angle
14	-3
16	-2
19	-1
21	0
28	1
31	2
48	1
53	0
62	-1
65	-2
70	-3
72	-4
92	-3
96	-2

Use the slider at the bottom right of the Flight Director screen to step through the frames and examine the bank angle. The bank angle is displayed at the right center of the screen.

Create a Helicopter and Other Objects

There are two ways to create a helicopter in 3D Studio: from scratch, or out of the box. Fortunately, 3D Studio includes a sample file with a helicopter already in it, which you can use for this demonstration. Figure 6.21 shows the helicopter loaded into the 3D Editor. The "screen" that will be used for the animation also is evident, particularly in the Top and Left views—it's right there in front of the helicopter. It's a simple box, but a very thin one. The animation image size is 320x200, so you should use the same proportion for the screen. Create it in the Front viewport to make life easy.

Figure 6.21.
A helicopter and
a screen in 3D
Studio's 3D
Editor.

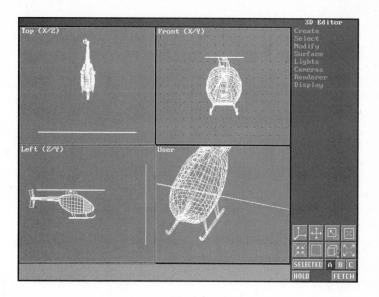

The helicopter is made up of three separate objects:[22] the main rotor, the tail rotor, and the helicopter body. There are two levels of animation involved. The rotors, naturally, must rotate in relation to the body. The body then must move up and down, and bank left and right to make realistic movements as determined by the analysis of the animation path.

The rotor animation should be considered part of the process of creating the helicopter. That way, it will be there when you need it. To create the rotor animations, determine the number of frames to use for one revolution; I used a setting of 30 frames, but you may prefer a faster or slower rotor. I chose 30 frames because that seemed to provide a sense of rotor motion. After moving to frame 30, I rotated each of the rotors through 360 degrees. That would only result in one rotation. To create a repeating rotation, click on the Key Info button at the bottom right of the screen and then on the rotor. This displays the Key Info dialog (see Figure 6.22).

Click the Repeat button to make this a repeating animation. That's all there is to it. Do the same for the rear rotor. Then use the Hierarchy/Link menu selection to link each of the rotors to the helicopter body. Now you have a helicopter, complete with rotors that rotate without any further fuss.

---

[22] Each of the objects has some individual elements, but they can be ignored for the purposes of this description. For example, the main rotor and the rotor shaft were created as separate objects, but they are joined together during all phases of the animation and thus can be considered as one object.

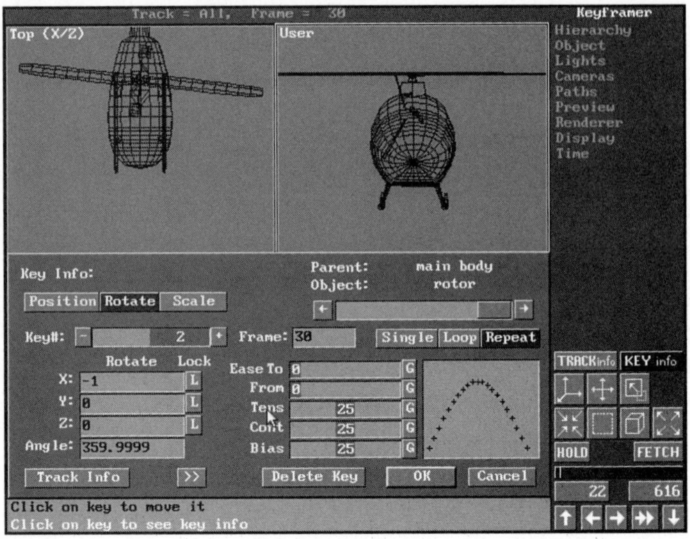

Figure 6.22.
The Key Info
dialog.

There are two more objects to create: a camera and a spotlight.[23] The camera requires only a little care to set up. The steps are:

■ Create the camera with the Camera/Create menu selection. Place the
camera directly behind the helicopter body. A longer lens setting works
best; try something in the range of 85mm to 135mm. Adjust the camera
position with the Dolly command until the right and left edges of the
screen are just outside the camera viewport.[24] Ignore the extra space at top
and bottom—the screen is matched to the image size, and if you also set
320x200 as the output size, the extra space will not appear in the rendered
frame even though you can see it in the viewport. See Figure 6.23 to see
what the camera viewport should look like at frame zero.

Figure 6.23 also shows the correct position of the spotlight for the beginning of
the animation. In the Top view, it is located at the right of the helicopter and slightly
forward. In the Front view, you can see that the light is also located slightly above
the helicopter. This angle, too, is derived from the sun position in the original file.

---

[23] It doesn't have to be a spotlight, but a spotlight creates shadows which add interest to the scene.

[24] You did remember to use Control-V to bring up the viewport dialog and make one of the views
a camera view, right?

Figure 6.23.
Setting up the
camera viewport.

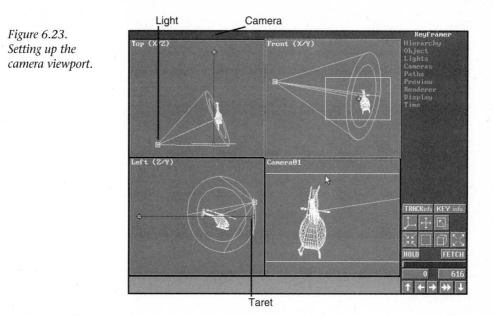

Just for fun, I have tilted the helicopter aggressively forward. This is not necessary, but gives the opening frame a sense of action and urgency. As a final touch, also link the spotlight target to the helicopter body. This will insure that the helicopter is always illuminated.

Animation as Texture Map

You can use an animation as a texture map using the same procedures as described earlier for bitmaps. Use the materials editor to create a new material, and select the .FLC file created with the pcx2flc utility (it comes with Vista Pro) as the texture map. Set the texture map slider to 100 percent. During rendering, each frame of the animation will use the corresponding frame from the fly-through animation in the .FLC file. It's all automatic.

All you need to do is use Material/Object/Assign menu selection to apply the material to the screen. If you want to avoid checking face normals, make the material two-sided.

Lighting

The light is the key to a realistic final result. With all of the analysis already performed, it's easy to animate the light correctly. With a worksheet similar to Figure 6.21 at hand, you can easily animate the light correctly. Look at Figure 6.24—it shows the desired result. If you look closely, you'll see that the key points along the light's path correspond to the points in Figure 6.21. To arrive at this happy conclusion, move to each frame listed in Figure 6.21 and move the light to a point corresponding to the orientation shown in the right column of Figure 6.21. When this is complete, display the path for the light. It should look like Figure 6.24. You may need to add key points, or move a few around, to get the best results.

Figure 6.24.
The fully
animated
spotlight.

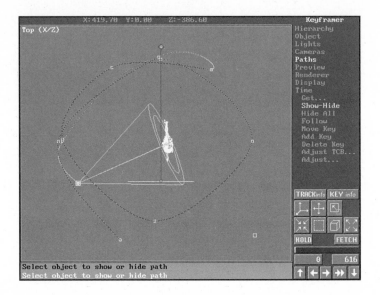

Animate Helicopter

There are two kinds of movement that you can apply to the helicopter. One is simple bobs and weaves based on the animation. The other is bank adjustments to adjust for turns. If you plan to add the bank adjustments, you should make them first. These are simple adjustments—move to the frames where the bank angle changes, and adjust the bank angle one degree plus or minus as needed. Once this is done, you can add all the bobs and weaves you want.

To change the bank angle, work in the Front viewport. Use the Rotate command to make the changes; press Tab to change the axis of rotation to the correct one. For bobbing and weaving, you can tilt forward and backward, or move the helicopter around. Figure 6.25 shows the path for the helicopter. The path doesn't show the numerous rotational changes, only the bobbing and weaving.

TIP

If you only make position changes in the Front view, you will keep the helicopter in the correct relationship to the screen—no closer, and no further.

Figure 6.25.
The path for the
helicopter body.

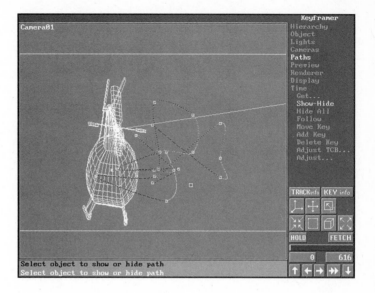

Render

Figure 6.26 shows four views of the helicopter at frame 503, near the end of the animation. Figure 6.27 shows a rendering (at 640x480, instead of the smaller 320x200 used for the animation) of the image for this frame. You also can render the animation at 160x100 if you want to have a much shorter rendering time and can settle for a lower resolution.

Figure 6.26.
Frame 503 in the
Keyframer.

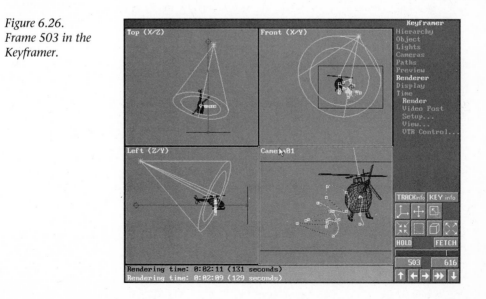

Figure 6.27.
A rendering of
frame 503.

Gallery

Figures 6.28 through 6.38 show the "key frames" identified for the lighting changes. Even if you aren't able to play the animation from the CD, you can see from these figures how the lighting angle, banking angle, and position changes are used to provide a realistic-looking helicopter addition to the fly-through.

Figure 6.28.
Frame 0 of the
animation. The
light is coming
from forward and
to the right of the
helicopter.

Figure 6.29. Frame 82 of the animation. This figure shows a bank of -4 degrees.

Figure 6.30. Frame 190 of the animation. This figure shows a bank of -5 degrees, and the helicopter has been moved to a low position in the frame. The lighting is now coming from behind the camera.

Figure 6.31. Frame 258 of the animation. The light is now on the opposite side of the helicopter from where it started.

Figure 6.32. Frame 299 of the animation. In this frame, the light is directly ahead, and slightly above, the helicopter.

*Figure 6.33.
Frame 335 of the
animation. The
helicopter has
come full circle,
360 degrees. The
lighting is now
back at the right
side of the
helicopter. The
bank angle is
zero.*

*Figure 6.34.
Frame 367 of the
animation. The
light is nearly
behind the
camera again.*

*Figure 6.35.
Frame 408 of the
animation. A
minor shift from
the previous
figure: the light is
now behind and
to the left. The
bank angle is -6.
This frame is a
particularly good
example of how a
correct bank
angle adds to the
realism of the
animation.*

*Figure 6.36.
Frame 514 of the
animation. I
added some spice
at this point in
the animation—
the camera has
begun to zoom in
on the helicopter.
The light is
nearly exactly
behind the
camera.*

Figure 6.37.
Frame 570 of the
animation. The
zoom is complete.
I moved the
helicopter to the
lower right corner
of the frame more
to keep it out of
the way during
the zoom than
for any other
reason.

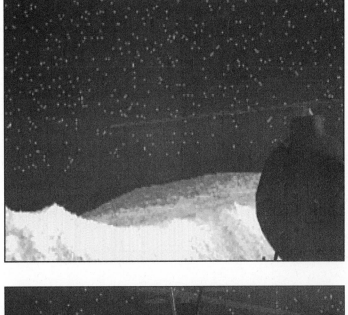

Figure 6.38.
Frame 615 of the
animation. To
conclude the
animation, the
helicopter jumps
quickly to the
center top of the
frame, and looks
over the entire
lake after coming
over the crest of
the ridge. This
was an attempt
to add a touch of
breathlessness to
the animation,
a feeling of
swooping into the
overview.

7

FRACTALLY YOURS

What Is a Fractal?

By now, almost everyone has heard of fractals. A few years ago, that wasn't the case, and fractals were a hot item. Perhaps you remember the image shown in Figure 7.1. This is the famous Mandelbrot set, a fractal universe whose exact dimension has never been determined.

Figure 7.1.
The Mandelbrot
set.

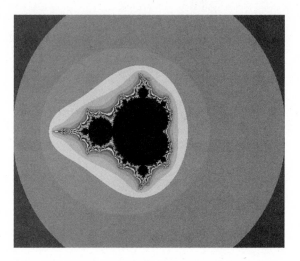

That statement requires a little explanation. A zero-dimensional universe consists of a single point (see Figure 7.2). There would be only one place to be, and that place would be infinitely small.[1] A one-dimensional universe exists as a single line, extending from infinity in one direction to infinity in the opposite direction (see Figure 7.3). A two-dimensional universe is a plane, a flat surface extending

---

[1]That's the nature of a point: it has no size.

outward in all directions[2] (see Figure 7.4). A three-dimensional universe extends everywhere in all directions, just like the one we live in (see Figure 7.5). A four dimensional universe would have to add another direction, but "where" it would go is pure conjecture. If we allow non-space dimensions, of course, we can add time as a dimension. Mathematically speaking, we can create and play with as many dimensions as we want.

Figure 7.2. A zero-dimensional universe.

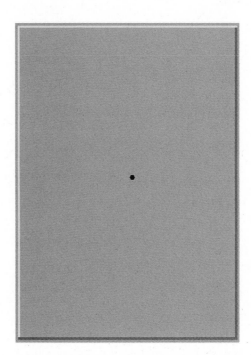

*Figure 7.3
A one-
dimensional
universe.*

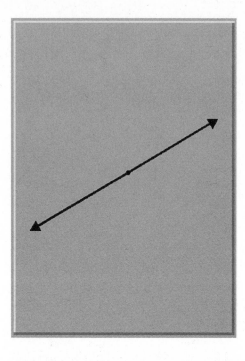

*Figure 7.4.
A two-
dimensional
universe.*

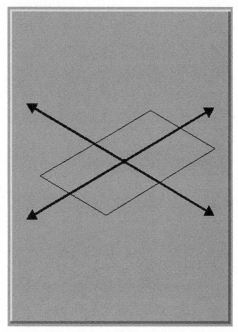

Figure 7.5.
A three-
dimensional
universe.

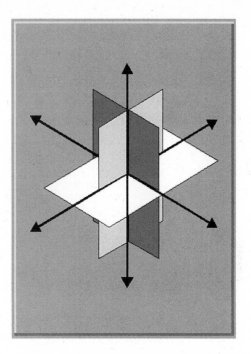

Despite their differences, all these universes share one thing in common: the dimension that defines them is a whole number. The word *fractal* comes from the concept of fractional dimensions.

What would a universe of, say, 2.3 dimensions look like? Well, it would look like Figure 7.6, since you asked. It has, as you might expect, a dimension between that of a plane and a 3D space.

This fractal object does look suspiciously like a mountain. To see exactly why it has a fractal dimension, we must delve a bit deeper into the nature of fractal reality. The Mandelbrot set offers a perfect example.

Figure 7.6.
An object with a
fractal dimension
of 2.3.

The Mandelbrot set is a collection of points that obey certain rules, specified by an equation. The mathematics of those rules are complicated, but they boil down to this: a point is in the Mandelbrot set if it obeys the rules.[3]

Certain characteristics of the Mandelbrot set are generic fractal characteristics. For example, look at Figures 7.7 and 7.8. Each of these figures contains four images based on the Mandelbrot set. Let's start with Figure 7.7. Each image is labeled *a* through *d*. Image *a* is the original Mandelbrot set, with the central region marked with a white square. Image *b* enlarges the part of image *a* in the square. Images *c* and *d* are further enlargements. Figure 7.8 continues this process. (That is, image *a* in Figure 7.8 is an enlargement of image *d* in Figure 7.7.)

---

[3]OK: if you really want to know, read on. The Mandelbrot set is defined in the complex plane. The traditional X-axis consists of real numbers, and the Y-axis consists of complex numbers. Coordinates are specified as a combination of a real and a complex number. To test a point, you plug it into the formula and see what happens. Each iteration of the formula yields a new point in the plane. If every new point generated from a test point lies within the defined region (+2 and -2 on both axes), the test point is in the Mandelbrot set. If even one of the new points wanders outside the region, it is not in the Mandelbrot set. The black area in a Mandelbrot image is the actual Mandelbrot set. Plugging one of these points into the equation yields an infinite series of points, all of which are between +2 and -2 on the x-and y-axes. The colored or shaded bands outside the black area are defined by the number of iterations of the formula required to find a point outside the region. That is, if it takes six applications of the equation to generate a point outside the region, then that point will be colored or shaded with color 6. The beauty of the Mandelbrot set in particular, and fractals in general, is that the level of complexity is infinite. That is, no matter how close together any two points are, they may be very, very different in their behavior.

*Figure 7.7.
Zooming in on
the Mandelbrot
set.*

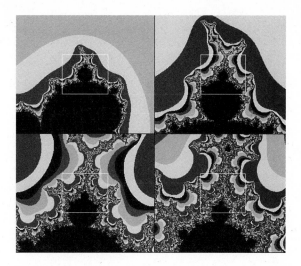

What is important about this sequence of images is that, no matter how far you zoom in,[4] the images have the same general character. In fact, you have to look carefully to see the difference between the various images.[5]

That is the basic nature of fractals, and that is what makes them so useful for virtual reality rendering. Instead of having to store the image of every leaf on every tree, of every rock on every mountain, you can use a relatively simple equation to generate any level of detail you need. It takes computing resources to generate fractal images, however, so there is a penalty to pay. However, when you can generate a complex landscape with less than 1K of data stored in the form of a few equations, that sure beats storing 2.5M of image data.

---

[4]Figure 7.8d is 8 levels deep. At each level, the zoom factor is 1/3. The zoom factor for level 8 is therefore (1/3)7. This means that if the size of the full Mandelbrot image were 1 foot square, the entire image 8 levels deep would be about four tenths of a mile square! And that's just getting started — we could zoom in indefinitely, and get the same general appearance each time.

[5]Interestingly, the Mandelbrot set contains itself many times over. If you hunt around, you'll find as many copies of the Mandelbrot set as you have time for.

Figure 7.8.
*Zooming in
still further.*

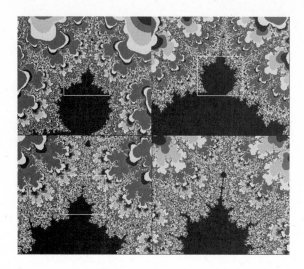

Armed with this knowledge, let's revisit the concept of fractal dimensions. Figure 7.6 showed a mountain with a fractal dimension of 2.3. Now let's examine a set of images with different fractal dimensions. Figure 7.9 shows a mountain with a fractal dimension of 2.04. Figure 7.10 shows a mountain with a fractal dimension of 2.3 (it's the same as in Figure 7.6). Figure 7.11 shows a mountain with a fractal dimension of 2.75, and Figure 7.12 with a fractal dimension of 2.99. Note the progression in complexity as the fractal dimension increases. At the lower fractal dimension, the mountains are relatively simple in character. As the fractal dimension increases, the level of detail and complexity increases as well. Think of it this way: as the fractal dimension increases from 2 to 3, the fractal tends to fill more and more of the 3D space.

Figure 7.9.
*A mountain with
a fractal dimen-
sion of 2.04.*

Figure 7.10. A mountain with a fractal dimension of 2.30. This is the same image as in Figure 7.6, and is repeated here for easy comparison.

Figure 7.11. A mountain with a fractal dimension of 2.75.

This means that we can define the fractal dimension of real-world objects, and then use fractal math to re-create the object. That means that the Rockies have a certain characteristic fractal dimension, as does a maple leaf or a fern.

It takes more than just a fractal dimension to define an object. For example, you can alter the distance between fractal points to create a coarser or finer fractal object. You can apply multiplication factors to the data, or other mathematical formulas to transform the numbers in interesting ways. You can even apply the same data in different situations.

Figure 7.12.
A mountain with
a fractal dimen-
sion of 2.99.

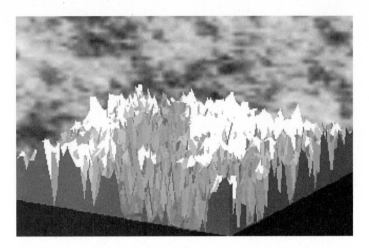

Fractal Possibilities

Once you calculate a series of values using fractals, you can apply those numbers to many different kinds of objects. For example, in the previous section we looked at fractal mountains. We could just as easily use that data to create fractal clouds, or a fractal world. Figure 7.13 shows a fractal mountain created with a certain set of criteria. Figure 7.14 shows the same data used to generate fractal clouds, and Figure 7.15 shows the same data used to create a planet. All these images, as well as the Mandelbrot images in the preceding section, were created using James Gleick's Chaos, The Software, from Autodesk. We'll look at some more examples using the program in this section as well.

Figure 7.13.
A fractal
mountain.

Figure 7.14.
A fractal cloud
generated using
the same fractal
data used in
Figure 7.13.

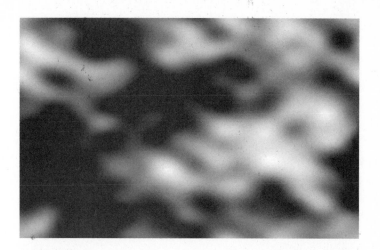

Figure 7.15.
A fractal planet
generated using
the same fractal
data used in
Figures 7.13
and 7.14.

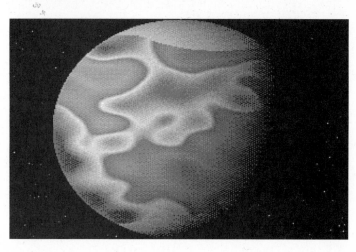

The purpose of this section is to illustrate how fractals can be controlled. To represent real-world objects, the various parameters involved in creating a fractal image must be tweaked and cajoled into doing what we want. The processes are quite chaotic, and small changes can create massive changes in the appearance of an image.[6] In fact, that is the very definition of chaotic behavior: small changes with big results. Running water is an excellent example of chaos in action.

---

[6]The science of chaos is interesting in it's own right, and involves much more than fractals. If you are interested in the subject, you could do a lot worse than to purchase the Chaos software used to illustrate the basics of fractals in this chapter.

Here is a small experiment you can try in your own home. Take a water-tight container that will hold about a quart or so of water. It could be a milk carton, a gallon-size plastic milk bottle, a coffee can, or (my favorite) a two-liter soda bottle. Put a small hole, about an eighth of an inch in diameter, into the side of the container very close to the bottom. Now head for the bathtub.

Fill the container with water, and then set it at the far end of the tub, away from the drain. Watch the path that the water follows from the container to the drain. You will most likely see a thin stream of water[7] that changes its course often. I used a video camera to capture this process in action, and you can see it on the CD-ROM in the directory for this chapter. Figures 7.16 and 7.17 show two frames from the video. As you can see, the course that the water follows is completely different between the two frames, even though they are less than one second apart. The input side, the flow of water from the container, is relatively steady, so you might not expect it to have much influence on the course of the water. This is chaos at work: even very tiny changes have large results in a chaotic system. If you wanted to render a flowing stream of water, this behavior would be something you would have to mimic.

Figure 7.16.
A frame from a
video of chaotic
streams of water.

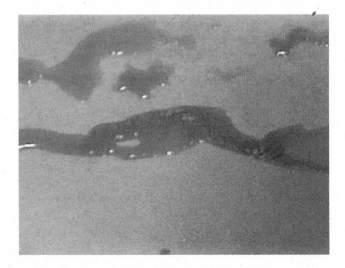

Chaos, The Software

Chaos, The Software, is a useful program for looking at how small changes can influence the appearance of images based on fractals.

---

[7]Or even two or three streams, for that matter, chaos being what it is.

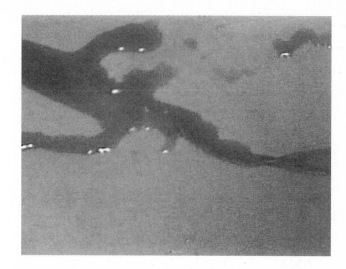

Figure 7.17.
A frame from the
same video in
Figure 7.16, less
than a second
later. Note
changes in water
flow pattern:
that's chaos at
work.

RECIPE

1 copy Chaos, the Software
1 VGA capability
1T patience

Instructions: Although this recipe takes time to prepare, the ingredients are simple and available in most kitchens. The graphics images are 16-color VGA or 256-color MCGA, but what you'll learn is much more important than the pretty pictures. A thinking person's kind of software, this is an inexpensive, no-frills main course. Makes a great snack, too.

There are actually six different programs within Chaos, each one focusing on a separate aspect of chaos. Only a few of these programs are covered here, but they are all interesting and fun.[8] The programs are described in Table 7.1.

Table 7.1. Chaos, the Software.

Program	Description
Mandelbrot Sets	Explore some of the classic fractal geometries, including Mandelbrot and Julia sets.
Magnets & Pendulum	Have fun with the chaotic interactions of virtual magnets and pendulums. Interactively experiment with creating large changes from small initial differences.
Strange Attractors	Watch as points in space attract other points with strange and unusual patterns resulting.
The Chaos Game	Explore the nature of fractal geometry. You can change a variety of parameters and see the results.
Fractal Forgeries	Use fractals to create images of clouds, mountains, and planets.
Toy Universes	Explore rule-based universes that you control.

The Chaos Game offers a unique opportunity to manipulate fractal images. A typical Chaos image is shown in Figure 7.18. This one is called Nautilus because it is reminiscent of the sea creature of the same name.

The Chaos Game isn't a game in any traditional sense. There is no arcade action, no questions are asked, and there is no score to keep. What you can do is press the F2 key to go to the Tweak screen, shown in Figure 7.19.

---

[8]Interesting means you will learn things you didn't have a clue about before you used the software, and fun means that you'll be surprised by what you find. Among other things, the documentation is superb. Not only will you find the information well-organized, clearly presented, and complete, but you will also enjoy the extended descriptions and mathematical digressions. You may not understand all of it, but it's fascinating stuff.

Figure 7.18.
A typical starting
image from the
Chaos Game.

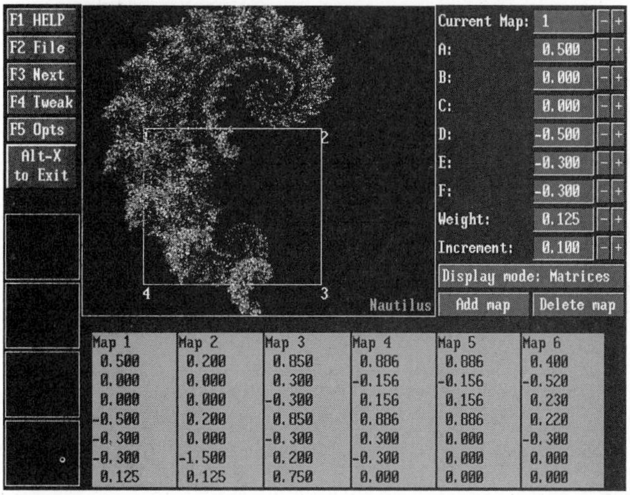

Figure 7.19.
The Tweak
screen in the
Chaos Game.

The top center of the Tweak screen shows a smaller version of the current image. At the right is a set of controls for the current *map*.[9] A summary of the settings for all maps is shown at the bottom.

The maps are the basis of each image in the Chaos Game. An image is created using multiple maps. Each map defines a different way to distort or change the

---

[9]Each image is built using multiple, weighted maps. The process will be explained shortly.

fundamental image. In fact, there are a defined set of simple transformations that are legal in the Chaos game: shrink, stretch, rotate, flip, and shear. Here's how it works: a point in the original image map is repeated in a second map, using one or more of the simple transformations. To add some spice, the decision about which rule to apply varies randomly. You can even assign weights to the various rules, so that some will occur more often than others. Given a set of rules, and a set of weights, such a random process will nonetheless always wind up creating the same image.[10]

Figure 7.20 shows the maps underlying the Nautilus image.[11] Each map acts as a rule, defining in some fashion the appearance of the image. The rest of this section will involve exploring the ways that an image can be altered by changing these maps.

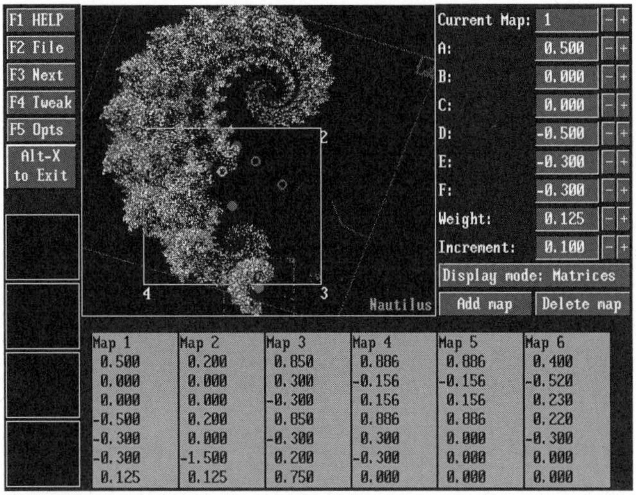

Figure 7.20.
The maps (rules)
that define the
Nautilus image.

F1 HELP			Current Map: 1	- +
F2 File			A: 0.500	- +
F3 Next			B: 0.000	- +
F4 Tweak			C: 0.000	- +
F5 Opts			D: -0.500	- +
Alt-X to Exit			E: -0.300	- +
			F: -0.300	- +
			Weight: 0.125	- +
			Increment: 0.100	- +

Display mode: Matrices   Nautilus   Add map   Delete map

Map 1	Map 2	Map 3	Map 4	Map 5	Map 6
0.500	0.200	0.850	0.886	0.886	0.400
0.000	0.000	0.300	-0.156	-0.156	-0.520
0.000	0.000	-0.300	0.156	0.156	0.230
-0.500	0.200	0.850	0.886	0.886	0.220
-0.300	0.000	-0.300	0.300	0.000	-0.300
-0.300	-1.500	0.200	-0.300	0.000	0.000
0.125	0.125	0.750	0.000	0.000	0.000

The reasons behind all of this is simple: fractals are chaotic, messy things. Learning to tune or tweak the parameters that define a given fractal image is essential if you want to represent real-world objects in a virtual world. The Chaos game will give you a taste of how involved that control is.

---

[10]The documentation for the Chaos Game describes the process as similar to walking into a room and randomly glancing about to determine what is in the room. No matter which places you look at, and in which order, the contents of the room are the same.

[11]Not all of the maps are shown in the figure. A map is shown more brightly if it has more weight, and some of the maps in the Nautilus image have very low weights, and are ,thus, nearly invisible. See the text for a discussion of weighting.

Table 7.2. The nine parameters of the Tweak screen.

Tweak Parameter	Description
Current Map	Determines which of the various maps uses the parameters listed below.
A:	Changes the height of the map.
B:	Squashes the map
C:	Stretches the map.
D:	Changes the width of the map.
E:	Changes location of the map.
F:	Changes location of the map.
Weight	Determines probability that the map will be used for calculating the next set of points.
Increment	Controls how much change will occur when you click the plus and minus buttons for the various parameters.

By adjusting these various parameters, you can arrive at distinctly different images. For example, Figure 7.21 shows a variation of the nautilus image that was created by simply increasing the weight value of map 6. No other parameters were changed. By increasing the weight of map (or rule) 6, that map is used more often to position points, and these new points cause a shift in the created image.

There are a total of six maps that control generation of the Nautilus image. You can display rectangles that represent the maps by pressing the M key at any time. This displays the maps shown in Figure 7.20. Figures 7.22 through 7.27 show each of the six maps that will generate the Nautilus image. For each map, note the values of the various parameters. Pay particular attention to the weighting parameters. This tells you how important each map is in defining the appearance of the image. Changes to maps with a large weight will have a large impact on the final image. The orientation of each map offers clues to how it will affect the image. For example, if the rectangle defining a map is twisted counterclockwise, the part of the image influenced by the map will twist counterclockwise. Because the rectangle represents multiple parameters, however, you cannot always gauge the result accurately.

Figure 7.21.
An image created
by changing the
weighting of
one map.

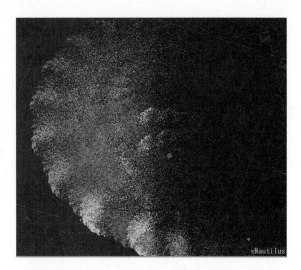

Figure 7.22.
Map 1 from the
Nautilus image.

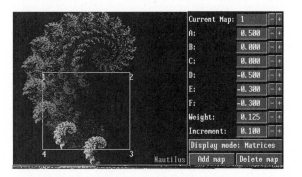

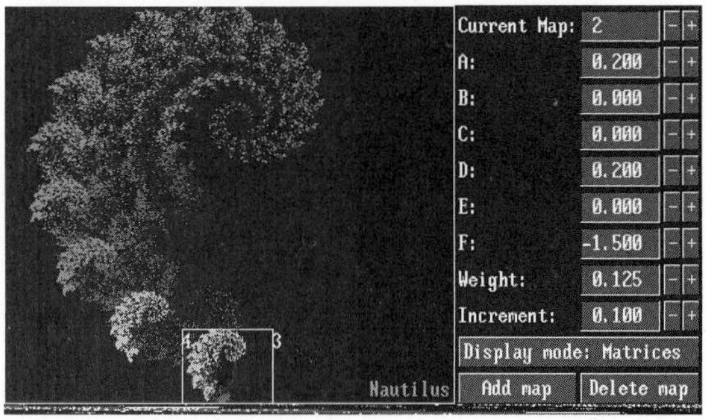

Figure 7.23.
Map 2 from the
Nautilus image.

Figure 7.24.
Map 3 from the
Nautilus image.

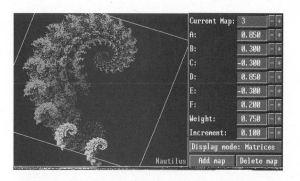

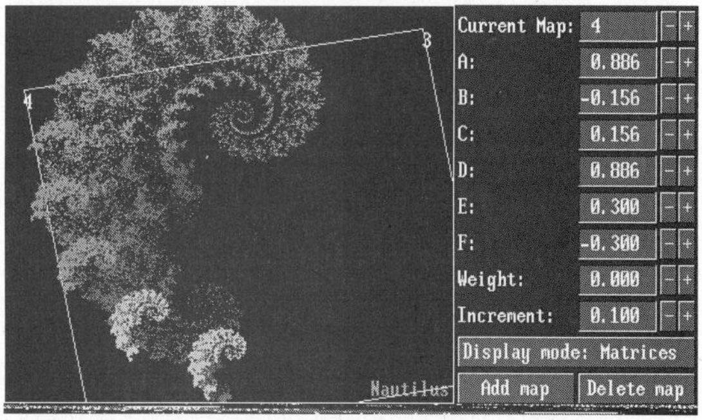

Figure 7.25.
Map 4 from the
Nautilus image.

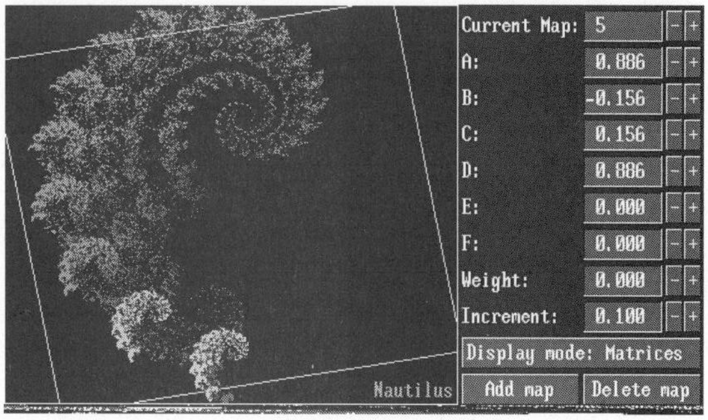

Figure 7.26.
Map 5 from the
Nautilus image.

Figure 7.27.
Map 6 from the
Nautilus image.

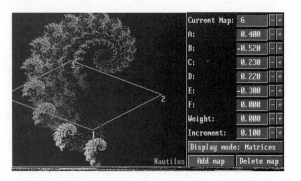

You can adjust map 3 so that the rectangle leans to the right (see Figure 7.28). The resulting image also leans in the direction. This is a graphic demonstration of the fact that all of the transformations allowed are simple, planar changes. Each change that you make to a single parameter in a single map will have a well-defined result. However, by adjusting several parameters, you can generate complex changes to the appearance of the image.

Figure 7.28.
Adjusting a
single parameter
of a map.

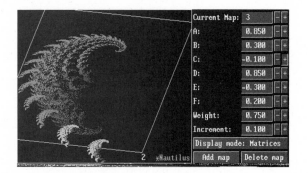

The most dramatic changes can be made by simply changing the weight of one or more maps. Figure 7.29 shows the nautilus image with map 6 weighted at 0.700. This completely changes the appearance of the image—it's barely recognizable as having anything to do with the original image.

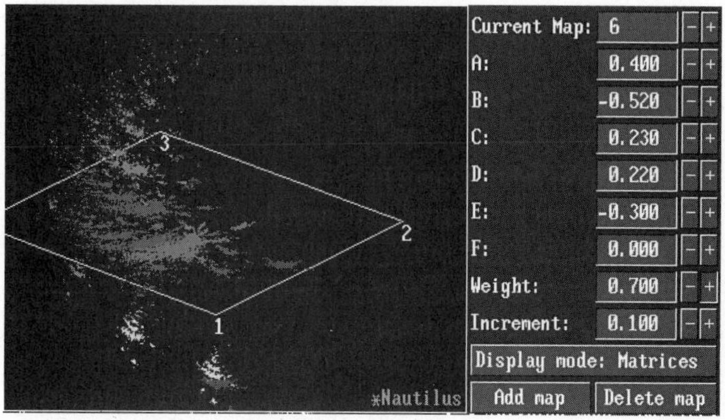

Figure 7.29.
Changing the
weighting of
map 6.

FERNS AND TREES

It takes some care to transform one fractal image into another, also useful image. In this section, we will tweak the values in the various maps of the Fern image, and create images corresponding, more or less, to different kinds of trees.

Figure 7.30 shows the basic fern image from the Chaos Game. The first thing I tried was to adjust the weight of map 1. The result is shown in Figure 7.31. In some ways, this second image is more natural; ferns aren't as fuzzy as shown in Figure 7.30.

I made further changes to the parameters for several maps, and was able to get the fern upright, the first step toward a coniferous tree image (see Figure 7.32). This was accomplished by de-rotating one of the maps. To find which map controls this aspect of the image, refer to Table 7.1 to find out which parameter controls rotation, and then adjust the parameter in each map until you find one that rotates the characteristic you want to change. I also tweaked several other parameters to achieve a more stick-like appearance.

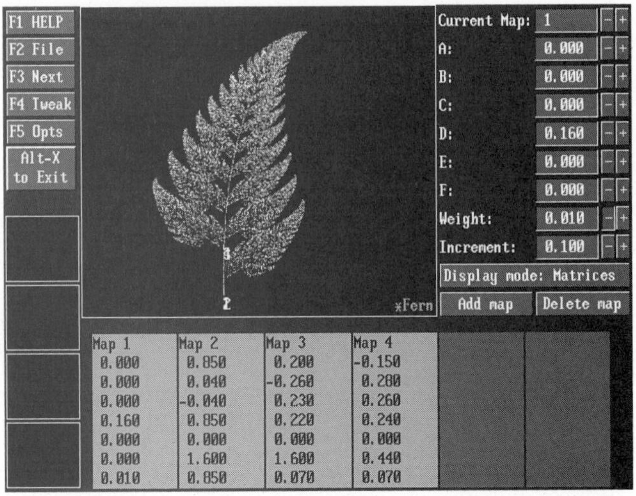

Figure 7.30.
The Fern image
from the Chaos
Game.

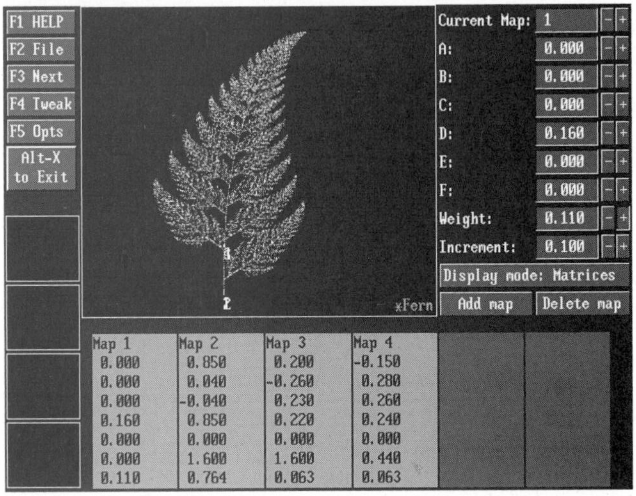

Figure 7.31.
A modified
Fern image.

Figure 7.32.
A further-
modified Fern
image.

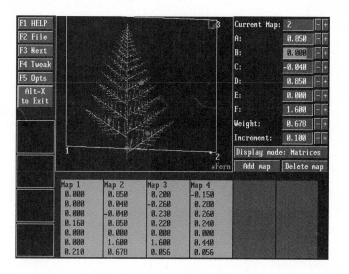

However, evergreens don't grow with their branches slanted up. Maps 3 and 4 control the left and right sides of the fern, respectively, and by changing the degree of rotation, you can set the proper branch angle for a tree. Figure 7.33 shows the right side horizontal (mostly), and Figure 7.34 shows both sides horizontal. There are some variations from horizontal, especially at the top of the "tree." This is influenced by other maps, and further tweaking would be required for perfectly horizontal branches.

Figure 7.33.
Further evolution
of the Fern image.

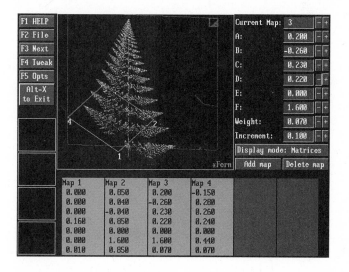

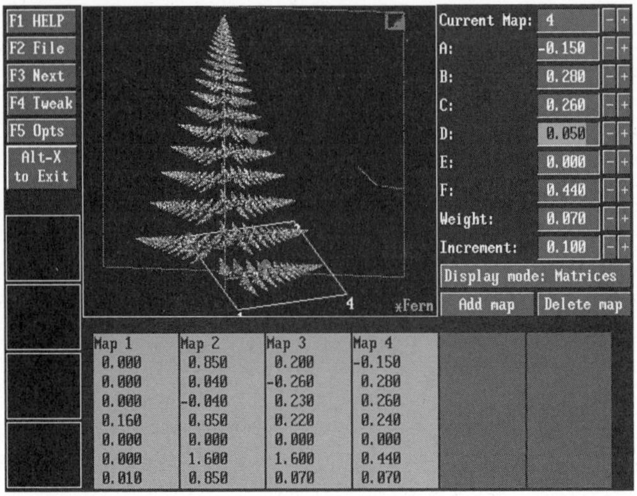

Figure 7.34.
"Son of Return
of Fern Image."

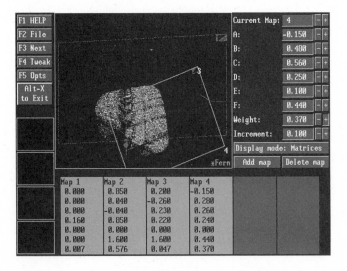

Just for fun, I made some major changes to numerous parameters, just to see if it was possible to take the process one step further and create a deciduous tree as well, using the same underlying basic image. The answer is: sort of. Figure 7.36 shows my best attempt.

Figure 7.35.
A modified
Fern image.

With the Chaos Game, you can get a sense of the methods involved in fractal tweaking. It should give you a good appreciation for the care involved in creating meaningful fractal objects, from mountains to trees.[12]

Fractals, Fractals Everywhere

Over the last few years, fractals have turned up in many places. They are being used to compress graphic images, for example, and are a big part of the Vista Pro program discussed in detail in Chapter 1. Fractal computations are very CPU intensive, and it has been the advent of increasingly powerful processors for personal computers that has made it possible to use fractals in a widening circle of applications. Time and again, you will bump into fractals as you explore virtual worlds. In some cases, you won't even notice.[13]

---

[12]Of course, cheating is allowed when it comes time to generate those gorgeous fractal landscapes. Many programs add bitmapped images to fractal technology to generate the best possible images.

[13]Would that this were so more often. One of the main purposes of this chapter has been to point out how hard it can be to use fractals effectively. Often, the secret to getting good results with fractals is nothing more than taking the time to tweak the various parameters involved — but that doesn't always happen. If any part of a virtual space looks a little too digital, there's a good chance that it's the result of fractal technology that didn't, or couldn't, go far enough.

8

SEEING IS BELIEVING

The human visual system is an electromechanical device. We seldom think of it that way, of course; we just know that we can see and we take that pretty much for granted. Each aspect of our visual system has some interesting flaws and loopholes. The eye itself, being mostly mechanical, has the most weaknesses. These can be exploited to fool the eye into thinking that what it sees is real when it is not. This means that a visual virtual reality need not be perfect to be perceived as real, which makes the job a lot easier.

There are numerous examples of optical illusions; Figure 8.1 shows an example. The two horizontal lines don't look like they are parallel, but they are. If you doubt it, just lay a ruler against the lines to verify it.

Figure 8.1.
An example of an
optical illusion.
The lines are
parallel, but
don't appear to
be so.

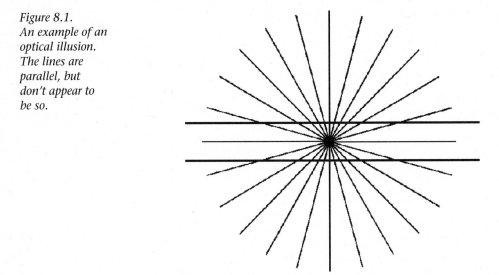

There is actually a wide variety of ways in which the eye can be fooled. By taking advantage of these flaws, the eye can be made to see color where there is none,[1] or to not see objects that are really there,[2] or to see the same object in completely

---

[1] The most common example involves spinning disks with concentric semicircles on them. The disk is white, and the circles are black.

[2] The most common reason to not see things that are there is the development of an afterimage. Try staring at a tile floor sometime—the lines between the tiles will come and go as the afterimage tends to cancel them out. This works best when the tiles, and the lines between them, are of contrasting colors or values.

different ways. For example, Figure 8.2 shows a drawing of a cube. Depending on how your eyes perceive the cube, you can see it from either the bottom or the top.[3]

Figure 8.2.
Another example
of an optical
illusion. The cube
will sometimes
appear to have its
top toward you,
and sometimes
its bottom.

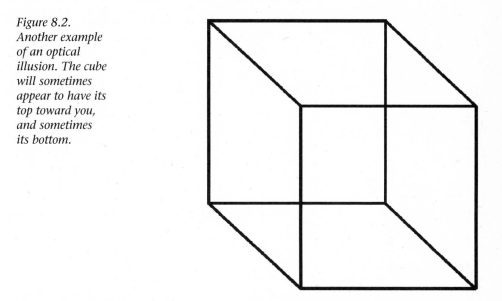

In this chapter, you'll learn how the eye can be fooled into thinking things are real, and you'll also learn about morphing, the art and science of making it appear as though one object were being turned into another.

Seeing Is Not Believing

There are two elements of perception involved in seeing an object in a virtual reality. The first, the physical and electrical systems, have been analyzed by various branches of science so that they are reasonably well understood. The second, our attitudes—the willingness to believe—is perhaps an even more important consideration.

The folks who analyze literature for a living use the term *suspension of disbelief* to describe the process of becoming involved in a story. When you open a book, sit

---

[3] If you don't see both forms, just stare at the image for a while—the image will usually flip by itself without you having to do anything.

in a movie theater, or observe a play, you know for a fact that what you are observing does not reflect reality. The book is just words on a page; the movie is just flickering light on a screen, and the actors are not who they seem to be. When you sit down at your computer to create or interact with a virtual space, you must likewise willingly suspend your disbelief. You must allow yourself to be deceived.[4]

However, it is impossible to quantify such things. The mechanics of seeing, however, being better understood than attitudes, suffer from no such limitation.

Motion

The first trick that is used to fool the eye is sequential imaging. You know the technique by the more common names in use: animation, movies, and video. All of these media use the same basic method to convince your eye that motion is occurring—putting a series of images in front of your eye so fast that your eye is fooled. The rate at which the images are presented is critical to the process. Movies and animation normally use a rate of 24 images per second, whereas video uses 30 frames per second.[5]

Digital video—video that has been converted to digital form and stored on a CD-ROM or a hard disk—is an emerging technology that has an increasing role in virtual reality. Digital video, however, must move from its current limitations—15 frames per second—to play a larger role. The wide acceptance of digital video (thanks in large part to Video for Windows technology) is leading to rapid advances.

---

[4] I like the phrase "allow yourself to be deceived" better than "suspension of disbelief" for several reasons. One, it is more accurate. Two, it avoids indirection. (That's an indirect way of saying, "it is direct." Get the point?) Three, I like going against the grain.

[5] Strictly speaking, this is not exact. Video is an interlaced technology. This means that half of the image is put onto the screen first—every other horizontal line of pixels. This is called a scan, and the horizontal lines are called scan lines. In the second scan, the rest of the image is put onto the screen. These two scans constitute a single frame; each of the scans is commonly referred to as a field. Thus, each frame has two fields. The process is called interlacing, and if you have ever tried to work with a 1024x768 video card using an interlaced signal, you know that the result of interlacing is flickering.

Thus, while video technology is the easiest to extend into virtual reality, it brings with it some potential flickering problems. Recent advances in television technology, such as HDTV, look more like the displays normally used on computers which do not use interlacing and are thus much more stable.

The frame rate is critical to the success of this trick. However, not all parts of the eye respond to the trick equally well—and this has some important ramifications for virtual reality technology. To simulate reality more effectively, a VR display system should wrap around the user's head. This adds peripheral vision to the simulation. But peripheral vision uses a different part of your eye, and that part doesn't work like the part that you use to see directly in front of you.

The eye has two kinds of light receptors: rods and cones. Cones are located mostly in the center of your eye, and they are very good at distinguishing colors. Rods are located mostly around the edges of the eye, and they are very good at distinguishing differences in brightness. Therein lies the problem. The most noticeable defect when using frames to simulate motion is the change in brightness that occurs when you change from one frame to the next. The sequence goes like this:

- Frame 1 is displayed

- Nothing is displayed

- Frame 2 is displayed

The problem is that nothing is in the middle. Depending on the medium, it will be more or less obvious. A movie uses a shutter to block the light while the frame is advanced, whereas video intermixes the frames somewhat. In either case, the rods at the outer part of the eye are particularly susceptible to the change in brightness that is associated with frame changes. This means that your peripheral vision is most likely to be affected by a visual system with excess flicker. It also means that a wraparound display must be better at flicker reduction than the typical computer monitor.

The Third Dimension

Once the object, and the virtual world, are in motion, the next consideration is to convince the eye that the world exists in three dimensions. This is easier said than done. The history of motion 3D can be summed up in a few lines:

- Red/blue glasses

- Polarized glasses

- Shutter glasses

Each of these techniques relies on a simple aspect of two-eyed stereo vision: each eye sees the scene from a slightly different point of view. The change in viewpoint, although small, is easy to see. Place your finger in front of your face, and put your other hand in front of one eye. You will see your finger against whatever background is behind it (see Figure 8.3 for the camera equivalent of this exercise).

Figure 8.3.
The view through
the left "eye."

Now, without moving your finger, shift the hand to the other eye. Note that the position of the vertical line against the background has shifted (see Figure 8.4).[6]

Combined-Image 3D

Your brain combines any two images it receives in separate eyes and creates the 3D effect right there in your head. This means that if we can:

■ Capture two sets of images, one for each eye, and each from a different viewpoint

■ Find a way to present the separate images to the correct eyes

then we can engage the brain to create a 3D image. Most 3D systems that use this method actually combine the two images into one image, and then use special glasses to send only the correct half of each image to the correct eye. The three

---

[6] The technical term for this is parallax.

kinds of glasses listed earlier use different techniques to achieve this result. The mechanism used to create images for each kind of glasses also differs.

Figure 8.4. The view through the right "eye." Note shift of vertical line against background.

Red/Blue Glasses

This is the easiest form of 3D technology, but it is also the least effective. To view the 3D image, you must wear glasses that use a blue film in one eye, and a red film in the other. The source image contains overlapping blue and red versions of the scene. Figure 8.5 shows such an image in black and white, but you can make out the two images easily.

To create the image, all that is needed is something called a *stereo pair*. This is just a fancy term for two images that represent what your own eyes would see if they had been there instead of the camera that took the pictures.[7] One image is encoded using blue colors only, and the other image is encoded using only red colors. When you view the image, the red image goes to one eye, and the blue image goes to the other eye—thanks to the colored filters in the glasses. The result is a so-so 3D image.

---

[7] This is not always exactly true. To enhance the 3D effect, you can increase the distance between the two cameras. Instead of using a few inches between the cameras to mimic the distance between our eyes, you can move the cameras several feet—or even more—apart. If the cameras are moved too far apart, this can destroy the 3D effect, however.

Figure 8.5.
A red/blue stereo
image.

Polarized Glasses

Polarized glasses also put both images into a single image, but instead of using color, this technique relies on the capability to polarize light.[8] It is most commonly used with movie projection. When the image for one eye is projected onto the screen, light polarized at a specific angle is used. The corresponding lens on the glasses has a filter on it that will only allow light polarized at that angle to enter. The image for the other eye uses a polarization angle that is different by 90 degrees. The corresponding lens on the glasses also has a matching polarizing angle. The result is that each eye only sees the image intended for it.

A significant advantage of the polarized technique is that you can use real colors in each image, so the resulting 3D view is much better than with red/blue glasses. The disadvantage, of course, is the need for equipment to polarize the light.

Shutter Glasses

Shutter glasses take a kind of brute force approach to the problem. Each lens contains a shutter that simply blocks the view of the eye on that side when the shutter

---

[8] If you are not familiar with polarization of light, here is a simple explanation. Light behaves like a wave. Normally, light waves vibrate every which way. A polarizer restricts the vibrations to one direction—for example, up and down. A beam thus polarized can be used for one image, and one polarized to a side-to-side vibration could be used for the other image. Each side of the glasses has a set of ultra-tiny parallel slits that only allow light whose polarization matches the slits to enter.

is closed. This method works well with video sources—if you recall, a video frame is actually made up of two fields. If we put the image for one eye in one field, and for the other eye in the other field, the shutter can be used to block the "wrong" field for each eye. The result is that each eye sees only the information that is intended for it.

The downside to shutter glasses is that they effectively cuts the vertical resolution in half. It also requires heavier, more complicated, and costlier glasses than either of the other methods. This is offset by the fact that little or no special equipment is needed to encode the images.

Options

As a general rule, there are two points in the 3D process where costs and technology get in the way: creating the image, and decoding the image. The best balance of quality, cost, and convenience is probably shutter glasses. Red/blue glasses are easy to use, but image quality is inferior. Polarizing is effective, but requires a projection system. Shutter glasses cost more than other kinds of 3D glasses, but they provide the ability to create images at a minimal cost.

Multiple Images

The ideal VR system would put a separate image in front of each eye. Wraparound, head-mounted displays will make this possible. Currently, this technology is going through a process that laptop LCD screens went through several years ago. The manufacturing capacity of the industry is waiting for demand, and demand is waiting for manufacturing capacity to increase and bring down prices.

Until there is an advance that will move this stalemate off dead center, the cost of even modest quality head-mounted displays will be high—more than $1,000. There are some head displays at lower prices, but they are basically just televisions that hang in front of your eyes.

The Morph the Merrier

Let's back away from 3D a bit to look at a fascinating technology that has only recently moved from the realm of the super computer to the desktop: morphing. Morphing is the art of appearing to transform one object or picture into another.

RECIPE

1 copy Photo Morph
1 starting image
1 final image
10-100 little square dots
1 Media Player or VidEdit

Instructions: This is a real taste treat. However, the recipe calls for a light touch—sort of like working up a soufflé, or a puff pastry. Take two images, roughly similar in outline if possible, then dot lightly with square dot-sprinkles. Careful positioning is a must! Serve the AVI output in Windows, or slice into DIBs for Animator Pro.

There are a number of commercial and shareware morphing products on the market. My favorite, hands down, is Photo Morph from North Coast Software. Good morphing software must not only follow the basic rules for morphing, but must be sensitive to various nuances of the morphing process. Photo Morph does the best job of balancing all of these requirements.

I have included a number of morph examples on the CD-ROM. One of the neatest features of Photo Morph is that it outputs AVI files. You can view these easily using Windows Media Player. I also have included a demo version of Photo Morph on the CD-ROM. You are limited to using just a few files, but it is otherwise a full-featured version of the software. This gives you a chance to test-drive Photo Morph before you decide whether or not you want to buy it. Along with Vista Pro, Photo Morph is very high on my personal must-have software list.

Figure 8.6 shows the basic Photo Morph program windows. The main window has nothing in it, and there is a separate window called the Project Editor.

Photo Morph is a bit like two programs in one. You can load bitmaps into the main window, where you can perform various operations on them as needed. You can add borders, change the contrast of an image, and so on. You will probably still use your favorite photo-paint software for major image manipulation, but you can always perform simple adjustments at the last minute in Photo Morph.

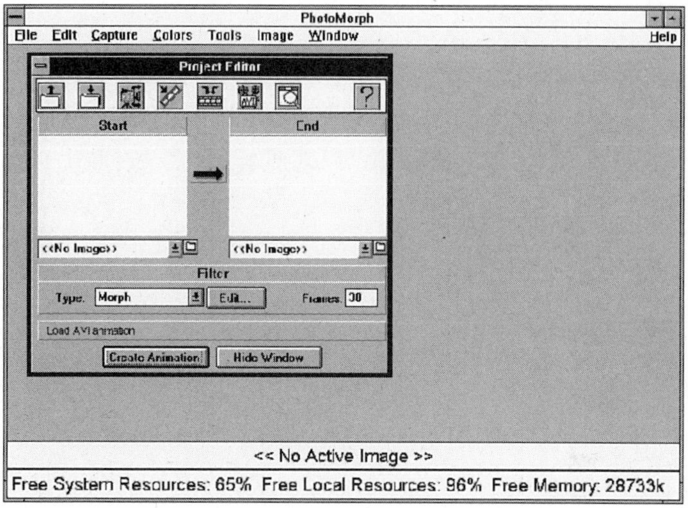

Figure 8.6.
The basic Photo
Morph windows.

Morphing is simple, and morphing is complex. The simple side involves the method used for morphing. You simply place a point on an image, and then tell the morph program where that point should wind up in the final image. After entering a series of points, you let the software perform the morph. The complex side involves the art of placing those points where they will do the most good.

Let's look at an example. There are two files on the CD that you can use for this example. They are dolphin.bmp and eye1.bmp. To load these images into the Project Editor, use the File/Project/Open menu selection to open the file d2eye.pmp. This will load the two image files into the main window, and into the Project Editor (see Figure 8.7).

There are numerous controls in the Project Editor window, and you'll learn about those in the next section. For now, simply click the Edit button at bottom center. This will display the editing screen (see Figure 8.8). I used the magnification icon to enlarge the eye portions of both images—this is where most of the morphing takes place. Note that there are square dots in both images. Only one dot in each image is active at a time, however. These are illustrated in Figure 8.8.

I carefully adjusted the position of each key dot in both images. If a dot was at the corner of the eye in the dolphin image, I made sure that the corresponding key dot in the other image was also exactly at the corner of the eye. Because the sizes of the eyes are different in the two images, this involved a lot of moving around of the dots.

Figure 8.7.
Two images
loaded into the
Project Editor.

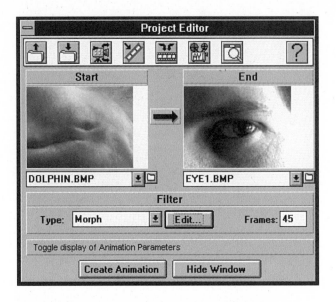

Figure 8.8.
The edit window.

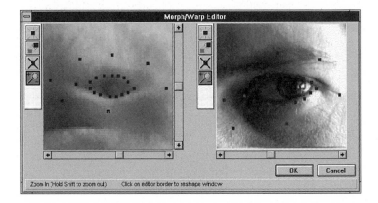

When I had the dots where I wanted them,[9] I saved the changes and returned to the Project Editor. I clicked the Create Animation button, and it took a few

---

[9] Where to put the dots is the subject of much of this chapter—don't expect to just lay down a few dots and get a world-class morph right away. By the end of this chapter, you will learn enough skills to allow you to have a good idea of where to put those dots for your own morph. However, you will probably find that there is a certain, irreducible amount of trial and error in the morphing process.

seconds for the AVI file to be generated.[10] This file (d2eye.avi) is on the CD-ROM; see the Appendix for information on accessing files. Figures 8.9 and 8.10 show two frames from the morph. As you can see, the images blend smoothly.[11]

Figure 8.9.
A frame from the
morph anima-
tion.

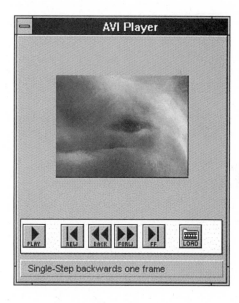

That's enough razzle dazzle for now. Time for a little hard reality: morphing is at least as much an art as a science. It's worth some time and effort to see exactly how morphing works before you try anything too fancy. A clear understanding of what the software does with all of those points will give you a good start to successful morphing.

The Square and the Circle

Figure 8.11 shows a simple project file loaded into Photo Morph. Note that the image files that make up the project are not only loaded into the Project Editor, but into the workspace of the main window as well. You can make changes to the bitmaps using the Image menu selection before morphing, should that be necessary.

---

[10] One of the nice features of Photo Morph is the speed with which it creates the morph output.

[11] This is much clearer if you play the AVI file itself. Still, black and white images cannot convey the subtlety of the morph.

Figure 8.10.
Another frame
from the morph
animation.

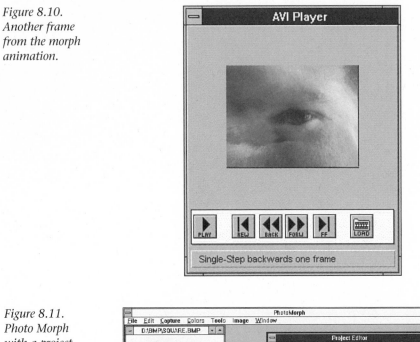

Figure 8.11.
Photo Morph
with a project
loaded.

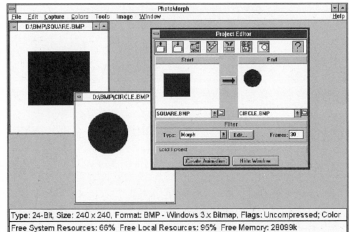

Before discussing the details of the dots, let's take a moment to list and describe the basic features of Photo Morph. Most of the morphing work is done in the Project Editor (see Figure 8.11). There is a row of buttons across the top of the window (see Table 8.1), and two image windows marked Start and End. The currently open images are listed under both of these windows for easy access. The little folder icon next to the filenames enables you to easily add more image files to the list.

Below the images is a section of the window called Filter. There are three controls here: the type of the filter (warp or morph), an Edit button, and a Frames control. A *warp* simply alters the pixel positions in an image, whereas a *morph* both alters the pixel positions and fades to a second image. The Edit button takes you to the editing screen where you place and move those little square dots. The Frames control tells Photo Morph how many frames to create in the AVI file. More frames means a smoother, but slower, morph.

At the bottom of the window are two buttons: Create Animation, and Hide Window. The former creates the AVI file, and the latter hides the project window.

Table 8.1. The Photo Morph Project Editor Toolbar (left to right).

Icon	Description
Load Project	Loads a project file from the disk.
Save Project	Saves the current project to disk.
View/Hide AVI controls	Displays additional controls related to AVI file creation, such as compression method. This is a toggle control.*
View/Hide all	Alternately hides and displays the animation and AVI controls.*
View/Hide animation controls	Displays additional animation controls. This is a toggle control.*
Play AVI file	Opens the AVI player.
Enlarge window	Enlarges the project window
Help	Access to help files.

* Note: The AVI and Animation controls are explained near the end of this section.

Now for the fun part: the dots. To place dots, click the Edit button in the Project Editor window. This displays the Morph/Warp Editor (see Figure 8.12).

There are four buttons at the left of each of the images. From top to bottom, these buttons:

- ■ Create a new dot
- ■ Move a dot

■ Delete a dot

■ Enlarge/reduce the image

Figure 8.12.
The Morph/Warp
Editor window.

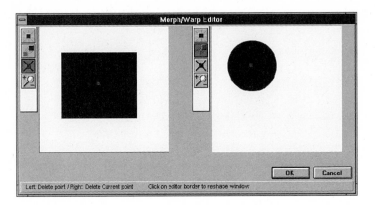

Clicking a button changes the operating mode of the window. For example, when you click the top button (Create a new dot), any time you click in that image, a new dot will be created.[12] If you click the enlarge/reduce button, the cursor changes to a magnifying glass, and will alter the scale of that image until you click a new icon.

The editing window is resizable, but you must use the enlarge/reduce icons to change the scale of an image.

In Figure 8.12, there is a single dot in each image.[13] The dots are located at the center of each object. Note that the image of the square has been enlarged, and the image of the circle has not. You can adjust the scale of each image independently.

Your first experiment is to find out what kind of morph takes place when you put dots in the center of corresponding objects. This is a simple example, but I have made it more interesting by using two completely different shapes. In a real morph, not only will the shapes have different characteristics, but there will be many different shapes. The circle and the square are mere teaching devices, sort of like using training wheels when you learn to ride a two-wheel bike.

---

[12] As a general rule, you should create one dot at a time. Adjust that dot's position in both images before you create another dot. If you create too many dots at once, you will lose track of which dot is which.

[13] When you create a new dot in an image, the corresponding new dot in the other image is created automatically.

To create the morph, click OK in the Morph/Warp Editor, and then click the Create Animation button in the Project Editor. A slider will appear in a small window showing you the progress of the morph operation, and you'll see a polite little window informing you when the operation is complete. To view the AVI file, you can simply click the Play AVI button in the toolbar. This displays the first frame of the AVI file (see Figure 8.13).

Figure 8.13.
The first frame of
a morph anima-
tion.

This is, as you would expect, simply the square that the morph is supposed to start with. Click the FORW button to step forward through the morph. Several frames in, you will see something like Figure 8.14.

There are two obvious things going on here:

- The image of the square is fading out, and the image of the circle is fading in.

- Both of the images are slightly deformed. The circle is somewhat more deformed than the square.

The deformation of the two objects requires some explanation. During a morph, there are actually two morphs going on at the same time. The square is being morphed into the circle, and, behind the scene, the circle is being morphed into the square. For example, if the morph takes ten frames, at frame one the image of the square has been deformed 10 percent toward the shape of the circle. In addition, the circle has been deformed 90 percent toward the shape of the square. In this case, we have only used one point to define the morph, and that doesn't give the program much information about the shape of either object.

Figure 8.14.
A frame from
the middle of
the morph.

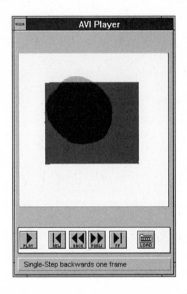

You see, the software doesn't look for the boundary of the square or the circle. The purpose of the dots is to tell the software where key points are—such as boundaries.[14] Because we have only defined one key point, the changes from frame to frame are not well controlled. This is the source of the odd deformation of the circle in Figure 8.14.

If you continue to step forward in the animation, you will get to a frame near the end that looks something like Figure 8.15. This frame also shows signs of an under-controlled morph. The circle is nearly right, but the edges of the square are going squiggly on us.

By the time we get to the next to the last frame (see Figure 8.16), the square has all but faded away, and the circle is in good shape.

---

[14] There are other kinds of key points, but it would only muddy the waters to talk about that here. Stay tuned.

*Figure 8.15.
A frame near the
end of the
animation.*

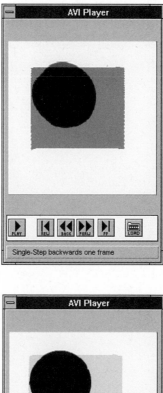

*Figure 8.16.
The next to last
frame of the
animation.*

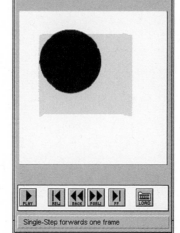

Clearly, if we want better control of the morphing process, we'll need more dots. This is a good time to rename the dots for what they really are: control points. The trick to creating a good-looking morph that will fool the eye is to place the control points where they need to go. The purpose of the rest of this section, where we will explore a seemingly endless succession of ways to place control points on these simple figures, is to show the effects of various placements on the resulting morph. So hang in there: all will be made clear.

Figure 8.17 shows a different setup in the Morph/Warp Editor. This time, instead of a single control point at the center of each object, there are four control points. There is one each at the corners of the square, and one each at corresponding points on the circle. The control points may be hard to make out, but they are there.

Figure 8.17.
Using four
control points.

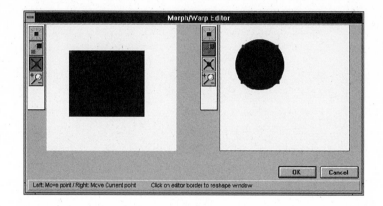

To see the results of this arrangement, click OK and then Create Animation. A check of the AVI file shows a frame like the one in Figure 8.18.

Figure 8.18.
A frame from the
new morph
animation.

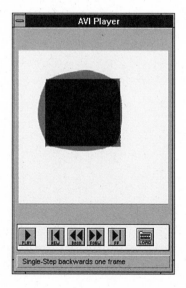

This is very different from Figure 8.14. Now there is a much better correspondence between the circle and the square. Still not perfect, but significantly better. The control points at the corners of the square are doing their job—the two objects are fairly well aligned at these points.

Still, the effect is not satisfactory. Let's try a slightly different arrangement of control points (see Figure 8.19). This time, the control points are located just outside of the square and the circle. (Compare with Figure 8.17.)

Figure 8.19.
A different
arrangement of
control points.

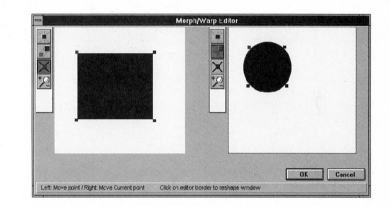

The result of the new placement is shown in Figure 8.20.

Figure 8.20.
A frame from
the new morph
animation.

The alignment at the corners is now very firm. However, the points along the edges of the square do not line up at all with the edges of the circle. Let's try more control points (see Figure 8.21).

Figure 8.21. Adding control points along the edges of the objects.

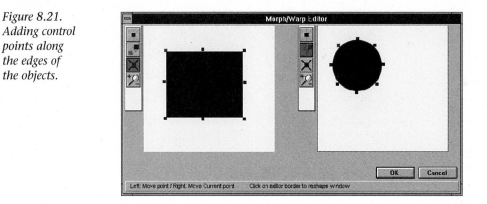

The result of the additional control points is shown in Figure 8.22. The morph is now much, much better—in fact, you could make a case for stopping here and calling it a morph. A close examination, however, shows a few minor flaws that may be worth some further attention.[15]

The lower left of the morph object shows a minor misalignment—there's a bit of black hanging out to the side that shouldn't be there. In addition, by adding the control points along the edges, we have lost some of the control we had at the corners of the square—these now extend out beyond the circle.

> New control points affect the action of existing control points. Be prepared to rearrange control points after adding new ones.

With this tip comes a side tip: check your work before you add too many new control points, so you can see what the effect of the new points is. You could wind up with a muddled mess if you try to do too much without checking your work.

You might try simply adding more control points (see Figure 8.23).

---

[15] If this morph were not so demanding, we probably could, indeed, stop here. However, you will sometimes find just such a high-contrast situation (black next to white in this case), and it will be useful to know how to handle it.

Figure 8.22.
A frame from the
morph with edge
control points.

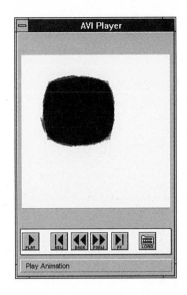

Figure 8.23.
Adding yet more
control points.

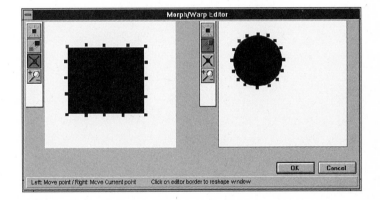

The result is shown in Figure 8.24. This is not good—the result is worse than it was before!

On a hunch, I tried the same number of control points, but arranged a little differently as shown in Figure 8.25. The extra control points have been moved much closer to the corners.

The result of this attempt at a fix is shown in Figure 8.26.

Figure 8.24.
The result of
adding more
control points.

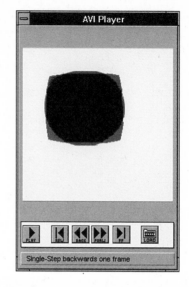

Figure 8.25.
Moving the
control points
around.

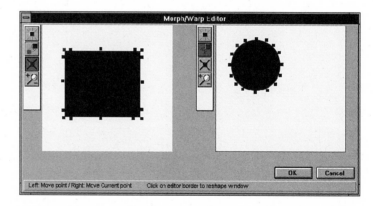

This offers some advantages that are worthwhile, but there is still some misalignment—the two figures are simply too different. The improvement comes in the form of straighter lines along the edges of the square, which will make for a more gradual and therefore more pleasing morph. To see the difference more clearly, compare Figures 8.24 and 8.26.

There are many lessons to be learned from this extended example. The following list summarizes them. However, the most important lesson to learn is that it is difficult and challenging to try to morph dissimilar objects. Ultimately, you can never do a perfect morph between objects that vary by too large a factor.

*Figure 8.26.
The result of
shifting the
control points
closer to the
corners.*

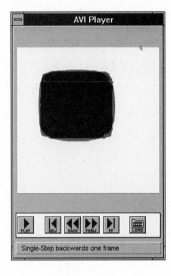

- Objects with corners need control points just beyond the corners.

- Straight lines need control points near their ends to preserve the straightness.[16]

- Odd morphing can usually be remedied by adding more control points.

- Check the effects resulting from the addition of new control points. It may change the effects of existing control points.

- When in doubt, more control points are usually better than too few.

One thing that was not covered in this example was the effect of having control points at very different locations on the start and end images. Such positioning required large-scale morphs. Here's another general rule: the farther apart matching control points are in the two images, the greater the risk of some fatal flaw that will spoil the morph.

The Frog and the Chick

Let's have a little fun with morphing: how about turning a frog into a chick? Figure 8.27 shows two images loaded into the Project Editor. The starting image is a frog, and the ending image is a chick.

---

[16] This assumes, of course, that the situation requires such preservation. By all means, locate control points away from the corners to speed up the transition to a curve when that is desirable.

Figure 8.27.
A more complex
morph in the
Project Editor.

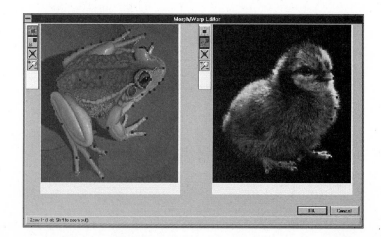

This morph presents some interesting challenges. The first step is to find areas in the images that correspond to one another—and there are more of them than you might expect. For example, look at the frog's two right feet. They match nicely with the chick's two feet. It would be a good idea to set up corresponding control points for each of the toes.

Other good places for control points would be eye-to-eye, and the overall outline of the animals. Figure 8.28 shows a good first attempt at control points. Some of the control points on the chick may be hard to see because of the black background, but they are there.

Figure 8.28.
Adding control
points in the
Morph/Warp
Editor.

However, these control points have at least one important problem: the frog's eye is not sufficiently controlled. Figure 8.29 shows a frame from the morph animation—the frog's eye has split. Part of it is migrating down to the chest, while the rest of it heads where it should: toward the chick's left eye.

Figure 8.29.
A frame from the
frog-to-chick
morph.

Figure 8.30 shows why this is occurring. Look at the control points around the frog's eye. There is only one control point for the lower-third of the eye. This would often be enough to give adequate control, but in this case the eye is very close to the control points along the lower jaw. The control points along the jaw have a long way to go to morph to the corresponding control points on the chick's chest. When you have this combination—control points moving in opposite directions, and moving over large distances—you often will need more control points to avoid problems.

You also can divide and conquer. By adding an additional row of control points in the area between the eye and the jaw line, you establish a boundary that reduces the impact of the eye/jaw control points on each other. Any given control point has the greatest influence on the control points immediately adjacent to it. If there is at least one control point between them, points will have much less impact on each other.

Figure 8.30.
A close-up of the
eye portion of the
morph.

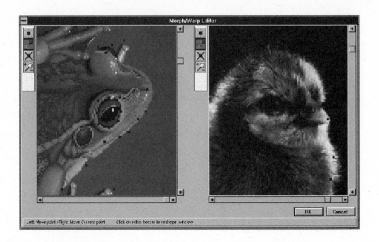

Now look at Figure 8.31. I have made both of the changes I suggested. There are twice an many control points around the frog's eye.[17] There are also three new points between the eye and the jawline.

Figure 8.31.
Revised control
points around the
frog's eye.

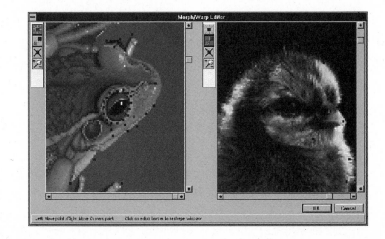

Figure 8.32 shows the result of adding the control points. The eye of the frog is now intact during the morph. Because the eye is red, it stands out and thus is a very important morph object. The human eye will follow the brightest or most colorful object in a scene. If you can identify the most prominent object in a morph,

---

[17] Remember: too many control points is seldom a problem, while too few almost always is a problem.

and control it carefully, the observer will be satisfied even if certain other aspects of the morph aren't quite perfect. This is especially true in the frog/chick morph because there are those extra frog legs at the top of the frog picture. As you can see in Figure 8.32, if you do not control them too tightly, they conveniently disappear.

Figure 8.32.
The frog's eye
now morphs
correctly.

The Circle and the Circle

The frog's eye was challenging to morph properly because it moves a large distance. Let's look at a more controlled situation. Figure 8.33 shows a morphing project with two circles, one at the upper-left (start) and one at the lower-right (end).

There is no shape changing involved in this morph. The starting object is a circle, and the ending object is a circle. Movement, however, is a critical consideration when morphing. To see the kinds of problems inherent in movement, let's add a single control point to each object (see Figure 8.34). This won't create a successful morph, but it will illustrate the kinds of problems encountered during a move.

Figure 8.35 shows a frame from the morph, about halfway through the animation. As you can see, the two objects are trying to move toward each other's initial position. This leaves a distorted trail of garbage behind.

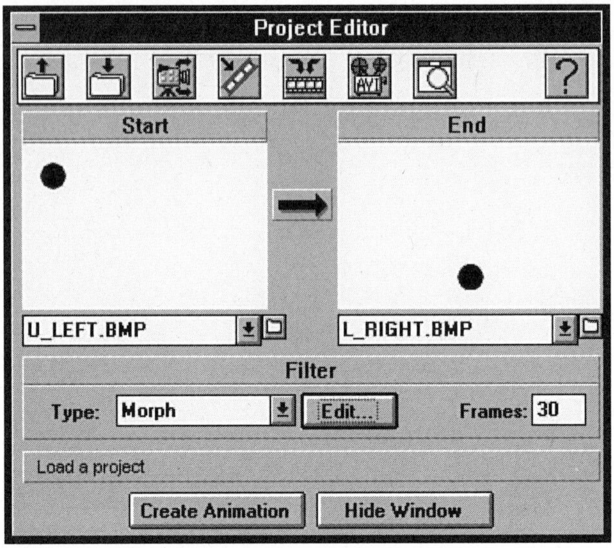

Figure 8.33.
A morph that
changes location,
not shape.

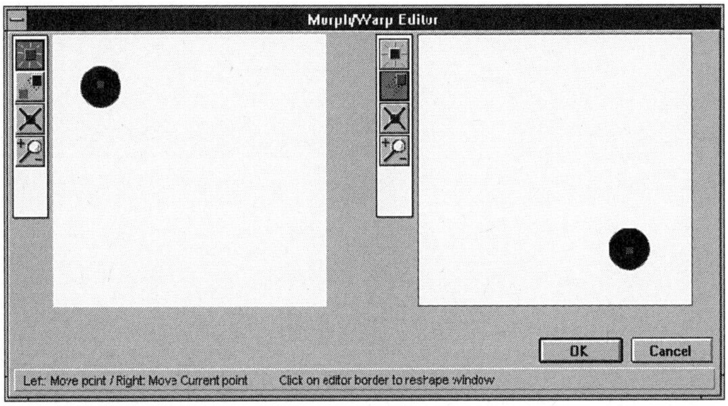

Figure 8.34.
A morph with
only a single
control point in
each object.

To get better control of the move, your first instinct would be to add more control points. A minimum of eight are likely to be needed, based on our observations in the preceding examples (see Figure 8.36).

However, as you can see in Figure 8.37, the result isn't quite right. There are two little "rocket jets" coming out of the end of the circle as it moves.

In Figure 8.38, I have zoomed in on the circles to show a slight change that I made to the control points. Because a bit of the object was getting left behind, so to speak, I added some white space to the area within the control points.

Figure 8.35.
The hazards of
an under-
controlled move.

Figure 8.36.
Using eight
control points.

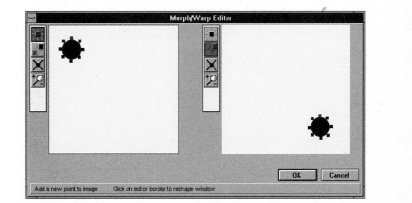

The result of what I'll call over-controlling is shown in Figure 8.39.

As you can see, we have reached the point of diminishing returns. The rocket jet is mostly gone, but now the object outlines do not coincide. This is a case where your own judgment must prevail—depending on the nature of the image, you can choose to under- or over-control for the best overall result.

Figure 8.37.
Some artifacts of
the move remain
under-controlled.

Figure 8.38.
Shifting the
location of a few
control points.

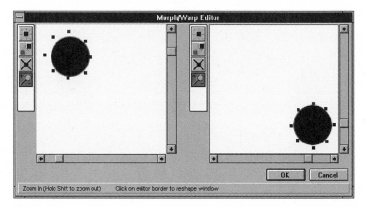

*Figure 8.39.
An over-
controlled morph
can also cause
problems.*

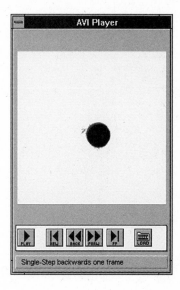

Summary

In this chapter, you learned about how the eye can be deceived into believing that images are more or less real. However, tricks and techniques are only part of the story—the eye's owner must be willing to be deceived. As demonstrated by morphing, the extra time it takes to smooth out the unreality of artifice can be well worth your while.

Because, just as the eye has a hard time accepting the transformation of a frog into a check, it is equally happy to be amazed if it sees nothing inherently wrong visually—if the motion is smooth, if there are no jumps, if the transformation is at least plausible, then the impossible can be made to seem real.

9

THE MODEL IS THE THING

Today's virtual reality hardware and software are really just models of reality. This takes me back to Chapter 2, where the subject was artificial reality instead of virtual reality. In many ways, the phrase *artificial reality* is much more appropriate for the technology available. The original idea of virtual reality was of an electronic (or otherwise) simulation that was, at its best, indistinguishable from reality. The reality of virtual reality is quite different. An analogy will serve to illustrate the differences.

Granularity

Weather forecasters use models to simulate the earth's weather systems. These models are extremely complex, and run on some of the fastest and largest computers in use today. These models are modeling reality, but not only are they *not* reality, they aren't even very close to reality. The reality of weather is that it is complex, chaotic, and, in truth, pretty much unpredictable. A model necessarily leaves out details. The term used to describe the accuracy of a model is *granularity*. This terms comes from the concept of graininess. For example, photographs use grains of silver compounds to create an image. Some grains are dark, and others are light. The smaller the grains are, the more closely the image will resemble the original. Figure 9.1 shows an image constructed of very large grains, and Figure 9.2 shows in image constructed of very small grains.

*Figure 9.1.
An image
constructed of
large grains.*

Figure 9.2.
An image
constructed of
small grains.

Granularity is easy to spot in a picture, but it is not always so easy to see in a model of something. Back to the weather simulation: granularity here involves the distance between the sensors used to record weather information. If the sensors are 100 miles apart, that means that aspects of weather smaller than 100 miles or so will not be part of the model—a grain is 100 miles in size.

The granularity of time is also a consideration when you create a model. If those weather stations sample the weather once a day, the model will have large "time grains." If the weather stations sample the weather every hour, that's a much higher granularity and a much more accurate model.

Both kinds of granularity are crucial factors when modeling any aspect of reality. Reducing the size of the grains in a model costs money, however. There is a general rule at work here: more grains means more CPU power, more bits of data, more time, and more money.[1]

A 486/66 computer, with a cutting-edge video display and the fastest hard disk available, isn't going to be able to create a simulation of reality that will fool anyone. The emphasis is on virtual and artificial, not on reality. Even if you spend $10,000 or more, the hardware can only do so much. This chapter, therefore, will

---

[1] It doesn't always cost more money, however. Today's computers are a hundred or more times faster than the original IBM PC, but they cost about the same. It has always cost about $2,500 for a decent computer—we just keep getting better computers at that same price.

be about what you and I can do on a reasonably fast computer, on our own, and not about what you *could* do "if only."

Rules and Conditions

Modeling reality goes beyond merely putting images on a computer screen or a head-mounted helmet display. It involves *rules*. The virtual objects in the model must obey rules that correspond to reality.[2]

In this chapter, you will learn how to use Virtual Reality Studio to create a model of reality. In keeping with the title of the book and my general tendency to look for the fun side of anything, it will be a slightly twisted reality.

Virtual Reality Studio uses rules, but it calls them conditions. Whatever the name, a rule is a rule: it specifies how an object responds or behaves. There are many levels of conditions in Virtual Reality Studio. You can associate conditions with an object, and you can create conditions that apply all the time to all objects, and there are also levels in between.

General conditions—These conditions apply everywhere in the artificial universe. They are useful for tracking purposes, such as timers and counters.

Local conditions—These conditions apply to one area.[3]

Object conditions—These conditions apply only to a single object.

Initial conditions—These conditions are applied when a session starts, or when a session is reset.

Procedures—You can create a library of procedures that can be used in conditions at all levels. For example, if the initial conditions make a certain object invisible, and the object itself becomes invisible under certain conditions, you could create a procedure that could be called from the Initial Conditions and the Object Conditions.

---

[2] Assuming, of course, that it is reality that you intend to model. If your intention is to model a fantasy world, then the rules can be whatever you like.

[3] VR Studio allows you to switch from one area to another. Each area has its own objects. For more information about areas, see Chapter 2.

Figure 9.3 shows the Conditions menu. It includes access to the conditions just listed, as well as several other features including animation. Animation is described in the Animation section of this chapter.

Let's begin by looking at object conditions. Use the Conditions/Object Conditions/ Edit menu selection to access the condition editor (see Figure 9.4). This is a simple text editor into which you can type commands. The example in Figure 9.4 shows a condition that responds to a "shot." If the object is shot, then it will fade. This condition is associated with object 118,[4] which is the roof of the house.

Figure 9.3.
The Conditions
menu.

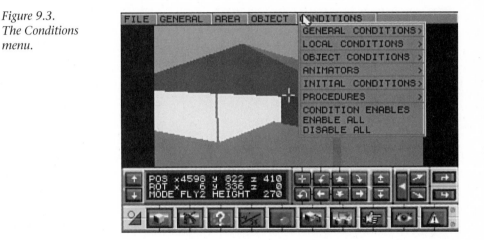

The idea of a "shot" requires some explanation. There are a total of three things that can happen to an object:

Shoot — To shoot an object, click it with the *left* mouse button.

Activate — To activate an object, click it with the *right* mouse button.

Collide with — A collision occurs when your point of view runs into an object.

The terminology reflects Virtual Reality Studio's origins as software designed to create 3D games. This makes for a fun combination. You not only get to create virtual worlds—you get to play in them!

---

[4] Yes, there are 118 objects in this scene! This is the same scene that was created in Chapter 2. The large number of objects required to create an interesting VR Studio scene required some patience and a good memory. A notepad is extremely handy for keeping track of things.

Figure 9.4.
Object condition
editor.

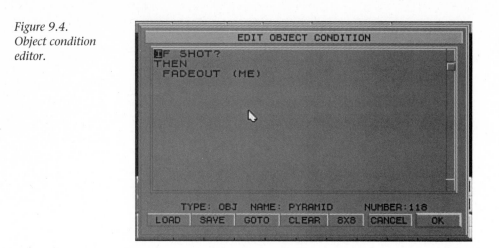

Return now to Figure 9.4. There are three lines of program code in the example. The first line is a test:

```
if shot?
```

The `if` command is a conditional command, and it is used like an `if` statement in any other programming language. The word `shot` is followed by a question mark. Some VR Studio commands can be used with or without the question mark. For example, the command `visit` means to set a flag saying that an area has been visited. The command `visited?` tests the value of the flag to see if the area was visited.

The next part of the command, `then`, is simply an announcement to VR Studio that the following command is to be executed if the `shot?` statement is true. The statement

```
fadeout(me)
```

is the action to carry out. Fadeout is one of many functions provided with VR Studio that changes the state, location, or appearance of an object. For example, you can move an object, turn it into a wire frame, and so on.

Once the condition exists, you can test it in VR Studio. Click on the roof with the left mouse button, and it will slowly fade to invisible. Of course, there's not much use in having an invisible roof if you can't put it back the way it was. Figure 9.5 shows an object condition I added to the vertical column that supports the roof.

Figure 9.5.
A second object
condition.

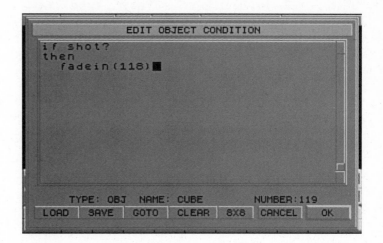

```
            EDIT OBJECT CONDITION
if shot?
then
    fadein(118)■




              TYPE: OBJ   NAME: CUBE          NUMBER:119
  LOAD   SAVE   GOTO   CLEAR   8X8   CANCEL   OK
```

The statements in this condition are similar to the statements in the roof condition. However, this time the action to be carried out is:

```
fadein(118)
```

The fadein will bring the object (the roof) back. There's another difference to note as well. In the first example, the fadeout was applied to me. This is a special variable that always refers to the object that the condition is attached to. Because we are clicking the column, it won't help much to have the column fade in. You can find the number of an object in many ways—the number is shown, for example, when you select an object, and is also shown in many operations (such as the object editor). You cannot use object names in conditions, hence my earlier suggestion that you keep a notepad handy to keep track of the details of your world.[5]

Thus, the statement

```
fadein(118)
```

will cause the roof to fade back into the scene. Figure 9.6 shows the pointer on the roof, and the roof fading out of the scene. Figure 9.7 shows the mouse pointer on the column, and the roof fading back into the scene.

---

[5] You can also take the time to name your objects, but this can be just as tedious as using a notepad. If you plan to develop a very complex scene, and to modify it over a long stretch of time, it will certainly be worth your while to create unique names for each object.

*Figure 9.6.
The roof fading
out after being
"shot."*

*Figure 9.7.
The roof fading
back in after
"shooting" the
column.*

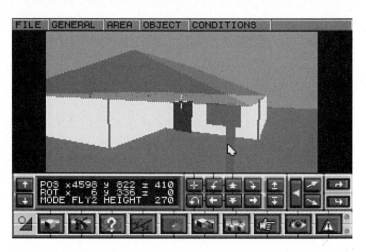

Fading in and out are only a small part of the types of things you can do with conditions. Virtual Reality Studio 2.0 comes with a large number of commands and
statements you can use. Table 9.1 lists some of the more interesting ones. There
are many more in addition to these examples. Collectively, these commands and
statements are known as the Freescape Command Language (FCL).[6]

---

[6] Have you ever noticed that almost all computer-related acronyms use three letters? We're getting awfully close to adding a new part of speech: nouns, pronouns, verbs, adverbs, three-letter
acronyms, prepositions...

Table 9.1. Freescape Command Language: Sample Commands.

Command	Description
activated?	Tests to see if the object was clicked with the right mouse button.
addvar	Adds a value to a variable.
loop/again	Loops through a set of commands a specified number of times.
border	Displays a specified border on the screen.
box	Draws a box on the screen of the specified size.
collided?	Checks to see if the current object has collided with anything.
defarray	Creates an array.
destroy	Destroys the specified object.[7]
for/next	Works like a for/next loop in BASIC.
if/then/else/endif	The familiar "if" control structure.
include	Includes an object in an animation.
goto	Moves the player to a specified entrance.
lockonto	Moves the player so that a specified object is centered on the screen.
moveto	Moves animation to a specified position.
pause	Pauses execution and wait for a specified keypress.
setground	Sets a new ground color.
sound	Plays a sound file.
startanim	Starts playing an animated sequence.
time	Gets system time; usually used for displaying time in *instruments*.

---

[7] This command also points to the roots of VR Studio as a game-creation product. This is a good thing—not only can you use VR Studio to create nifty virtual spaces, you can then turn them into games and have some fun as a reward for the effort you put into its creation.

So far, you have learned about three ways that you can interact with an object and cause the condition to execute: shooting, activating, and colliding. You also can make an object into a *sensor*. To experiment with sensors, create two cubes and shape them as flattened, floating buttons as shown in Figure 9.8. Both objects are poised over the entry to the house. They should be placed so that you will pass under one object or the other when you try to enter the house.

Figure 9.8.
Creating objects
to use as sensors.

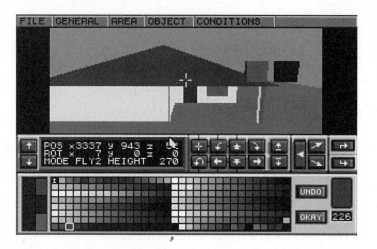

Use the Object/Attributes menu selection to display the dialog box shown in Figure 9.9. There is a group of buttons on the right side of the dialog.[8] Click the SNS button at top right. This stands for sensor. The button will turn dark, and the Sensor button at bottom center of the dialog will be activated. Click the Sensor button, which will display the dialog box shown in Figure 9.10.

A sensor does what its Star Trek-like name implies: it senses your movements. The top-half of the dialog box allows you to specify the directions that the object will sense in, and the lower-half of the dialog box allows you to define the characteristics of the sensor. By default, all the directional buttons are in black, meaning that they are activated. To select one or more active directions, make sure only the directions you want to use are darkened. For example, to specify that the example sensor will only sense when the player moves below it, click all the buttons but the Below button to turn off sensing in those unneeded directions (see Figure 9.11).

---

[8] If you are curious about the function of these various buttons, all will be explained shortly.

Figure 9.9.
The Object
Attributes dialog.

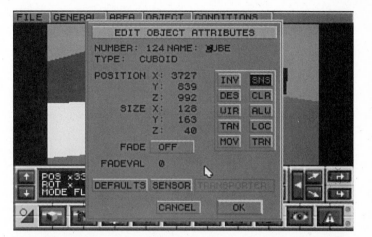

Figure 9.10.
Editing the sensor
attributes.

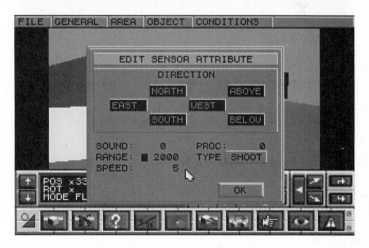

The remaining entries in the dialog box control the characteristics of the sensor:

Sound—Determines which sound, if any, is to be played when the sensor is activated.

Range—The distance over which the sensor operates. The sensor will not detect anything until the player moves within this distance in a direction which is "on."

Speed—How quickly the sensor will react, in 50th's of a second. For example, a setting of 5 indicates that the sensor should respond on 1/10th of a second.

Proc—Which procedure is to be called when the sensor is activated.

Type—There are two types of sensor: detect and shoot. A shoot sensor gives a visual indication when it is activated, and a detect sensor does not. In all other respects, they are identical.

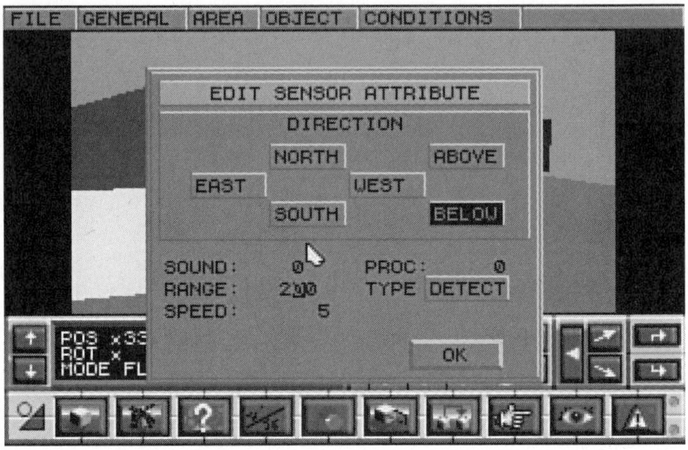

Figure 9.11.
Adjusting the
directions for
sensing.

You can use sensors simply to play sounds, of course, but the best way to use sensors is to have them call procedures. As explained earlier in this chapter, a procedure is a small, independent program that can be called from anywhere in a condition, or from a sensor. To create a procedure, use the Conditions/Procedures/Create menu selection. To edit the procedure, use the Conditions/Procedures/Edit menu selection (see Figure 9.12).

Figure 9.12.
Editing a
procedure.

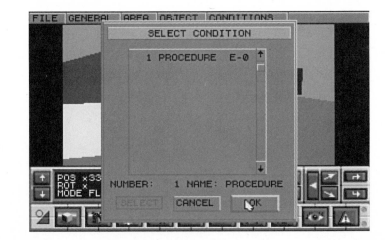

This displays a list of available procedures—in this case, just the one we created. You must create new procedures before you can edit them. Procedures are referred to by number—another good use for that notepad I keep telling you to have handy. To edit the procedure, click on the line in the list box. (There is only one line in this case.) Then click the OK button. This displays a dialog box just like the condition editor (see Figure 9.13). You can enter commands and statements just as you did in the condition editor.

Figure 9.13.
Entering a
command into a
procedure using
the procedure
editor.

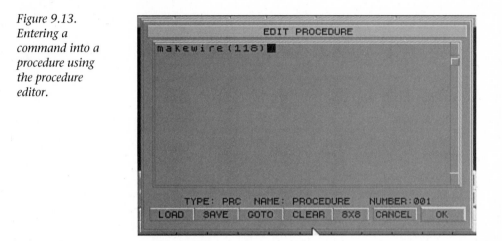

This procedure contains just one statement, but you could enter multiple statements just as easily. The statement is

```
makewire(118)
```

The number is an object number, and it is the roof again. Moving under the sensor will cause the roof to be displayed as a wireframe object instead of as a solid object. Figure 9.14 shows a cube in both solid and wireframe modes.

To complete the example, you can add the statement

```
makesolid(118)
```

to a second procedure. You then can change the sensor attributes for each object to point to the appropriate procedure number (see Figure 9.15, which shows procedure number 2 being set as the active procedure for a sensor).

Figure 9.14.
Examples of a
cube in solid (a)
and wireframe
(b) modes.

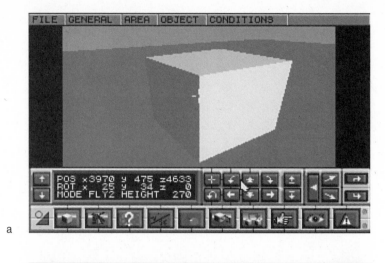

a

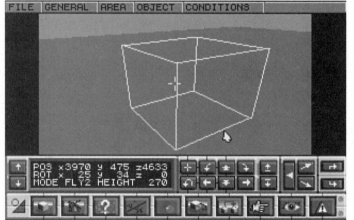

b

In the previous examples, we have put opposite statements in different objects, which allows the player to reverse actions. You can put the reversal action in a single object condition. To do this, you must first test to find out the current state of the object. Figure 9.16 shows a condition that tests to see if an object is invisible. First, the condition checks to see if the object has been shot.[9] If it has, the rest of the code is executed. If not, nothing happens. If the object is invisible, it is faded in. If the object is not invisible, it is faded out.

---

[9] If you recall, a shot consists of a click with the left mouse button.

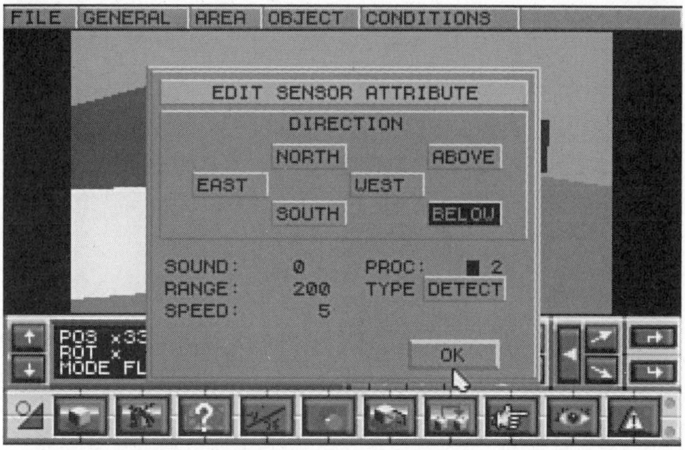

Figure 9.15.
Setting the
procedure number
for a sensor.

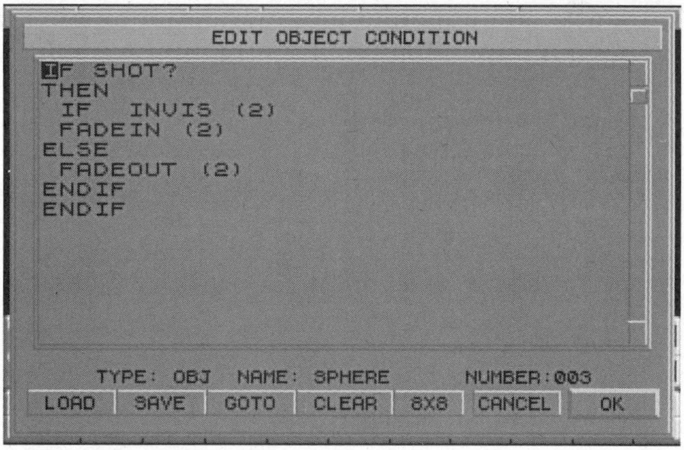

Figure 9.16.
Testing the state
of an object
before acting
on it.

Backgrounds and Borders

To recap, you have learned about two important aspects of Virtual Reality Studio so far. One, you can use it to build 3D virtual environments. Two, you can create rules that the object must obey while a "player"[10] moves through the space. Now you will learn about a third way that you can control the virtual space: backgrounds and borders.

---

[10] This term, like many in VR Studio, is derived from its origins as a game creation tool.

Don't be deceived by those simple terms. As it happens, a VR Studio background/border[11] is actually quite an active place. For starters, you can have a whole collection of borders in your world, and switch from one to the next using conditions. Typically, you would use a background with a specific area. For example, if you were creating a space journey, you might have one background represent a launch control center, and another background represent the inside of the space vessel. You can use the border command in FCL to change the border at any time.[12]

A border also can have controls placed on it, just like the controls in VR Studio itself. You'll learn how to create such controls in this section. Before you do, however, let's look at one of the borders that comes with VR Studio to see how everything works together.

Start by adding a border. This is a rather round-about process, unfortunately. Begin with the menu selection File/Borders/Locate. This is where you tell VR Studio where the borders are located.[13] Now you can use File/Borders/Add to actually add the border. This displays a modified file dialog box (see Figure 9.17). The buttons for navigating to other drives and directories are disabled. Unfortunately, you can't preview the border to see what it looks like until *after* you have added it.[14]

For this example, choose the file spacevga.lbm and click OK. This displays the dialog box in Figure 9.18, which allows you to set various attributes of the border. The most important one to note is the one labeled Freescape Window. Set it to off. This tells the program to ignore the current 3D window, and load the entire background. If it is set to On, the portion of the screen covered by the 3D window will be black when you load the file.

---

[11]Backgrounds and borders are really the same thing in VR Studio. The menu uses the name border, but it's really a background. All will become clear shortly.

[12] If all you want to do is display an image, you also can use the loadscreen command. It will load an image file, and you may optionally display the 3D window on top of it.

[13] Oddly enough, they are located in the borders subdirectory. Why this is not the default, I'll never know. Every other operation that accesses files does fine with the usual methods for loading files, so this unique method for handling borders is completely mysterious.

[14] Yet another odd and frustrating aspect of using borders. It's a good thing that, once I had a border loaded and set up, I liked the result. A clear case of the end justifying the (oddly designed) means.

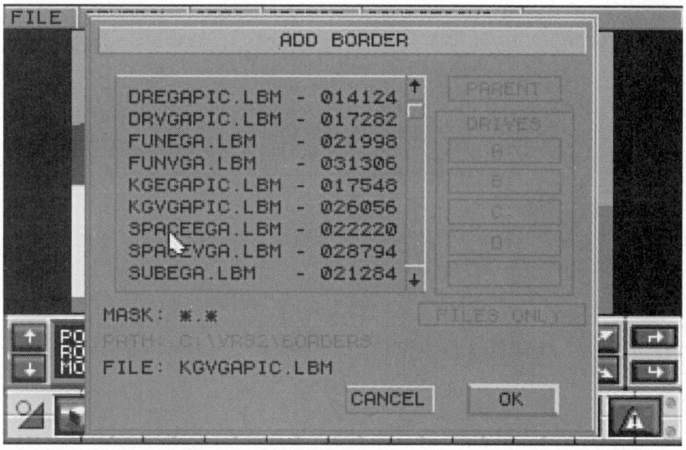

Figure 9.17.
Adding a border
file.

Figure 9.18.
Setting border
attributes.

You may have noticed that the border number of the example in Figure 9.18 is 2. That happened because I wound up creating two borders without realizing it. The way that borders are handled is, no question about it, confusing. If you get lost, you are not the first person to have that happen. I do think that borders add a lot to the finished product, however, so it is well worth your time to persevere.

To view the border, use the File/Borders/View menu selection. This displays the dialog box shown in Figure 9.19.[15] Click the border you want to view, and then click OK.

Figure 9.19.
Selecting a
border.

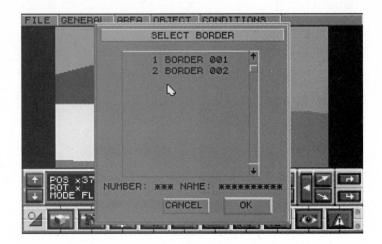

The border should now be displayed on your screen (see Figure 9.20).[16] As you can see, the "border" occupies most of the screen real estate. The black area in the center of the screen is where the 3D world will be displayed.

The next step is to tell VR Studio where that black part of the image is so it can use it as the equivalent of a view screen. Use the General/Set View Window menu selection to display the dialog box shown in Figure 9.21.

There are four numbers in this dialog: the x and y coordinates for the upper-left corner of the window, and the width and height of the view window. Despair not. You do not have to enter these numbers by hand. Click the Set button, which will give you the display shown in Figure 9.22.

---

[15] The user interface of VR Studio is a bit quirky, and I have tried to include as many illustrations as possible to make your use of the product easier. The documentation leaves too much to one's imagination.

[16] The image is of a space control center. The 3D space you will be viewing is of the house created in Chapter 2. If you find this an odd mixture, imagine if you will that a space probe has just landed on a strange planet where the entire land surface is covered with suburban tract houses, and that the folks in the control center are about to launch a remote robot probe to explore the area. Now everything makes perfect sense.

Figure 9.20.
A sample VR
Studio border
image.

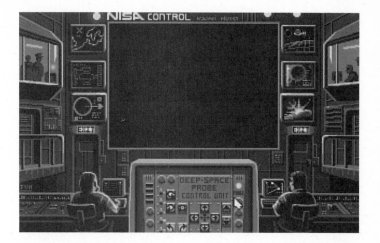

Figure 9.21.
Setting the view
window.

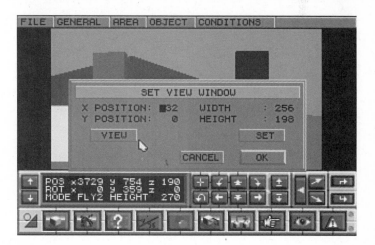

NOTE The numbers from the dialog shown in Figure 9.21 are repeated at the bottom-right corner of Figure 9.22. The thin lines indicate the size and position of the view window corresponding to these numbers.

It would be much easier to adjust the view window if you could see the background. Click on the gray box at the bottom right to open the Select Border dialog, and select spacevga.lbm again. It is displayed along with the outline of the view window (see Figure 9.23). This allows you to match the outline of the view window to the background. To move the window, click and drag it. To change its size, click carefully in the little box at the bottom right of the outline.

*Figure 9.22.
Setting the view
window visually.*

*Figure 9.23.
Adjusting the
view window over
the background.*

Right-click on the screen to return to the Set View Window dialog, and click OK to accept the new values. To test your handiwork, click the eye icon at the lower right of the main VR Studio screen. The view window appears (see Figure 9.24).

Oops—there's no border! This is by design. You can test features of your virtual environment without wasting time loading a border. To see the border, you'll have to get back to the VR Studio screen. Press F1 to do so.

Use the General/Defaults menu selection to open the dialog box shown in Figure 9.25. This dialog box is used to set up the state of your world when it is loaded or reset. There are two areas to pay attention to. At the bottom, enter the number of the border you want to be displayed at startup. Just above that, you can set the default mode. I prefer Fly 2 for its flexibility, but you can set any appropriate mode here. Note also that you can set a default entrance and area. This is important for establishing the initial position in your world. You can accept the default of area 1, entrance 1, or change these values to anything you wish.

Figure 9.24.
Testing the size and position of the view window.

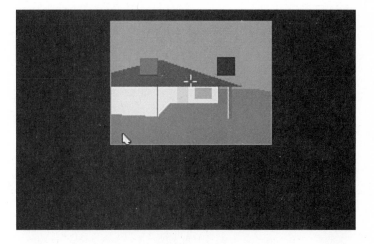

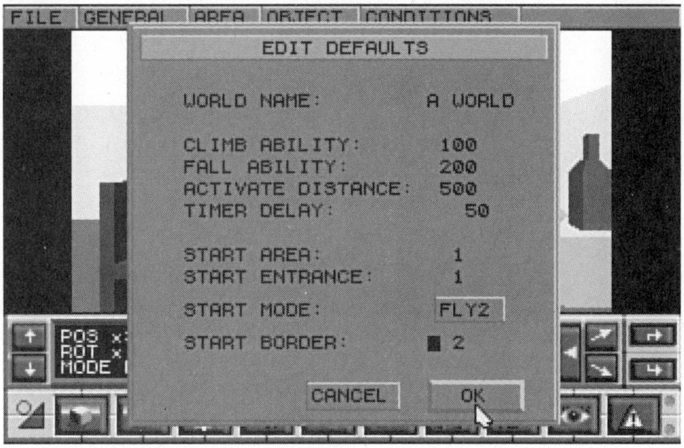

Figure 9.25.
Setting the defaults for your virtual world.

Let's test the view window again. Click the eye icon, and then press the escape key to reset your world. The following should happen:

■ The border is displayed.

■ You are positioned at the area and entrance numbers you set.

The result is shown in Figure 9.26.

Figure 9.26.
The border and
view window
working together.

Controls

Now you can see the benefit of being able to locate your own controls on the border. As things stand, there is no way for you to move around in the 3D world you have created. There are controls included at the bottom-center of the border, but they don't do anything—they are just pretty pixels, with no powers. You need to tell VR Studio where to put the controls using the General/Controls menu selection. This displays the Edit Controls dialog box (see Figure 9.27).

Figure 9.27.
The dialog for
editing controls.

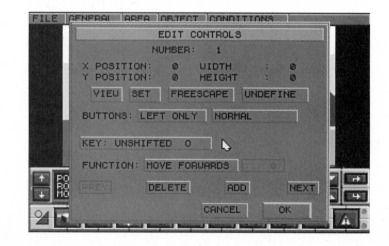

There is a lot going on in this dialog box. Table 9.2 lists the various controls in the dialog and explains what they do.

Table 9.2. Edit Controls Dialog Explained.

Control	Description
X/Y Position	The upper-left corner of the control.
Width	Width of the control.
Height	Height of the control.
View	Works like the View button for borders.
Set	Works like the Set button for borders. It takes you to a screen where you can set the size and location of the control area visually.
Freescape	Sets the size of the control to be the same as the 3D view window.
Undefine	Returns the values of the control to the state they were in originally.
Buttons	Establishes which mouse buttons are used for the control.
Key	Indicates whether there is a keystroke associated with the control, and, if so, which one.
Function	Specifies what the button does. There are a number of built-in functions, or you can add your own.
Prev	Moves to the previous control.
Delete	Removes the control.
Add	Adds a new control. You will be asked to specify a procedure to be called when the control is activated.
Next	Moves to the next control.

Most of the actions you need already exist as pre-defined controls. Figure 9.27 shows the Move Forward control. To tell VR Studio where this control is located, click the Set button. This will display the screen you used to set the view window. Click on the gray box at the lower right to select and view the border, and then move/ change the size of the control outline. Figure 9.28 shows the control outline where it doesn't belong. It is just like the outline for the view window. To move the control around, click and drag. To change the size, click and drag in the little box at the lower right of the box outline.

Figure 9.28.
Adjusting the size
and position of a
control.

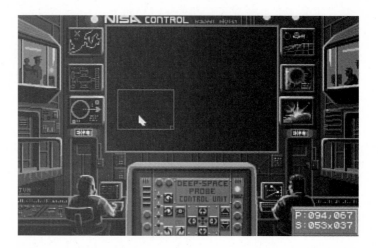

Drag and size the outline until it exactly covers the small arrow pointing up (the "Move Forward" control) on the control panel at the bottom center of the screen. Then repeat this process to set the "Move Backward" control.[17] With these two controls, you now have primitive movement capabilities: forward and back. Figure 9.29 shows the initial entrance point for the world, and Figure 9.30 shows the change in viewpoint that results from a few clicks on the Move Forward control.

Instruments

In addition to controls, you can create instruments that use dials, numbers, or text to display information. For example, you could create a control to display the time. To create a control, use the General/Instruments/Create menu selection, and then use General/Instruments/Edit to change the settings. Figure 9.31 shows the Edit Instrument dialog box.

---

[17] To access this control, just click the Next button in the Edit Controls dialog.

*Figure 9.29.
The initial view
of the world.*

*Figure 9.30.
A changed view
after pressing
Move Forward a
few times.*

Table 9.3 describes the function of the various controls in the dialog.

Table 9.3. Edit Instruments Dialog Explained.

Control	Description
Number	The sequential number for the instrument. Like most things in VR Studio, each instrument has a unique number.
Name	Unlike many things in VR Studio, each instrument can have a name.

continues

Table 9.3. continued

Control	Description
XPOS	The x coordinate for the instrument's upper-left corner.
YPOS	The y coordinate for the instrument's upper-left corner.
Variable	The numeric variable that will contain the data to be displayed in the instrument.[18]
Value1	The minimum value the instrument's variable can have.
Value2	The maximum value the instrument's variable can have.
Col1	Foreground color.
Col2	Background color.
Font	Font to use.
Type	The kind of instrument. Examples include numbers, text, or a dial.
View	Views the instrument.
Delete	Removes the instrument from the list of instruments.
Set	Works like the View button for borders. It takes you to a screen where you can set the size and location of the instrument visually.
Prev	Edits the previous instrument.
Store	You *must* click this button to store the changes you make to an instrument.
Next	Edits the next instrument.

In this example, because we plan to use the instrument to display time (specifically, seconds), the minimum value should be set to 0, and the maximum to 59.

---

[18] This is the first mention of variables in VR Studio. You will note that even variables have numbers. To refer to a variable, append the letter V to the number. In this example, V30 would be used. If you are not familiar with programming, a variable is like a container. It holds a value, and that value can be changed in the program. The opposite of a variable is a constant—a value that doesn't change. The number 5, for example, is a constant.

The other values can stay as they are. To position the instrument, click the Set button and use the same techniques you used for controls. Position it just above the control console at bottom center of the border.

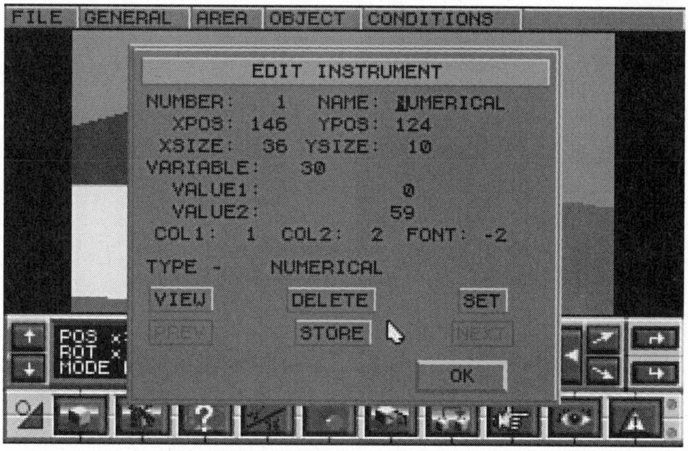

Figure 9.31.
The Edit
Instrument
dialog box.

The key to controlling the instrument is the variable, in this case V30.[19] The value of the variable will be displayed in the control. All we need is some method to update the variable with the current time while the program runs.

Fortunately, VR Studio provides just that opportunity in the General conditions. If you think of a VR Studio session as a kind of live, interactive movie, the General conditions are executed between frames. First, create a new General condition using the Conditions/General Conditions/Create menu selection. Then edit it using the Conditions/General Conditions/Edit menu selection. Select the condition you just created, and click OK. This displays the dialog box shown in Figure 9.32.

Yes, it is the familiar condition editor. I have taken the liberty of adding the time function. It takes three variables, one each for hours, minutes, and seconds. We don't care about the hours and minutes, so I have used dummy variables (V31 and V32) for them. The variable defined for this instrument, V30, is in the seconds position of the function.

---

[19] The first 30 variables, from v0 to v29, are system variables with special meaning. They are explained in the documentation for VR Studio, and need not concern us here.

When this condition is executed—and thanks to the frame orientation of VR Studio, that will be frequently—it will update the instrument we created with the current time. If you wanted to display hours, minutes, and seconds, you would use three interments. Figure 9.33 shows the clock instrument in place, displaying a value of 32.

Figure 9.32.
Editing a Global
condition.

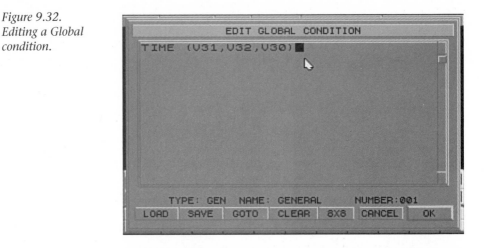

Figure 9.33.
An operating
instrument.

In addition to numbers, you also can display text in instruments. If you were to truly create your world as a game, you could display comments to the player as well as a score.

Animation

Virtual Reality Studio supports two kinds of animations. You can animate objects (or groups of objects), and you can play small 2D animations on the border. The former are referred to simply as animations, whereas the latter are called brush animations.

Object Animations

Object animations are based on conditions. In fact, there is a special set of conditions for animations. To access them, use the Conditions/Animators/Create, and Conditions/Animators/Edit menu selections. The basic structure of an animator is as follows:

- Include the objects for the animation.[20]

- Start command.

- The commands for the animation.

- End command.

For example, the following set of commands would move a single object continuously, 10 units at a time.

```
Include(2)
Start
Loop (30)
Move (0,0,10)
Again
End
```

To play the animation—for example, from a sensor or object—create a condition and add a set of commands like this:

```
if shot?
then
startanim(1)
endif
```

Substitute the actual number of the animation for the value of 1.

That's all there is to creating and using an animation. The key, of course, lies in using the various FCL commands to create the appropriate movements. However, these animations open up a whole range of possibilities for the worlds you create.

---

[20] These can be any objects or groups on the 3D space you created.

Brush Animations

Now let's take a look at brush animations. These apply only to the border, not the 3D space.

The process of creating a brush animation is awkward, with a lot of details. You begin by using the General/Brushes/Cut Brush menu selection to load an image. The file worldvga.lbm is a good example. Once you have selected the file, you'll see the screen shown in Figure 9.34.

Figure 9.34.
Cutting a brush
for an animation.

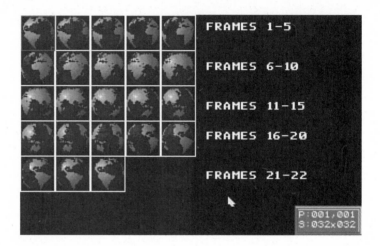

You'll see a thin outline around the first image in the animation. Make sure that it corresponds to the exact outline of the image, then click the right button to complete the cut. Add the brush to the list of brushes, and then go back to the cut screen to cut the next frame. Repeat this process until all frames have been cut.

What you now have is a set of brushes. The next step is to create a brush animation, and then add the brushes to the animation. Use the General/Brush Animation/Create to create the animation, then General/Brush Animation/Edit to work with it. The dialog box shown in Figure 9.35 is used to build the animation brush out of the brushes you cut.

To add the individual brushes, click the Add button and select them from the list of brushes, one at a time. When you have loaded all of the brushes, click OK. You can preview the animation (as shown in Figure 9.36) by clicking the Preview button.

*Figure 9.35.
Editing an
animation brush.*

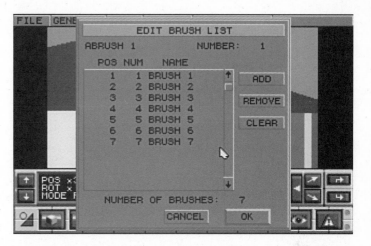

*Figure 9.36.
Previewing a
brush animation.*

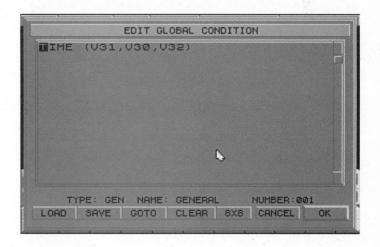

You can then place the brush animation using the same techniques that you used for the view window and the controls/instruments. To access the dialog for adjusting the position and size of the animation, use the General/Brush Animation/Edit menu selection, and click the Set button. The animation will play—single, repeat, or random, depending on the setting in the edit dialog—automatically (see Figure 9.37).

Figure 9.37.
An animation
playing auto-
matically (that's
it at the upper
left).

Summary

Virtual Reality Studio has many features of the bigger VR programs. In fact, it was created by a company in England that has developed high-end, sophisticated VR simulations. I have a love/hate relationship with VR Studio. On the plus side, it offers an inexpensive way to explore virtual spaces. On the negative side, there are some bugs that need to be resolved, and the interface is, at best, awkward. On the whole, however, and considering the cost, VR Studio offers a decent value, and an easy entry into virtual reality.

III

VIRTUAL REALITIES

10

YOU ARE
THE STAR

This chapter will show you how to combine video with virtual reality.[1] This involves putting real objects into a virtual space.[2] For example, in this chapter you'll learn how to put a video of yourself into a landscape created with Vista Pro, or into a 3D Studio animation. The road to this objective winds around a bit, but the end result makes the journey well worth while. You'll start with an introduction to Media Merge, an exciting new video editing package from ATI. After learning how to work with Media Merge, you will learn how to set up a simple video studio.[3] Finally, in the last section of this chapter, you'll find out how to put all of the pieces together to create your own VVRs (Video Virtual Realities).

Video Basics

Everyone agrees about one thing when it comes to using video on a computer:

> **Video allows you to *show* what you mean, instead of just describing it.**

If you have a new product, you can show your customers how it works, and how it will benefit them. If you supply technical equipment, now you can show your users how to perform maintenance. In both cases, using video to get your message across is smart, because it's almost impossible to describe something that the reader hasn't *seen* before. In the case of virtual reality, the virtual spaces you create may never have been seen by anyone before.

These advantages of video led to Stage One of video on a PC: the video clip. A video clip is a self- contained bit of video that shows one thing, and one thing only. This is good, but it's not enough.

Media Merge is Stage Two: the video production. With Media Merge, you can now show not only what you mean, you can tell a story—and you have the tools to tell it very well.

---

[1] Which raises a question: what does one call such a hybrid? Virtual Video springs to mind, but isn't terribly accurate. I lean toward VVR—Video Virtual Reality. Let's face it: just about everything else has a three-letter acronym.

[2] "Objection, your honor! Video objects are not real objects," the defense attorney says, jumping from his seat. "Overruled," the judge says, adding, "everyone knows that video is real. Don't you watch reality TV?"

[3] That's an interesting concept: setting up your own video studio. Be honest now: did you ever think you would be reading a book, thinking to yourself, "Hmmm...should I set up a video studio this weekend?" The fact that one can now rationally consider such possibilities points up how far we've already gone toward virtual reality.

For example, some folks have complained that the size of a PC video window is small—usually somewhere between 160x120 and 320x240. At most, this covers one quarter of the screen. If what you have in mind is watching the latest Indiana Jones movie, this argument has some merit. But if the video window is sharing the screen with such things as interactive menus and buttons, text blocks, and bitmaps—video in a window suddenly becomes even better than full-screen video. For example, you could create a virtual space, add video elements to it, and then place it within the context of a text story line, or combine it with still images, add music or narration, etc.

Learning to work with video is like any other skill: a little time and repetition will go a long way toward making you good at it. This chapter will show you the basics of putting together a real video production, and then apply those skills to virtual reality.[4] The title of the video is "Kayak Self Rescue." The video footage comes from a demonstration of one of the popular sports in my hometown. I chose this subject for several reasons:

- The subject is not widely known, so it will be a good proof of the concept that video is useful for communicating about new ideas.

- The subject is graphic: boats, paddles, water, and the paddler are all easily seen and comprehended even in a small, 160x120 format video.

- The subject is inherently interesting: if you are planning on kayaking in the ocean, knowing how to rescue yourself is pretty important stuff.

I will take you step by step through the process of creating a video using video files included on the CD-ROM that comes with Media Merge. They are all located in the tutorial directory—feel free to peek at them ahead of time. The files are described individually in the section *Working with Media Merge* in this chapter.

Video Concepts

In one sense, all of us are video experts. Think about how much television you've seen over the years: every commercial, every sitcom, every movie you have ever

---

[4]This chapter started out as a "guest chapter" in the documentation for Media Merge. I was very impressed with the capabilities of Media Merge, as well as it's potential for combining virtual reality and video. I've added a lot of additional material to the portions of the chapter that cover Media Merge, including some tricks and tips that are not covered in the Media Merge documentation.

seen has been part of your education for working with video on a computer. Like most of us, the only thing lacking is a framework of knowledge that will help you decide what video techniques to use in your own productions. That will come with time, of course, but this section will give you a jump start.

There are five key areas that you should think about before you begin to produce video:

■ Moving Images—Video shows movement. Use that movement to your advantage. Don't rely on static, boring subjects in your video clips— when was the last time you saw a commercial that didn't jump and dance and dazzle you? With Media Merge, you can mix and match static and dynamic content.

■ Transitions—A video production is made up of several video clips. How you make the transition from one clip to the next is important.

■ Content—Video moves and is therefore interesting in its own right. Don't use that as an excuse to use boring material. Seek out subjects that are interesting—that will double the impact of your final production.

■ Timing—Unlike a book or a document, a video production rolls along in real time. Timing of various events—music, narration, dramatic moments, etc.—is critical.

■ Pace—Finding the right pace for your video is important. Short clips that whiz by will confuse, and long, similar clips risk boredom.

Each of these topics is described in detail in this section.[5]

Moving Images

Video *is* movement. Unlike static images, video allows you to show life in action. To create videos with impact, you'll want to put as much action in your videos as possible.[6] The key to using movement is simple: tell your story with actions, not words, whenever possible.

---

[5]My earlier book, *PC Video Madness*, includes an extended treatment of a variety of video issues, including how to use a camera, how to light a scene, and other topics.

[6]That is not strictly true, although if you will only be doing television commercials you can assume it is always true. Action is a good thing; too much action is usually confusing. In general, it is easier to err on the side of too little action.

For example, there will be times when you simply must use a video clip of a "talking head." That's any video that simply shows someone talking. Instead of sitting that person behind a desk, why not have him look up as they he starts speaking, or perhaps he could be walking, or pointing at the subject he is talking about. Even adding an interesting background—a seacoast, a factory floor, a busy workplace—adds visual interest.

Another important aspect of movement involves movement within the frame from one scene to the next. One scene can contain a subject at the upper left; the next can use a subject at the lower right. Use such motion to add interest—but be careful not to overdo it with stuff coming from all directions. For example, you could have a series of three subjects move into the frame from the left, and then have one subject come in from the right to offer a summary.

Finally, movement is not the ultimate answer for every video clip. You may want to emphasize something by allowing it to be perfectly still during a clip.

Transitions

The best videos are made up of a number of video clips. The example video in this chapter, for example, uses eight clips. Normally, you won't just chop from one video clip to the next; you'll add transitions between clips. Transitions include such effects as wipes and fades, and Media Merge makes it very easy to add transitions to your video productions.

There are three major types of transitions:

- Same-subject transitions
- New-subject transitions
- Breaking transitions

You should use different kinds of wipes and fades for each type of transition.

A *same-subject transition* occurs when you have two clips that are very closely related. For example, the first clip might show a complete picture of a product, while the next clip shows a close-up of a particular part of the product. Generally, you should use soft, unassuming effects for same-subject transitions. A dissolve is a good technique to use in these situations.

A *new-subject transition* occurs when you have two clips that do not relate closely, but have some relationship to each other. For example, the first clip might show how to load paper in a new printer, while the second clip might show how to attach a FAX device to the printer. Both clips are about the printer, but they are also about different topics. This is a more abrupt change, and you can signal the abruptness of the change by using an appropriate transitional effect. In this example, a wipe would be a good choice.

A *breaking transition* occurs when two clips are about very different subjects. For example, if you have a series of six clips that show different aspects of a printer, and then have five clips that show different aspects of a copier, you should use a transitional effect that makes it clear that a major break is occurring. You may also want to add a title sequence to alert the viewer to what is going on. In this example, the Media Merge Boxes effect would work well—especially if you use color between the videos. You could easily put title text on a solid color.

Content

There is sometimes a temptation to rely on the movement in a video image to keep the viewer's interest. It's true that video alone is interesting simply because it moves. But if you want your productions to stand out, keep a sharp eye out for interesting content as well.

People make particularly interesting video subjects, but not if they are nervous about the experience. Help the subject of the video relax by minimizing the impact of the video taping process—don't constantly start and stop recording. Set everything up in advance, and let your subject act naturally.

For inanimate objects, get as close as you can to the object. Fill the frame! PC video sizes are small, and you don't want to lose detail if you can avoid it. If the subject is large—like the kayaks in the tutorial later in this chapter—keep the background simple so the outline of the subject is clear.

> TIP   Take some close-up shots of various details. You can use some of them later during production to emphasize these details.

Timing

As you work with video, you will automatically develop a sense of timing. It is one of the most important assets you can have for creating video productions that are strong and effective. Knowing when to end a video clip, and start the next one, is something of an art. However, there are a few basic rules that will get you started.

- A good starting point usually involves action. You don't need a lot of tape prior to the beginning of the action. In fact, the only reason to use any slack time at the beginning or end of a clip is to use it as part of a transition, such as a fade from black.

- Every clip has a start and an end; you just have to find out where they are. Don't settle for just any ending point. Here's a trick: count the action beats in a clip. A beat is anything that happens—he picks up a pen, he touches his hat, he pauses for effect, he points at the audience. Everything that happens is a beat. End a clip on a strong beat.[7]

- Good things come in threes. A three-beat clip is often perfect. Or try two clips to set up the idea, and then hit hard with a third clip. Use same-subject transitions between the three clips, and follow the third clip with a new-subject transition.

Pace

It's very important to find the right pace for each video production you create. I am speaking here of the overall video, not individual clips. If the video moves too slowly—if the story is being told too slowly—your viewers will lose interest. If the video is too fast, your viewers will miss important information.

Keeping a video on a useful pace can be difficult if you don't have experience with video production. Fortunately, there's a simple cure. Find someone you trust to view your material and give you feedback about the pacing. Here are some questions you can ask yourself to get started:

- Does each video clip move the story along?

- Is each video clip part of the same story?

- Is there any part of a clip that seems to be just hanging out, serving no useful purpose?

- Is each video clip long enough to make a clear point? Is it short enough to hold interest?

---

[7]Sometimes, the clip must serve other masters. For example, a clip may have a natural ending, but the script requires that you hold that subject for more time. Perhaps the narration is complex at that point, and the clip has to last at least long enough to explain the subject. If the clip is truly boring, you might be able to use one of those detail shots I mentioned earlier. While you are in the field videotaping, it's always a good idea to collect more shots than you think you'll need.

The Viewer over Your Shoulder

With experience, you will learn to be your own best viewer. Until then, sit down to look at your video-in-progress with an imaginary viewer looking over your shoulder at your work. Ask yourself if the video you are creating will be interesting and useful to that viewer.

Working with Media Merge

Media Merge provides two tools for working with video files: the Story Board and the Scene Editor. The Story Board is used to arrange your video clips in the right order, and to put transitions between clips. The Scene Editor is used to merge multiple audio and video clips into a single clip. You can create some very interesting effects using the Scene Editor.

RECIPE

1 Story Board Editor   1 Video camcorder or VCR
1 Scene Editor   1 solid color background
1 Sound editing program   1 tripod
1 Video capture card

Instructions: Toss images into camcorder (use a tripod for best results) and blend well. Select best chunks and capture to hard disk. Merge clips using Scene Editor, and create sequence using the Storyboard. Serve and watch your guests smile. For a gourmet touch, add virtual animations instead of one or more video files.

Let's start with the Story Board. It's very easy to use, and all by itself it gives you a lot of power.

The Story Board

The concept behind the Story Board is simple. There are two kinds of slots, as you can see in Figure 10.1. The big boxes are slots for video clips, and the little boxes are slots for transition effects. To create a video production, you just put all of your video clips into slots, and then select transitions to use between the clips.

Figure 10.1.
The Story Board window.

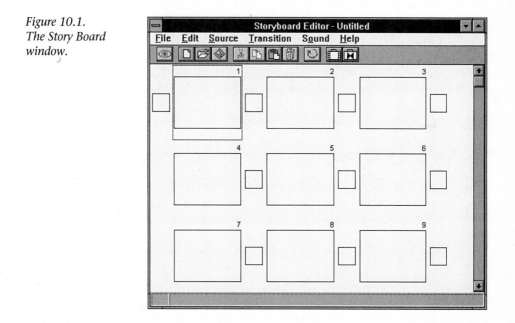

Let's add a video to the first large box (it has the number one at the upper-right corner). Double-click the box to display the dialog box shown in Figure 10.2.

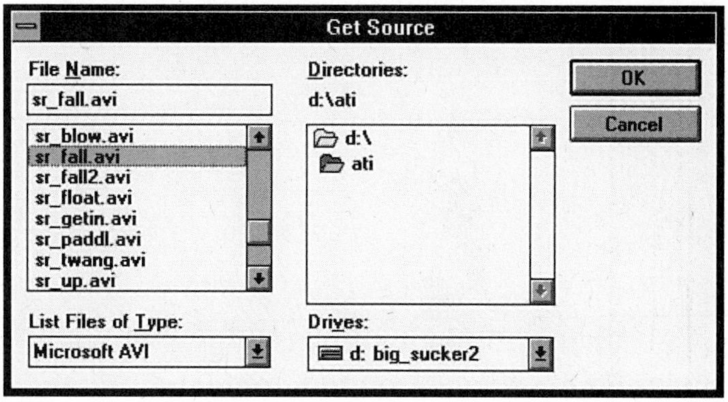

Figure 10.2.
Selecting a source video to add.

This is a standard Windows Open File dialog, and you can use it to locate and load a video clip. If you would like to follow along, find the file \tutorial\sr_fall.avi on the CD-ROM that comes with Media Merge. Click on the filename, and then click on the OK button to load it. A small image of the first frame will appear in the box, as shown in Figure 10.3.

Figure 10.3.
A file has been
added to the
Story Board.

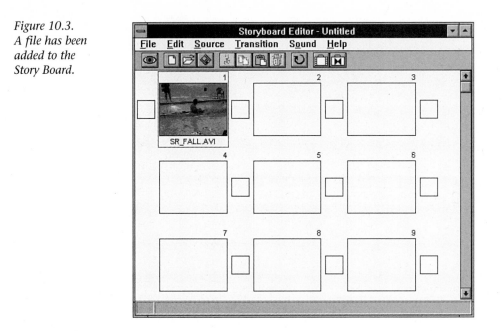

You can edit the clip easily. If you have not already done so, use File Manager to create a file association between .avi files and videdit.exe. Then, when you want to edit the clip, just double-click it to launch VidEdit.

Even though you only have one clip so far, you can add a transition effect. You'll put it in the small box to the left of the file you just loaded. To create a transition, double-click the small box now. This will display the Transition Browser dialog box (see Figure 10.4).

There are nine kinds of transitions you can use. Each transition has options that you can set to vary the effect. Table 1 lists all of the transitions, and suggests ideas for using them effectively.

A dissolve is often a good choice for an opening transition. Double-click on the Dissolve icon to display the dialog box shown in Figure 10.5. The top half of the dialog box is used to set the parameters for the transition, and the lower half is used for setting the style of a transition. A dissolve doesn't have any style settings.

*Figure 10.4.
Using the
Transition
Browser.*

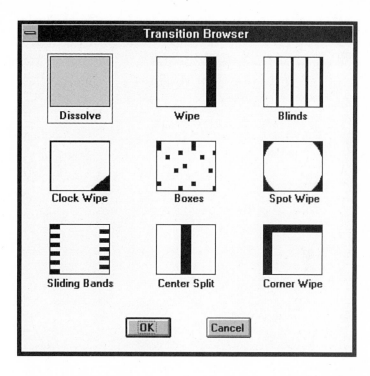

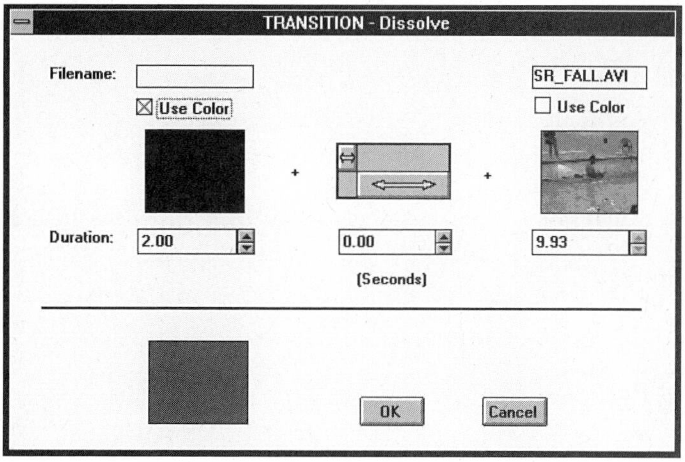

*Figure 10.5.
Setting options
for the Dissolve
transition.*

The top half of the dialog box is divided into three sections. The preceding video clip is controlled in the left section, the next video clip is controlled in the right section, and the length of the transition is controlled in the middle section.

Unlike most transitions, an opening transition has no video on the incoming side. The Story Board automatically supplies a solid color in place of the missing video clip. (Note that the check box "Use Color" is checked in Figure 10.5.) To change the color, just double-click on the black box. "Use Color" means that when the .avi file is created, you will see the color shown for the time indicated at "Duration." In this case, the duration of the solid color is two seconds. You can change this value by typing, or by using the up/down arrows at the right.

The video clip that will follow the transition is shown at the right of the dialog box. Under the image is the length of the video clip (9.93 seconds in this example). The filename appears above the image.

In the center of the dialog box is a little contraption that controls the duration of the transition. The top half shows the preceding video clip, and the bottom half shows the next video clip. The duration is initially set to zero, so the blocks representing the two video clips do not overlap. The time you enter as a duration is the time that the two video clips will overlap. During the overlap time, the transition will be "in progress." This means different things for different transitions.

In the case of a dissolve, the image on the left—solid black—will dissolve to the image on the right—the video clip. For example, if you enter a value of 1.5 seconds into the box below the contraption, the contraption will change its appearance as shown in Figure 10.6a. Figure 10.6b shows frame 13 from the transition—the image is still dark, and we are slightly more than halfway through the transition. Because the duration is 1.5 seconds, and the video was created with 15 frames per second, there are a total of 22 frames in the transition. Frame 1 will be completely black, and frame 22 will be completely from the video file.

Figure 10.6a.
A dissolve with
a duration of
1.5 seconds.

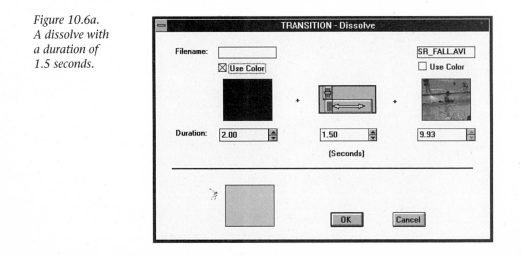

Figure 10.6b.
A frame from
about the middle
of the transition.

Note (in Figure 10.6a) that the bars representing the two videos now overlap. If we were to create a video file right now, we would see:

- .5 seconds of black

- 1.5 seconds with the video clip sr_fall.avi fading in from the black

- 8.43 seconds of the rest of the video clip sr_fall.avi.

The contraption is designed to help you visualize the relationship of the three pieces: the previous video clip, the transition, and the next video clip.

> **TIP** Adding a transition to a video production does not add additional video to the production. A transition is applied during the time that two video clips overlap.

Click on the OK button when you have all of the durations set correctly. The Story Board screen now looks like what you see in Figure 10.7. The appearance of the small box has changed to show that a transition exists. To edit the transition, just double-click the small box.

Figure 10.7.
The Story Board
with one video
clip and an
opening
transition.

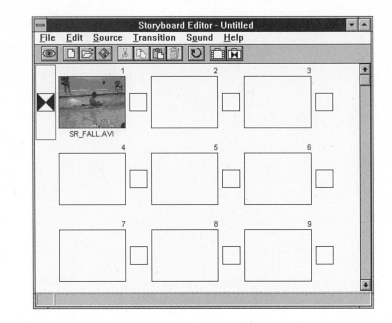

This is a good time to look at table 1, which explains the various transitions and how to use them effectively. Although the terms "video 1" and "video 2" are used to refer to the video clips, either or both can also be a solid color for any of the transitions.

Table 10.1. Transition effects in the Story Board.

Icon	Transition	Description
	Dissolve	Fades from video 1 to video 2 over the time specified. Useful for same-subject breaks between clips, but it also functions well in breaking transitions if you use a solid color as one part of the fade.
	Wipe	Moves one video over another. Different style settings allow you to control which video moves. You can slide the next video over the previous video, or you can push one video clip with the other. Useful for new-subject transitions. You can wipe from eight directions: top/bottom, left/right, or the four corners (diagonal wipe).

Icon	Transition	Description
‖‖‖‖	Blinds	The transition looks just like Venetian blinds, and can be done horizontally or vertically. This is a fairly dramatic transition, and is best for new-subject and breaking transitions.
	Clock wipe	A radial wipe.
	Boxes	Random boxes appear to create the transition from one clip to the next. Can be used almost anywhere, but don't overuse it because it is a very noticeable effect.
	Spot wipe	Video 2 appears over video 1 in a growing spot; the spot can have several different shapes. This is a useful transition for video clips that have the subject located in the center of the frame. Best for breaking transitions, but in the right situation (dramatic is the key word here) it can be effective as a new-subject transition.
	Sliding bands	Numerous bands interlock like the teeth of a comb, with video 2 sliding over the top of video 1. A good new-subject transition, although it is sometimes effective as a same-subject transition, too.
	Center split	A very good breaking transition. Video 2 (or, often, a solid color) comes in from both sides like a closing door.
	Corner wipe	Video 2 slides over video 1 from one of the corners. This is an effective new-subject or breaking transition. You also can use it to create a shuffle effect with a sequence of same-subject videos.

Each of these transitions has its own individual style settings. For example, you may be able to select the direction the effect moves from, or how one video clip replaces another during the transition.

There are seven more files used for the complete Kayak Self Rescue video, as shown in Figure 10.8. I also have added transitions for each of the video clips, as indicated by the shading of the small boxes.

Figure 10.8.
The complete
Kayak Self
Rescue video in
the Story Board.

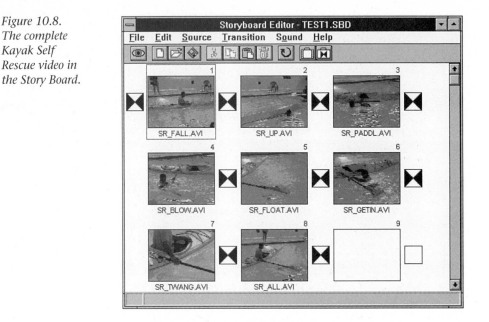

Let's take a look at how I arrived at the choice for some of these transitions. This will give you some insight into the factors that will play a role in your own selection process when you create your own video productions with the Story Board.

You often can determine what transition to use simply by examining the ending and beginning segments of the adjoining video clips. For example, Figure 10.9 shows the ending frame of the video clip sr_fall.avi. Figure 10.10 shows the starting frame of the video clip sr_up.avi.

These images are very similar. Both show the kayak upside down, and the position of the paddler is similar, although we can't see much of him in Figure 10.9. I chose to use the Sliding Bands transition because it adds some texture during the transition, which would otherwise be a very boring transition. Blinds also might be a good choice—there are no hard and fast rules about which transition is best. A dissolve wouldn't be effective, however, because it would look like the person in Figure 10.10 was appearing out of nowhere. In some situations, of course, this would be exactly the right effect, but not here: this is a serious subject!

Figure 10.9.
The ending frame
of sr_fall.avi.

Figure 10.10.
The starting
frame of
sr_up.avi.

Figure 10.11 shows a frame from the midpoint of this transition. The textural quality of this transition is evident. It adds interest to an otherwise mundane transition.

Figure 10.11.
A Sliding Bands
transition at the
midpoint.

Let's look at another transition. There is a same-subject transition between the clips sr_blow.avi and sr_float.avi. Figure 10.12 shows the last frame of sr_blow.avi. The paddler is inflating a small flotation device that he attached to his paddle. Figure 10.13 shows the first frame of sr_float.avi, which is a close-up of the float on the paddle. I chose a dissolve to make the transition as smooth and unobtrusive as possible.

Figure 10.12.
The last frame
of the file
sr_blow.avi.

Figure 10.13.
The first frame
of sr_float.avi.

Figure 10.14 shows the middle frame of the transition, with the two images super-imposed. The paddle image is gradually fading in.

Figure 10.14.
The last frame
of the file
sr_blow.avi.

TIP

> Use longer durations (1 to 2 seconds) for same-subject transitions, and shorter durations for new-subject and breaking transitions (.5 to 1.5 seconds, or less).

And remember: as with all rules, there are times when you will need to break the rules. Only you can decide when the time is right!

The Scene Editor

The Scene Editor is an extremely powerful tool. If you haven't worked in a video studio (and that includes just about everyone), the concepts may be completely new.

There are two important concepts used in the Scene Editor: *time line* and *keying*.

A time line is a method of representing a video project on your screen. The starting time (zero) is at the left of the screen (see Figure 10.15). Keying allows you to selectively add or remove portions of the video image. It is the process used to place the weatherman in front of the weather map on the evening news. You'll learn how to use keying later in this section.

*Figure 10.15.
The Scene Editor
screen. The time
markers are at
the top, beneath
the toolbar.*

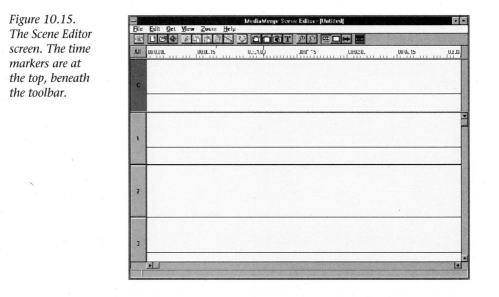

The Scene Editor consists of the time markers and time lines. The time markers are located at the top of the screen, just below the toolbar. These mark time as explained in the section *Time Lines Explained* that follows. The time lines are the horizontal bars below the time markers. The top time line is labeled with a "C" at the left edge. This is the *composite* time line, and it shows how the final video will look. The other time lines are slots that can hold video clips, audio, bitmaps, or text.

When you produce a video using the Scene Editor, the various objects in their various time lines will be combined into the final video production.

Time Lines Explained

The individual frames are marked with tic marks at the top of the window, just beneath the toolbar. The starting time is marked as 00:00.00. This is a special form of time-keeping. The first two digits are hours, and the second two digits are minutes. The last two digits are frames.

There are 30 frames in one second. That means that time is represented like this in the Scene Editor:

> 00:00.00—Starting time
> 00:00.15—Halfway through the first second
> 00:01.00—The first second
> 00:01.15—Halfway through the second second
> 00:02.00—The second second

To represent each frame, time is shown like this (see Figure 10.16):

> 00:00.00—The first frame
> 00:00.01—The second frame
> 00:00.02—The third frame
> ...
> 00:00.29—The thirtieth frame
> 00:01.00—The thirty-first frame

The kind of video you see on your television uses 30 frames per second. Most of the time, on your computer, you won't work with a full 30 frames per second, but because that is the maximum number of frames per second, that's what the Scene Editor must use. The most common rate you will work with is 15 frames per second. In that case, each frame will occupy two ticks on the time line.

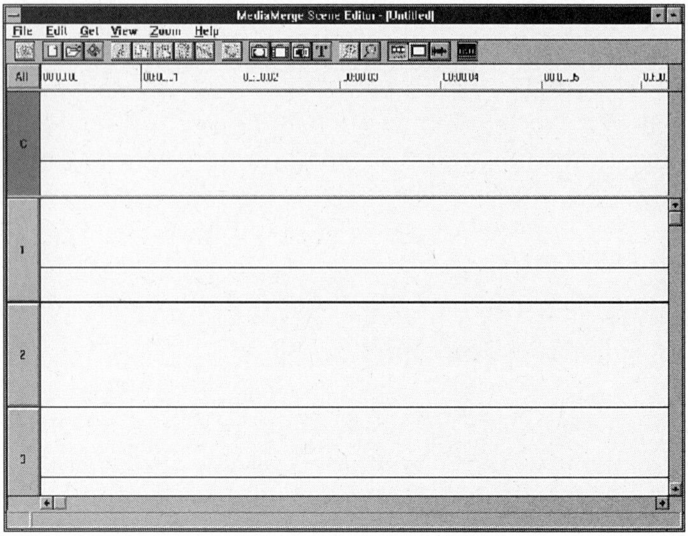

*Figure 10.16.
A time line
expanded to
show every
frame.*

You can adjust the scale of the time line easily in the Scene Editor. You can zoom in to see every frame, or you can zoom out to see the entire scene at a glance. Each tick on the time line can represent a single frame, or many frames. The zoom menu lets you choose how many frames you will see at one time. During this tutorial, you will learn how to adjust the scale of the time line.

The time line comes into play when you load one or more video files into the Scene Editor. It will show you how long each video is. You can use the time line to set the starting time of a video, or to check the ending time of a video. The time line gives you precise control over the composition of a video scene.

A video scene can be made up of any of the kinds of resources shown in Table 10.2. You'll learn how to use each of them in this section.

Table 10.2. Scene Editor resources.

Resource	Description
Video clip	Any .avi file. The video clip may or may not have any audio in it.
Audio clip	Any .wav file.
Still image	A bitmapped image. Valid file formats include .bmp, .pcx, .gif, .tif, .tga, .eps, and .wmf.

Resource	Description
Text	The Scene Editor allows you to create a moving or scrolling text object.

Video Clips

You can use the Scene Editor to combine video clips using overlay techniques. The first step is to load in the base video clip using the Get/Video menu selection. The cursor will change to a little hand—click at the left edge of time line number one to place the video file. The result is shown in Figure 10.17. The loaded clip is sr_all.avi, from the tutorial directory of the CD-ROM disc. It is one of the clips used in the Story Board example.

Figure 10.17.
A single clip
loaded into the
Scene Editor.

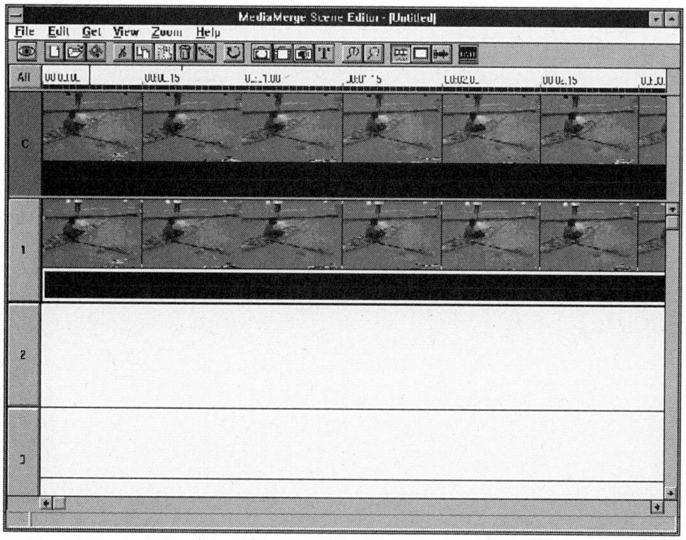

The top half of time line #1 contains the video clip, and the bottom half of time line #1 contains the audio portion of the .avi file. The composite time line shows the same images as time line #1 because there is only one clip loaded. Now load a second video clip, sr_strok.avi. Place it in time line #2, as shown in Figure 10.18.

Now look at the composite time line. It contains the same images as time line #2. The images from time line #1 have been completely lost. This is temporary. The important point to notice is that the images in each successive time line are placed on top of the images in the preceding time lines.

*Figure 10.18.
Two clips loaded
into the Scene
Editor.*

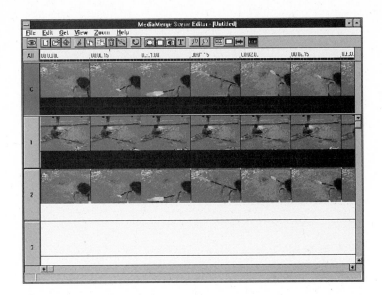

Here is where you learn to use keying techniques. Click on time line #2 to select it
(if it is not already highlighted). Use the Edit/Set Overlay Option menu choice to
display the dialog box shown in Figure 10.19.

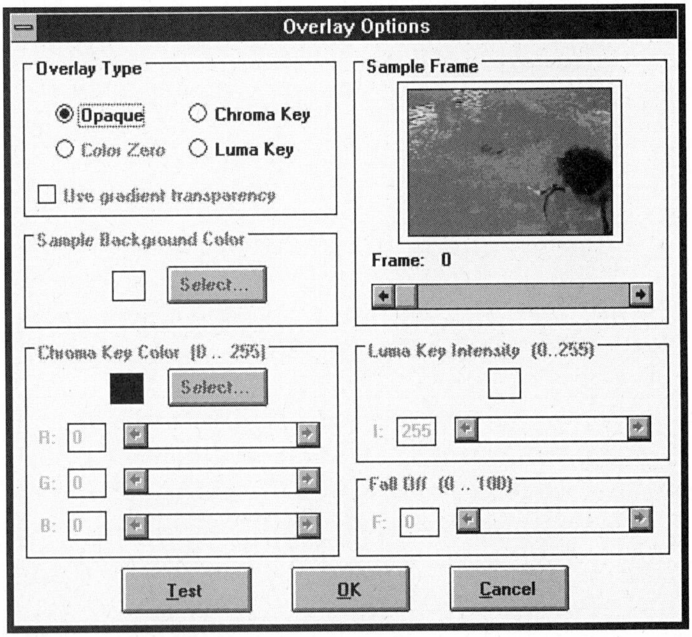

*Figure 10.19.
Setting overlay
options for a
video clip.*

This dialog box is the heart of the Scene Editor. You'll learn about all of its capabilities elsewhere in this documentation. Right now, you'll learn how to use it to create a Chroma Key. This uses color to select which portions of the video image will stay, and which will be dropped.

Click the Chroma Key radio button. It's in the Overlay Type box at the upper left of the dialog. Now move the mouse to the small image in the sample frame box. The cursor changes to a small dropper, which you can use to select the Key color. Click in the large green area just above the paddle. The values for the Red, Green, and Blue portions of the color should match those shown in the box Chroma Key Color (see Figure 10.20). If they do not, click again on a slightly green shade, or enter the values using the keyboard.

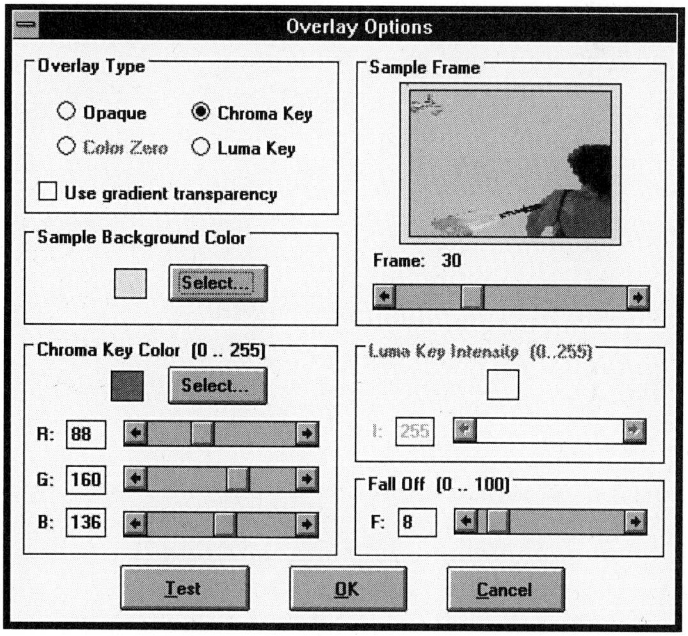

Figure 10.20.
Setting Chroma
Key options.

When you select a Chroma Key color, that color is used to select the portion of the video image to drop. Try clicking on various colors. You'll see that all portions of the video image matching that color seem to disappear. Here's the trick: *any video image in another time line will show through wherever the Chroma Key color exists.* This is true only for time lines with lower numbers than this time line. In this example, setting a Chroma Key color in time line #2 allows us to see the image in time line #1 wherever the Chroma Key color exists.

Selecting only one color value to use as a Chroma Key won't actually give you useful results in most cases. The Fall Off box at the lower right of the dialog box allows you to expand the Chroma Key effect to similar colors. In this example, there are a range of green colors that need to "disappear." A fall off setting of 8 is about right.

When you have all of the settings—Overlay Type, Chroma Key Color, and Fall Off—set correctly, the sample frame should look like the example in Figure 10.20. Click OK to save the settings. The Scene Editor now looks like Figure 10.21.

Figure 10.21.
The Composite
time line has
been altered by
the use of
Chroma Key.

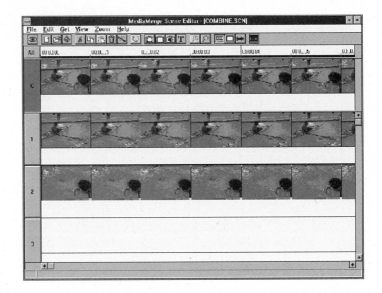

The Composite time line looks completely different. The video clip in time line #1 now shows through the areas that contain the Chroma Key colors. As objects move from frame to frame, only those areas that contain the Chroma Key colors will allow the first video clip to show through.

Because this is a time line, you may want to set the starting point of the overlay video clip in time line #2 so that it ends at the same time as the first video clip. To do this, you will need to change the zoom factor. In Figure 10.21, the time line has been zoomed all the way in to show each individual frame. To zoom out, select the Zoom/1 second (30 frames) menu selection. This will show the full video clips in the time lines. You can click and drag the clip in time line #2 until its ending point matches that of the video in time line #1, as shown in Figure 10.22.

Figure 10.22.
Adjusting video
clip timing in the
Scene Editor.

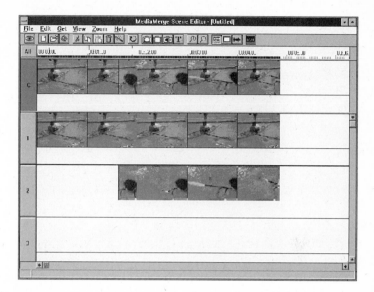

You can use multiple video clips to create multi-layered effects. Figure 10.23 shows three video clips loaded, and key colors have been created for two of them, allowing the underlying video clips to show through.

Figure 10.23.
Using three video
clips to create
multi-layered
effects.

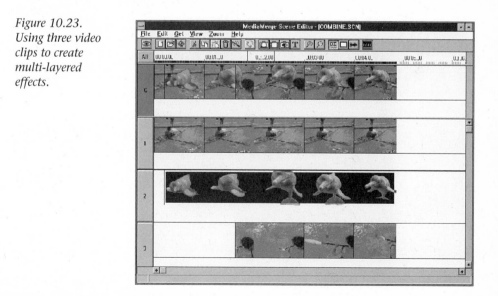

> **TIP**
>
> You can adjust the starting or ending point of a video clip (or audio clip, for that matter) by clicking and dragging the beginning or ending edge of the clip in its time line.

Note that the video in time line #2 has a black background behind the dolphin. There is a story behind this video that explains how to work with videos that do not work well with conventional keying. The dolphin was swimming in a huge tank at the Pittsburgh zoo when I shot the video. The water and the dolphin are nearly the same color. Chroma Key not only made the water disappear—it took most of the dolphin with it. But the dolphin was such a nice clip that I took some extra time to create a black background for each frame. The process is time-consuming but well worth it if you have an image you really need to use with keying.

My favorite program for this process is Adobe Photoshop. The Windows version includes a number of tools that make the process much easier. To modify the individual frames, use VidEdit to save the frames as bitmaps first. Then, you can load each bitmap into Photoshop, make the changes, and then load all of the revised bitmaps back into VidEdit.

To save the video sequence as a series of bitmaps, use the File/Extract menu selection in VidEdit. Choose DIB Sequence from the list of options at the lower left of the dialog. Enter a base filename for the sequence, such as dolph001.bmp. It will take a few moments for VidEdit to create all of the bitmap files. They will have sequential names—dolph001.bmp, dolph002.bmp, etc. Figure 10.24 shows one of the bitmaps (frame 57) loaded into Photoshop.

Although the goal is to select the background and fill it with black, I find it easier to select the dolphin, and then invert the selection. Because the color of the dolphin and the color of the background are so similar, you cannot use the magic wand in Photoshop for this purpose. Instead, choose the lasso tool. Hold down the Alt key while you click along the dolphin's outline, and then double-click to create the selection. The dolphin will be outlined by a dotted line (see Figure 10.25).

Use the Select/Invert menu selection to invert the selection. This causes only the background to be part of the selection (see Figure 10.26).

Make sure the background color is black, and then use the Edit/Fill menu selection to fill the selected area. Use the settings shown in Figure 10.27.

Figure 10.24.
A frame con-
verted to a
bitmap and
loaded into
Photoshop.

Figure 10.25.
The dolphin has
been made into
a selection.

Figure 10.26.
Inverting the
selection.

Figure 10.27.
Fill settings for a
solid black
background.

The result of the fill operation is shown in Figure 10.28.

Because there is usually only a small difference in the position of an object from frame to frame, you can use Photoshop's ability to copy a selection to your advantage in this situation. Rather than go through the tedious process of outlining the dolphin by hand in the next frame, you can use the Image/Calculate/Duplicate menu selection to copy the selection. Figure 10.29 shows the dialog box that you will work with.

*Figure 10.28.
The filled
selection.*

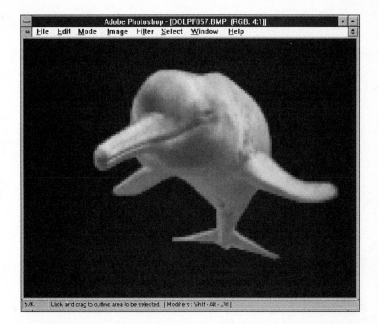

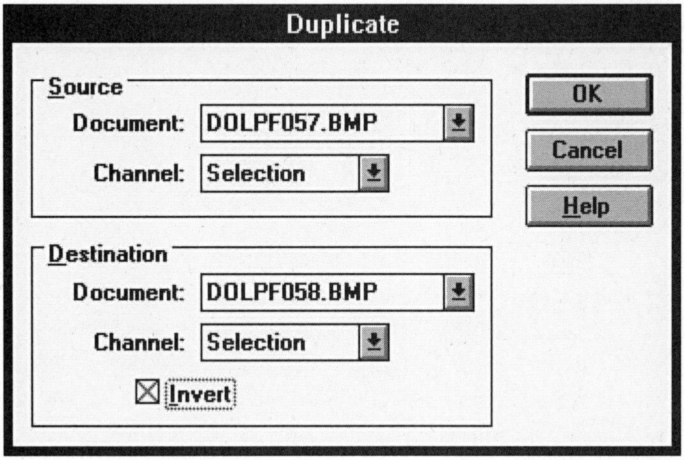

*Figure 10.29.
The Image/
Calculate/
Duplicate
dialog box.*

To copy the selection boundaries without copying its contents, you must use the settings shown in Figure 10.29. The source document should be the bitmap you just worked with; the selection must still be active. The channel must be Selection—otherwise you will wind up copying the image, or a single color channel. The

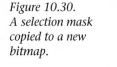

destination document—which must already be open, by the way—should be the bitmap for the next frame. The channel for the destination should also be the selection. I highly recommend using the Invert button, located at the bottom of the dialog box. The current selection is the background. You will almost certainly have to make minor edits to the selection in the new bitmap, and edits are much easier when you are working with a selection area that matches an object. Inverting the selection should make it nearly match the outline of the dolphin in the new bitmap. The result of the operation is shown in Figure 10.30.

Figure 10.30.
A selection mask
copied to a new
bitmap.

Note that the outline is offset quite a bit from the new image. However, this was due to camera shake (the camera was hand-held). Grabbing and moving the selection to cover the position of the dolphin makes a nearly complete match. A few minor edits, and the selection mask is complete, as shown in Figure 10.31. You can now proceed to invert, fill the background, and copy the mask to the next frame.

Occasionally, the difference from frame to frame will be large, and you will have to re-create the selection mask from scratch. Even so, this is far less tedious than re-creating the mask for every frame.

When you have completed the process, and have filled the background for every frame, you can use VidEdit to File/Insert the DIB Sequence and save it as an AVI file. Figure 10.32 shows a sequence of frames from the modified video sequence.

Figure 10.31.
The copied and
modified
selection mask.

Figure 10.32.
The modified
video sequence.

When used in Media Merge, the modified sequence will look something like Figure 10.33.

Figure 10.34 shows yet another use for video overlay. The first video sequence (in time line #1) is the finished production from the Story Board section of this chapter. Time line #2 contains a "talking head." Instead of just using a narration, I used the talking head to give the piece a focus and a little personality. The audio track is in time line #2.

The result of this scene is shown in Figure 10.35. The entire video from the Story Board section appears to play in the background. Figure 10.36 shows this more dramatically. Even the transition effects are located completely behind the head.[8]

---

[8]That's my head, of course.

Figure 10.33.
An example of a
modified frame
in use.

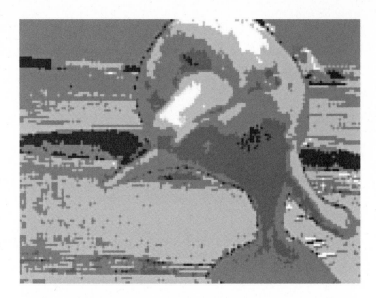

Figure 10.34.
Integrating a
"talking head"
into a video clip.

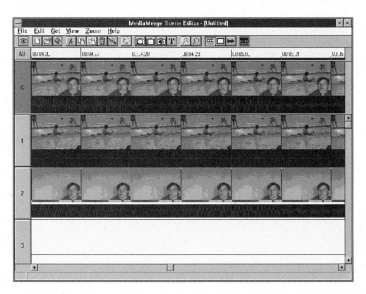

Figure 10.35.
A frame from the
combined video.

Figure 10.36.
Another frame
from the com-
bined video. Note
that the effect is
completely in the
background of
the "talking
head."

If you must use talking heads, this gives you a powerful tool for making them much more interesting!

Audio Clips

Audio clips are very easy to use in the Scene Editor. In fact, you can use the Scene Editor to mix multiple audio sources. To add an audio source, use the Get/Audio menu selection. As with a video clip, the cursor will change to a little hand. Click in the audio portion of a time line to place the audio clip.

Figure 10.37 shows an audio clip placed into time line #2, where a video clip was already placed. Because the video clip did not have an audio track, there was an open spot for adding audio. Note that the audio track shows up in the composite track. The Scene Editor will mix the various audio tracks into a single track for you when you File/Produce the video.

Figure 10.37.
Adding an audio
clip to the Scene
Editor.

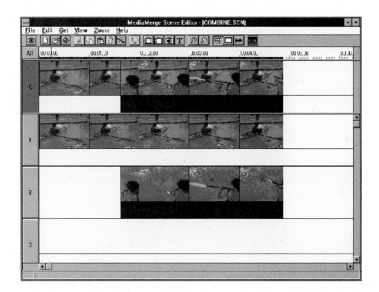

Still Images

Still images are also easy to use. Use the Get/Still menu selection to load a still image. As with video and audio clips, the cursor will change to a little hand, and you can then drop the still image into a time line. It will initially occupy a single frame, as shown in Figure 10.38. (I have used Chroma Key to allow the kayak frames to show through the new frame. That's me, Mr. Author, in the still.)

Figure 10.38.
Adding a still
image to a frame.

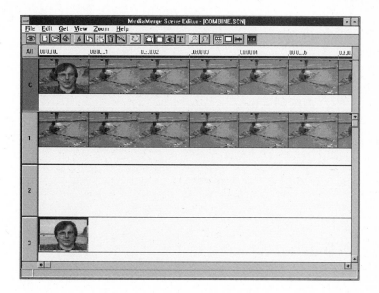

You can expand the duration of the still image by simply clicking and dragging the right edge of the image in the time line. This adds the still image to additional frames, as shown in Figure 10.39.

Figure 10.39.
Extending the
duration of a
still image.

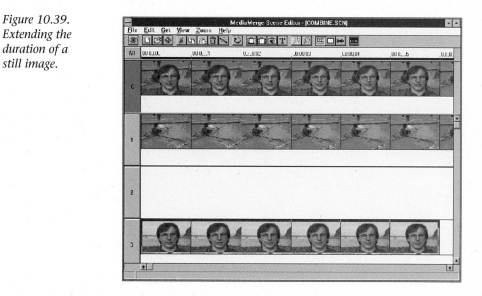

Text

Text has many uses in a video production—titles, credits, explanations, identifiers, and more. For example, you can use text in a video to:

- Identify a speaker
- Identify a product
- Explain an action

Traditional titles and credits can be created in the Scene Editor. For example, you could create a title for the Kayak Self Rescue video by using the Get/Text menu selection. This displays the dialog box shown in Figure 10.40.

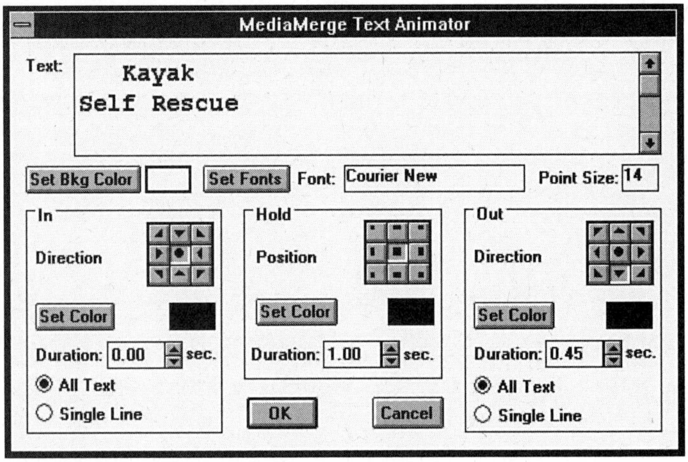

Figure 10.40.
Adding text
to a scene.

The top portion of the dialog box allows you to enter text and choose fonts (including style and size). The lower portion of the dialog box contains three boxed areas that can animate your text.

The In box let's you choose the direction the text will enter (or use the central dot to create stationary text). You can choose the text color, and the duration of the entry. This is useful for such text as scrolling credits.

The Hold box allows you to define a position where the text will stay put, and you can set a color and duration. This is useful for titles. You can also combine In and Hold—slide the text in from any direction, and then hold it in place.

The Out box is similar to the In box. You can determine what direction the text will take to exit the screen, and set color and duration. You can combine the Out settings with In and/or Hold.

Let's look at an example of animated text. In Figure 10.27, there is no In setting, so the text will appear within the frame in the position marked by the Hold setting (the center of the frame). The duration of the hold is 1 second. After 1 second, the Out setting will be used. It calls for the text to scroll downward over the course of .45 seconds.

Figure 10.41 shows several frames from the Scene Editor showing the result of these text animation settings.

Figure 10.41.
Text animation
in the Scene
Editor.

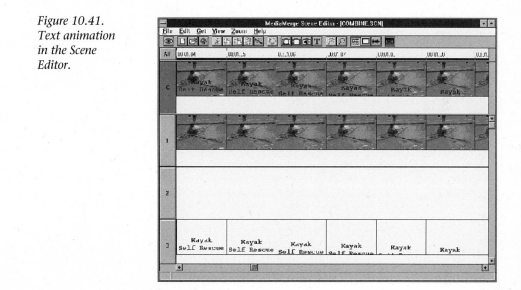

Your Own Video Studio

If you already own a video camera of any description, you now have half of what you need to put yourself in a virtual space. The other (and less costly) half is a card for your computer that will capture video. Setting up the physical studio is the easiest part of all.

Video Camera

I have yet to meet a video camera (camcorder) that isn't up to the task. Whether you have a large, VHS camera or one of those miniature 8mm or VHS-C cameras, there are only two output signals that you will encounter in North America:

composite and S-Video.[9] Most video capture cards will handle either, and all of them will handle a composite signal. There's no need to understand the technical nature of these signals.[10] All you need to know is that S-Video uses a higher resolution than composite, and that either one is fine for video capture because at 160x120 or 320x240 you're hardly pushing the capabilities of either kind of signal.

Video Capture Card

There are two video capture cards available that I use and like: the Video Spigot[11] and the Smart Video Recorder.[12] Each has specific advantages and disadvantages.

The Video Spigot is the best of its class. It is one of several cards that captures incoming video signals without compressing them. After the video is captured, you compress it using a *codec*.[13] Compression is essential for working with video. Uncompressed video creates huge data files that are just too much for most computers to handle. Compression allows you to shrink the size of the video file enormously. This does affect image quality, but the better codecs minimize the damage.

The image quality of the Spigot (as it is affectionately known) is very good, and installation and ease of use are also very good.[14] The board has also proven itself to be reliable in heavy use. Perhaps the best part of owning a Spigot is the Cinepak codec that comes with it. This codec is one of the best when you have to squeeze the data rates really low. However, be warned: Cinepak tends to have a somewhat digital appearance. It yields very sharp images, which means that the individual pixels stand out well. This is great when you have things like text or buildings in a video, and not so great for faces.

---

[9]Neither of these have anything to do with RF signals. Radio Frequency signals are used for broadcast television. Newer televisions have the usual RF input as well as composite and, sometimes, S-Video inputs.

[10]For example, I don't.

[11]From Creative Labs.

[12]From Intel.

[13]Codec stands for either encode/decode or compress/decompress—depends on who you ask.

[14]The bane of video capture cards is that they must use things like IRQs and memory addresses. Unfortunately, it is up to you to find unused IRQs and memory addresses. The Spigot installation software tries to help, but it can only go so far. You may have to check your installed hardware to determine what IRQs and memory addresses are available. If you can't solve the problem, some of the engineers who designed the Spigot have been known to hang out in the Multimedia forum on CompuServe.

The Smart Video Recorder is also the best of its class. It is one of a few cards that capture and compress in one step. Like the Spigot, the SVR (as it is affectionately known) is easy to install and use, and it has excellent image quality. It is also very reliable, and comes with the Indeo codec—another excellent choice for compression. Indeo tends to generate a softer image, with less sharpness. This is great for faces, and not so great for text.

I tend to favor the SVR for much of my own work, as the real-time compression from the on-board i750r chip saves a lot of time. For example, compressing with the Cinepak codec after capture can add 30 to 60 minutes of compression time for each minute of video. Cinepak is a great codec, however, and there are times when the wait is well worth your while. You won't regret owning either of these capture cards.[15]

The Studio

Once you have a video camera and a video capture card, it's time to set up your studio. I set up mine in my garage, but you can use any space that has at least one blank wall. One advantage of the garage is that I can often just open the garage door to get plenty of natural light. Figure 10.42 shows my basic setup.

The only critical piece is that square thing in the middle of the picture. It's a piece of bright blue fabric used for Chroma Key. With the solid color in the background, it's easy to use Media Merge to blend in any object I can videotape. I added weights to the bottom of the cloth to keep it from fluttering (especially when the garage door is open!), and you might also want to add a long, thin strip of wood to the bottom edge. This adds weight, and helps keep the cloth from showing fold marks.

I added a few other bits and pieces to complete my simple studio. I invested in a simple color monitor (a Panasonic 1379 is a good and inexpensive choice) that I

---

[15]Of course, that only means that one of my readers will get the proverbial bad apple, and complain. No one, least of all a hardware manufacturing company, is perfect. One other point: neither of these cards does video overlay, which is a completely different ballgame. Video overlay involves adding the video signal to your existing video display, rather than capturing the video to a hard disk. Completely different hardware is used for capture and for overlay. If you require both, look into the Bravado 16 from Truevision. I've used it, and it does a great job. Also a completely different process is outputting your VGA display to videotape. If that's your bag, try the Video VGA from Truevision, or the VGA Producer from Magni Systems.

use to preview the video image, a microphone, and a video tripod.[16] The tripod is a critical piece of equipment. Without it, camera jitter can ruin your video footage and make it useless.

Figure 10.42.
A simple video
studio setup in
a garage.

This setup is easy to use. Place the object—yourself, for example—in front of the blue screen, and turn on the camera. That's all there is to it. If you want to have the object appear to move within the virtual landscape, you can move the camera instead of the object. For example, if you want the object to start out at the lower left of the video frame, and then move to the upper left, tilt the camera instead of moving the object. This gives you very tight control over the location within the video frame.

Going Virtual with Media Merge

You now have everything you need to go virtual: the software, the hardware, and a studio to create the video. It's time to do some serious virtual video. There are four steps involved:

---

[16]Don't settle for just any old tripod. A video tripod uses a fluid head that makes for smooth panning and tilting. Regular tripods don't have this feature.

- Create the virtual space
- Make the videotape
- Capture the video
- Merge it!

Create the Virtual Space

There are a variety of ways to create a virtual space, but not all of them will work with the methods described in this chapter. File formats are the backbone of the process of combining video and virtual reality.

The video file doesn't present any problems. It can be loaded directly into Media Merge. The problems, if any, crop up when you try to use the animation output from the software you use to create the virtual space. That animation must be converted ultimately to an .AVI file. That's not a problem if the software can output using the .FLI or .FLC file formats. For example, Vista Pro outputs single frames as .PCX file, but it comes with a utility program that will convert the .PCX files into a .FLC file. If you don't already know what file formats your software supports, check the documentation.

It's easy to use Media Merge's Scene Editor to combine the video file with the animation file, but it's not so easy to make the blend look realistic. For example, as you learned in Chapter 6, the lighting in the virtual space must be matched when you videotape the real object that you plan to include. If you don't do that, the difference in lighting angle can be jarring to the viewer. If the lighting angles are too complex, you can minimize the effect by using an overhead light in both the virtual space and for the videotaping. Such lighting casts minimal shadows, and movement of objects causes only minor changes to shadows.

If the animation of the virtual space uses a camera, and you change the camera angle, you'll need to duplicate the camera angle when you videotape.

All of this may sound like a lot of bother, but it's really just basic bookkeeping. A little time taken to jot down frame numbers and camera or light angles, for example, can add a real sense of reality to your creation. The techniques you use can be based on the examples in Chapter 6.

Make the Videotape

There are several levels of camera technique that you can use when you are photographing a real object that will be added to a virtual space. These range from the simple to the complex.

- Stationary camera, stationary target
- Stationary camera, moving target
- Moving camera, stationary target
- Moving camera, moving target

Each of these has different uses and applications, and a different level of difficulty.

Stationary Camera, Stationary Target

This is the easiest way to get started. Because neither the camera nor the target is moving, the logistics are very simple: position the object/target, aim the camera, make the tape. If you need to move the lighting during filming, that adds a bit of complexity, but once you start the camera you've got two hands free.

Stationary Camera, Moving Target

There are different ways of moving an object, and each of them creates different challenges. If the object is moving in the same place—that is, it does not change its distance from the camera—the only question is the mechanism for moving the object. You do not want any of the support system showing up in the video. If you must have a visible support, make sure the support is covered with the same color and kind of fabric you used for the background. You can, for example, make a glove for your hand, and drape cloth across your arm or shoulder, and move the object the old-fashioned way: by hand.

If the distance between the camera and object changes, the issues become more complex. The biggest priority is to keep the object in focus. If your camera has auto focus, that will keep the object in focus in most situations. However, there are several special situations where auto focus may not be adequate. For example, some auto focus systems use the center of the frame for focusing. If the object is at the edge of the frame, the camera may try to focus on the background cloth—a hopeless task, since the cloth is uniform in color and lighting.

Moving an object away from the camera also presents special problems. The further away you are from the object, the bigger the background must be. This can create a practical limit to how large an object you can videotape. For example, putting all of your body into the frame requires a very large background—most likely from floor to ceiling. If possible, use a continuous strip of background material and curve it to cover part of the floor and ceiling—this will avoid any creases that may be difficult to remove in Media Merge. Most fabric is only 60 inches wide, and this can cause problems, too.

If you are serious about using large objects, you have two choices: build a larger studio, or remove the background in each frame using a program like Photoshop.

Moving Camera, Stationary Target

Instead of moving the object, you can move the camera in such a way that it looks like the object is moving. This is the technique that was used to animate the various star fighters in the movie *Star Wars*. The movie studios rely on computers and motorized camera transports to work their magic. If you try this technique, you will have to think through the necessary camera motions very carefully, and you will probably need to move the camera by hand. This can be very unsteady, and you would need to create tracks to even out the camera movement. Some motions can be done using a tripod, but they aren't the useful ones. Panning and tilting will seldom give you the effect you want.

There is a class of moving camera shots, however, that are easy to take. These involve the opposite of what I have been describing so far. Instead of adding video to a virtual space, you can add virtual objects to a video. In this case, you are free to do whatever you want to do with the camera. When you have the tape you want, you can add the virtual object. For example, if you create a bizarre space alien in Imagine, and then animate it in the foreground[17], you can use Media Merge to put the alien into any video. Or, you might hold the camera while walking along a path, and then add a floating spacecraft, or a pair of robot arms, to the foreground. Let your imagination run wild.

Moving Camera, Moving Target

There should seldom, if ever, be a need for this combination. Almost any movement can be accomplished using either a moving camera or a moving target.

---

[17]With an appropriate single-color background, of course.

Capture the Video

Once you have your video tape, the next step is to capture the video sequence to your hard disk. You'll need a pretty fast computer to handle video capture. I recommend at least a 486/33, although the Intel Smart Video Recorder may work satisfactorily with slower hardware because it off-loads some of the work to its onboard video compression chip. A fast hard drive is critical. I use a disk with an average seek time of 10ms.[18] Any disk under 15ms is acceptable, but 12ms or less is better. A fast video display card is very desirable for playback, but it won't have much impact on capture.

Here are some hints on video capture from my book *PC Video Madness*:

- Test the capabilities of your system before you try to capture for any real projects. Start easy—try to capture at 160x120 using 256 colors and 15 frames per second as a beginning. If that works, try 24 and then 30 frames per second. Verify that you are getting reliable performance. Then you can try such things as 24-bit color codecs like Indeo and Cinepak. You won't get the benefits of 24-bit color, of course, unless you have a video display adapter than can handle it.

- If you use the Intel Smart Video Recorder, set the following options in VidCap for capture: Indeo codec, highest quality setting, and key frames set to 1. This almost always gives you the best results. The key frame setting is critical for the Indeo codec Version 2.12 to correct a potential problem with ghosting when the frame contents change dramatically from one frame to the next. After capture, use VidEdit to save the file using No Change as a compression option using the data rate of your choice.

- Use a permanent capture file. To create a permanent file, start by defragmenting your hard disk with a utility like Speed Disk from the Norton Utilities.[19] Then run VidCap, and from the file menu choose Set Capture File. The dialog box allows you to set the size of the capture file. Allow from 10 to 25 megabytes per minute of capture, depending on such things as image size, frame rate, and bit depth. If you will be using the Intel Smart Video Recorder, or another board that compresses in real time,

---

[18]The "ms" stands for milliseconds, and refers to average seek time. I use a Micropolis 2112A, with a 1.05 gigabyte IDE drive. The SCSI version, the 2112, is also a good choice.

[19]Having a fragmented hard disk slows down access times because files wind up being in several pieces. In the case of a large video file—say 50 megabytes or so—a fragmented hard drive can mean that the file is cut into hundreds of pieces.

you'll need less space—usually at least one-third less than for uncompressed (also called raw) capture. After you capture a video sequence to the permanent capture file (which will now always stay defragmented until you erase it), use Save As in VidEdit to save the file with an appropriate name after you have made any necessary changes. This preserves the capture file for future use.

■ Unless you need to play the video files from a CD-ROM, don't use the Pad for CD-ROM feature in the compression options. However, the 150K data rate is a good target if you want the file to be playable on a variety of machines. Any file with a data rate over 300K per second may not play well on the majority of machines—such high data rates demand the fastest computers, hard disks, and video systems. In general, don't compress until you create the final video—use uncompressed files throughout development to preserve image quality.

Merge It!

Once you have the two files, you can merge them with Media Merge's Scene Editor. The process is exactly like the example earlier in this chapter. To refresh your memory, I'll list the steps again:

1. Load the file with the virtual space animation in time line #1. In this case, it is a Vistapro landscape animation.

2. Load the file with the video object in time line #2. I am the object in this example.

3. Load any additional video objects into the appropriate time lines. In this case, I wanted a dashboard effect; I used a bitmap between the video of me and the landscape animation.

4. Set the overlay properties for each video object. Select the background color as the Chroma Key color, and then adjust the fall off until the background disappears completely. You may want to experiment with the feathering options located in the upper portion of the dialog box.

5. Check the appearance of the results in the Composite time line. Figure 10.43 shows the kind of results you can expect. The Composite only uses 8-bit color, so don't be alarmed if the images there don't look as detailed as you were expecting. If what you see is what you want, use the File/Produce menu selection to create the final product. In figure 10.43, The video in

track 1 is already a composite video: I added a still image of a cockpit as an overlay using Chroma Key. I then loaded the resulting video in for a second overlay. I could have overlaid all three videos in one step, of course. In this case, I wanted to do several versions using the same cockpit. The dashboard bitmap is shown in Figure 10.43b.

Figure 10.43.
Several video files
loaded into the
Scene Editor.

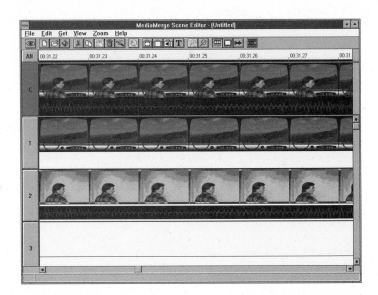

Figure 10.43b.
A bitmap used to
create a dash-
board for the
composite video.

Figures 10.44 and 10.45 show single frames from the video produced using the files loaded into the Scene Editor for Figure 10.43. These images have been compressed, so the detail is not as crisp as in the original. Note that all three elements of the composite are integrated into the images: the Vista Pro landscape, the dashboard, and the video of me, Mr. Author (or, in this case, tour guide—play the file meetme.avi on the CD-ROM in the VRMAD directory).

Figure 10.44. A single frame from the produced video.

Figure 10.46 shows a frame from the original video I made in my garage studio. The surface behind me is the blue cloth I used as a backdrop. It is not quite exactly uniform in color, but Media Merge allows you to make adjustments for this using the Falloff slider.

*Figure 10.45.
Another single
frame from the
produced video.*

Summary

The list of possibilities for working with a combination of virtual space animations and video files is endless. The ability to layer multiple images with Media Merge gives you a powerful tool for creating never-before-seen images. Whether you add video to a virtual space, or enhance a video by adding virtual objects, you will likely find yourself on the cutting edge of computer technology for quite some time.

Figure 10.46.
A frame from the
original video,
before making
the composite.

11

VIRTUAL
VIRTUOSITY

From total immersion to 3D morphing, from flights of fancy to detailed pseudo-realities, virtual reality is as much an art as a science. Life on the cutting edge has always been that way. There are few prefabricated solutions on the cutting edge. Virtual reality is completely different from hum-drum, every-day programs like spreadsheets and word processors.

Once upon a time, of course, spreadsheets and word processors were new, fun, and exciting. But as the various programs from the various vendors look more and more alike with each new version, virtual reality is a mere babe in the woods. Like multimedia, virtual reality still has room for the home-grown product, for the enthusiast to go places no one has ever gone to before. In the case of virtual reality, of course, the latter is literally true.

Today's VR tools, as limited and experimental—and sometimes costly—as they are, still offer enormous possibilities to anyone who is willing to put in the time and effort to stretch the limits. Out there, in the trenches, the Cezannes, Van Goghs, and Picassos of virtual reality are sweating out the details in front of their computers, trying to find a sense of style, a way of doing things that breaks completely new ground.

These are the virtual virtuosos. These are the people who aren't willing to wait until someone else gives them the tools to build new worlds—they'll build them now, either by finding new ways to use the tools available or by creating their own tools out of their impatience.

In this chapter, you'll learn about stretching and bending tools to get what you want, when you want it. This chapter features the high end of 3D modeling software, 3D Studio from Autodesk. A morph here, a reflection there, and pretty soon you can have your own virtual creatures.

For this example, you will build a cylinder in a sparklingly technological-looking environment, and then make it come to life. It will bend down toward you, and then shake its "head" threateningly at you. After the example, I'll show you some possibilities for adding even more pizzazz to the animation.

The results will be first-class stuff because 3D Studio is used by many professionals to create the artificial realities you see on television, in commercials, and in movies.

The Column that Ate the Animator

You will create just a handful of objects in this scene, but the results will make it look like it took forever to do. Begin by setting the values for a cylinder using the Create/Cylinder/Values menu selection, as shown in Figure 11.1.

RECIPE

1 copy 3D Studio 2.01
1 highly developed sense of imagination
1 conception of a virtual space and its inhabitants.

Instructions: The recipe can only suggest where to go with this gourmet item. Begin by visualizing a scene that has some impact—something that hits you in the gut. For example, pretend you have been hired to create a scene in a movie where an inanimate object comes to life. What would it look like? How would it move? Then work at it and work at it until it appears to come to life in an animation. Serve only when really, *really* ready.

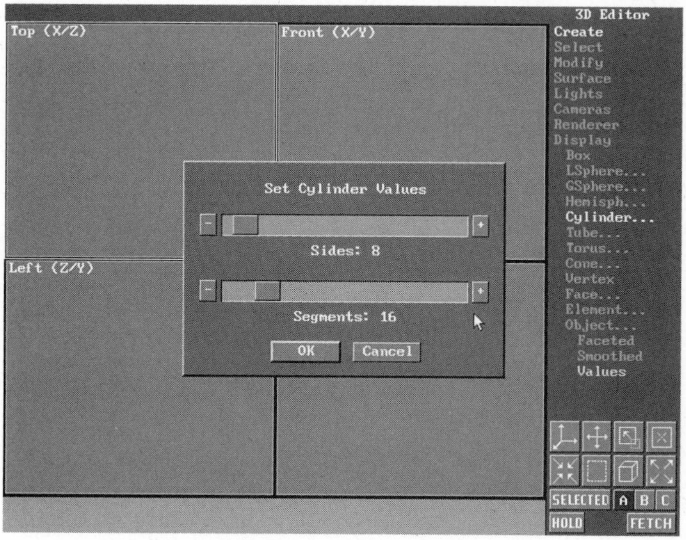

*Figure 11.1.
Setting values for
a new cylinder.*

To create the cylinder itself, use the Create/Cylinder/Smoothed menu selection. When asked, use the name Cyl01. Make the cylinder tall and thin, as shown in Figure 11.2. Apply the material Blue Glass[1] to the object.

Figure 11.2.
Creating a tall,
thin cylinder.

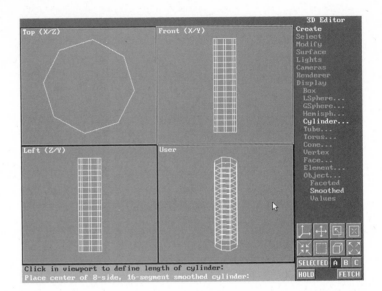

Let's cover a little background information before proceeding. To animate the column, you're going to use a little trick. You will actually use a morph[2] to transform the column into various versions of itself. Instead of animating a single column, you will create different versions of the column, and then morph from one to the next.

Create four copies of the column. The easiest way to do this is by cloning. Use the Modify/Object/Move menu selection, but hold down the shift key when you select the column for moving. This creates an exact copy of the column, including the surface material. Name each of the cylinders appropriately, such as cyl02, cyl03, and so on. You can use any of the viewports for the moving and cloning operations, as shown in Figure 11.3.

---

[1] These are just suggestions; feel free to adjust the mapping and materials to suit your own concept of a column that will come to life. By the way, you need not specify the same material for the object copies—morphing has no affect on the surface characteristics of an object.

[2] See Chapter 8 for more information about morphing.

Figure 11.3.
Five identical
cylinders.

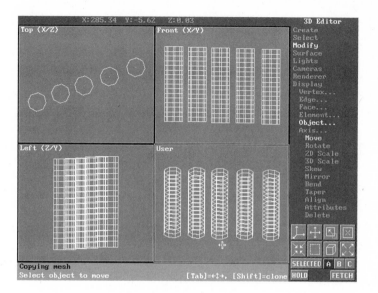

Now use the Modify/Object/Bend menu selection to bend cylinder #2 30 degrees. Make sure that the cursor that appears has a little arrow pointing up. If the arrow points in a different direction, press the tab key until it points up. Figure 11.4 shows the cylinder as it looks during the bend operation. A shadow cylinder shows the degree of bending. Check for the exact degree of bending in the status line at the top of the screen.

Figure 11.4.
Bending a
cylinder.

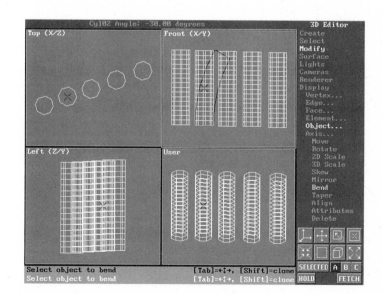

Now move to cylinder #3, and bend it to 60 degrees. Bend cylinder #4 to 90 degrees and cylinder #5 to 120 degrees. Once you have bent all of the cylinders, the screen should look something like Figure 11.5.

Figure 11.5.
Different degrees
of bending on the
cylinders.

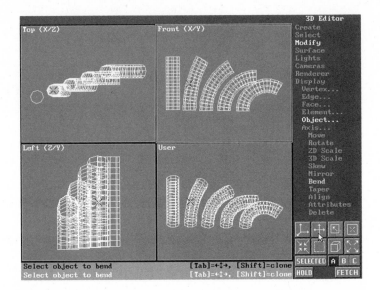

Press the F5 key to go to the Keyframer, 3D Studio's animation tool. Use the Display/Hide/Object menu selection to hide each of the bent cylinders.[3] The only remaining object is the original cylinder, as shown in Figure 11.6.

This is the point where you apply the morphing. Move to frame 30, and then go to the Object/Morph/Assign menu selection. Click on Cyl01, which will display the dialog box shown in Figure 11.7. This is a list of the objects in the scene that are valid morph objects for Cyl01.

Click on Cyl02, and then click OK. The cylinder now appears bent, as shown in Figure 11.8.

Move to frames 60, 60, and 120, and morph the cylinder to cylinders 3, 4, and 5. In frame 120, the cylinder appears nearly bent over (see Figure 11.9).

---

[3] Simply click on each cylinder to hide it.

Figure 11.6.
The bent
cylinders have
been hidden.

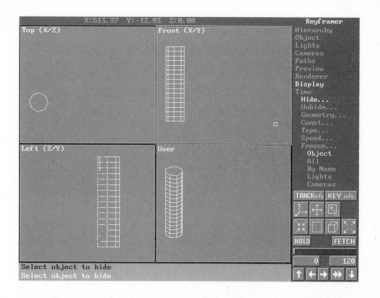

Figure 11.7.
Selecting an
object to
morph to.

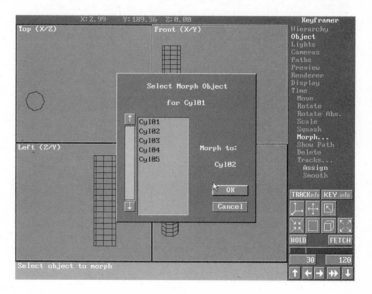

Figure 11.8.
The cylinder
appears bent in
frame 30.

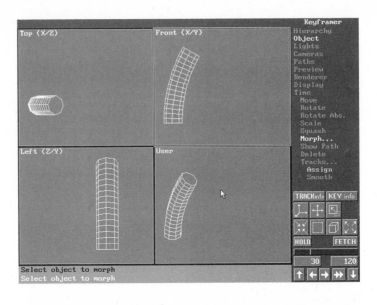

Figure 11.9.
The completed
morph.

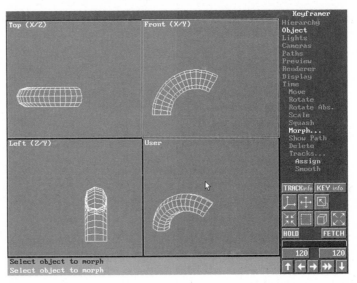

Throughout the morph, the cylinder did not move. It did not, for example, move to the location of cylinder #2 when morphed to that cylinder. Morphing is actually a limited action. It does not affect the surface properties of an object, nor does it affect position. In fact, morphing does only one thing. A morph merely moves the vertices of one object to the (relative) positions of the vertices in the second object. In other words, all that a morph does is change the shape of an object to match the shape of a second object.

One side effect is that you can only morph objects that have the same number of vertices. When you click on an object to morph it, you are presented with a list of the objects in the scene that have the same number of vertices. If you want to morph, say, a sphere into a cube, you will first have to add vertices to the cube—lots of them, as a matter of fact, because the typical sphere may have hundreds, while a stock cube has but eight.

One of the best ways to create objects with the same number of vertices is to copy them, as we have done here, and then make changes to the copy. Another method is to use the 3D Lofter (another 3D Studio tool) to create the two shapes, and then loft them into 3D objects. This offers more flexibility, but can take much more time.

Now you can set about getting the most out of the morph. Return to the 3D Editor by pressing the F3 key. Use the Cameras/Create menu selection to open the dialog box shown in Figure 11.10.

Figure 11.10.
Adding a camera
to the scene.

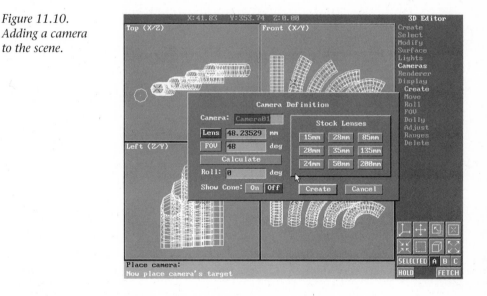

There are a number of lenses to choose from, and the lens you select will affect the appearance of the bending column. A wide-angle lens[4] will make the column look far away—it won't show the effect to its best advantage. A telephoto lens[5] will

---

[4] The lens focal lengths from 15mm to 35mm are considered wide angle.

[5] The lens focal lengths from 85mm to 200m are considered telephoto.

show the column in close up, but if we get too close, the morphing will not be seen in its entirety. In this case, the so-called normal lens is best—50mm. Select this lens by clicking on it.

To make one of the viewports show what the camera sees, press Control-V to display the dialog box shown in Figure 11.11. Click the Camera button, and then click in one of the viewports at the lower left of the dialog. The viewport marked with a U would be a good choice because the User point of view isn't needed when you have a camera viewport.

Figure 11.11. Changing the contents of a viewport.

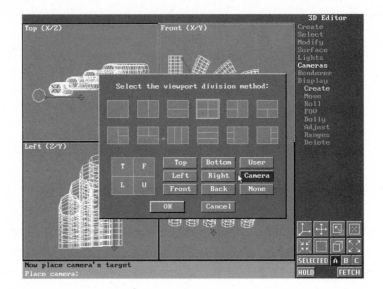

Place the camera at a low level, looking up at the column. You should also add a light to the scene. A spot light would be nice because it casts shadows, which will add depth to the scene. Figure 11.12 shows the light and the camera in position in the 3D Editor.[6]

The light from above, however, may not be enough. This leaves the underside of the column in shadow as it bends. Because the camera sees mostly the underside of the column, it would be a very boring animation—not at all appropriate for a movie scene. You can add a second spotlight below the bending column, as shown in Figure 11.13. Note that this illuminates the area right in front of the camera at the end of the sequence.

---

[6] You may need to change the position of both objects depending on exactly where and how the column moves during the morph.

Figure 11.12.
The scene with a
light and camera
added.

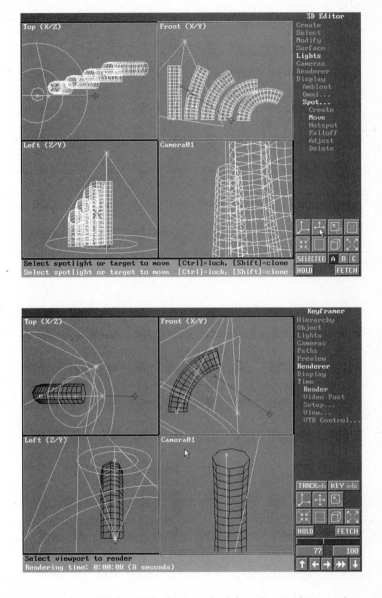

Figure 11.13.
Adding a second
spotlight under
the column.

The animation as it now stands is OK, but it lacks punch. A bending column, after all, doesn't have much personality. If we want this column to really look like it is coming alive (and we'll have to if we ever want to see our payment from the movie's producer), we'll have to add more motion. Time to head back to the 3D Editor.

Create two copies of cylinder #5—the one that is bent farthest. Figure 11.14 shows the two additional objects (best seen in the Top viewport) after they have been bent a second time, this time sideways.

Figure 11.14.
Adding two more
bent cylinders.

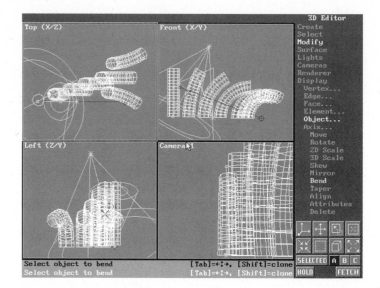

These two new cylinders can be used to add some rather interesting morphs. Return to the Keyframer and add 60 additional frames (for a total of 180). Move to frame 135 (see Figure 11.15) and add a morph to one of the new objects.

Move to frame 165 and add a morph to the other object, and then to frame 180 and morph to cylinder #5. Now hide the two new objects using the Display/Hide/Object menu selection. Figure 11.16 shows how the cylinder looks in wireframe view in frame 165.

If there is anything about the animation that you are not satisfied with, the easiest way to make adjustments is with the Track editor. To use the Track editor, click the Track Info button at lower right, and then click on the cylinder. This displays the Track Info dialog box (see Figure 11.17).

Note that there is a dot at each frame where you created a morph. To edit a morph, simply click on the Key Info button at the lower left of the dialog, which will display the Key Info dialog box (see Figure 11.18).

Figure 11.15.
The view in the
Keyframer before
hiding the new
objects.

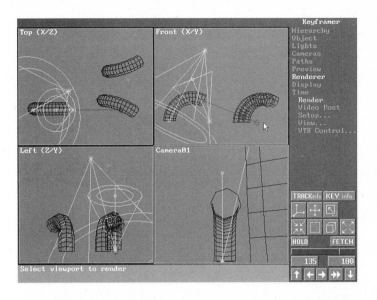

Figure 11.16.
A view of the
cylinder ending
both down and to
the side.

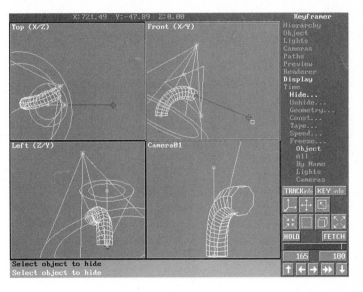

Figure 11.17.
The Track info
for the cylinder.

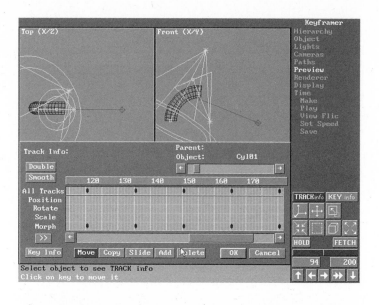

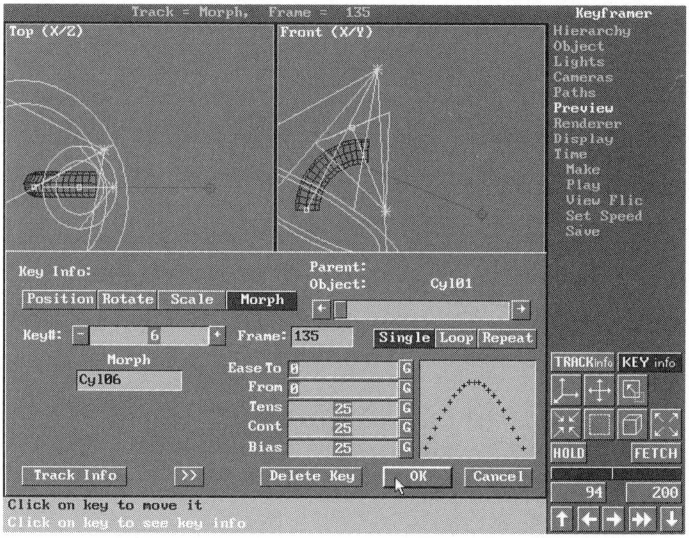

Figure 11.18.
The Key Info
dialog box.

Using the Key Info dialog, you can change the object you are morphing to, and you can also change the Ease To settings. This can give you a high degree of control over the pace of motion during the morph. The Ease To value affects the velocity with which an object (or, in this case, a morph) approaches a key frame. If the value is zero, there is no change in velocity. If the value is 50 (the maximum), the change in velocity will be as high a possible.

The Ease From setting also affects velocity. A high setting (50 is also the maximum here) will increase velocity leaving the key frame.

In other words, if you increase the Ease To setting, the pace of the morph will speed up as it reaches the key frame. If you increase the Ease From setting, the pace of the morph will be fast as it leaves the key frame, and then slow down. You can use these controls to change a boring, same-speed morph into a dynamic, unpredictable virtuoso performance.

There are three other settings in the same area of the Key Info box that can be useful:

Tension—This control determines how abruptly a transition occurs. A setting of 50 means the transition is very abrupt, 25 is average, and 0 means that motion will even go in reverse, if necessary, to make the transition as smooth as possible.

Continuity—This control determines how smooth the changes will be at the key frame. A setting of zero means the change will be abrupt—all in one frame. A setting of 25 means the change will be smooth, and a setting of 50 forces an overshoot prior to and after the key frame.

Bias—This control determines whether the settings that apply to a given key frame will apply equally to entry and exit, or favor one or the other. A value of 50 emphasizes entry, a setting of 25 is neutral, and a setting of 0 favors exit.

These settings, which were designed primarily to control motion, can have either interesting or ruinous effects on a morph—experimentation is the only useful guide.

As interesting as we have managed to make the morph so far—a snake-like column wobbling dangerously from side to side—we are not done. We can add substantial mood to the morph by creating a suitable background. If you recall, the specifications called for a "sparklingly technological-looking" background. The first order of business is to create the background object. I opted for a simple background, consisting of a floor and one wall (see Figure 11.19).

The objects are simply boxes created in the 3D Editor using the Create/Box menu selection. I adjusted the size and position of the boxes to make sure that they filled the camera view. I then assigned suitable materials to each of them—Blue Marble to the floor, and a material I created for the wall using pattern #150 as a texture map. Figure 11.20 shows a rendering of the scene.

Figure 11.19.
Adding objects
for a background.

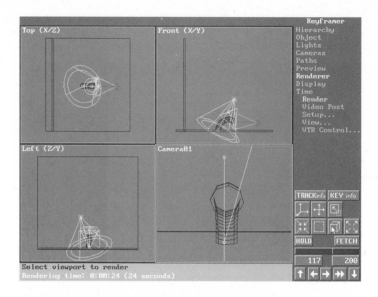

Figure 11.20.
A rendering of
the first frame in
the morph.

All three objects can be seen in this rendering. The blue glass is nearly transparent, however, and may not be an ideal choice. We'll return to this subject in a moment. For now, see Figure 11.21, frame 107 of the animation. The cylinder is bent at a little bit more than 90 degrees.

Figure 11.21.
Frame 107 of
the morph.

In Figure 11.22, the cylinder is bent completely to one side.

Figure 11.22.
Frame 134 of
the morph.

There are some things you can do to improve the appearance of the animation. I made the following changes, and then rendered the image in Figure 11.23.

- Added an automatic reflection map to the blue glass material and increased its shininess.

- Added a bump map to the blue marble to create some highlights and shadows in the surface and added automatic reflection mapping.

- Added shininess to the pattern of the wall and added a bump map.

Figure 11.23. Frame 135 with changes to the characteristics of the materials.

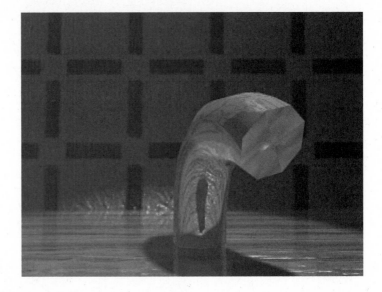

As you can see, this adds quite a bit of atmosphere to the scene. We are almost there, but not quite. For a final touch, add a spotlight that illuminates the wall in the background. Place the light so it is above and nearly in the same plane as the wall—this will cause harsh shadows that emphasize the texture of the wall. The final result is shown in Figure 11.24, and can be found on the disk as bend.avi.

Summary

This scene is really just a basic morph in 3D Studio. I have added a few extra touches to give the animation more impact. But there are more things that you could do. For example, you could join a face to the top of the cylinder using the Create/Object/ Boolean menu selection. 3D Studio comes with a large number of sample files, several of which contain heads or faces that would be useful in this situation, or you could create your own from scratch.

Figure 11.24.
A light has been
added to
emphasize the
texture of the
background wall.

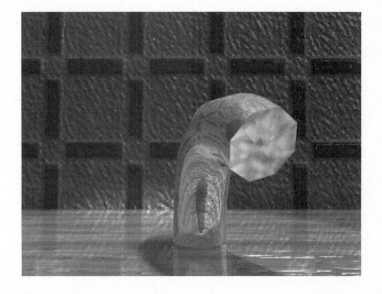

You could also add other objects to the scene and have the cylinder interact with them. For example, a ball could roll in from the side, and then get eaten by the cylinder when it bends down.

You could also replace the simple patterning of the back wall with a rock wall that looks like a dungeon, or a sparkling, futuristic metallic look. You could add objects—lights, paintings, decorations, architectural details—to the back wall or the floor.

The bottom line is this: The more you put into a scene, the more you are going to get out of it. Of course, knowing when you are done—when adding even one more detail would be too much—is just as important!

12

CYBERSPACE/
CYBERPUNK

Reality may have already sprung a leak. To my knowledge, there is no little Dutch boy to put his finger in the dike and stem the flood—quite the contrary. There are hoards of cyberpunks scratching and clawing to widen the breach any way they can.

If that paragraph seems odd, or lacks meaning or a point of reference, read on. All will be made clear.[1]

Let's begin with two words: *cyberspace* and *cyberpunk*. Both words owe their origin to the word *cybernetics*, a term coined decades ago by Norbert Wiener of MIT. This term originally referred to the study of control/feedback systems. It, in turn, is based on the Greek word *kybernetes*, meaning helmsman.

Over the years, the root portion of these words, *cyber*, gained a life of its own. Words such as *cyborg* [2]—half man, half machine—began to crop up in the world of science fiction.[3] In the last decade, William Gibson used the term cyberspace to describe what he calls "a consensual hallucination." It is "a graphic representation of data abstracted from the banks of every computer in the human system."[4]

If you could connect all of the computers in the world, and then find a way to put your own mind into that space, that would be cyberspace. In some ways, this is already happening, though not to the degree it has been depicted in science fiction. You can connect almost anywhere these days using Internet, a BBS, CompuServe, or just plain old electronic mail. But you can't find yourself in a graphically vivid alternate reality composed of the very stuff of computers.

The Moral Dilemma

Even if the reality falls short of the virtual promise, there is a lot going on in the first bits of cyberspace today. More and more people rely on some form of electronic communication and/or virtual presence to get work done, communicate about personal issues, or just raise a little hell. Cyberspace is uniquely suited to the latter—you are there, and you are not there. In most cases, you can walk away from an electronic conversation without anyone knowing who you are, or where you

---

[1] Or, to be more accurate, one man's (considered) opinion will see the light of day.

[2] A contraction of *cyb*ernetic *org*anism.

[3] Or, as Harlan Ellison and many of his contemporaries preferred, *speculative fiction*.

[4] For a less concise, but much more visceral, exploration of the concepts of cyberspace, read Gibson's novel, *Neuromancer*, winner of all three of science fiction's highest awards: the Hugo, the Nebula, and the Phillip K. Dick awards.

came from. This is just one way in which a cyberspace virtual reality is different from garden-variety reality.

Given that the two are different, the question can be asked: what are the implications of virtual reality in general, and cyberspace in particular?

VR Versus TV

There is a vocal minority that would like us to believe that violence on television is ruining the youth of America. Whether you agree with that point of view or not, the same is likely to be said about virtual reality and cyberspace. The truth is that most of us alive now have grown up with television, and are either ruined or not, as the case may be. The generation coming along right now will be the first to grow up with virtual reality at their (literal) fingertips. What are the implications of that?

Both more and less than you might think. I'll begin with less.

My son Justen is a good example of a typical Nintendo/Genesis child. He has access to both systems, buys[5] three or four games a year for each system, and pesters his parents to death regarding every hot new game that is advertised. He will willingly spend hour after hour glued to the television playing the games. He will play them alone; he will play them with friends. He will play them when the weather outdoors is ideal; he will play them when it rains. In short, if someone doesn't come along and roust him from his reverie, he will play them until his thumbs fall off.[6]

As a matter of fact, some of the most accessible VR technology can be found in games. Game vendors are competing with each other for the kids' parents' money, and the game that sounds, looks, or works more like reality— or, more often, some enhanced form of reality—is what catches the kids' attention.

Time-out: let's mull this over. It's been said that we humans enjoy play because a small effort leads to a large reward, giving us pleasure. That's a dry description of play, but it makes a valid point. It also explains the allure of TV, video games, VR, and cyberspace. In the real world, a reward is married to effort. In any kind of artificial reality, the rules can be as artificial as the reality. The rules can be shaped to enhance the experience. A VR experience isn't like a vacation at all—it can rain on your vacation, or you can stub your toe on some coral while wading in a

---

[5] Well, we buy for him...

[6] And sometimes beyond. There was the night he came to me to show me the blisters on his fingers from playing a new game hour after hour after hour. I was reminded, and I don't know if there really is a connection, of John Lennon's scream at the end of *Helter Skelter*, "I've got blisters on my fingers!"

Caribbean lagoon. In VR, the experience is guaranteed. You fire the missile, you punch the bad guy, then you get the reward. In short, today's VR is predictable.[7] Not entirely predictable, of course—there is always a need for some thrilling surprises.

Of course, I could go on endlessly about *why* kids, and some of us adults, enjoy video games. The bottom line is obvious: kids love them. The *why* may not be so important, but the results are.

I think the most serious potential problem with virtual reality is mistaking it for reality, and I think most of us are relatively immune to that mistake. In that sense, VR, cyberspace, cyberpunk, and so on are no more—and no less—dangerous than something like cigarettes or alcohol. Most people who use these things get enough pleasure out of them to offset both the risks and the potential for problems. Of course, there is a minority that does not find itself in this comfortable position.

There are going to be folks who get hooked on alternate realities, for whatever reason. There are going to be folks who indulge in it more than they know they should. And there will be most folks, who will take it or leave it, as it suits them.

In other words, I don't think there's any more of a moral dilemma involved in virtual reality than in any other civilized pursuit. By *civilized*, I mean pursuits that are the fruit of civilization. There are many such, positive and negative.

- A teenage girl spending half her after-school day on the telephone giggling over things.

- An adult watching the evening news, and then turning the TV off in disgust when a vapid sitcom comes on.

- A teenage boy smoking when his parents aren't around.

- A book editor playing a game of Tetris to calm down after a lengthy editing session.

Here is what I see as the "real" bottom line:

Virtual reality will have the same joys and pitfalls as actual reality because the same user is running both operations: a person.

I must temper that opinion with another consideration, however. Without balance, without some actual reality to balance the virtual reality, sterility is a real concern. No one mistakes the urban jungle for the real jungle. Graffiti is nature's

---

[7] This will not always be the case, or so most of us expect. The addition of even crude artificial intelligence to games and software changes the rules in a different way.

way of trying to put the equivalent of leaves on flat, sterile buildings.[8] Unfortunately, it's a hopeless task. I would prefer that we do a better job with virtual reality than we have with actual reality, and I think I am not alone in that hope.

Ultimately, virtual reality appeals to, and satisfies, only a portion of the human psyche. If we as a society neglect to offer a balanced menu, or if individuals fail to choose a balanced menu, the end result can only be pain and trouble. We should do everything we can to avoid that.

More Questions than Answers

I relied on William Gibson for a definition of cyberspace, but I'll provide my own definition of cyberpunk. Cyberpunk is nothing more than young folks applying youthful energy and creativity to computers, art, and virtual reality. This isn't very different from what went into the beat generation, hippies, and yuppies. The beat generation applied their energy to finding the boundaries of imagination, hippies to finding the boundaries of personal freedom, yuppies to finding the boundaries of personal success. Each youthful generation is supplied with the enthusiasm and emotional tools for unremitting pursuit of the farther edge of some aspect of life. This generation is no different—it just wants to push what we take for granted to the edge, and then maybe a little bit further.

This is the nature of adolescence. One effect of such single-minded pursuit is that it creates new territory. Whether that territory be jazz, beat poetry, acid rock, folk music, detailing of a BMW, surfing lingo, performance art, or virtual communities, it represents enormous vitality. It is the grass roots effort to build the future, and I believe it will have a profound effect on the nature and timing of our virtual future.

Where might that future lead? Consider the possibilities, both mundane and exotic.

Virtual Communities

A virtual community is a collection of individuals who communicate electronically. Such a community takes many, many forms. Within a company, several people may work together on a project without ever meeting face to face—they simply send electronic mail (e-mail) to one another during the course of the project to "talk" about goals, problems, and the like. Or a group of individuals interested

---

[8] Take me literally at your own peril.

in music of the later 18th century might communicate via their modems on a bulletin board. There are hundreds of such communities on the CompuServe Information Service, Genie, America Online, and other such services.

The power of such virtual communities can be profound. Communication is a powerful tool. Not only does it transfer knowledge; it also acts as a catalyst for the generation of new ideas, and creates possibilities where none existed before.

Virtual Art

The range of art produced in the field of virtual reality is vast. Ranging from full-blown multimedia extravaganzas to intimate works, the field is hardly definable. Almost any aspect of computers, multimedia, or virtual reality is seen as a valid medium by many artists. And science fiction literature is rampant with cyber artists of every description, ranging from artists who sculpt with human emotion to creators of complete virtual systems.

Sensory Stimulation

So far, multimedia means only sight and sound. The future holds the promise of adding stimulation of other senses, either directly or electronically. What would be the results of linking smell or touch to a computer simulation? How would it change our daily experience if such things became common—if the television migrated from "the box" to a suit you wear?

These possibilities are far down the road, but they could shake the foundations of what it means to be human.

Hypertext

Hypertext is the ability to link similar information by electronic means. Today, it is used by products like Encarta[9] for more than text. You can, for example, look up "cat" and you will find not only references to specific breeds that you can access with a click of the mouse, but animations, sound recordings, and pictures as well. All are *hyper-linked* to the text.

The future possibilities for hyper-linking are endless. It could be applied to television, for example. You could be watching a program that reminds you of an old Jack Benny show, and you could jump to that show using a search tool, and then return to the show you were originally watching without missing a second of it.

---

[9] A wonderful multimedia encyclopedia from Microsoft.

Medical Simulations

Today, the first simulations of the human body are appearing in medical schools. Sometimes referred to as a "virtual cadaver," these simulations allow medical students to explore human anatomy without ever touching a real body, dead or otherwise. Surgeons can use such simulations to practice surgical techniques.

At the far edge of such simulations is the conversion of data from CAT scans and other high-tech tools into 3D or virtual simulations. This allows a physician to examine the inside of a body as though the enclosing skin and muscle were not present.

Virtual Sex

Yes, there is virtual sex, too—whether you like it or not, this powerful human drive is very much a part of the virtual scene. You can already purchase 3D video tapes rated XXX, and there are interactive "games" that feature or emphasize sexual content. Simulated sex seems as likely to find its way to market as any other kind of simulation.

Robotics

There are many uses for robots in places where it would be dangerous or difficult to put a human being. For example, robots are already being used to handle nuclear and chemical clean-up duties. The development of virtual reality and *telepresence*[10] will enhance an operator's ability to maneuver such robots. Planetary exploration also offers a unique opportunity for development of virtual reality techniques—it is much safer to send a robot probe controlled by a person to a planetary surface than that same person. In fact, planetary models are currently under development that would use miniature vehicles to allow researchers to explore a planet from a human perspective, and perhaps learn new ways of interpreting existing data.

Data Police

If we are to have data highways, then surely there will be data highway patrolmen to guard them. Security issues have dogged business use of computers from the very beginning, and that isn't likely to change. As reality becomes more and more

---

[10] Telepresence refers to maintaining a presence in a distant environment using robotic equipment and sensors. This might range from having a remotely operated camera in a different room to using a robot that looks like you to attend a meeting.

artificial, someone has to hold the patents and create the technologies to make it possible.

Virtual Underground

And just as surely as there will be a virtual community, there will have to be a virtual underground—a place for the dissidents and rebels. This is evident even today in the existence of the virtual equivalents of Greenwich Village, Berkeley, and Soho.

Hacker's Dream, Hacker's Nightmare

Whatever the future holds, I'll make one prediction: It's going to be more or less unpredictable. It will be a hacker's[11] dream because there will be enormously interesting challenges to be met. It will be a hacker's nightmare because the proliferation of proprietary technologies likely to emerge will keep some technologies out of people's hands for decades.

Roots and Possibilities

If the roots of the figure are already present, there is very little that is certain about where virtual reality is going. Talk about *data highways*[12] is now a common part of business discourse. Businesses are competing for these data highways the same that railroad barons competed for land to put railroads on. And just as the railroads changed forever how the American landscape was viewed and used, the data highways of the future will alter forever the nature of the human landscape, both inside and out.

Humankind must always keep one toe on the ground. That's where our roots are, and that's where our values are formed. It is our reference point, the measure of all things. If virtual reality is exciting or fun or useful or profound, it is in relation to what it adds to real experience, not the other way around.

---

[11] If you aren't familiar with the term, a hacker is someone who basically builds his own hardware or software from the ground up—someone who knows the technology inside out. In the media, the term has earned a negative connotation, having been used to refer to people who crack into computer systems illegally. I much prefer the earlier use of the term to refer to knowledgeable insiders.

[12] These are the physical links between the sources of data and your television set. Cable television is just the tip of that iceberg. How about a fiber-optic cable coming into your home, and connecting with a "television" that has the power of a personal computer inside it?

13

THE VIRTUAL FUTURE

The virtual future holds a lot of promise, and there's no telling how much of the promise will actually come true. You can, however, get a real taste of that future today. You can even do it without spending a lot of money. Consider the recipe for this chapter.

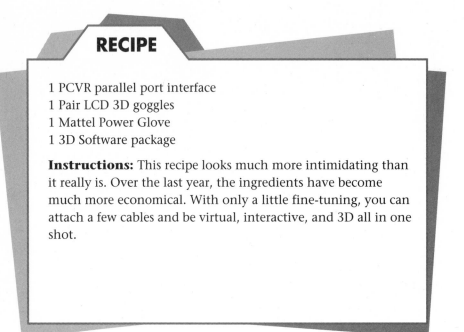

RECIPE

1 PCVR parallel port interface
1 Pair LCD 3D goggles
1 Mattel Power Glove
1 3D Software package

Instructions: This recipe looks much more intimidating than it really is. Over the last year, the ingredients have become much more economical. With only a little fine-tuning, you can attach a few cables and be virtual, interactive, and 3D all in one shot.

You might think it would cost a lot of money to acquire that list of ingredients, but that's not the case. For example, consider the costs of a basic 3D system:

LCD[1] goggles	$350
3D Software	Free[2]
Mattel Power Glove[3]	$100
Computer Interface for above	Included with goggles

That means your total investment in 3D VR is less than $500. Let's talk about what you get for your money.

LCD Goggles

LCD goggles work on a very simple principle. They are a pair of glasses with LCD panels in place of lenses. As explained in Chapter 8, most 3D systems must find a way to present different images to each eye. By switching electrical current to alternate LCD panels, the computer can control which eye sees the computer screen. Here's what's happening:

■ The computer displays an image for the left eye on the monitor. At the same time, it sends a timing signal to the interface that controls the glasses, usually through the parallel port.

■ When the glasses receive the timing signal, it opens one LCD panel and closes the other.[4]

■ The computer displays the image for the right eye on the monitor, and sends another timing signal.

---

[1] LCD stands for Liquid Crystal Display, and this is the same technology that is used in watches, laptop computer screens, and hand-held calculators. The idea is simple: when an electrical current is applied to and then removed from the liquid crystal, it toggles between transparent and opaque. In typical applications, the crystals are shaped into letters and numbers. Electrical currents are turned on and off to make portions of the LCD panel opaque, thus making readable text or numbers.

[2] You can download Rend386, for example, from the Compuserve forum CYBERFORUM. This program is explained later in this chapter, but only from the user-interface point of view. For complete information about Rend386, look for the book Virtual Reality Creations from the Waite Group. It is written by one of the authors of Rend386, David Stampe. If you want to spend a little money, you can create stereo images with Vistapro as well.

[3] This item is no longer manufactured, but it remains in heavy circulation among VR enthusiasts. You can find them locally by watching the classified section of your newspaper, or you can buy them on the very active VR market. Several companies are stocking large quantities of used Power Gloves. I ordered one, and when it arrived, it still had all of the original equipment and manuals.

[4] This system does not guarantee that the correct panel will be open. Most such systems have a simple way for you to reverse the currently open panel—often nothing fancier than a simple toggle switch.

■ The glasses switch panels—the one that was open is now closed, and the one that was closed is now open.

This process continues at very high speed. If you were to view the monitor without the glasses, you would see both images at once—sort of like double vision. You need the glasses to make sure that each eye only sees what it is meant to see.

The glasses are often referred to by VR enthusiasts as "Sega goggles" because Sega was one of the first companies to come out with such a product. However, this is not an accurate name at all, because most such goggles are now used on computers, not game machines.

Figure 13.1[5] shows a pair of LCD goggles that I received from the 3D TV Corporation.

Figure 13.1.
3D LCD glasses
from 3D TV
Corporation.

I found it very easy to set up and use the glasses. In fact, it took just a few minutes to be up and running with the glasses. The glasses interface using several different available black boxes. The one that I received from 3D TV is called the PCVR interface. It consists of a switch box (see Figure 13.2) and several cables. The PCVR is ideal if you will be using the Power Glove because you can connect both the glasses

---

[5] Many of the figures in this chapter were created using PC Video Capture technology. For those who are interested, the videos were recorded on Hi8 tape with a Canon A1 camcorder, and then captured with a Video Spigot card from Creative Labs. The images were captured at 640x480 as single frames and saved as 24-bit bitmaps.

and the Power Glove to the PCVR. If you will not be using the Power Glove, and just want 3D, you can try one of the other products listed in the "Alternative" sections later in this chapter.

Figure 13.2.
The PCVR
interface unit for
3D glasses and
Power Glove.

The front panel of the PCVR looks a bit intimidating, but most of what you see never needs any attention. To use the PCVR, you must make the following connections:

- Connect the PCVR to the parallel port of your computer, using the cable supplied.

- Connect the 3D goggles to the front of the PCVR (cable supplied).

- Connect the Power Glove cable (supplied) to the back of the PCVR.

- Connect the power cord (supplied) to the back of the PCVR, and plug it in.

- Optional: Connect your printer cable to the PCVR.

- Optional: Add a cable between your video display card and your normal video cable, and connect one end to the PCVR for better frame synchronization.

Figure 13.3 shows the rear panel of the PCVR, with the various connection ports just described.

Figure 13.3.
The rear panel of
the PCVR.

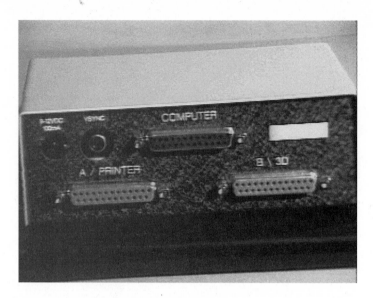

The front panel of the PCVR has a large rotating switch. This works just like the rotating switch on a printer switch box—to use your parallel printer, rotate the switch to the Printer setting. To use the Power Glove, rotate the switch to the B 3D setting.

There are also two indicator lights. A red light indicates that the power is on, and a yellow light tells you when the proper synchronization signal is present for the glasses.[6] Just in case the timing signal is off, there's a switch you can use to make sure that the right and left eyes get into proper synchronization.

The whole process is much simpler to do than it is to describe. Once you connect the cables, you should be up and running. One place where you can run into trouble is with a non-standard port address for your parallel port, but that's easy to fix. If you connect everything correctly, and don't get a yellow light, check the "3D Software" section later in this chapter.

Figure 13.4 shows the goggles in use.[7] I expected the cable to get in the way, but it is light, thin, and very flexible, and wasn't much of a problem. However, a cable is a cable, and it is at best a minor annoyance.

---

[6] The yellow light also lights up when data is being sent to your printer—just thought you should know.

[7] That's my wife, Donna Brown, under those goggles. She helped out in a million different ways with this book, but this is the only help you can actually see.

Figure 13.4. The 3D LCD goggles in use. Note the connecting cable dangling from the left side of the goggles. This is the cable that connects to the PCVR.

There is a noticeable flicker when you use the goggles. This is not unexpected, considering that the goggles are basically flickering on and off to do their job. To reduce flicker, keep room lights low, and don't crank up the brightness setting on your monitor. Generally, I found that the 3D effect was quite good.

The Mattel Power Glove

3D is fun, but getting right into the action is better. Using the Power Glove, you can interact with your computer in completely new ways.

However, before I get you all excited about the possibilities, a few words of caution are in order. The Power Glove, after all, started out as a toy. Real computer gloves use sophisticated tracking methods to allow fairly precise interpretation of your hand movements. For example, one model of a professional glove uses fiber optic cables strung along your fingers. The surface of the cables is etched to allow a slight loss of light. The more the cable is bent by your finger, the greater the loss of light. Separate cables are used for each knuckle and joint on your hand. The result is a precision tool, and the cost is many thousands of dollars.

The Power Glove, on the other hand,[8] uses cruder techniques for detecting finger movements. The Power Glove offers much lower precision in tracking finger

---

[8] Pun, as usual, intended.

movement—it can detect when your fingers are straight, and when they are bent, and that's about it. Instead of fiber optics, it uses resistive coated mylar—as your finger bends, the resistance of the coating changes. This is simply not as effective as fiber optics. But the price is much better: about $100 for a typical used Power Glove. (They are no longer manufactured.)

Figure 13.5 shows the Mattel Power Glove. The unit consists of a glove for the hand, a sending unit attached to the back of the hand, and a data-entry section over the wrist. It is connected to the computer by a cable at the base of the wrist section.

Figure 13.5.
The Mattel Power
Glove.

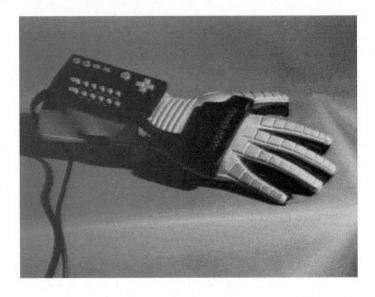

The underside of the glove is shown in Figure 13.6, attached to a hand. The straps are easy to attach using the hook and eye (more commonly but incorrectly known by the trademarked term Velcro) straps.

I have very long fingers, but I had no trouble using the glove—as you can see, the finger tips are open, allowing long fingers to simply stick out. This was not uncomfortable.

In normal use, you must do two things before using the glove with your software: flex and center. Flexing—making a fist a few times, as shown in Figure 13.7—allows the glove to adjust to the size of your hand.

Figure 13.6.
The underside of
the Power Glove.

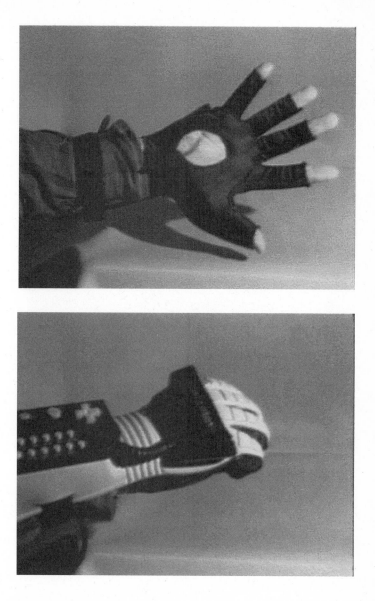

Figure 13.7.
Flexing the glove
to adjust to the
size of your
hand.

Centering is done by relaxing your hand and leveling it, with the fingers spread in a relaxed manner (Figure 13.8). When the glove is comfortable and level, press the Center button on the control panel of the glove with your other hand. A beep will confirm that you are centered.

*Figure 13.8.
Centering the
glove should be
done with a
relaxed hand.*

Proper centering requires that you point the glove at the middle of the stationary receivers. The little black box attached at the back of the hand generates ultrasonic signals that the stationary receivers translate into positional information. Figure 13.9 shows the stationary receivers. There are three of them, and they must be oriented as shown. Normally, you drape them over your monitor. Because the average computer monitor is smaller than the average TV, you may need to add a book or something similar to balance the receiver properly on your monitor. Later illustrations show the use of a large dictionary for exactly this purpose.

To center properly, make sure that the glove points at the middle of a rectangle defined by the three black boxes of the receiver.[9]

To verify that the glove is working properly, either plug it into a Nintendo Entertainment System (for which it was originally designed) or check to see that the LEDs[10] at the upper right of the receivers follow the movement of the glove.

You can also test the glove visually with your software, since Rend386 displays the current position and gesture of the glove on screen. Pointing is a good test (see Figure 13.10). This is a gesture which is very useful in Rend386.

---

[9] Yes, you only need three points to define a rectangle.

[10] LED stands for Light Emitting Diodes, and are not to be confused with LCDs, which emit no light of their own.

Figure 13.9.
The stationary
receivers used
with the Power
Glove.

Figure 13.10.
The pointing
gesture.

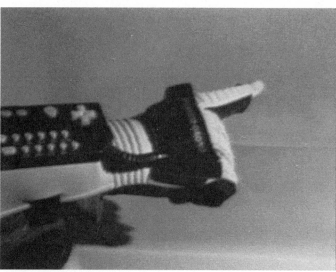

Using the Power Glove

Once you have the Power Glove centered, you can begin using it with your software. Different software uses different glove gestures to manipulate objects. Figure 13.11 shows the glove in use.

Figure 13.11.
Using the Power
Glove.

In general, we found that the glove was easiest to use standing up. This makes typing awkward, and you can't type very well with the hand wearing the glove. This is part of the price you pay for using the glove.

Figure 13.12 shows the glove in use with the Rend386 program. The glove is in the centering position. If you look carefully, you can see that the glove on the screen matches the position and orientation of the real glove.

Figure 13.12.
Using the Power
Glove with
software.

Figure 13.13 shows the glove made into a fist, and the corresponding fist of the glove in the software.

Figure 13.13. The physical glove and the on-screen glove match gestures.

If you move to the left of the screen (see Figure 13.14), the on-screen glove follows. If you make a pointing gesture, the on-screen glove points, too.

Figure 13.14. Moving the glove side to side.

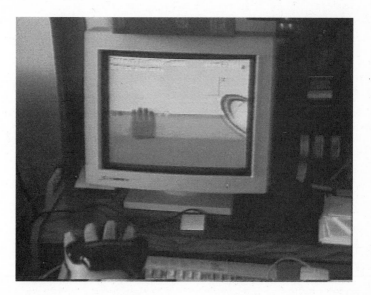

Figure 13.15.
Making a
pointing gesture.

Moving the glove toward and away from the screen moves it into and out of the scene.

Alternative 3D Connections

The PCVR is just one way to connect your 3D goggles to your computer. The folks at 3D TV[11] make several other devices that work just as well—and if you won't be using a Power Glove, these are quite economical.

Alternative #1: The PC3D

The goggles kit that comes with the PC3D is $250, a full $100 less than the PCVR kit. The PC3D is a serial interface for the goggles, and is extremely compact (see Figure 13.16).

The PC3D is extremely easy to use. It takes its power from the serial port, so all you need to do to use it is to connect it to your serial port and plug in the 3D glasses. As with the PCVR, if your computer doesn't use standard port addresses, or if you aren't using COM1 as your serial connection, you may have to edit a few lines in the configuration file of the software.

---

[11] You may be wondering why I keep mentioning 3D TV—am I ignoring other companies? It's because this is an infant industry, and 3D TV is by far the most prominent supplier of inexpensive VR technology. If it weren't for 3D TV, VR would not be as accessible as it is.

Figure 13.16.
The PC3D serial
interface for 3D
goggles.

Alternative #2: The Model 3000

The Model 3000 is an interesting device. The unit I tested was a prototype (see Figure 13.17). This unit costs $175 (in addition to the cost of goggles).

Figure 13.17.
The Model 3000
3D goggle
interface.

The Model 3000 is an interesting hybrid. It interfaces your goggles with the video port only—there is no parallel port connection involved. It senses the sync signal by tapping into the video cable using an adapter supplied with the unit. It also comes with a power unit for its AC connection.

The Model 3000 also supports viewing of 3D video from your VCR. To use it in this manner, you need only run a cable from the video out of your VCR to the Model 3000. You can then plug the 3D goggles into the Model 3000. 3D TV markets a number of 3D videotapes which are listed in the appendix.[12]

How does 3D Video look? When the source material is recorded using a 3D video camera, the effect is the best I have ever seen. Converting 3D movies to videotape is not as effective.

3D Software

The world of 3D software is in its infancy. It wasn't until 1993 that inexpensive hardware became commonly available, and, as in the past, software is busy trying to catch up to what the hardware can do.

Software Options

Software options are currently limited to several programs. Two of the more interesting ones are Vistapro, whose virtual reality aspects were covered in Chapter 1, and Rend386. Each program takes advantage of 3D goggles in a completely different way. Of the two, only Rend386 takes advantage of the Power Glove.

Vistapro

To use Vistapro with 3D glasses, you would create stereo pairs in the normal manner (see Chapter 1). However, instead of combining the pair into a single red/blue color image, you would convert each the the PCX files to the GIF format and then combine them using the PCGV program supplied by 3D TV for viewing with 3D goggles.

---

[12] The quality of the tapes is mixed, and the content is idiosyncratic. However, when the content and quality of the material is just right, the effects are some of the best 3D I have ever seen.

Rend386

Rend386 is a remarkable program. Created by David Stampe and Bernie Roehl, it is not available in any stores. It isn't shareware, either, and it isn't freeware. Rend386 is a collective project of many individuals, and is available for downloading from Compuserve's Cyberforum.[13] The program is almost always evolving to support new stuff in virtual reality, so the features you see here may not reflect the state of the program when you download it.

Rend386 has two personalities. One is very friendly, and one is very technical.

The friendly side consists of a program you can use to move interactively through relatively simple 3D spaces. The technical side involves the creation of 3D spaces. Rend386 uses a fairly complicated mechanism to specify the objects in a 3D space and their properties. On the plus side, it is very powerful. On the minus side, it takes a lot of perseverance to create a 3D world for Rend386.[14]

Figure 13.18 shows a screen from the Rend386 program that you can use to tour a 3D world. The scene is one that comes with the Rend386 disk from 3D TV, called pool.wld. This is one of several worlds that are included. Another favorite is an animated version of the solar system, solarsys.wld, that is also highly recommended.

Figure 13.18.
A Rend386
screen.

---

[13] It is also available for downloading via anonymous ftp from sunee.uwaterloo.ca in the pub/rend386 directory—if you can handle such things using Internet.

[14] If you are interested in exploring world creation with Rend386, I strongly suggest you look into the book *Virtual Reality Creations* from the Waite Group Press. It is essential for a solid understanding of Rend386 at this level. Because of the unique nature of the development of Rend386, this book will actually serve, in effect, as the program's documentation.

As you can see, the glove is shown on the screen. In this example, the glove is making the pointing gesture.

Setting Up Rend386 for the Goggles and the Power Glove

If you run Rend386 and the glove and/or goggles don't work properly, the most likely problem is that the default port settings aren't right for your setup. These can be edited with a text editor in the configuration file rend386.cfg.

The most common problems involve port addresses. For example, the default port address for LPT1, the parallel port, is 378 hex. In my case, my machine was using 3BC as the port address for LPT1. I simply edited the lines in rend386.cfg that reference this port address:

```
segaport 3BC 04 04 00 00 00
pgloveport 3BD 3BC 3 0 2 1 3 10 00
```

As you can see, the contents of rend386.cfg aren't exactly plain English, but there are lots of comments in the file to help you out. You probably won't need to change much to get yourself started. Don't try to change any lines that start with a pound sign (#)—it indicates a comment.

Exploring with Rend386

You can move around easily in Rend386. The arrow keys rotate your point of view left and right, and the up and down arrows move you into and out of the virtual space. There are also key combinations you can use for vertical and sideways movement.

You can also select objects in the virtual space and move them around. You can select with the mouse, or by pointing to objects with the glove. If an object is moving, selecting it with glove takes some dexterity—the first touch selects, and the second touch deselects. If the object is moving rapidly, a touch on the leading surface will select, but a touch on the trailing surface will deselect. Figure 13.19 shows the glove touching an object with the pointing gesture to select it.

*Figure 13.19.
Selecting an
object by
touching it with
the glove.*

Figure 13.20 shows a lounge chair near the pool that has been selected—the construction lines are now highlighted.

*Figure 13.20.
A selected item is
highlighted. The
glove can be seen
at the right of the
screen.*

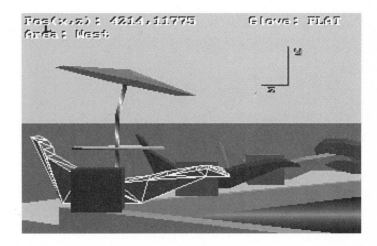

To move a selected object or objects, simply make a fist with the Power Glove and move it—up or down, left or right, in or out of the virtual space. Figure 13.21 shows the lounge chair lifted up. Figure 13.22 shows the lounge chair pushed further back into the scene using the glove.

Figure 13.21.
An object moved
upward with the
Power Glove.

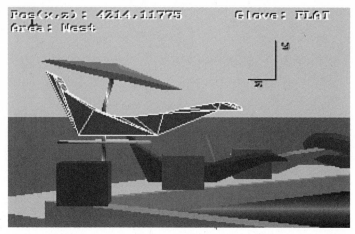

Figure 13.22.
An object moved
farther back
using the Power
Glove.

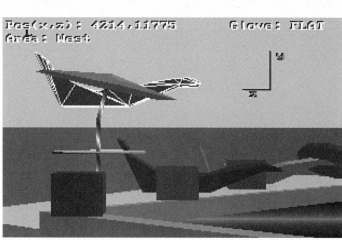

In Figure 13.23, a second lounge chair has been selected using the pointing gesture of the glove, and pulled toward the viewer.

Throughout these operations, the glove appears on the screen,[15] mimicking the current position and orientation of the real glove. For example, in Figure 13.24, the glove can be clearly seen at the right of the screen.

---

[15] If you move the glove too far in any direction, it will move off of the screen. To bring it back, simply move it back within the boundaries of the receivers.

Figure 13.23.
An object moved
forward using the
glove.

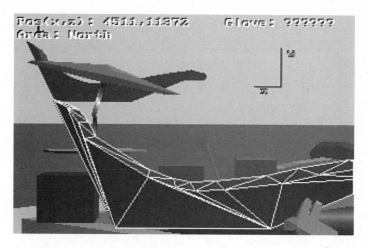

Figure 13.24.
An object moved
forward using the
glove. The glove
can be seen at
the right of the
screen.

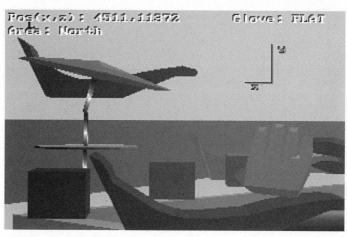

Even if you move very far from the center of the scene, the glove still maintains the same relative proportion of the screen at various physical positions. For example, Figure 13.25 shows the point of view moved thousands of units up and out from the pool, but the glove stays right with the point of view.

*Figure 13.25.
The glove
maintains a
constant
relationship with
the local point of
view.*

Summary

In this chapter, you learned about technology that is at the cutting edge of affordable VR hardware and software. Throughout this book, I have tried to present tools that are within the reach of the average computer user. The barriers—cost and complexity—that kept VR tools out of the mainstream of computing are falling all around us. You have the opportunity, right now, to get involved in the development and use of virtual worlds.

Whatever the implications of adding virtual reality capabilities to personal computers may turn out to be, you are in a position to start finding out today.

A

THE "MADNESS" CD-ROM

The CD-ROM that accompanies this book has a wide variety of material on it. There are virtual reality worlds to explore, demos of commercial programs, 3D and VR games, animations, videos, and a whole lot more.

The material on the CD is easy to access. This appendix will be your guide to finding the information you want, and making use of it.

The VR Madness Menu

Most of the product demos and other software are DOS products and need to be run from a DOS prompt—not from within Windows. There are also several Windows-based products and an exciting Windows multimedia applications that you won't want to miss.

The DOS software on the disk can be accessed by running the *VR Madness!* menu. This menu will allow you to navigate through the selections on the CD-ROM. You can run programs or install the software to your hard drive, if needed, from the menu.

Follow these steps to start the *VR Madness!* menu:

1. Change to the drive containing the CD-ROM. For example, if your CD-ROM drive is D:, type **D:** and press Enter.

2. Type **MAINMENU** and press Enter.

3. The *VR Madness!* menu will appear and present you with the choice of running it in text mode or graphics mode. To run the menu in graphics mode requires VGA or SVGA graphics. Choose one of the options by using the arrow keys to highlight your choice and pressing Enter.

4. You will see the main page of the menu. From here, you can choose to navigate into the different sections of the CD-ROM. Each choice will take you to a new menu.

The top line of the menu tells you which menu you are at. If a menu contains many items, a scroll bar will appear to the right of the choices, indicating that there are more choices. The final choice in each menu will be Return to Main Menu. To exit the menu and return to DOS, press the Esc key.

If you wish, you can explore the areas of the CD-ROM without using the *VR Madness!* menu. You can go to the directory where a product is stored, read the documentation files, and run or install the software. If you don't feel comfortable rooting around in directories and exploring software on your own, it would be best to resort to the menu.

Working Demos

The software demos in this section are special versions of commercial products that let you take the full product for a test drive.

Mars Explorer

Virtual Reality Laboratories, Inc.
2341 Ganador Court
San Luis Obispo, CA 93401

Category: Commercial demo

Location on disk: \MARS

Documentation: MARSXDMO.TXT

Command to start the program: GO

This software is a sample version of the full Mars Explorer package from Virtual Reality Laboratories, the makers of Vistapro. The full package contains low to high resolution images of the surface of Mars, pieced together from NASA's Viking missions. Images can be saved in PCX format for use with other programs, including Microsoft Windows applications.

PhotoMorph

North Coast Software
P.O. Box 459
265 Scruton Pond Road
Barrington, NH 03825

Category: Commercial demo

Location on CD-ROM: \WINDEMOS\PMORPH

Documentation: README.TXT

Command to install the program: INSTALL

PhotoMorph is the easy-to-use Windows-based morphing software from North Coast Software. PhotoMorph can easily create morphs of various types and in different formats, including Video for Windows .AVI format. The quality of morphs created with this software can rival what you see in movies and on television.

This demo has most of the functionality of the retail version, with some restrictions. Read the documentation file for more details. See the section "Bonus Software", later in this appendix, for information on some sample morphs included on the CD-ROM.

NOTE

You need to run the INSTALL.EXE program in this directory to install the demo to your hard drive. If you have not installed Video for Windows drivers, see the section "Windows Access," later in this chapter. These drivers must be installed before you can access all the functions of this demo.

Vistapro 3.0

Virtual Reality Laboratories, Inc.
2341 Ganador Court
San Luis Obispo, CA 93401

Category: Commercial demo

Location on disk: \VP3

Documentation: VPDEMO.TXT

Command to start the program: VPDEMO

This demo is an interactive tutorial and trial version Vistapro 3. After working with the full version of Vistapro 1, included on this CD-ROM, this demo will give you a feel for how version 3 works. By the way, there was no version 2 of Vistapro.

Distant Suns

Virtual Reality Laboratories, Inc.
2341 Ganador Court
San Luis Obispo, CA 93401

Category: Commercial demo

Location on disk: \DSUNS

Documentation: DSDEMO.TXT

Command to install the program: INSTALL

Distant Suns is the Windows-based desktop planetarium that displays the night sky from anywhere on the planet from 4173 BC to 10000 AD. One of the new features in Distant Suns 2.0 is the off earth mode that can display the heavens from anywhere in the solar system.

> You need to run the INSTALL.EXE program in this directory to install the Distant Suns demo to your hard drive.

Virtual Worlds

In this section, you'll find dozens of interesting virtual worlds to explore, many of them interactive. Nearly all of these worlds were created with commercial virtual reality products. Some of them were even created with Virtual Reality Studio, which is included on this CD-ROM.

Superscape VR

Dimension International
Zephyr One, Calleva Park
Aldermaston
Berkshire
ENGLAND RG7 4QZ

Category: Commercial demo

Location on disk: \SUPERVR

Documentation: README

Command to start the program: DEMO

This software is a demo of the commercial Superscape virtual reality software. The demo allows you to control one of several objects in a industrial complex. You have your choice of driving around in one of two cars (either from the driver's seat, or from above), flying a helicopter, or controlling a walking man.

This demo was created specifically for VGA cards, but the actual product is a high-resolution interactive environment that runs on high end graphical workstations. In the back of the book you'll find an advertisement for this software.

Virtual Reality Studio Creations

(various authors)

Location on disk: \VRSDEMOS

Documentation: (each demo has its own documentation)

Command to start the menu program: VRSMENU

You'll find a number of interactive virtual worlds here that were created with versions 1 and 2 of Virtual Reality Studio. Some of them are complex games, others are worlds meant for exploration.

These creations will give you a taste of the types of virtual reality worlds that can be put together with Virtual Reality Studio.

Each virtual world is stored in its own separate subdirectory. Change to the \VRSDEMOS directory, type VRSMENU and press Enter to start a menu which allows you to explore each of these worlds in turn. You can also access this menu from the main *VR Madness!* menu.

Stunt Island Movies

Disney Software, Inc.

Category: Commercial demo

Location on disk: \STUNT

Documentation: STUNT.DOC

Command to start the player program: PLAYONE

These movies are examples of the types of interaction that can be created with Stunt Island, from Disney Software. Stunt Island allows you to become your own movie director by creating complex action scenes and stunts. After setting up the action, you film it from different angles and locations, edit the film and view the final result.

For more information on Stunt Island, read Chapter 4 of this book.

> The player is configured to run with Sound Blaster music and sound. It will run this way if you don't have a sound card.

Fly the Grand Canyon

Fred Tuck
5508 Chimney Hollow
Norcross, GA 30093

Category: Commercial demo

Location on disk: \FLY

Documentation: (the program will display instructions)

Command to start the program: FLYDEMO

This program is a demo version of Fly the Grand Canyon. This is a flight simulator-type program that lets you take a flying tour of the Grand Canyon. You can let the program fly you around, or take your chances at flying yourself.

The Grand Canyon appears as wire-frame contours and you can use 3D glasses to view the scene in three dimensions. This demo shows just a part of the complete program. The full program allows you to fly through the entire Grand Canyon, not just a small portion of it. The complete Fly the Grand Canyon also has other added features, such as a record mode and more detailed graphics.

VR Games

Arcade-type virtual reality games are beginning to appear in places like shopping malls and video arcades. Virtual reality games are also beginning to be available for home computers. In this section, you'll find a variety of virtual reality games, from action games to interactive games that can be played over phone lines.

Because most of these games need to save files when they're running, you must first install a game to your hard drive before running it. You can install these games from the *VR Madness!* menu.

Mate

VRontier Worlds
809 E. South Street
Stoughton, WI 53589

Category: Shareware

Location on disk: \VRGAMES\MATE

Documentation: README.TXT

Command to start the program: SMATE

Mate is a true Virtual Reality Chess Game that allows two players to interact in a single virtual environment. In addition, you don't have to live close to your opponent. You can call them with your modem and play over the telephone lines. All the telephone functions are built into the program.

Each player must have an 80386 or higher IBM compatible computer, a mouse and a 2400 baud or higher modem. In addition, a math coprocessor is recommended—it speeds up the program.

Megatron

John Dee Stanley
6959 California Ave SW
Seattle, WA 98136

Category: Shareware

Location on disk: \VRGAMES\MEGATRON

Documentation: MEGA.DOC

Command to start the program: MEGA

Megatron is a two-player combat game. The object of the game is simple—hunt down your adversary and destroy his assault robot. You can either play against the computer, or you can use your modem to play against another computer over the phone lines.

Megatron requires VGA graphics. A 386 or better computer system is strongly recommended.

Ken's Labyrinth

Epic Megagames
10406 Holbrook Dr.
Potomac, MD 20854

Category: Shareware

Location on disk: \VRGAMES\KENSLAB

Documentation: HELPME.DOC

Command to start the program: KEN

Ken's Labyrinth is a 3D arcade maze game featuring high-res 256-color graphics, music, and digital sound effects. Before playing, you need to run SETUP to tell the game what hardware you have. Simply type "SETUP" and press Enter, then go through the menu and select your hardware from the lists of choices.

Ken's Labyrinth requires VGA graphics and a 286 or better computer system.

Wolfenstein 3D

Apogee Software Productions
P.O. Box 496389
Garland, TX 75049

Category: Shareware

Location on disk: \VRGAMES\WOLF3D

Documentation: When you run the program, select the "Read Me" option on the main menu.

Command to start the program: WOLF3D

Wolfenstein 3D is a technology breakthrough in PC games—you play your character in first-person perspective in a 3D world. As an escaped prisoner in a Nazi war prison, you will move smoothly through a world full of amazing detail and animation.

 Wolfenstein 3D requires 256 color VGA graphics and a 286 or better computer system.

Alone in the Dark

Interplay Productions
17922 Fitch Avenue
Irvine, CA

Category: Commercial demo

Location on disk: \VRGAMES\ALONE

Documentation: README.TXT

Command to start the program: TATOU

Alone in the Dark is a sophisticated virtual reality based commercial game, which features 3D ray-traced characters which interact with each other in a gothic-horror novel setting. This demo version allows you to play out only one of the many rooms and scenarios in the full game.

 Alone in the Dark requires 256-color VGA graphics and a 386 or better computer system.

Pictures

The \PICTURES directory contains a large number of graphics that were created with products discussed in the book. You can view these pictures from the *VR Madness!* menu. The SVGA shareware program is used to display the images— you'll be able to see the resolution of each file and read a brief description of the image.

Files that end with a _ character are graphics that have 16 million colors, are 1024x768 in size, or both. There is a 640x480 256 color version of each of these high-resolution images. If you have a 256-color system, the lower-resolution versions will look much better. The \PICTURES\BMP directory contains BMP files that work great as Windows wallpaper. There are 640x480, 800x600, and 1024x768 versions of most pictures.

Utilities

These utilities were used in creating the *VR Madness!* menuing system and the on-line documentation for Vistapro 1 and Virtual Reality Studio 1. The complete distribution versions of these shareware programs is included on the CD-ROM. As with any shareware, please read the documentation for the product and register the program if you find it useful.

SVGA

John P. Silva
3429 Maywood Dr.
Richmond, CA 94803

Category: Shareware

Location on disk: \UTILS\SVGA

Documentation: SVGA.MAN

Command to start the program: SVGA

SVGA is an easy-to-use image viewer that can view a variety of graphics file formats. It's designed to help you quickly browse through a collection of image files. This image viewer is used to view some of the graphics images when you are running the *VR Madness!* menu. SVGA works with VGA and SVGA graphics systems with at least 512K of video memory. It also offers support for VESA compatible graphics cards.

When you are viewing an image in SVGA, there are several keys that can help you:

- The F9 and F10 keys will toggle between sizes of the image being viewed.

- You can use the arrow keys to scroll around the image when the image is larger than the graphics resolution on your computer.

Menu Media

> EFD Systems
> 304 Smokerise Circle SE
> Marietta, GA 30067
>
> *Category:* Shareware
>
> *Location on disk:* \UTILS\MMEDIA
>
> *Documentation:* MM.DOC
>
> *Command to start the program:* MM

Menu Media is a simple-to-use menuing system that runs in text, ANSI graphics, and VGA graphics modes. This program is used to create the *VR Madness!* menus for this CD-ROM.

NOTE
> You cannot distribute or use the full version of Menu Media for your own use. You *can* use the version in the \UTILS\MMEDIA directory—it is the unregistered shareware version.

FView

> Chris Gordon
>
> *Category:* Freeware
>
> *Location on disk:* \UTILS\FVIEW
>
> *Documentation:* FVIEW.DOC
>
> *Command to start the program:* FVIEW

FView is a simple program that displays a text file. It allows you to page through the file and search for particular words. It is used for viewing the on-line manuals for Vistapro 1 and Virtual Reality Studio 1.

Windows Access

There is one entry point to all of the files that are accessible in Windows. It is an application called *VR Madness!*. It allows you to see all the figures that appear in this book in glorious living color, and to play numerous video and animation files that illustrate the principles covered in each chapter. Not all chapters have video or animation files, however.

A few words of warning are in order. Many of the images created for the book are in color, and many of them use large numbers of colors. If you are using a 256-color (also called 8-bit) video display adapter, you won't be able to enjoy the full range of colors in these images, and you may sometimes see incorrect colors as well. This is a result of the limitations of working with 256 colors.

To see all the colors in the images, you will need a 16-bit (65,000 colors) or 24-bit (16 million colors) display adapter. This was necessary in order to preserve the high level of detail in the original images.[1]

As a general rule, I'm a big fan of 16-bit or better video displays. It's hard to beat the superior color rendition, especially for video files. Another advantage is the lack of palette switching that is so annoying in 8-bit color modes. With only 256 colors available, the color palette has to be changed for each image displayed, with consequent flashing and color changing in any images displayed elsewhere on the screen.

All of the files for the VR Madness application are located in a single directory, <*d*>:\VRMAD, where <*d*> is the drive letter of your CD-ROM drive.

Before you run the VR Madness application[2], run the INSTALL.EXE program found in the \VRMAD directory. Follow these steps:

1. Select File + **Run** from the Program Manager menu.

2. Type <*d*>\VRMAD\INSTALL and press Enter. For example, if your CD-ROM drive is D:, type D:\VRMAD\INSTALL.

Follow the instructions in the installation program, and it will install the files that run the VR Madness application to your hard drive. The installation program will also create a VR Madness group in Program Manager.

---

[1] Many of the more interesting images are included as .BMP files on the CD-ROM. Look for them in the \BMP directory of the CD-ROM.

[2] It was created in Asymetrix Toolbook, if you are curious.

To run the application, double-click on the Configuration icon in the VR Madness Program Manager group and follow the instructions in the file. Then you can double-click the `VR Madness Application` icon.

The Opening Screen

The opening window of the VR Madness application is shown in Figure A.1. There is a message box at the center of the window, and a number of buttons at the bottom. The message box provides some information you'll need for viewing the figures. I used Compel to display the figures, and the information in this box explains the basics of using Compel.

Figure A.1.
The opening
window of the
VR Madness
application.

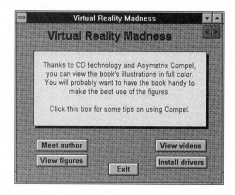

There are five buttons at the bottom of the window:

- ■ *Meet author*—Plays a video file I created to introduce myself to you. You must have Video for Windows, or the runtime for Video for Windows, already installed to play the video file.

- ■ *View figures*—Takes you directly to the page that allows you to view the figures for the various chapters.

- ■ *View videos*—Takes you directly to the page that allows you to view the various video and animation files included with the VR Madness application.

- ■ *Install drivers*—Takes you to a page that allows you to install the Video for Windows runtime, the Cinepak video codec, and the animation drivers.

- ■ *Exit*—Quit VR Madness.

Installing Drivers

I have provided several video and animation drivers that you may or may not already have on your system. They are all the very latest versions of these drivers, as of August, 1993. To view many of the pages in the application, you must first install these drivers on your system. Otherwise, some parts of the application will not work.

The *Install drivers* page, shown in Figure A.2, allows you to install the various drivers.

Figure A.2.
The Install
drivers page of
VR Madness.

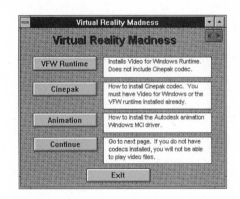

You can install the following drivers:

VFW Runtime—This installs the complete Video for Windows runtime. Just as I was finishing this book, Intel announced a new release of Indeo, which is included when you install the Video for Windows runtime. This new 3.0 version of Indeo is a great improvement and you should have it on your machine if you want the best colors and performance from your video files.

Cinepak—The Cinepak codec for Video for Windows, from SuperMac, was recently included in the list of drivers that can be distributed as a runtime. Clicking on this button tells you how to install the runtime Cinepak driver. You'll need to use the Control Panel's Drivers applet to do the installation.

Animation—If you do not already have a driver for playing .FLI and .FLC files (otherwise known as Autodesk animation files), click this button for instructions on installing the Autodesk animation MCI driver. You'll need to use the Control Panel's Drivers applet to do the installation.

Continue—This button will take you to the View Figures page, without installing anything.

Viewing Figures

If you click the *View figures* button, you will see the page displayed in Figure A.3.

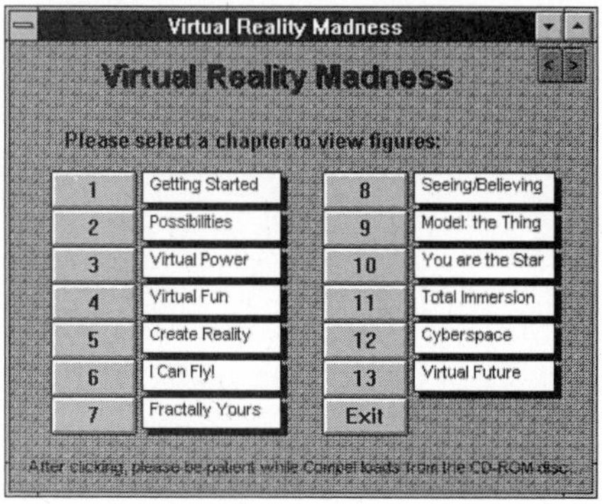

Figure A.3.
The View figures
page of VR
Madness.

To view the figures for a specific chapter, click on the numbered button corresponding to the chapter number. Brief chapter titles are located next to each button. This will start the Compel runtime; be patient while it loads. For information about working with the Compel runtime, see the Compel section later in this chapter.

Viewing Videos

If you click the *View videos* button, you will see the page displayed in Figure A.4.

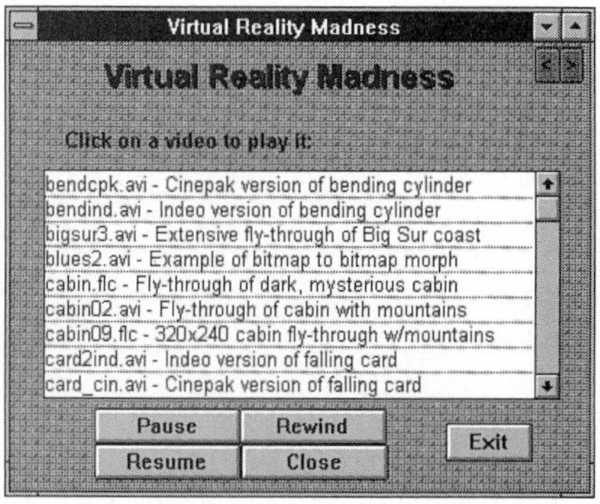

Figure A.4.
The View
videos page of
VR Madness.

The video page is simply a list of the videos in the \VRMAD directory, with a short description of the videos. Most of the videos are playable from the Compel presentations for each chapter, but I thought you might like to be able to play the videos by selecting them individually.

I've added a few "bonus" video files that I created at the last minute; these are only accessible from the video page. My favorites among the bonuses are the Jupiter and Saturn animations.

To play a video, simply click on its name. It will start playing automatically.[3] You can the use the four buttons at the bottom of the video page to control playback:

- *Pause*—Pauses the video at the current frame.

- *Resume*—Resumes playback after pausing. Has no effect if a video file is not paused.

- *Rewind*—Moves the video to the first frame, and leaves it in pause mode.

- *Close*—Closes the video file.

You do not have to close one video file before opening another; it's done automatically.

Working with the Compel Runtime

When you click on a chapter number button on the View Figures page, VR Madness loads and runs a Compel presentation. Each presentation contains a number of elements:

- All of the figures for that chapter.

- Captions (some are expanded from the book) for each figure.

- Additional text to explain the figure or the concepts behind it.

- Videos or animations related to the chapter.

The presentation consists of one page for each figure. You can move from page to page in a variety of ways:

- By clicking the page with the left mouse button (you must click in an inactive area of the page).

---

[3] To play videos, you must have installed Video for Windows or the runtime. Some of the video files require the latest drivers for Indeo and Cinepak. These drivers are included on the CD-ROM, and can be installed from the Install drivers page (see Figure A.7).

■ Pressing the right arrow and control keys simultaneously.

■ Using the "twin click" floating controller (more about this soon).

When you start one of these Compel presentations, you'll see a box that explains some of the basic concepts behind the presentation of the figures. At the bottom of the screen, you are advised to view the presentation at 800x600 or larger "for best results." This requires a bit of explanation.

Many of the figures were created by capturing standard VGA screens. As a result, the typical figure is 640x480 pixels—the same size as a VGA screen. If you view the figure—and the captions, titles, explanation, etc.—on a 640x480 screen, the figure will appear slightly reduced, and will not be as clear as it could be. In other words, you can view the presentation at 640x480, but you may miss a few details in some of the figures.[4]

If you choose to use a screen size larger than 640x480, there are some things you should know about Compel. The most important: Compel requires a lot of memory for large screen sizes. You will want at least 8 megabytes of RAM if you are viewing at 800x600, and 12 megabytes for 1024x768. Otherwise, the time it takes to store screen data in virtual RAM on your hard disk will make the presentation very, very slow.

A second consideration is color. You should have at least 256 colors available, but you will get much better results if you can use 16-bit or 24-bit color.

Figure A.5 shows a typical Compel page, taken from the Chapter 9 presentation.

Special Features of the Compel Runtime

The Compel runtime offers you a few special services that are worth knowing about. They are located in the Control menu. You can access the Control menu by pressing the Alt and Space keys simultaneously. The menu is shown in Figure A.6.

The Slide Show Setup menu choice opens a dialog box that allows you to make the slide show automatic (by default, it is interactive, requiring you to press a key to move to the next page). You can also show a range of slides, and change the presentation from full-screen to windowed.

---

[4] Some of the figures are actually much larger than 640x480. The largest figures were created at 1024x768. These will look better on larger screens, too.

Figure A.5.
A sample page
from the Compel
presentation for
Chapter 9.

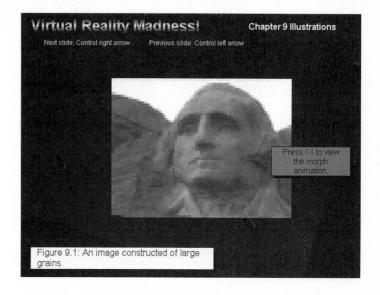

Figure A.6.
The Compel
Control menu.

If you have any problems running any of the sounds, videos, or animations in the Compel presentation, you can use Check Media Links in the Control menu to verify that you have support for the various multimedia features required. Any problems will be noted in the section titled "Media Link Status."

> If Compel can't find a media file, you can use the Set Directory button to select the \VRMAD directory on the CD. If you do not have a sound card or a video codec installed, you'll need to go through the installation procedure before that aspect of the Compel presentation will work properly.

One of the nice features of Compel is that it will not complain if you don't have the right multimedia setup to play a multimedia file. It will simply gracefully decline to play the file. If this happens, you can use Check Media Links to diagnose the problem.

The System Information dialog box is another useful diagnostic tool. You can display it with the System Information selection on the Control menu. It will tell you what multimedia hardware and software drivers you have installed, as well as the drivers used in the presentation.

Playing Media Files

Figure A.7 shows how most media files are played in the Compel presentations. Text boxes that say "Click me" in red will play a video, sound, or animation. The mouse cursor changes to a pointing hand when you move it over something that you can click. In some cases, you will be instructed to click an image to play a media file. You will know that the mouse is correctly positioned when the cursor changes to a pointing hand.

Figure A.7.
A sample figure
from Chapter 11
showing how
media files are
played.

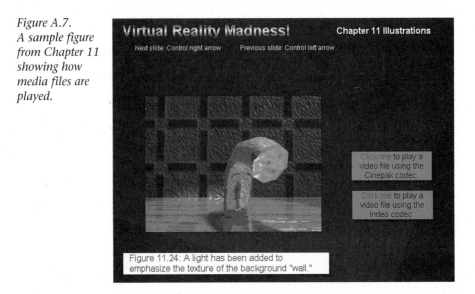

Figure A.8 shows a clever feature of Compel—the Twin Click floating controller. You can open the controller at any time by clicking simultaneously on the left and right mouse buttons.

Figure A.8.
The Twin
Click floating
controller.

You can use the controller to move forward and backward using the two small page icons at the lower right and left of the controller. You can also use the icons at the top of the controller to pause the presentation, blank your screen, or to load a new presentation. To move to a specific slide in the presentation, click on the current slide number at the bottom center of the controller.

That about covers the possibilities for Compel runtime. Have fun!

Music on the CD-ROM

I wanted to find some appropriate music to add to some of the presentations on the CD-ROM. I recently moved to the Puget Sound area of Washington, where I met a very talented harpist, David Michael. You'll find some of his music on the CD-ROM; you'll encounter it automatically when you start the Windows application.

The music is from David's album *New Zealand*, and features David on solo harp. Just on the chance you find it as pleasing as I did, here is some background on the album from David's promotional materials:

> *New Zealand*—A solo harp album, inspired by and celebrating the scenic splendor and peoples of New Zealand. Multi-instrumentalist David Michael chose the Celtic harp to convey his impressions of this magic land with its uncluttered landscapes and crystal-clear skies. The title cut "New Zealand" was the first piece he composed upon his return. Along with the original melodies, David offers fresh new arrangements of the ever-popular "Pachelbel Canon" and the Celtic classic "Song of the Silkies." The album is drawn to a close with the majestic piece "Aotearoa" (the Maori name for New Zealand), which means "land of the long white cloud."
>
> **About the Artist:** David Michael is a composer and multi-instrumentalist with skills on myriad stringed instruments. His degrees include a B.A. in music from Evergreen State College and an M.A. in Arts and Media Technology from Antioch University West. David performed in ensembles in the Seattle area, throughout the '70s and early '80s, which received art grants and were featured on numerous radio and television programs. In

1983 he moved to the San Francisco Bay area where he has been involved in many studio recording projects. He is well known for his Fortuna Records release with flutist Randy Mead, *Petals in the Stream*, which received rave reviews: *Heartsong Review* hailed it as "a masterpiece of inspiration, talent and love." Victory Music Review called it a "romantic listening feast." W.A. Mathieu, San Francisco Sufi Choir director and Windham Hill recording artist, refers to David as "a gifted musical groundbreaker." David Darling, former cellist with the Paul Winter Consort and founder of Music for People has "always enjoyed David Michael's beautiful and sensitive music."

I would like to extend a hearty thanks to David for letting me use his music on the CD.

If you would like to get more information about David's music, please contact Purnima productions at PO Box 317, Port Townsend, WA 98368. David has numerous albums, and the folks at Purnima would be glad to send you a catalog. You can also call at 206-379-9732, or FAX at 206-385-4874.

Contacting the Author

Both Virtual Reality and Multimedia are quickly evolving fields. That makes it important to have access to the latest information. The best way I have found to provide that access is on the CompuServe Information Network. If you are not already a member of Compuserve, you are missing out on a great source of information.

You can access CompuServe with your modem. Almost every modem sold today comes with a CompuServe membership offer. If you haven't already taken advantage of it, dig through the package that came with your modem and find it! If you don't own a modem, you can get even a very fast (9600 or 14.4k baud) modem very cheaply.

You can find me in the Multimedia forum of CompuServe (GO MULTIMEDIA). You can send me email at my CompuServe ID: 75530,3711, or you can send me a message in the Hands-on Multimedia section of the Multimedia forum (or use section 1 if you are new and don't know your way around yet). I prefer receiving messages in the Multimedia forum because when I answer your questions there, other people also get to learn things. Please only use email for private messages.

You may also want to visit the CYBERFORUM, where you will find ongoing discussions about virtual reality. There are a number of interesting shareware applications in both the Multimedia and Cyber forums.

Happy modeming!

At the Last Minute...

One important piece of information came my way too late to include elsewhere, so I'll include it here. In Chapter 3, I described the Autodesk Home Series, including the program 3D Plan. Autodesk has shipped a new version of the software that includes some additional features.

I still have a problem with the small number of available colors in the 3D mode. However, you can now edit the 16 colors (you are not stuck with the default VGA colors), out of a total palette of 64 colors. In addition, 3D Plan is now integrated into the various Home Design modules, so you do not need to purchase it separately.

These new features—and many more involving the floor plan modules only—are important, and increase the value of the software. If you are planning any changes around the house, or if you just want to play around with floor plans or landscapes and then view them in 3D, the Home software series provides a lot of utility and fun at a very low price.

Bonus Software

In the \EXTRA directory, you'll find a variety of bonus files:

- AVI files—morphing videos created with PhotoMorph.

- A Vistrapro flyby—At the DOS prompt, type FLYBY to view this file. Press any of the number keys to speed up or slow down the animation. Press Esc to exit.

B

VISTAPRO

In this appendix, you'll find information on installing and getting started with Vistapro, which is included on the *Virtual Reality Madness!* CD-ROM.

Vistapro is a three-dimensional landscape simulation program. Using data from the U.S. Geological Survey (USGS) Digital Elevation Model (DEM), Vistapro can accurately recreate real world landscapes in vivid detail. As a fractal landscape generator, Vistapro can create landscapes from a random seed number.

Vistapro supports over four billion different fractal landscapes. Simply by changing a number, you can simulate whole new worlds. These virtual worlds can then be customized. For instance, by clicking on several buttons, rivers and lakes can be created in a landscape where none existed previously.

The Vistapro software included with this book is the complete version of Vistapro 1.0. You can upgrade to the newest version for a special price—see the Vistapro registration card in the back of the book.

NOTE

If you don't have access to a CD-ROM drive, you can order special floppy-disk versions of Vistapro and Virtual Reality Studio. You'll find a disk offer form near the back of this book.

You might want to refer back to Chapter 1, "Getting Started With Virtual Reality," which goes into more detail about how virtual landscapes can be created with Vistapro. That chapter talks about the latest version of Vistapro, but most of what's shown in the chapter can be duplicated with Vistapro 1.0.

License Agreement

Vistapro is being provided to you through a special arrangement with Virtual Reality Laboratories, Inc. This software is not public domain and you must abide by the terms of the company's license agreement:

> *The program Vistapro and the related user manual are copyrighted. You may not copy, modify, distribute, transfer, or transmit this program or the related manual except as is expressly provided in this agreement.*
>
> *You have the non-exclusive right to use this program on a single computer. You may make one backup copy of this program to protect against media damage. Call Virtual Reality Laboratories for use on local area networks—usually there is no charge.*

This program is sold as entertainment, without warranty as to its suitability to be used as any other purpose.

This license agreement shall be governed by the laws of the United States of America and the State of California.

How Vistapro Works

Vistapro uses a combination of artificial intelligence, chaotic math, and a user-definable set of values to simulate landscapes in their natural state. At present, the USGS has converted about 40% of the United States to DEM files that potentially may be used with Vistapro. Vistapro is a single frame generator, meaning that it acts like a camera; point and click the camera and Vistapro will render a new view of the landscape.

Landscapes can be viewed from a practically infinite combination of heights, angles, and distances. Using the combination of user-controllable values and Vistapro's built-in routines, landscapes can be made as realistic or as surreal as desired. It is easy to alter tree and snow lines, haze, exposure, rivers, lakes, and light sources to customize the appearance of the landscape.

For generating its images, Vistapro uses data derived from United States Geologic Survey Digital Elevation Mapping files. These files contain coordinate and elevation data at 30-meter (roughly 100 ft.) increments. Each file used in Vistapro contains about 65,000 elevation points and 130,000 polygons.

Vistapro doesn't know anything about what covers the terrain. It doesn't know where the trees, roads, or buildings are. It does its best to color each polygon (based upon a few numbers that you input) in a realistic way, but it still can't draw each rock and tree where they are in reality.

Installing Vistapro

At a minimum, you must have the following hardware and software to run Vistapro:

- IBM PC-compatible computer with 640K memory
- MS-DOS or PC DOS operating system
- Microsoft compatible mouse and driver
- VGA, Extended VGA, or Super VGA graphics capability
- DOS hard-disk partition with at least 3M free space

Vistapro must be installed on a hard disk before it can be run. A hard-disk installation program has been included on the CD-ROM. The installation files for Vistapro are located in the \VISTAPRO directory.

To run the install program, place the *Virtual Reality Madness!* CD-ROM in your CD drive and follow these steps:

1. From the DOS prompt, type **drive:\VISTAPRO\INSTALL** and press Enter. For example, if your CD drive is D, type D:\VISTAPRO\INSTALL and press Enter.

2. You'll be given the option to change the drive where the programs will be installed. Use the arrow keys to select drive C: or D: and then press Enter.

3. The install program will display an introductory message; press any key to begin installing files.

4. A message will appear when the program is finished.

The following section provides more details on the memory requirements of Vistapro.

Memory Usage by Vistapro

Vistapro requires a lot of memory (RAM) to run. It must have about 540K of free memory. You can determine how much memory is free at the DOS prompt by using the DOS CHKDSK command. DOS 5 and DOS 6 users can also use the MEM program to obtain the total and free amounts of memory.

The amount of free memory should be greater than 540,000 bytes for Vistapro to run properly. Most users should have enough memory available, but if you don't, you will have to do something to free up some memory.

The simplest option is to remove some memory resident programs from memory. You might also try removing unused device drivers. ANSI.SYS is often installed but not used. A RAM disk may be eating up some conventional memory, and even though it is desirable to have Vistapro put its temporary files on the RAM disk, you may want to remove it if the existence of the RAM disk eats up too much memory.

All these solutions require editing your CONFIG.SYS or AUTOEXEC.BAT files and rebooting your computer. Caution: If you are not familiar with these files, we don't recommend fiddling with them.

Another good way to free up some memory on 80286, 80386, and 80486 systems is to upgrade to DOS 5, DOS 6 or DR DOS 6.0. All of these solutions require that you buy these packages and then spend the time installing them—and probably backing up your hard disk, too.

Advanced Setup Options

Vistapro uses several temporary files while it is running. These files contain data that is used internally and a copy of the graphics screen after a picture is rendered. We recommend placing these files on the fastest available drive or partition.

If the environmental variable VTEMPDIR is not defined, Vistapro will create these files in its default directory, usually C:\VISTAPRO. If VTEMPDIR is set to a valid drive and pathname, Vistapro will place these working files at that location. These files may consume as much as 1.2M of memory.

If you can spare the memory, we suggest setting VTEMPDIR to point to a RAM disk that is big enough to hold all the temporary files. For example, if your RAM disk is drive D and is 1.2M or greater, type:

```
SET VTEMPDIR=D:\
```

Vistapro will run a little faster and more smoothly with its temp file on RAM disk. If VTEMPDIR is set to a drive or directory that doesn't exist, Vistapro will complain and abort. You can erase the environmental variable with the following command:

```
SET VTEMPDIR=
```

This will force Vistapro to return to using the default directory for its temporary files.

The screen modes you plan to use (see Table B.1) will determine how big a RAM disk you need for the temp files.

Table B.1. RAM disk sizes for each graphics mode.

Graphics mode	Bytes needed
320x200	520K
640x400	700K
640x480	750K
800x600	930K
1024x768	1.17M

For example, if you will only be using the lowest resolution graphics mode (320x200), your RAM disk need only be 520,000 bytes.

Note that the RAM disk must be in EMS or XMS and that Vistapro will still need about 540K bytes of DOS program memory.

You may also use VTEMPDIR to select another hard disk for the temp files. Many people keep their permanent files on one disk or partition and their transitory files on another disk or partition. We suggest putting the temp files (via VTEMPDIR) on your fastest available device.

Graphics Modes

The 320x200 VGA graphics mode can be used with a standard VGA system. For resolutions that are higher than this, you must have either a VESA-compatible VGA system or a system that has VESA capability.

With systems that have VESA capability, a special VESA software driver must be run before starting Vistapro. Your video card manufacturer may have supplied you with such a driver with the video card. If not, there are a number of VESA drivers supplied with Vistapro.

The VESA drivers are located in the VESA subdirectory of your Vistapro directory. The drivers are arranged by manufacturer; for example, the drivers for ATI cards are located in the \VISTAPRO\VESA\ATI subdirectory. Read the text file in the subdirectory for your card manufacturer. This file will explain how to set up the driver for your card.

Getting Started

To start Vistapro, you need to be at the DOS prompt. Type the following commands, pressing Enter after each line:

```
C:
CD \VISTAPRO
VISTAPRO
```

If you installed Vistapro to a hard drive other than C, substitute that drive letter for C in the preceding commands.

You will be ready to start when you see a screen with the gray Control Panels on the right hand side and the empty green topographical map on the left.

Vistapro Menus

Vistapro's menus are accessed via the buttons at the top left of the main screen. (See Figure B.1) To see the menus, place the mouse cursor over one of the buttons and press the left mouse button. A menu with several selections appears immediately below the button. This menu will remain on the screen as long as the left mouse button is held down.

*Figure B.1.
The opening
screen of
Vistapro.*

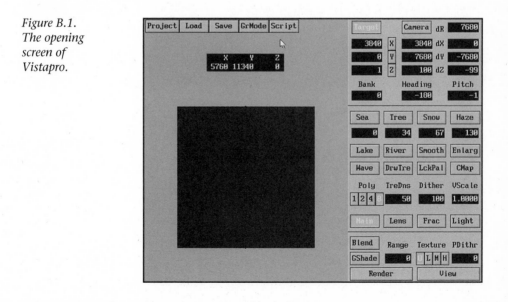

To select a menu item, move the mouse pointer down over the menu and release it when the cursor is over the desired item. (For more general information on using the menus, see the Graphical User Interface section that is located in Chapter 2 of the online manual. This manual is installed to your hard drive when you install Vistapro from the CD-ROM.)

There are five menus in Vistapro:

■ The *Project Menu* allows access to DOS, information about Vistapro, information about the currently loaded landscape, and the Quit Vistapro function.

■ The *Load Menu* allows loading of landscapes, colormaps and pictures.

■ The *Save Menu* saves landscapes, colormaps, and pictures.

■ The *GrMode Menu* is used for selecting graphics and animation modes.

■ The *Script Menu* is used for creating and executing Scripts.

Loading a Landscape

When Vistapro is first loaded, it starts out with a flat landscape. To quickly view an actual landscape, you can load one of the DEM (Digital Elevation Model) files that are included with Vistapro. These files are in a format used to represent landscape data.

To load a landscape, position the mouse pointer over the Load button at the top of the screen. Press and hold the left mouse button. The Load menu will drop down to reveal several options. Move the mouse pointer (while still holding the left button) to the first option, Load DEM, and release the button.

Now you will see the Load Vista DEM *File Requestor*. (See Figure B.2) The File Requestor is used anytime a file is to be loaded or saved.

The Load Vista DEM button is this File Requestor's confirm button. Clicking on it means to go ahead and load the file. The label on the confirm button varies depending on the File Requestor. The Abort button is used to exit the File Requestor without taking an action.

The single up arrow button scrolls up one line, and the single down arrow button scrolls down one line. The three up arrows scroll up one page, and the three down arrows scroll down one page.

Figure B.2.
The Load Vista
DEM File
Requestor screen.

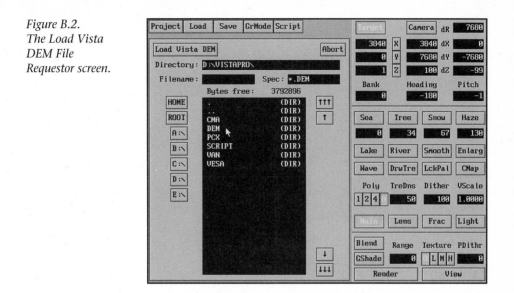

Find the DEM directory in the list, position the mouse pointer over it, and click the left mouse button. You will now be presented with a list from the DEM directory.

Find the file HALFDOME.DEM, and click it. Click the confirm button, which is the button labeled Load Vista DEM at the top left of the File Requestor.

The screen will switch back to the topographical map, and Control Panel and Vistapro will begin loading the landscape. It could take several seconds to complete.

Once Vistapro is finished loading the landscape, you will see a topographical view of the landscape in the box near the left side of the screen. The topographic map is colored by elevation. Dark greens represent the lowest altitudes, browns represent the middle altitudes, and gray-whites are the highest altitudes.

Locate the Render button at the lower left corner of the lower control panel. Press and release this button with the mouse, and Vistapro will begin to render the scene you loaded.

After a few seconds, you'll see the screen switch to the View screen. At first it will be blank, then you will see Vistapro draw the sky and ground. Then it will draw a landscape.

At the current settings (assuming you haven't changed anything), this landscape of Halfdome in Yosemite will look very blocky. As you learn more about Vistapro, you'll learn how to make scenes like this more photo-realistic. You'll also learn how to create fly-throughs and animated sequences.

To switch back to the Control Panels and topographical map, just click the left mouse button.

You now need to read the Vistapro online manual, which is discussed in the following section. It contains full details on how to use the many features of Vistapro.

The Online Vistapro Manual

When you install the Vistapro software from the CD-ROM, the online user's manual will also be installed. It will be located in the \VISTAPRO\MANUAL subdirectory of your hard drive.

The manual comprises the following series of text files, arranged by chapters and appendices:

        CH1.TXT
        CH2.TXT
        CH3.TXT
        CH4.TXT
        CH5.TXT
        CH6.TXT
        CH7.TXT
        APPA.TXT
        APPB.TXT
        APPC.TXT
        TUTOR1.TXT
        TUTOR2.TXT
        TUTOR3.TXT
        TUTOR4.TXT

The file TUTORIAL.TXT steps you through the creation of Vistapro landscapes, explaining about most of the controls and features of the program.

To view the manual, change to the \VISTAPRO\MANUAL subdirectory, type MANUAL and press Enter. You will see a menu of choices, which represents a table of contents for the manual. When you select a choice, the text for that chapter will be displayed.

The viewing program offers several features that will help you as you use the manual. Access these features as follows:

■ Use the PageUp, PageDown, Home, End, and arrow keys to navigate through the text.

■ Pressing the F key will let you search for a particular word in the text. After you have found the first instance of this word, press N to search for the next and P to search for the previous occurrence.

■ Pressing the Esc key will exit the program.

If you want to print the manual, you can print it by using the DOS PRINT command. You will need to print each individual chapter.

You can also read these files into your favorite text editor or word processor and then print them.

C

VIRTUAL REALITY STUDIO

In this appendix, you'll find information on installing and getting started with Virtual Reality Studio, which is included on the *Virtual Reality Madness!* CD-ROM.

Virtual Reality Studio allows you to create interactive virtual-reality worlds on your home computer. You can even add animation, sound, and teleportation effects to your worlds.

You can use the Editor to create, test, and edit your custom worlds. Then, you can create stand-alone versions of the worlds that can be run on any compatible computer.

The version included with this book is version 1 of Virtual Reality Studio; you can upgrade to the newest version for a special price—see the advertisement in the back of the book.

> If you don't have access to a CD-ROM drive, you can order special floppy-disk versions of Virtual Reality Studio and Vistapro. You'll find a disk offer form near the back of the book.

You'll find more details of how Virtual Reality Studio can be used in Chapter 2, "Virtual Possibilities." That chapter deals with the latest version of the software, but much of what's shown there can be duplicated with version 1.

License Agreement

Virtual Reality Studio is being provided to you through a special arrangement with Domark Software. This software is not public domain and you must abide by the terms of the company's license agreement:

> *This computer software product (the "Software") is provided to the customer under license from Domark. The Software and the on-line manual are subject to the following terms and conditions, to which the customer agrees by opening the package of the software.*
>
> *The software is copyrighted 1991 by Incentive Software. The user manual is copyrighted 1991 by Domark. All rights are reserved. Neither the software or the manual may be duplicated or copied for any reason. The Customer may not transfer or resell the software or the user manual. Except as provided above, Incentive Software makes no warranties, either express or implied, with respect to*

the Software. Domark makes no warrantees either express or implied, with respect to the user manual. Incentive and Domark expressly disclaim all implied warranties, including without limitation, the warranty of merchandisability and/ or fitness for a particular purpose.

Installing Virtual Reality Studio

At a minimum, you must have the following hardware and software to run Virtual Reality Studio:

- IBM PC-compatible computer
- MS-DOS or PC DOS operating system, version 2.0 or higher
- Microsoft-compatible mouse and driver
- VGA, EGA, CGA or Tandy graphics

The software also supports a mouse, joystick and Ad Lib-compatible sound boards.

Virtual Reality Studio must be installed on a hard disk before it can be run. A hard-disk installation program has been included on the CD-ROM. The installation files for Virtual Reality Studio are located in the \VRSTUDIO directory of the CD-ROM.

To run the install program, place the *Virtual Reality Madness!* CD-ROM in your CD drive and follow these steps:

1. From the DOS prompt, change to the drive that holds the CD-ROM. For example, if this drive is D, type D: and press Enter.

2. Type \VRSTUDIO\INSTALL, and press Enter.

3. You will see a menu that asks you to choose the VGA, EGA, CGA or Tandy version of the install program. Use the arrow keys to highlight the choice that corresponds to the type of video display you have, then press Enter.

4. You'll be given the option to change the drive where the programs will be installed. Use the arrow keys to select drive C: or D: and press Enter.

5. The install program will display an introductory message; press any key to begin installing the files to your hard drive.

6. A message will appear when the program is finished. Press any key to continued.

Running Virtual Reality Studio

After you've installed the software from the CD-ROM, you can start Virtual Reality Studio by typing the following commands at the DOS prompt (remember to press Enter after each line):

```
C:
CD\STUDIO
STUDIO
```

If you installed the software to a drive other than C, substitute that drive letter for c in the preceding commands.

This will bring up the Virtual Reality Studio Editor, which is where you will create and test your virtual creations. The following section of this appendix will give you an overview of how the Editor operates. (You'll find more details on how to create and program worlds in the special online documentation, which is discussed later in this appendix.)

You can get a good feel for the kinds of worlds this software can create by looking at the Virtual Reality Studio creations that are included on the CD-ROM. Refer to Appendix A for more information on these virtual worlds.

The Virtual Reality Studio Editor

Virtual Reality Studio is designed to be user-friendly, with icons and pull-down menus enabling the user to quickly understand the working environment. When you load the program, you will see the main screen (Figure C.1), which is divided into several areas.

The menu selector is the top text line, which contains the headings for various menus. To access one of the menus, simply move the mouse pointer over the desired heading and the relevant menu will open below the heading. Moving the mouse pointer over the options within the menu will highlight them, and then pressing the mouse button will select the option currently highlighted. Moving the pointer out of the boundary of the menu will cause it to retract.

Figure C.1.
The Virtual
Reality Studio
main screen.

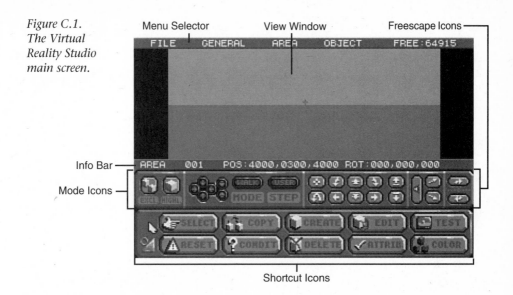

You can use Virtual Reality Studio without a mouse, although it will be more cumbersome. The cursor keys on the numeric keypad will move the mouse cursor around the screen. To move faster, press either shift key at the same time. The Insert and Delete keys on the numeric keypad act exactly like the left and right mouse buttons.

The joystick options act in a similar manner—the stick moves the cursor and the buttons correspond to the mouse buttons.

View Window

Below the menu selector you will see the main View window. This area is always used to display the current Freescape view, as seen from whichever camera is currently selected. Here is where you will see the objects in the world you are creating and editing.

Information Bar

Below the View window is the Information bar. This shows the current area, your present viewpoint coordinates (X, Y, and Z), and the angle of view (yaw, pitch, and roll). When in edit mode, this line will change to read the object name you are editing, its position in the environment, and its size. This information will be especially useful when animation or other more advanced uses of the system are employed.

Icons

Immediately below the Information bar, you will see a series of icons, comprising the Mode and Freescape group of icons. The Mode group is on the left half of the screen.

EXCL is useful when editing objects. Clicking on this icon will exclude all background information and leave the currently selected object to be edited.

Just to the right of this you will see HIGHL, which will highlight the selected object for ease of identification during work.

To the right of these icons, you will see a set of small icons in the form of arrows. These icons are very useful. When an object is selected, if these arrows are activated, they will lock onto the current object from the front, rear, sides, top, or bottom.

To the right of the arrows, you will see the MODE and STEP icons. MODE toggles between the following modes, which affect your movement:

> WALK allows you to move along the ground, with the restriction of gravity. You can climb onto objects and fall off them. Your height above the floor is restricted to between 64 and 280 units, corresponding to a crouched and standing position.

> FLY1 removes restrictions on gravity. You can now fly as if you were in a helicopter, with complete freedom in three dimensions. Forward motion is restricted to a horizontal plane, so that you can fly forward and look down at the same time.

> FLY2 is very similar to FLY1, except that you can now fly in exactly the direction you are looking, as though you were in a an airplane.

> CAM1 through CAM5 control five "cameras" which can be placed anywhere. Control is similar to FLY1, except that the cameras are allowed inside objects and outside the area. When you change to another view, the camera's position is saved, so that on returning to that camera, the view position is retained.

> WALK, FLY1, and FLY2 have collision detection built in. They will not travel through solid objects. These modes are the only three possible modes within a runnable program or the test screen.

STEP toggles between USER and FINE, which affect the size of movements as follows:

USER affects the standard speed of operation and movement, which is initially set by the PREFERENCES menu on the GENERAL menu bar item.

FINE is used for fine work when only a small movement is required in editing or movement.

To the right of the Mode icons, you will find the Freescape icons. The first of these is a set of directional arrows which are used for your movement in an environment. Using these arrows, you can move left, right, forward, or backwards, rotate left, rotate right, make a complete U-turn, move up or down, and toggle the crosshair cursor on and off.

To the right of these icons, you will see the rest of the Freescape icons, which control your view movement. These allow you to look up, look down, and roll. Clicking on the center "eye" icon will return your view to the center view.

The Edit and Freescape icons remain on the screen and can be used at most times during editing.

Below the Mode and Freescape icons, you will see the shortcut icons (see Table C.1). These icons duplicate the more commonly used functions, which are also available from the menus.

Table C.1. The Editor's Shortcut Icons.

Shortcut icon	Menu
SELECT	OBJECT
COPY	OBJECT
CREATE	OBJECT
EDIT	OBJECT
TEST	GENERAL
RESET	GENERAL
CONDITION	OBJECT
DELETE	OBJECT
ATTR	OBJECT
COLOR	OBJECT

The Studio Game

The Studio game is a Virtual Reality Studio world that has been included as an illustration of some of the possible environments that can be constructed. The object of the game is to escape from the mysterious world in which you find yourself and return to Earth. Some sort of space vehicle will probably come in handy. See if you can complete the game without cheating.

This game features advanced use of animations and conditions, and these can be examined and edited using the relevant functions of the editor. In addition, the tutorial section at the end of the online manual takes you through the beginning of the game and explains how the program was written.

To load the game, follow these steps at the main screen of the Editor:

1. Go to the FILE menu and select LOAD DATA. When the file selector box appears, click on the DATA directory.

2. Select the Studio game filename. The file is named VGAGAME.STU for VGA installations, EGAGAME.STU for EGA or Tandy, and CGAGAME.STU for CGA.

3. Go to the FILE menu and select LOAD BORDER. When the file selector box appears, click the box-shaped icon next to the file list. This will move you up one directory level, back to \STUDIO.

4. Select the BORDERS directory.

5. Select the appropriate file for your system. The border file is named SGVGAPIC.LBM for VGA installations, SGEGAPIC.LBM for EGA or Tandy, and SGCGAPIC.LBM for CGA.

6. Press F1 or select the TEST icon. This will start the game.

To exit the game, press F1, go to the FILE menu, and select CLEAR ALL.

The Online Virtual Reality Studio Manual

When you install the Virtual Reality Studio software from the CD-ROM, the online user's manual will also be installed. It will be located in the same \STUDIO\MANUAL subdirectory of your hard drive.

The manual is a series of text files, arranged by chapter, as shown in Table C.2.

Table C.2. Online Manual Files.

Filename	Contents
CH1.TXT	Introduction
CH2.TXT	Introduction to Freescape
CH3.TXT	Introduction to the Editor
CH4.TXT	Creating and Editing your first Object
CH5.TXT	The user interface
CH6.TXT	File Menu options
CH7.TXT	General Menu options
CH8.TXT	Area Menu options
CH9.TXT	Object Menu options
CH10.TXT	The Freescape Command Language (FCL)
CH11.TXT	The Animation Controller
CH12.TXT	Examples and Variables
CH13.TXT	Sound effects
CH14.TXT	Studio game tutorial
CH15.TXT	Additional Information

To view the manual, change to the \STUDIO\MANUAL subdirectory, type MANUAL, and press Enter. You will see a menu of choices, which represents a table of contents for the manual. When you select one of the choices, the text for that chapter will be displayed.

The viewing program offers several features that can be accessed as follows:

- Use the PageUp, PageDown, Home, End and arrow keys to navigate through the text.

- Pressing the F key will let you search for a particular word in the text. After you have found the first instance of this word, press N to search for the next and P to search for the previous occurrence.

- Pressing the Esc key will exit the program.

If you want to print the manual, you can print it by using the DOS PRINT command. You will need to print each individual chapter.

You can also read these files into your favorite text editor or word processor and then print them.

I

INDEX

Symbols

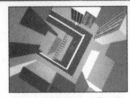

On the CD in this book,
you'll find a full working copy of

Vistapro 1.0
the incredible virtual reality landscape generator

**Turn in this registration card for version 1.0
to become eligible to upgrade to Vistapro 3.0**
for the regular upgrade price of $45.00 <u>plus</u> shipping!
Please see coupon opposite.

VISTAPRO 1.0 IBM REGISTRATION CARD
Please take a few moments to register your FREE software.

Date _____

Contact Name _____

Business Name _____

Street Address/P.O. Box _____

City _____ State/Province _____ Zip/PC _____

Country _____ Phone _____ FAX _____

Where did you hear about VISTAPRO?   Store   Review   BBS   Friend   VRLI

User Group (which?) _____   Trade Show   Magazine (which?) _____

Where did you buy VISTAPRO?

   Store   Mail Order   VRLI   Trade Show   User Group   Other _____

What processor do you have?   386   486   586

How much memory does your PC have? _____ What size is your hard drive? _____

Do you own a CD ROM drive? Yes No

Comments _____

_____

What is your primary use for Vistapro? _____

_____

BUSINESS REPLY MAIL

FIRST CLASS MAIL PERMIT NO. 496 SAN LUIS OBISPO, CA

VIRTUAL REALITY LABORATORIES, INC.
2341 GANADOR COURT
SAN LUIS OBISPO, CA 93401-9826

NO POSTAGE
NECESSARY
IF MAILED
IN THE
UNITED STATES

Add to Your Sams Library Today with the Best Boo
Programming, Operating Systems, and New Techno

The easiest way to order is to pick up the phone and ca

1-800-428-5331

between 9:00 a.m. and 5:00 p.m. EST.
For faster service please have your credit card available.

ISBN	Quantity	Description of Item	Unit Cost	Total
0-672-30318-3		Windows Sound FunPack (Book/Disk)	$19.95	
0-672-30310-8		Windows Graphics FunPack (Book/Disk)	$19.95	
0-672-30249-7		Multimedia Madness! (Book/Disk CD-ROM)	$44.95	
0-672-30248-9		FractalVision (Book/Disk)	$39.95	
0-672-30305-1		Computer Graphics Environments (Book/Disk)	$34.95	
0-672-30361-2		Virtual Reality and the Exploration of Cyberspace (Book/Disk)	$26.95	
0-672-30315-9		The Magic of Image Processing (Book/Disk)	$39.95	
0-672-30345-0		Wasting Time with Windows (Book/Disk)	$19.95	
0-672-30301-9		Artificial Life Explorer's Kit (Book/Disk)	$24.95	
0-672-30352-3		Blaster Mastery (Book/Disk CD-ROM)	$34.95	
0-672-30320-5		Morphing Magic (Book/Disk)	$29.95	
0-672-30308-6		Tricks of the Graphics Gurus (Book/Disk)	$49.95	
❑ 3 ½" Disk		Shipping and Handling: See information below.		
❑ 5 ¼" Disk		TOTAL		

Shipping and Handling: $4.00 for the first book, and $1.75 for each additional book. Floppy disk: add $1.75 for shipping and handling. If you need to have it NOW, we can ship product to you in 24 hours for an additional charge of approximately $18.00, and you will receive your item overnight or in two days. Overseas shipping and handling adds $2.00 per book and $8.00 for up to three disks. Prices subject to change. Call for availability and pricing information on latest editions.

11711 N. College Avenue, Suite 140, Carmel, Indiana 46032

1-800-428-5331 — Orders   1-800-835-3202 — FAX   1-800-858-7674 — Customer Service

Book ISBN 0-672-30391-4

	Cost

Virtual Reality Madness! **Disk Offer**

If you don't have access to a CD-ROM drive, you can order the *Virtual Reality S*
dio and *Vistapro* software on floppy disks. The disks contain the complete softwa
for these programs, including the special on-line manuals.

The cost is only $12 (add $4 for international orders).

You can only order these disks by mail and you **must** return this page
with your order—photocopies of this page will not be accepted.

To order the disks, complete this form and mail it to:

> **Sales Department—Disk Offer**
> **Virtual Reality Madness!**
> **11711 North College Ave.**
> **Carmel, IN 46032**

Enclose a money order or check for $12 (add $4 for international orders).

Name _____

Company (for company address) _____

Street _____

City _____

State _____ ZIP or Postal Code _____

Country (outside USA) _____

ISBN # 0-672-30391-4D

*u-
re

The Virtual Reality Madness! CD-ROM

The CD-ROM contains **two** award-winning commercial virtual reality programs, which retail for more than **$150**. You'll find a complete version of these award-winning VR programs—*not* demos!

Virtual Reality Studio
by Domark Software and New Dimension International
The leading virtual reality creation software for home computers. You can design your own interactive virtual reality worlds. Version 1.

Vistapro
by Virtual Reality Laboratories
The three-dimensional landscape simulation program. Create and explore real-world landscapes with vivid details. Version 1.

Both programs include special on-line versions of their complete manuals.

If you don't have access to a CD-ROM drive, you can order floppy disk versions of Virtual Reality Studio and Vistapro. You'll find an order form near the back of the book.

Plus—The CD-ROM is a treasure chest of additional virtual reality demos, programs, and samples—more than 400 megabytes of software. Here's just a sample of what you'll find:

- Demo versions of popular commercial VR programs
- VR worlds you can explore and interact with
- VR games, including programs that feature two-player interaction over phone lines
- Animated fly-bys of virtual worlds
- Videos of virtual worlds
- A complete multimedia presentation of VR creations with animations, video, graphics and sound.

For information on the CD-ROM, and how to use the programs on it, read Appendix A in the book.